Rethinking Halal

Muslim Minorities

VOLUME 37

The titles published in this series are listed at *brill.com/mumi*

Rethinking Halal

Genealogy, Current Trends, and New Interpretations

Edited by

Ayang Utriza Yakin
Louis-Léon Christians

TUTA SUB AEGIDE PALLAS · 1683 ·

BRILL

LEIDEN | BOSTON

Cover illustrations: Galleria Cittorio Emanuele II, Milan, photo by Marr Lauren.
Halal Certificate, issued by the European Islamic Halal Certification.
Certificate of Halal Products, issued by EuroHalal, Office of Control and Halal Certification.
Halal certificate, issued by Halal Expertise, European Research Centre for Halal Industry.
Halal certificate, issued by Halal Food Council of Europe.

Published with the support of the Research Institute Religions, Spiritualities, Cultures, Societies (UCLouvain)

Library of Congress Cataloging-in-Publication Data

Names: Yakin, Ayang Utriza, 1978- editor. | Christians, Louis-Léon, editor.
Title: Rethinking halal : genealogy, current trends, and new interpretations / edited by Ayang Utriza Yakin, Louis-Léon Christians.
Description: Boston : Brill, 2021. | Series: Muslim minorities, 1570-7571 ; 37 | Includes bibliographical references and index.
Identifiers: LCCN 2021002164 (print) | LCCN 2021002165 (ebook) | ISBN 9789004459229 (hardback) | ISBN 9789004459236 (ebook)
Subjects: LCSH: Muslims–Dietary laws. | Halal food. | Halal food industry–Certification.
Classification: LCC BP184.9.D5 R48 2021 (print) | LCC BP184.9.D5 (ebook) | DDC 297.5/76–dc23
LC record available at https://lccn.loc.gov/2021002164
LC ebook record available at https://lccn.loc.gov/2021002165

Typeface for the Latin, Greek, and Cyrillic scripts: "Brill". See and download: brill.com/brill-typeface.

ISSN 1570-7571
ISBN 978-90-04-45922-9 (hardback)
ISBN 978-90-04-45923-6 (e-book)

Contents

Acknowledgements VII
Abbreviations VIII
Notes on Contributors X

1 Rethinking Halal: Critical Perspective on Halal Markets and Certification 1
Ayang Utriza Yakin, Louis-Léon Christians, and Baudouin Dupret

PART 1
Halal Market: Genealogy and Current Trends

2 Rethinking Halal: Hegemony, Agency, and Process 25
Harun Sencal and Mehmet Asutay

3 Halal Practices at the Dawn of Southeast Asian Modernity: Some Cases of Halal Fatwas in *al-Manār* in the Beginning of the Twentieth Century 56
Jajat Burhanudin

4 Halal Issues, *Ijtihād*, and Fatwa-Making in Indonesia and Malaysia 80
Syafiq Hasyim

5 Developing the Halal Market: China's Opportunity to Strengthen MENA Ties and Address Uighur/Hui Issues 108
Zaynab El Bernoussi

6 Science, Politics, and Islam: The Other Origin Story of Halal Authentication in Indonesia 128
En-Chieh Chao

PART 2
Halal Certification: New Interpretations in Critical Perspective

7 Halal Certification, Standards, and Their Ramifications in Belgium 153
Ayang Utriza Yakin

8 The Italian and Spanish Legal Experiences with Halal Certifying Bodies 196
Rossella Bottoni

9 The Process of Eating Ethically: A Comparison of Religious and National Food Certifications in Italy 221
Lauren Crossland-Marr

10 Halal Certification as a Source of Intra- and Inter-Group Tensions among Muslims in Poland 241
Konrad Pędziwiatr

11 Living Halal in the Volga Region: Lifestyle and Civil Society Opportunities 265
Matteo Benussi

Index 295

Acknowledgements

The book originated from the conference 'Rethinking Halal: Genealogy, Current Trends, and New Interpretations' held at the Catholic University of Louvain (UCLouvain), in Louvain-la-Neuve, Belgium, on 18–19 June 2018. Organising this conference was part of the three-year post-doctoral of Ayang Utriza Yakin's research project 'Halal Economy in French Speaking Countries' (2017–2019) funded by 'The MOVE-IN Louvain Programme' of UCLouvain, co-financed by the European Union Commission's Marie-Skłodowska Curie Actions programme. The organisation of the conference benefited from support received from the Belgian National Fund for Scientific Research (Fonds de la Recherche Scientifique, FNRS). The publication of this edited book was made possible thank to support of the Research Institute of Religions, Spiritualities, Cultures, Societies (RSCS) and the Chair of Law and Religion at UCLouvain.

Many individuals offered various forms of support from the inception to the publication of this volume. At the Research Institute of RSCS UCLouvain, we thank Christine Plateau, Aurore Marion, Leopold Vanbalingen, Martin Dutron, and Ima Sri Rahmani for their help and support during the organisation of the conference. Ayang Utriza Yakin wants to thank especially to Baudouin Dupret for productive discussion during his research and stay in Louvain-la-Neuve. Our deep thanks go to Joern Thielmann, a series editor of Muslim Minority (MUMI) at BRILL, who became interested in this project and accepted it to be included in the series. Our special thanks go to Nienke Brienen-Moolener, editor Middle East and Islam in BRILL, for introducing us to the world of BRILL's publication process and working with us during the publication process.

We are immensely grateful and thank wholeheartedly all the authors for their patience in the long journey of this volume's publication, which took three years. We are indebted to our authors for their trust in us and for their hard work to make the final version of their chapters far more readable and sharper than the original. The editors and contributors are very grateful to all the anonymous reviewers in the first and second stages for their constructive comments and criticism that improved the quality of chapters and their argumentation. We also thank tremendously Pat FitzGerald for her diligent copyediting work to refine the text according to British English and for the indexing. Last but not least, we have adopted the system of IJMES (International Journal of Middle East Studies) for Arabic transliteration and Chicago Manual System 17th edition for notes and references.

Ayang Utriza Yakin
Louis-Léon Christians

Abbreviations

ASBL	Association Sans But Lucratif (non-profit organisation/NPO)
BENELUX	Belgium, The Netherlands, and Luxembourg
BKI	Bijdragen to de Taal-, Land-, en Volkenkunde
BPJPH	Badan Penyelenggara Jaminan Produk Halal (National Agency of Halal Product Assurance)
BRI	Belt Road Initiative
CICB	Centre Islamique et culturel de belgique (Centre for Islam and Culture of Belgium)
Co.Re.Is	Comunità Religiosa Islamica (Islamic Religious Community)
COVID-19	Corona Virus Disease 2019
D.O.P.	Denominazione di Origine Protetta (Protected Designation of Origin)
DNA	Deoxyribonucleic acid
ECtHR	European Court of Human Rights
EIHC	European Islamic Halal Council
EMB	Exécutif des musulmans de Belgique (the Executive of the Belgian Muslims)
EU	European Union
GMO	Genetically modified organism
GCC	Gulf Cooperation Council
GSO	Gulf Standardization Organization
GVI	Główny Inspektorat Weterynarii (General Veterinary Inspectorate)
HIA	Halal International Authority
HAACP	Hazard Analysis Critical Control Point
HCB	Halal Certification Body/ies
HFB	Halal Federation of Belgium
HFCE	Halal Food Council of Europe
ISO	International Organization for Standardization
ICFA	International Council of Fiqh Academy
ICS	Islamic Commission of Spain
IFI	Islamic financial institution
IME	Islamic Moral Economy
ISEAS	Institute of Southeast Asian Studies (Singapore)
JAIN	Jabatan Agama Islam Negeri (State Department of Islamic Affairs)
JAKIM	Jabatan Kemajuan Islam Malaysia (Department of Islamic Development Malaysia)
JMBRAS	Journal of Malaysian Branch of Royal Asiatic Society
LBM	Lembaga Bahsul Masa'il (Fatwa Institution of Nahdlatul Ulama)

LM	Liga Muzułmańska w Rzeczpospolitej Polskiej (Muslim Leagu)
LP-POM	Lembaga Pengkajian-Pangan, Obat-Obatan, dan Kosmetika (the Assessment Institute for Foods, Drugs, and Cosmetics)
MAIN	Majlis Agama Islam Negeri (State Council of Islamic Affairs)
MAS	Modern Asian Studies
MENA	Middle East and North Africa
MHS	Malaysian Halal Standards
MKI	Majlis Kebangsaan bagi Hal Ehwal Ugama Islam Malaysia (National Council for Islamic Affairs)
MSG	Monosodium glutamate
MSKK	Muzułmańskie Stowarzyszenie Kształcenia Kulturalnego (Muslim Association of Cultural Education)
MUI	Majelis Ulama Indonesia (Indonesian Council of Ulama)
MZR	Muzułmański Związek Religijny w Rzeczpospolitej Polskiej (Muslim Religious Union)
NAM	Non-aligned movement
NFC	National Fatwa Council of Malaysia
NU	Nahdlatul Ulama (The Awakening of Ulama, a traditionalist-moderate Sunni Islam movement in Indonesia)
OBOR	One Belt, One Road
OIC	Organization of Islamic Cooperation
OTOZ	Ogólnopolskie Towarzystwo Ochrony Zwierząt (The All Polish Association for Animal Protection)
PDI-P	Partai Demokrasi Indonesia Perjuangan (The Indonesian Democratic Party of Struggle)
PERSIS	Persatuan Islam (Union of Islam)
PIH	Polski Instytut Halal (Polish Halal Institute)
SACF	Sino-Arab Cooperation Forum
SEZ	Special Economic Zone
SJM	Stowarzyszenie Jedności Muzułmańskiej (Association of Muslim Unity)
SMIIC	Standards and Meteorology Institute for Islamic Countries
SSM	Stowarzyszenie Studentów Muzułmańskich (Association of Muslim Students)
UGM	Universitas Gajah Mada (Gajah Mada University)
UIII	Universitas Islam Internasional Indonesia (Indonesian International Islamic University)
WHA	World Halal Authority

Notes on Contributors

Ayang Utriza Yakin
is Visiting Professor in Arabic and Islamic Studies at the Department of Languages and Cultures, Section Middle-East, Ghent University, Research Associate at the Research Institute 'Religions, Spiritualities, Cultures, Societies' (RSCS) of the Université Catholique de Louvain (UCLouvain), Belgium, and *chargé de recherche postdoctoral* at Sciences-Po Bordeaux, France. He studied Arabic and classical Islamic studies, Islamic law, history, and philology in Indonesia (1990–2001), Egypt (2001–2002), and France (2003–2005 and 2008–2013). He was visiting fellow and postdoctoral researcher at Oxford (2012), Harvard (2013), Tokyo (2016), and Louvain-la-Neuve (2016–2019). He has published two books in Indonesian (both published in Jakarta in 2016 by Kencana PrenadaMedia), and numerous articles and book chapters in Indonesian, French, Arabic, and English.

Baudouin Dupret
is Directeur de recherche, Centre National de la Recherche Scientifique (France) and Visiting Professor at the Catholic University of Louvain, Belgium. He has published extensively on the sociology and anthropology of law on topics including legislation and media, especially in the Middle East, is the author of multiple books, and has also edited or co-edited numerous volumes. His publications include *Adjudication in Action: An Ethnomethodology of Law, Morality and Justice* (Ashgate, 2011), *Practices of Truth: An Ethnomethodological Inquiry into Arab Contexts* (John Benjamins, 2011), *Ethnographies of Islam: Ritual Performances and Everyday Practices* (Edinburgh University Press, 2012), *Law At Work: Studies in Legal Ethnomethods* (Oxford University Press, 2015), *What Is the Sharia* (Hurst, 2018), and *Ethnographies du raisonnement juridique* (LGDJ, 2018).

En-Chieh Chao
is a cultural anthropologist, currently Associate Professor of Sociology Department at National Sun Yat-sen University, Taiwan. Her research interests focus on the intersections between religion, gender, race, and modernity. Her book *Entangled Pieties: Muslim-Christian Relations and Gendered Socialities in Java, Indonesia* was published by Palgrave Macmillan in August 2017. More recently, Chao has undertaken a project to study Islam with science, technology, and society in the Indo-Malay world. She explores the overlooked multi-species sciences of halalness—the dynamics of Islamic ritual purity in modern life

involving animal physiology, molecular biology, and chemistry—to expose the social contingencies that gave birth to novel scientific practices and religious understandings.

Harun Sencal
holds a PhD in Islamic Finance from Durham University, UK. He graduated from the Computer Engineering Department of the Yeditepe University in 2007 and obtained an MBA degree from the same university. He teaches both conventional and Islamic economic courses. He works as an assistant professor at the Istanbul 29 Mayis University, Turkey. His main research area includes both qualitative and quantitative aspects of Islamic economics and finance. In particular, his research focuses on risk aspects of Islamic financial instruments and moral foundations of Islamic financial institutions, and has presented papers on his research at several international conferences.

Jajat Burhanudin
is Professor in Islamic History, Faculty Adab and Humanities, Syarif Hidayatullah State Islamic University Jakarta, with special expertise in the history of Islam in Indonesia and Southeast Asia. He earned his doctoral degree at Leiden University, The Netherlands, in 2007. His recent works include 'Converting Faith, Connecting People: The Kingdoms and the Dynamics of Islamization in Malay-Archipelago' (*Studia Islamika*, 2018); *Islam dalam Arus Sejarah Indonesia: dari Negeri di Bawah Angin hingga Negara Kolonial* [*Islam in the Course of Indonesian History: from the Lands below the Winds to the Colonial State*] (Prenada, forthcoming).

Konrad Pędziwiatr
is Senior researcher at the Center for Advanced Studies of Population and Religion and Professor in the Department of International Affairs Cracow University of Economics. He is the author of numerous publications on religion and ethnicity in the processes of migration, Islam, and Muslims in Europe, and the politicisation of Islam in Europe and the Middle East and North Africa, including the monographs 'Transformation of Islamism in Egypt and Tunisia in the shadow of the Arab Spring' (2019), 'Polish Migration Policy' (2015), 'The New Muslim Elites in European Cities' (2010), and 'Muslims in Western Europe' (2007).

Lauren Crossland-Marr
received her bachelor's degree from the University of Maryland, College Park in 2007. In 2014, Lauren received an MA in anthropology from the Catholic Uni-

versity of America and in May 2020 received her PhD in cultural anthropology from the Washington University in St Louis. She is currently a post-doctoral researcher on an EU-funded project that explores public awareness and acceptance of new biotechnology use in agriculture. From 2017–2018 she conducted participant observation on the halal certification industry in Milan, Italy to determine the impact of local cultural foodways on certification schemes meant for global markets.

Louis-Léon Christians
is a legal scholar and Professor at the Université catholique de Louvain (Belgium), where he is head of a Chair for Law and Religion. From 2012 to 2019, he was also president of the UCLouvain Research Institute for Religious Studies (RSCS). He has also been an expert in religious affairs for the Council of Europe, United Nations High Commissioner for Human Rights, and the European Union. In 2020, he was appointed head of a new Public Agency for the Promotion of Islamic Studies (IPFI) by the Belgian Government. His research interests, publications, and teaching cover the fields of religious freedom, churches' and states' relationships in Europe, and international law and comparative religious laws.

Matteo Benussi
is a Marie Skłodowska-Curie Global Fellow based jointly at the Universities of California, Berkeley and Ca' Foscari, Venice. Matteo is a social anthropologist specialising in religion in post-socialist Eurasia. His doctoral project (University of Cambridge) dealt with Islamic piety movements and the politics of virtue amongst Muslims in Tatarstan (Russia) and is now in the process of becoming a book. Building on that experience, Matteo is currently researching Muslim topographies, temporalities, and subjectivities in Inner Russia's borderlands. Previously, Matteo carried out ethnographic research into vernacular Orthodox Christianity in post-Chernobyl Ukraine.

Mehmet Asutay
is a Professor of Middle Eastern and Islamic Political Economy and Finance at the Durham University Business School and is the Director of the Durham Centre in Islamic Economics and Finance. Mehmet's recent research includes the construction of Islamic moral economy and Islamic political economy and their articulation in economic and sustainable development. In addition, his research has focused on locating Islamic banking and finance within the expressed ideals of Islamic moral economy by essentialising sharing and collaborative economy nature of Islamic finance. Mehmet is also involved in

empirical research in various aspects and dynamics of Islamic banking and finance.

Rossella Bottoni
is Associate Professor at the Faculty of Law, University of Trento. She has published extensively on law and religion and comparative ecclesiastical law in academic journals, and has edited volumes. Author of two monographs in Italian language (*The Principle of Secularism in Turkey. A Legal and Historical Perspective*, 2012, and *Law and Religion in the European Space*, 2019). Co-editor of *Religious Rules, State Law, and Normative Pluralism* (Springer, 2016), and *Routledge Handbook of Religious Laws* (Routledge, 2019).

Syafiq Hasyim
is Lecturer and Director of Library and Culture at the Indonesian International Islamic University (UIII) and lecturer at the Faculty of Social and Political Sciences, UIN Syarif Hidayatullah Jakarta. He is currently Visiting Fellow on the Indonesia Studies Programme of the ISEAS—Yusof Ishak Institute. From 2018 to 2019, he was Visiting Fellow at RSIS, NTU, Singapore. He obtained a DPhil in Islamic Studies from Freie University, Berlin, Germany and MA in Islamic Studies from Leiden University, The Netherlands. His research fields are on fatwa in Muslim and non-Muslim countries, Islamic commodification, democratic life, political Islam, Islamic feminism, and shariʿa life-style.

Zaynab El Bernoussi
is professor of international studies at Al Akhawayn University (Morocco). Her research focuses on dignity politics. She holds a Masters degree in finance from IE Business School (Spain), a Master of Public Administration from Columbia University (USA), and a PhD in political and Social Sciences from the Université catholique de Louvain (Belgium). El Bernoussi was a Carnegie visiting scholar at the Carolina Center for the Study of the Middle East and Muslim Civilizations, Harvard University, and Smith College. She lived in China for two years and has published encyclopedia entries on Islamic Bioethics, with her mentor, Dr Baudouin Dupret.

CHAPTER 1

Rethinking Halal: Critical Perspective on Halal Markets and Certification

Ayang Utriza Yakin, Louis-Léon Christians, and Baudouin Dupret

Etymologically, halal means 'permitted'. Looked at logically, everything should be considered as permitted unless or until proven otherwise. However, halal today pervades the life of most Muslim societies, for many reasons. Religiously, it corresponds to what many Muslims consider as the good performance of their beliefs. Economically, it creates new opportunities for business. Politically, it corresponds to times in which identity issues became paramount. Socially, it relates to the need to cope with new realities without losing one's right to define the norms of the community. Legally, it is linked to the framing of 'traditional' norms in modern terms and categories. The outcome is that nowadays, the principle has been inverted and everything is taken as non-halal until proven otherwise. A no-trust principle is assumed and nothing can be accepted until certified as halal by a relevant body.

The phenomenon of halal is part of a process of 'positivisation' that directly affected Islam and Islamic normativity, often called the shariʿa. In a continuum stretching from the most local to the most global, and from the legal to the technical and quasi-managerial, we can illustrate the many forms taken by this positivisation process. In its first stage, this process resulted in the transformation of the shariʿa into 'Islamic law', that is, in a hierarchical, comprehensive, codified, state-centred, and unified system of positive rules of law. The example of the 2000 law governing *khulʿ* divorce in Egypt is paradigmatic of the transformation of the *fiqh* into Islamic law, that is, a norm originating from Islamic sources interpreted according to the procedures and standards of positive law. Another illustration can be drawn from the law-making process, which in many Muslim-majority countries included the shariʿa or the *fiqh* in constitutions as sources of legislation, showing that nowadays, the components of the shariʿa must be spelled out in the constitutional text in order to become legally meaningful and consequential within the realm of positive law. The arena of international law, e.g. several rulings of the European Court of Human Rights, can also prove illustrative, since it shows how courts do not refer to the shariʿa *per se*, but to the shariʿa made-into-positive-law. A last illustration, that of the ruling of the International Criminal Court in the Al-Mahdi case, illustrates how

 | DOI:10.1163/9789004459236_002

the Islamic normativity, while being both reified and positivised, is at the same time made illegitimate with respect to international and globalised legal standards.

In its second stage, the process of positivisation created and affected other types of norms. These include technical and managerial norms, which have had a deep and global impact on the governance of contemporary societies. This holds true for norms inspired by Islam and Islamic doctrine which, through this positivisation movement, were reconceptualised and transformed. Within a framework of normative hyper-densification of social life, the use of such technical and managerial norms, taking the form of indicators and standards, complements or conflicts with legal norms. Islamic finance is a first example. While the justification for the search for a specifically Islamic form of financing is derived from Muslim jurists' opinion that revenue is only considered legitimate if it is the outcome of a real sharing of the risks that have enabled the revenue to be generated, it has led to Islamic financial institutions offering a variety of products such as association, leasing, and limited companies and creating standards that serve as guides and models for the 'shariʿa boards' responsible for the assessment of the Islamic conformity of products. The domain of bioethics represents another example of this standardisation of the world. In the case of Muslim societies, several thinkers and scholars have based their answers to questions relating to bioethics in the Qur'an and hadith, and several fatwas have also contributed to broadening the interpretation of some of these Islamic rulings. The speed of developments in the medical field has prompted a systematic collaboration between biomedical scientists and Islamic institutions, emphasising the role of biomedical scientists in a 'normative' interpretation of the Qur'an and the Sunna from their own understanding.

Halal is a paramount instance of such a positivisation process. The contemporary phenomenon of halal corresponds to this move, through which the Islamic tradition started to be read through the positivist lens, both legal and technical, through which many areas of norms that were either not or were loosely addressed by the shariʿa came to be increasingly regulated in Islamic, though positivistic, terms. Although 'commanding the good and prohibiting the evil' has been known and practised in Muslim societies since the beginnings of Islam, it has taken on a particular dimension in the current period of expanding commodification and commercialisation. In a period of widespread industrialisation, merchandising, changing consumption patterns, and evolving dietary worldviews, within an increasingly global market, determining the criteria governing what foods are permitted is both sensitive and problematic. It has triggered 'the development of new halal regulations, the rise of the halal consumer and certification industry, and the construction of a "halal cuisine".[1] These regulations are currently developed by international actors: state, international, transnational, and other organisations, which produce standards defining what constitutes halal. As well as Islam, these standards can encompass many types of sensitivities (e.g. organic, vegan, ecological), transforming the question into a syncretic, multilayered issue. What must be emphasised here is that the issuance of such standards constitutes a thoroughly normative, though not necessarily legal, enterprise. It represents 'bureaucratic scripts by which major halal players with hegemonic aspirations in the Islamic world and ambitious economic expectations govern religion. These standards are also indicative of what have become halal dicta under the purview of the modern state and the influence of global capitalism'.[2]

1 The Glocalisation of Halal

Historically speaking, the 'question' of halal sprang up in the late 1970s and early 1980s. However, it is only in the past 20 years that it has become a salient concern, especially in Europe and Asian non-Muslim countries, mainly for business and other economic purposes. During that time, halal has progressively encompassed all aspects of modern human life, including halal food-processing, halal hotel, halal sauna, halal cosmetics, halal drugs, halal fashion, halal taxis, halal airlines, and so on. This 'halal phenomenon' has been characterised by the emergence of new institutions: halal certificate bodies (HCBs), Islamic marketing, and Islamic finance. These new practices required new kinds of scholars ('ulama') in charge of linking religious scholarship and technological developments in food, pharmaceutical, and cosmetic industries. Shariʿa boards started issuing fatwas on such issues, which either did not previously exist or were different in nature and content from classical-*fiqh* discussions. For centuries, 'ulama' were not concerned with modern halal issues. This recent development can be explained by the evolution of science and technologies, especially in the domain of food production. It became difficult for Muslim-majority states not to regulate and legislate on halal. In that respect, these states became important agents in the field of halal. Other states (i.e. European) chose not to specifically regulate halal, but it opened a new market with its own legal issues and judicial conflicts.

1 Armanios and Ergene, *Halal Food: A History*, p. 17.
2 Armanios and Ergene, *Halal Food*, p. 17.

The transformation of halal in the world should be read as a 'glocalisation' problem, that is, the outcome of a dynamic exchange between the global and the local. Glocalisation is

> the twin process whereby, firstly, institutional/regulatory arrangements shift from the national scale both upwards to supranational or global scales and downwards to the scale of the individual body or to local, urban or regional configurations, and secondly, economic activities and inter-firm networks are becoming simultaneously more localised/regionalised and transnational.[3]

The concept of glocalisation captures the idea that 'capitalistic production for increasingly global markets [involves] the adaptation to local and other particular conditions'.[4]

The spread of halal compliance is not only due to the increasing influence of Salafi-Wahhabi or Islamic neo-fundamentalism, as some suggest.[5] Rather, it is the combination of different elements that led to the widening of its meaning. At the beginning, 'halal' was limited to the domain of food allowed to be consumed by Muslims. Later, the word underwent a semantic extension to other products and services, stretching from economic (e.g. banks, insurances) to social institutions (e.g. marriage). The religious concept 'halal' contains, as a normative concept, many transformatory possibilities. Every concept has a history of usage. In this sense, there is neither contradiction nor paradox in observing the evolving religious content of halal as a norm able to include new kinds of practices progressively. In other words, there is no contradiction in affirming simultaneously that halal is a religious concept and that it is a socially living, constructed, invented, and reproduced concept, undergoing a long process during which the word, the idea, the meaning, and understanding are continually reshaped and adjusted.

Halal reflects an anthropological revolution, that of the scientising, standardising, and normalising of social life. Scientising in the sense that religious truth has become a scientific issue, as exemplified by creationist theories. Standardising, meaning that technical standards based on the consensus of certain groups are developed to maximise quality and thus commodification.

---

3 Swyngedouw, 'Globalization or "Glocalization"? Networks, Territories and Rescaling', p. 25.
4 Robertson, 'Glocalisation: Time-Space and Homogeneity-Heterogeneity', pp. 28–29.
5 See, for instance, Bergeaud-Blackler, *Le Marché Halal ou l'invention d'une tradition*.

Normalising, as the development of such technical norms and standards proves to be not only a coordination issue but also that of stating a norm that *has to be* followed.

2 Beyond the Dichotomy Opposing Essentialism and Instrumentalisation

Halal is a normative phenomenon that must be studied in parallel with new economic and social modes of production and consumption, including the development of market economy. Historically, the rise of halal corresponds to the formation of new fields in positive law, like consumer law and trademark law; we should also mention the adoption of the Single European Act and the creation of the European Single Market, in the early 1990s. This is a dynamic that aims at both protecting consumers and promoting business competition. The same phenomenon can be observed at a global level: harmonisation of national laws, inter- and transnational covenants, regulated competition in a market economy.

It is sometimes thought that the economic dimension of the halal issue affects its religious nature and reduces it to an instrumentalised process. The risk of such a notion is that the multiple and polymorphic capacities of religious phenomena are missed. To disqualify the religious nature of the phenomenon because of its transformative capacities would be tantamount to a petition of principle: namely, that there are only intangible religions. Following such a presupposition, religious phenomena could be analysed only in terms of a dilemma: either reduction to an absolute intangibility, which would condemn religion to the fundamentalist incapacity of any reflexivity; or characterisation as non-religious, confining it to an imposture, religiously inauthentic, or politically instrumentalised.

Such a binary approach is curious. Far from denying any conjunctural instrumentalisation effect, we suggest that we should take seriously how religion—understood as a living tension in the quest for meaning and transcendence, both individual and collective—can mobilise capacities for evolution, mutation, and even co-instrumentalisation. In short, how it shows capacities for self-transformation in its maintaining its place in the world within new contexts (e.g. capitalist). This perspective allows us to understand better the contemporary capacity of the evolution of Islam, which is both geographically and conceptually glocalised.

The extension of the halal referent, by going beyond the traditional prescriptions, actually comes to dematerialise them and to extend them to processes rather than to products. Some see it as a primarily economic achievement, others as a collective identity quest or even a political project. There is also the possibility of an ethical approach. In this case, the halal referent would not simply give force to an extended orthopraxis of Islam, but to a methodical and deontological approach open to new processes of reflexivity. It would invite the entire community to a process of collective responsibility in the light of tradition, complex and varied processes of authority building, and technological developments. The extension of the halal referent does not only raise questions about its material perimeter or even the effects of the economic situation; it also concerns much broader foundations that bring into play the modes of reflexivity specific to Islamic doctrines. In particular, the question arises of the generalisation of a deontological dimension to the practice of halal, extending its ethics to all economic issues.

2.1 *Halal in Secular Systems*

The deployment of the halal referent does not remain without consequences for its legal status, including in secular legal systems. Certain questions are classical, for example, those concerning fraud and consumer protection. How could a secular judge rule on the religious authenticity of a product? The classical answer is well-known: it involves checking the labelling of the product and verifying the identity of the certifying authority and the traceability of the process. The recent jurisprudence of the Court of Justice of the European Union has given a new dimension to these labelling controls by supporting the existence of a 'negative label'. Indeed, the court decided that the European 'BIO/ORGANIC' label would no longer be compatible with ritual slaughter practices for animal meat. In other words, the European BIO/ORGANIC label now constitutes the proof of lack of the halal property.[6]

However, the extension of the halal reference will raise many more issues than those traditionally linked to product characteristics. Let us give just one example, involving a potentially holistic legal understanding of the European halal business. In 2000, a European directive renewed the definition of what had previously been referred to in the literature as 'TendenzBetrieb' and is now referred to as 'public or private organisations whose ethics are based on religion or belief'. This new definition applies not only to organisations whose purpose is the dissemination of religious doctrine (such as a school or a newspaper), but to all companies whose production respects some religious ethic. The exten-

6 CJEU, Judgment of 26 February 2019, C-497/17

sion of scope is significant and constitutes a major stake for the halal economy, having been excluded from the previous scope of application but potentially included by the new.

However, this new classification is associated with an exceptional legal regime. Indeed, within an enterprise for which this qualification is retained, 'a difference of treatment based on a person's religion or beliefs does not constitute discrimination when, by the nature of these activities or by the context in which they are carried out, religion or beliefs constitute an essential, legitimate and justified occupational requirement with regard to the organisation's ethics'. Moreover, such enterprises may 'require persons working for them to adopt an attitude of good faith and loyalty towards the organisation's ethics'.[7]

Applied to halal businesses, the European 'faith-based' status could profoundly affect the identity of their staff and the nature of their management. It would indeed be possible to justify that an essential part of the staff must indeed be Muslim and that these employees have an obligation to be publicly loyal to their company and their religion. Moreover, the extension of religious normativity to all aspects of the company could be imposed in this way, at least according to the rules of proportionality and good faith provided for by European law. One example should be mentioned here: a famous judgement of the Paris Court of Appeal of 25 May 1990,[8] in which one of the employees (a religious food controller) was able to successfully invoke Jewish religious rules to justify an extension of the leave of circumstances for the religious funeral of his father (three days according to French law; three weeks according to his Jewish status). The Jewish employer, who intended the leave to be calculated according to French law, was defeated: the Court of Appeal allowed a three-week absence. The court reasoning, linked to the rule of the French Civil Code providing for the good faith execution of agreements, was based on the coherence of the contract in relation to the religious normative system: the religious rule could not be applied only to the quality of the product and not also to the duration of the funeral rites. The sincerity of the company presupposes the full application of religious law.

2.2 *Between Halal Markets and Certification*

The present volume shows how necessary it is to confront a diversity of analyses of this plural reality of halal, between a top-down approach (religious normativity, processing economy, scientific expertise, customisation of import

7 COUNCIL DIRECTIVE 2000/78/EC of 27 November 2000 establishing a general framework for equal treatment in employment and occupation, art. 4.

8 *Arbib v. Brami*, *Recueil Dalloz*, 1990, 596, in this case concerning a Jewish kosher restaurant.

and export markets, binary certification, foreign accreditations, legal framework, and political stakes) and a bottom-up approach (demography linked to immigration, emergence of Muslim middle-classes, need for socialisation of communities, consumer expectations, attitude of believers, local recognition practices). These two paths address themselves in very different ways between minority Islam and majority Islam, realities that are themselves in global tension. At their crossroads, the religious referent will be at the heart of the attention of this book: we will show that this religious referent does not necessarily lock itself into a black box, which would either be neglected by the actors or abandoned to opaque games of power. Nor is it condemned to a binary perspective in which classical Islamic thought did not lock it up, unlike some more recent economic facilities. The regression of this religious referent is not linear: after recalling how the marked term, which was that of haram (forbidden), with a general presumption of conformity (halal), has been reversed into an inverse presumption of absence of conformity in the absence of certification, we will underline with several contributors how the main stake in the deployment of halal may not be played out in binary presumptions and oppositions, but in more refined, continuous, and thoughtful assessments.

Wouldn't it be a contribution of Islam not to confinement to certainties and binaries, fast and risky, but on the contrary to the opening of an ethical and thoughtful renewal, for example, the sustainable development of a responsible economy? IME (Islamic Moral Economy), *taḥsīniyya*, *ṭayyib*, but also *ḍarūra*, or in the opposite direction *iḥtiyāṭ* (precaution), seem to be gradually coming together with halal reference and creating a new space for interaction, not only towards goods (markets) but also towards people (workers, managers, and clients, Muslims and non-Muslims) and finally environment (creation). However, how can one not see in these openings a dangerous abandonment of the precautionary principle, and a risk of infidelity to tradition, as in the debates on the concept and practices of 'delusive *maṣlaḥa*', but also those of pious compensatory practices? Here again, a work of Islamic sciences is necessary that is not hostage to economic stakes, but builds the Islam capacity to rethink the various paths of an economy attentive to its ethical growth and not only to its capitalist efficiency. The extension of the field of halal is progressively accompanied by its transformation into a reflexive ethical moment that is rooted in the richness and diversity of the lived traditions of Islam.

This perspective will gradually emerge around several themes in the book. First, halal certification. It addresses: (i) the study of halal certification bodies around the world, in both Muslim-majority and Muslim-minority countries; and (ii) their role in creating standards and norms in halal matters. This theme attempts to answer different questions: who are the actors of halal certification bodies? What are the standards? Do they create new norms for halal? What is the role of 'ulama' in the process of certification? Who is the authority deciding the 'halalness' of a product? Does the standardisation of halal neglect traditional Islamic institutions? Do halal certification bodies marginalise the role of 'ulama'? Do halal certification bodies become a profit-seeking rather than community-service enterprises? What is the financial dimension of the halal certification process? Second, the 'glocalisation of halal'. This has to do with people's daily practices. Local factors, cultures, and traditions are at work within a context of globalisation. The issue of halal is driven by a mechanism that is much more complex than a mere 'domino effect'. This theme attempts to answer the following questions: To what extent do local factors determine the debate and the practice of halal? How do global and local factors interact in halal debates and practices? Third, it explores the development and evolution of fatwas on halal in both classical and modern *fiqh*, as well as debates among 'ulama' organisations and shari'a committees around the Muslim world, their impact in non-Muslim countries, and vice-versa. The theme answers such questions as: how is halal interpreted in Islamic theology? How do halal practices of Muslim communities differ from discourses in Islamic theology? What are the fatwas in the contemporary Islamic world? In what way do they differ from those in classical *fiqh* and why? How do various fatwa committees in different Muslim countries perceive halal? How do 'ulama' react to a rapidly growing halal economy? What are the differences in opinions pertaining to halal among fatwa committees? How do 'ulama' deal with the fast-growing halal market in issuing halal fatwas on products?

In short, contributors to this volume analyse the genealogy of halal, the current trends of this phenomenon, and its recent interpretations by contemporary Muslim scholars. The volume also discusses how the main stakeholders in halal ('ulama', states, halal certificate bodies) are producing new norms and standards. This leads to thinking about how they become moral agents aiming to control, guide, and dictate what is lawful and unlawful for individuals, communities, and corporate societies. It explores the production of fatwas on halal, interpreting halal issues in the face of scientific and technological discoveries and findings.

2.3 *What Is New about This Book?*

The chapters in this book come from a variety of disciplines and cover very different geographical and cultural areas, from Muslim-majority countries to countries with Muslim minorities. Despite this diversity, a common thread runs through the book and constitutes its originality as compared to the existing literature. Rather than limiting itself to the elucidation of doctrinal traditions addressing the issue of halal/haram or, on the contrary, focusing only on the external economic, financial, political, or demographic factors that explain historical and current changes, the volume helps to show the interrelated working of religious doctrine, on the one hand, and economic and political factors, on the other. In that sense, this volume is a good example of a scholarly third way that seeks to explore the many constituents of practices in contexts characterised as Muslim (sometimes abusively), between 'islamologism', that is, the explanation of everything that takes place in such contexts by Islam and its doctrinal rules, and 'sociologism', i.e., the explanation of the same questions by the work of only sociological (including economic and political) factors.

Far from opposing these two sets of realities, the book shows their non-severable interaction. It shows, for example, to what extent the capitalist practices of the market economy put pressure on shariʿa experts, to what extent certification agencies can claim to give mechanical priority to the (increasingly insignificant) calculations of scientific standardisation, and to what extent political contexts, including ethnical identities, must be taken into account. The volume underlines the relevance and significance of Islamic sciences and questions of doctrinal interpretations. Doctrinal readings can support interpretations that sometimes validate capitalist practices, but at other times challenge and have an impact on them. It is important for shariʿa boards and religious experts to secure real independence in order to carry out their scholarly function, according to their belonging to one of the many schools and traditions; such independence is itself a condition for a reflexive religious understanding of halal conformity. The book thus shows, chapter after chapter, the persisting link, in the Islamic doctrine, between economic tenets and religious principles.

The interrelatedness between religious and socioeconomic factors suggests a second originality. The evolution and extension of the halal referent, through its uses in various commercial and socioeconomic fields, does not lead the doctrinal approach to focus only on the substance of new products, but to enlarge itself into a much wider ethical assessment, not simply of products quality but of entire production processes. Halal started to encompass the relationship between halal and *ṭayyib* and between halal and Islamic economic ethics. This progressive transformation of the halal reference leads halal thinking in the domain of quality ethics and common good. Accordingly, and contrary to an increasingly 'microscopic' perspective carried by a techno-scientific fascination, Islamic doctrine contributes to a global economic ethic, in a dialogue nourished by the diversity of its own traditions.

Most of the chapters based on ethnographic work in various European countries show the formation of halal norms, through certification, in parallel to the social and economic ascension of Muslim communities in minority contexts. This halal certification brought the subject of religion into scientific logic, something that never happened in the past since halal was regarded as a religious matter only. The volume demonstrates that Islam underwent a process of positivisation, that is, a kind of reframing of its rules and principles through the lens of a characteristically modern standardising, scientificising, and systematising mind.

2.4 *Contributions at a Glance*

The book invites to rethink certain aspects of halal, and in particular the issue of the halal market and halal certification in Muslim-minority contexts. The book is divided into two parts, each of five chapters, after this Introduction. The first part focuses on genealogy and new interpretations from a wide variety of angles, approaches, and perspectives. How do religious concepts still really shape the deployment of the halal referent? Are there doctrinal keys in Islam to facilitate (or to confront) the domination of capitalist economic uses?

Chapter 2, 'Rethinking Halal: A Fuzzy Logic Perspective', aims to describe an old and yet still controversial Islamic financial concept, *tawarruq*, which is used in the capitalist market to fit the market's demands. In this chapter, Harun Sencal and Mehmet Asutay trace the basic arguments in classical Islamic legal philosophy (*uṣūl al-fiqh*) and the concept of *maṣlaḥa* (public interest) and examine its compatibility as product and service with the objective of shariʿa. Quoting Sencal and Asutay: 'The most important feature of delusional *maṣlaḥa* is that it can be contrary to the verses of the Qur'an or the sayings of the Prophet Muhammad, but as long as jurists consider this solution as a *maṣlaḥa* or public utility, it is considered as valid, as such a fatwa is rendered on emerged issues.' As a consequence of this delusional use of the *maṣlaḥa* concept, they conclude that 'it is capitalism rather than the shariʿa scholars that remains sovereign over Islamic law and IFIs [Islamic Financial Institutions] in such a state of exception'. Such a religious ability to give prevalence to exceptions on Islamic principles shows that the existence of shariʿa governance or shariʿa boards (SBs) in modern IFIs is insufficient for religion to challenge the hegemony of the capitalist system. After carefully examining the history of the concept of *maṣlaḥa*, the authors come to justify the transformation of the role of shariʿa scholars. Once renowned and irreplaceable in their expertise, they are now subject to economic power. Customers usually do not seek information regarding members of SBs since, for them, the *existence* of a SB is sufficient condition for shariʿa compliance of an IFI. In order to overcome these structural inadequacies of halal certification, the authors construct an important alternative by suggesting to complete this expertise by a civil society-based regulatory mechanism to evaluate the shari'a compliance of the products and services of IFIs. For Sencal and Asutay, 'rather than deciding whether a certain product is *ḥalāl* or *ḥarām*, this mechanism mainly aim to decide as to what degree a certain product or service is compatible with the morality of shari'a', by considering various stakeholders currently kept beyond the decision frame such as environment, employee-employer relationship, production process, etc. This transformation of the halal referent is a major challenge for its evolution, the authors show the major stakes in finer and more continuous ethical evaluations. In this sense, they evoke the concept of embellishment (*taḥsīniyya*) and that of Islamic Moral Economy, which is resolutely non-binary. Sencal and Asutay's study, however, acknowledges the difficulties and limits of this alternative model, but they underline that it is part of the constant deployment of a plural economic ethic within the framework of a social responsibility to which Islam must contribute. This chapter, resolutely placed at the beginning of this first part of the book, must remain in the background of all the contributions, as it constitutes a normative background for measuring the diverse evolutions that are taking place across the various countries studied in the book.

Chapter 3, entitled 'Halal Practices at the Dawn of Southeast Asian Modernity: Some Cases of Halal Fatwas in *al-Manār* in the Beginning of the Twentieth Century', discusses the request for fatwa (legal opinion) on the halal food consumption by Southeast Asian Muslims to the journal *al-Manār*, then under the editorship of Rashīd Riḍā in Cairo, Egypt. In this chapter, Jajat Burhanudin elaborates the reason for the fatwa and how, together with the changing circumstances in Southeast Asia, this fatwa affected the concept and practice of halal in the country. If, for the Muslims of the period, halal was not an issue to be concerned with since the food they consumed was homemade in nature, issues have been emerging since the beginning of the twentieth century through the modernisation process of South-East Asian cities. Burhanudin shows that requests for fatwa to the Cairo *'ālim* Rashīd Riḍā dealt mainly with the significance of the new invention out of modernity for Muslims' socio-religious life. The questions were concerned with way Muslims handled new developments that started coming into their life, such as the use of gramophones, the creation of paintings and photographs, the wearing of European dress, and the like. Burhanudin concludes that modernity appeared as the prime factor behind the rise of fatwa requests on the halal issues to the journal *al-Manār*. No similar question, therefore, could be found in the fatwa collections of the nineteenth century. The author thus shows that the evolution of the halal referent in a purely religious framework does indeed respond to particular historical circumstances, but that traces of this already existed at the beginning of the twentieth century, well before the current developments linked to other later mutations, albeit offering the same exogenous character, while underlining the specificities of South-East Asia.

Chapter 4, 'Halal Issues, *Ijtihād*, and Fatwa-Making in Indonesia and Malaysia', highlights the development of *ijtihād* and its application in dealing with halal issues in the context of Indonesia and Malaysia. In this chapter, Syafiq Hasyim examines the practice of using the various methods of *ijtihād* for their halal issues by the Council of Indonesian Ulama (MUI) in Indonesia and the Department of Islamic Development (JAKIM) in Malaysia. Here again, the questioning focuses on the major concepts of Islam and the more or less open resources of interpretation, in a comparison that shows the differences and specificities of the different systems in Malaysia and Indonesia. It is therefore first of all the diversity of positions regarding the closure of *ijtihād* that is exposed, as a classic question, and then the difference in these capacities of interpretation between the two systems, according to variable declinations (*istinbāṭ al-aḥkām* or *tarjīḥ*, *taḥqīq* or *taqrīr*). Malaysia has a stricter tendency towards the Shāfiʿī school of Islamic law, while Indonesia remains open to the thoughts of other *madhāhib*, although the majority groups of Indonesian Islam follow the Shāfiʿī school of Islamic law as well. In the case of halal fatwa, based on his study, Indonesia can accept Ḥanafī and Mālikī schools of Islamic law. The concepts of *istiḥāla* (transformation) and *istihlāk* (dilution), which are essential keys to the contemporary evolution of halal in the face of the processing industries, are then discussed: the first being rejected by both systems, the second being accepted by Malaysia alone. The *ijtihād* and fatwa-issuing on halal employed by both Indonesian and Malaysia fatwa authorities in terms of *istiḥāla* places them in opposition to the broader position of international ʿulama' in the Middle East. The diversity of Islamic conceptions is very explicit here. Once more, *maṣlaḥa* is a key concept for Malaysian *ijtihād*, but not for Indonesian *ijtihād*, in which *maṣlaḥa* is rarely used as a legal reason and argument. Another major discussion addresses the relationship of religious interpretation to scientific expertise. A double validity is systematically claimed. The author concludes that there are three elements that reflect the use of the collective *ijtihād* principle in the fatwa-making of MUI in halal issues: the presence of shariʿa experts (*muftī*), the presence of non-shariʿa experts, and the presence of food auditors as data investigators. Two other concepts are presented to underline yet another source of diversity: *ḍarūra* and *iḥtiyāṭ*. The use of *ḍarūra* (emergency) is a kind of safety valve for cases for which a precedent cannot be found in Islamic legal reasoning to determine their lawfulness, according to similarly derived criteria in Malaysia and Indonesia. The same closeness can be seen for the concept of *iḥtiyāṭ*: conceptually speaking, *iḥtiyāṭ* is used by Muslim jurists to explain the importance of considering precautions in the practice of Islam in daily life. The author concludes that 'the stricter *ijtihād* of halal adopted in both Indonesia and Malaysia reflects loyalty to the textual reading of the sources of Islamic law on one hand, but it also indicates the ignorance of new findings in science and technology related to bio-technological and chemical issues and other new scientific findings'. (Note that the comparison with Indonesia is discussed up to the new 2014 legislation, which comes into effect in 2019, and under which the National Agency of Halal Product Assurance is fully responsible for the issuance of halal certification and MUI retains the function of *ijtihād* and fatwa-issuer. This brings us back to the major issue of the gradual distinction between bodies specialising in the question of religious interpretation and those concentrating on standardised certification issues.)

The last two chapters begin a transition to the second part of the book. They attest to the importance of contexts when considering the means of religious interpretation about the halal referent. The importance of religious referents and their discussion depends indeed on structures and institutions that vary according to socio-historical contexts. The absence of such systems in China is examined in turn and this relative emptiness is contrasted with the rich circumstantial history of Indonesia.

Chapter 5, 'Developing the Halal Market: China's Opportunity to Strengthen MENA Ties and Address Uighur/Hui issues', discusses China as a halal product producer and its capacity to supply halal demands. In this chapter, Zaynab El Bernoussi argues that China would be able to take the opportunity of the halal business to strengthen its relationship with the MENA region, yet has to deal with internal human right issues affecting its Muslim population (i.e. the Uighur issue) that will undermine its share of the halal business. The author shows both how the halal issue is internally politicised by the issue of minorities and externally by Uighur China's desire to deploy economic relations with MENA countries. But priority is given by this chapter to a bottom-up view, showing that the development of halal is not just a top-down issue. The feelings of Muslim minorities are presented, including the way of life and external discrimination of the Uighurs. Faced with a way of life that is extremely close to the sources of local production, the halal issue hardly arises. In comparison, the substantial mechanisms for the benefit of other Muslim minorities (Hui), which are better dealt with, raise different issues, more related to middle-class needs. In both cases, however, it is yet another issue that hinders the development of even a minority local religious interpretation: there has been great controversy about the Chinese halal labelling as 'fake'. Such a reputation thwarts any internal success and refers back to external relations. For their halal labelling, many Chinese Muslims have greater trust in imported products from Malaysia, Singapore, Indonesia, and beyond than in local Chinese halal products. A lack of confidence among the population seems to explain why a more complex religious referencing of halal has slowed down (with the sole exception of Hong Kong, linked to its foreign Islamic tourist deployment). More generally, the author shows to what extent the convergence of halal/*ṭayyib* operates in a positive perspective of well-being and ecology, notably around the question of animals' well-being throughout their life. The fact remains that China is still not a major player in the halal market: it has no halal certification bodies or national authority for its halal market, no halal ports, and it still suffers from distrust of its halal production.

The final chapter in this part, 'Science, Politics, and Islam: The Other Origin Story of Halal Authentication in Indonesia', discusses how making 'halal certification' a scientific enterprise is a very recent phenomenon. In this chapter, En-Chieh Chao shows convincingly that scientific halal certification was created by a complicated process of 'co-production' among different actors, including food scientists, inter- and intra-national politics, Chinese-owned factories, and Muslim religious scholars, as well as the logic of scientific certification. She suggests treating the origin story as 'a site of political struggle that is conditioned by specific socio-cultural contexts'. The focus will be a localised history of the birth of halal certification in Indonesia, which is more precisely inseparable from scientific intervention and ethno-religious politics. The author shows that it was a social panic linked to the dissemination, in 1988, of a scientific discovery establishing the presence of impurities in well-known and reputable products that brought the halal issue to the Indonesian agenda. The researcher who is the source of this information and whose name is now celebrated as the founder, was at the time called subversive—proof that the scientific refinement of halal was not considered commonplace at the end of the 1980s, or even adequate. The MUI then gradually reversed its principles: the need to prove the haram nature in order to prohibit it was to be replaced by the obligation of prior certification of the halal nature of this property. The category of *mushtabihāt*, or doubtful things would fade away. This was the first attempt to incorporate scientists, full-time technicians, and laboratory experiments into the references for the issuing of fatwas with regards to the question of halal authenticity. But other considerations have also come into play to explain this scientific eagerness: while some companies are assumed halal, others are often doubted, and Chao shows this has much to do with ethno-religious politics, mainly due to a suspicion about the Chinese, easily extended from Chinese restaurants to Chinese-owned factories. From this perspective, halal certification has come to be seen as a tool to prevent potential ethno-religious conflict and socio-economic unrest and was in practice only popular among some sectors of the market, ethno-religiously marked, and it remained so for years. Chao then shows the importance of another scandal in 2000, concerning a food-processing process using enzymes derived from pork but not integrated into the product itself. In a plain language, there is no trace of porcine DNA in it. In 2000, many scientists took the same stance. But this time, their opinion did not count. The real question was, rather, how to judge contamination found in an indirect place. This was indeed a religious interpretation effect concerning the doubt of contamination. But Chao also shows the extent to which this decision is linked to the troubles in Indonesian society at the time, in a difficult democratic transition after the end of the Suharto regime. 'Neither a natural Muslim desire nor simply rising religious conservatism, halal authentication in Indonesia today is always already a socio-material process in which technoscience and ethno-religious politics have played an important role', concludes Chao.

The second part of the book focuses on current trends of halal issues in a minority context, such as in Belgium, Italy, Spain, Poland, and Russia. The question addressed here is less that of Islamic doctrinal content for the interpretation of the halal referent. The chapters in this second part of the book show how the diasporic effects of Muslim minorities, concerning settlement and internal consumption, will be combined with various export themes to predominantly Muslim countries. As we have already seen, albeit negatively in the Chinese case, this link between local and transnational halal certification is constructed not only according to external economic policies but also internal religious policies. However, as soon as the halal issue is deployed within states that are themselves secular, the door of Islamic science is not the first one, but rather the progressive institutionalisation of the representative structures of Islam in these countries, with great diversity as we shall observe. As for the social circumstances, they are not the result of scandals concerning false certifications, but of other polemics, such as that relating to slaughter without stunning and the dominant argument of animal welfare. Several authors will point out that the principles of Islam are traditionally concerned with animal welfare throughout the life of the animal, 'from farm to fork', rather than only at the time of slaughter. However, the Islamic internal doctrinal argumentation is resolutely second in these secular frameworks. On the contrary, it is a new opportunity for scientific debates (on animal welfare) and economic practices (related to consumer information and product labelling).

Chapter 7, 'Halal Certification, Standards, and their Ramifications in Belgium', discusses halal certification bodies, standards of halal, certification processes, and their ramifications in Belgium. In this chapter, Ayang Utriza Yakin addresses the issues of HCBs, the process of making their standards, and the halal certification process. He argues that these standards of halal and halal certification had ramifications, such as the shift of religious authority and the threat to the pluriversality of halal. The first observation made by Yakin puts Belgium in the category of countries where Islam is a minority (7 per cent of the population): while an official representation of Islam has been built up from the recognition of Islam as a religion with preferential public status, the recognition of halal status has progressively been governed by private organisations commonly referred to as halal certification bodies, and not, as was originally the case, by the official representation of Islam recognised by the Government. Only the question of slaughter without stunning is the subject of intervention by the representative body of Belgian Muslims, parliamentary debates, and legal disputes (still unfinished at the time of writing). In Belgium, as elsewhere, private certification procedures, linked to accreditation for South-East Asian standards, result in the shift of the religious authority from the 'ulama' toward HCBs and the neglect of the diversity of opinions within Sunni orthodoxy and of halal practices among all Muslims. After recalling the successive conditions for the settlement of Muslim populations in Belgium, mainly from 1964 onwards, Yakin shows that the debates related to halal only really emerged in the 2000s. He explains the results of a field analysis of the HCBs currently active in Belgium. In fact, the development of halal issues in Belgium is part of the *glocalisation* problem—the dynamic exchange between global and local. Export capacity to Muslim-majority countries is linked to the issue of domestic consumption and vice-versa. One of the major findings of this chapter is the gradual shift from religious authorities to specialised agencies, whose legal qualification (not very convincing) is that of non-profit organisations. Of the 17 HCBs detected by Yakin, only some are actually active, and only one has international accreditation. The standards used depend mainly on the export destination. One of the major observations is the total absence of religious experts during the certification processes by these Belgian agencies. In fact, all of the auditors-certifiers have been educated in science, technology, and economics, at various academic levels. Although each HCB has a religious board, this is just a formality. One of the main conclusions of the chapter is the decline of the pluriversality of halal that was previously deployed through the richness and variety of religious debates and the importance of subjective individual and community experiences, replaced today by technical standards devoid of reflexivity.

Chapter 8, 'The Italian and Spanish Legal Experiences with Halal Certifying Bodies', examines the Italian and Spanish experiences with halal certifying bodies from a legal perspective. In this chapter, Rossella Bottoni discusses the legal regulation of religion regarding halal certification and their implications by describing two interesting experiences, namely Halal Italia in Italy and Junta Islámica's Marca de Garantía Halal in Spain. The economic crisis of 2008, new export opportunities, and the controversies surrounding animal welfare are highlighted as factors for change. However, the analysis offered by this chapter is resolutely of a legal nature. The analysis is conducted according to the three dimensions of the European legal regimes of religions: individual freedom of religion, respect for the doctrinal autonomy of religions and, finally, selective cooperation between the state and certain religions. On the subject of individual freedom, the author stresses in particular that the issue of respect for the dietary rules prescribed by one's religion or belief has been expressly addressed by Italy's National Bioethics Committee: food differences related to ethnic origins or religious or ideological beliefs deserve protection, because they express a person's or a group's identity. The most important point for halal certification is respect for the doctrinal autonomy of religions. Consequently (unlike in the USA, for example), Italy's and Spain's internal legal systems refrain from providing a legal definition of halal and leave this issue entirely to private actors (companies and religious authorities). However, consumer protection remains, particularly with regard to information, labelling and fraud prevention. The result is a wide variety of halal labels and relative uncertainty as to their actual scope. Bottoni, along with others, points out that Muslim consumers have differing degrees of religiosity and attitudes towards animal welfare and, thus, different expectations about halal food. Finally, both countries offer legal regimes favourable to certain religions, but only Spain has a specific agreement with representatives of Islam, which includes provisions on the halal denomination. However, bilateral relations exist in both countries, and Italy has also recognised the relevance of some Muslim bodies in halal certification. This is the case of Trademark Halal Italia linked in 2010 to an Inter-Ministerial Unilateral Convention for the Support of the Initiative 'Halal Italia'. Halal Italia is a trademark registered in 2010 by Comunità Religiosa Islamica (Co.Re.Is.)—an already existing Muslim organisation and active since the 1990s to cater for the general needs of Muslims. It is one of the three certifying authorities linked to Islamic organisations. Bottoni describes the development of this certification mechanism that, according to guidelines, does not have the purpose of endorsing a specific interpretation of what halal is, as this matter ultimately belongs to the concerned religious authorities. Public support for the initiative is clearly of a purely economic nature. The minister responsible for religious matters is not a signatory. Even in this case, the halal nature of a product cannot be discussed as such before a state judge. Only the existence or not of a halal certification can be verified, as well as its possible fraudulent nature. As regards Spain, Bottoni describes the creation of the Marca de Garantía Halal de Junta Islámica, resulting from Article 14 of the cooperation agreement with the Islamic Commission of Spain (ICS) in 1992. ICS does not have a guaranteed monopoly and remains inactive, but other organisations have registered halal trademarks since 2003 (currently more than 50). The rationale for the endorsement of a specific Muslim organisation's halal certifying body has been the protection of religious freedom in the Spanish case, and the promotion of economic interests in the Italian one. However, in Spain, linking the recognition of Islam with a capacity to define halal has only led to internal blockages within the recognised body and has led other (economic) actors to ensure this certification on the basis of common trademark law. This is in line with the Italian situation. It can be seen that relations between religious bodies, public authorities, and economic players remain extremely variable and uncertain. Bottoni concludes by explicitly pointing out the tensions, in Italy or Spain, of the diversity of Islamic traditions versus the progressive homogenisation linked to standardisation.

Chapter 9, 'Ethics as Process: The Case of Religious and National Food Certifications in Italy', continues the analysis of the Italian situation but from a very different, more anthropological, perspective. It focuses on halal certification by HCBs and its halal consumption as an ethical process in Italy. Lauren Crossland-Marr highlights that halal-acceptable food is part of long and continuous debate on eating ethics between certifiers, consumers, and producers in Italy. The previous chapter explained the legal conditions for the birth of the Halal Italia trademark from a top-down perspective. Crossland-Marr's chapter highlights the effect inherent in bringing the two concepts, Halal and Italia, together as a factor of consumer confidence, from a bottom-up perspective. Exploring debates about ethics, this chapter seeks to merge the anthropological study of the halal sector with larger questions in food studies, arguing that an ethics of eating is continual and that debates are an expected part of this process. The concept of halal is again brought closer here with ideas about 'good', 'healthy', and 'correct' production, processing, and distribution at many levels (local, regional, national, and global). Crossland-Marr shows how the notions of halal are co-created by certifiers and consumers, and reinforced by the label Made in Italy. The author attempts a comparison of the two labels and their joint effects. While halal audit bodies emphasise religious ethics, Food Italy recognises ethical foundations found in the national realm. For example, both labels rule out GMs crops and derivatives because there is no scientific consensus on whether GMOs are safe. More generally, the observation of an irreducible diversity is also made here: 'The lack of a global, unified standard in both Made in Italy and halal audit bodies means that standards vary and are influenced by the local cultural attitudes regarding the value of certain foods.' But it is the underlying interpretation that is most remarkable: for the young consumers, halal is an ethical orientation that is *also* religious practice. Individual trust is at the heart of the process, with multiple sources ranging from labelling to trust in the neighbourhood Muslim butcher, even without certification. In the same line, they believed that the rise of certifications like organic and vegan should also allow for halal to be present in the Italian context. Among young people, this trust is increasingly based on the use of the internet and social networks, such as halal food bloggers-known as 'haloodies', although consensus is rare. Once again, the concept of '*ṭayyib*-halal ethos' is at the heart of the conclusions of Crossland-Marr's analysis.

Chapter 10, 'Halal Certification as a Source of Intra- and Inter-Group Tensions among Muslims in Poland', shows the development of the halal market and certification strategies by various Muslim groups in Poland (around 0.1 per cent of the Polish population). In this chapter, Konrad Pędziwiatr addresses how halal food production and halal certification became a source of tension and internal conflict within the Muslim community in Poland, and examines the status of the Tatar minority, which comprises smaller but historically more anchored Muslim communities in Poland. As a result of the immigration processes already starting to emerge in the late 1950s (mostly in the form of student migrations) and conversions to Islam, the Muslim community revived and started to become increasingly diversified. At the beginning of the twenty-first century, the largest group within the Muslim population in Poland are no longer Tatars, but immigrants and their children and grandchildren as well as Polish citizens who have embraced Islam. The historical leadership of the Tatar minority will gradually be questioned, especially on the occasion of the halal certification, which will generally escape the Tatar minority in favour of the Muslim League established in 2001 and recognised as the 'religious community' in 2004 by the Department of Denominations and National Minorities at the Ministry of Internal Affairs and Administration. Until the end of 1990s, membership of the traditional (and Tatar-driven) Muslim Organisation of Poland was open only to Muslims with Polish citizenship. The end of communism, the emergence of a middle class, including Muslims, the controversies surrounding stunless slaughter, and the importance of Poland's halal export capacity to Muslim countries are all factors that the author examines to present the context. But the most striking fact is about Tatar identity: an identity and a traditional leadership threatened by the growing halal certification authority of a concurring organisation (the Muslim League). This change is explained by a number of cyclical factors, including financial flows and their lack of transparency. Pędziwiatr shows how they became a very important source of inter- and intra-group disputes. The creation of the Polish Halal Institute has taken over the part of the market traditionally serviced by the Muslim League. The organisation has developed dynamically since 2010 and has acted as one of the major factors reconfiguring some groups within a diverse Muslim community in Poland, the community as a whole and its relations with broader society.

The last chapter, 'Living Halal in the Volga Region: Lifestyle and Civil Society Opportunities', describes the phenomenon of 'the halal movement' in Russia. In this chapter, Matteo Benussi explores how the 'halal boom' in Russia emerged as a historical novelty in the post-socialist era, and highlights both the challenges and the opportunities of civil society in these new and alternative forms of virtuous subjectivity. Despite being steeped in a region's long Islamic history, the halal boom in the Tatar Central Russia's Idel-Ural region represents a whole new chapter of that history. The findings of this chapter are in line with the cross-cutting observations that are at the heart of this work, as regards the first signs of an ethical transformation of the halal reference more than ethnic or even purely religious. The success of halal discourses indicates a rise in ethicised religion at the expense of the vernacular devotionalism and localism that characterised Soviet-era approaches to Islam. Benussi observes that the idiom of halal, with its universal categories, and its emphasis on conduct, personal choice, and individual rectitude, resonates deeply with the existential needs and aspirations of a bourgeoning, cosmopolitan Muslim middle class. At the same time, this success reveals Tatar Muslims' sincere commitment to ways of living Islam that, though scripturally informed, have not been linked to political militancy, 'grand civilisational goals', or mediation of Russia's Spiritual Directorates. Benussi shows how Muslim consumers use 'ethical' halal as a guiding principle in a post-Soviet landscape of newly formed, still unruly markets, as well as a fertile ground for experiments in Islamic capitalism, in order not to become identified as 'non-traditional for Russia'. But all these evolutions in Tatarstan are, from Bernussi's observations, as much a product of social change in post-Soviet, neo-capitalist Russia as they are heir to the many centuries of Muslim history in this region.

At the end of this overview, many cases and contexts will have shown not only how different approaches and various actors are articulated but also how religious interpretation can seem to be abused, sometimes by reinterpretations favourable to the dominant economic structure, sometimes by a vicious circle of scientific techniques. Religious interpretations are sometimes themselves frozen by a strong precautionary principle. A tension has also been observed between international halal standardisation, linked to macro-economic relations, and individual or community anthropological reconstructions, linked to questions of identity and integrity but also, more broadly, ethical forms of life. Throughout the various chapters, the call for a reflexive deployment of the halal referent, less binary, but open to the construction of an Islamic economic morality, integrating the principle of religious precaution into fidelity with the diversity of Islamic traditions more than to the diktats of two supposedly new sovereign rulers, Science and The Market, have been pointed out.

Bibliography

Armanios, Febe and Bogac Ergene. 2018. *Halal Food: A History*. Oxford: Oxford University Press.

Bergeaud-Blackler, Florence. 2017. *Le Marché Halal ou l'invention d'une tradition*. Paris: Seuil.

Robertson, Roland. 'Glocalisation: Time-Space and Homogeneity-Heterogeneity'. In *Global Modernities*, edited by Mike Featherstone, Scott Lash, and Roland Robertson, 25–44. Sage: London, 1995.

Swyngedouw Erik. 2004. 'Globalization or "Glocalization"? Networks, Territories and Rescaling', *Cambridge Review of International Affairs* 17, no. 1: 25–48.

PART 1

Halal Market: Genealogy and Current Trends

CHAPTER 2

Rethinking Halal: Hegemony, Agency, and Process

Harun Sencal and Mehmet Asutay

1 Introduction

During the last decades, we have witnessed the competition of Islamic Financial Institutions (IFIs) with the conventional financial sector at the global scale, particularly after the 1990s. As a result of this competition, developing 'efficient' products and services with 'low transaction cost' while providing shariʿa compliance at the same time has become the main challenge for IFIs. In responding to this challenge, *maṣlaḥa* (public utility) is utilised as the main justification method for the controversial products and services to sustain shariʿa compliance.

While *maṣlaḥa* is not a new concept or ground in justifying a fatwa (issuing a ruling), we argue that, in a modern context, it has been transformed into a new meaning. The most distinguishing feature of the modern meaning of *maṣlaḥa* is that it does not have to comply with the two main sources of Islam, namely the Qurʾan and sunna (tradition of the Prophet of Islam). Rather, the legitimacy of *maṣlaḥa* stems from the evaluation of a case as '*maṣlaḥa*' or public utility by shariʿa scholars without any further supporting evidence from the Qurʾan and sunna. Ramaḍān al-Būṭī[1] used the term 'delusional *maṣlaḥa*' (*maṣlaḥa mawhūma*) to define it due to its contradictions with the verses of the Qurʾan or sunna. Some jurists have utilised delusional *maṣlaḥa* to justify exceptional cases. These cases are considered as an 'exception' since none of the schools of thought in Islamic law approves them.

In an attempt to render justification for these exceptions, shariʿa scholars in IFIs implicitly or explicitly appeal to the principles of modernity and capitalism such as low transaction cost and efficiency (as the example of organised *tawarruq* articulates) rather than the principles of shariʿa agreed by many scholars throughout history. Another important criterion to determine an exception, particularly in the contemporary context, is the utilisation of shariʿa scholars' opinion as a collective body with different intellectual and cultural backgrounds, such as The International Council of *Fiqh* Academy, as a

1 al-Būṭī, *Ḍawābiṭ al-Maṣlaḥa fī al-Sharīʿa al-Islāmiyya*, 412.

 | DOI:10.1163/9789004459236_003

benchmark. Since such organisations are non-profit organisations with members from all around the world, they have relatively less pressure from governments and businesses compared to the IFI-based shariʿa scholars, and enjoy an intellectual environment of discussing a variety of opinions to reach a conclusion. Such an exception is similar to that defined by Schmitt.[2] We argue, therefore, that the jurists who apply delusional *maṣlaḥa* decide an exception in Islamic law. This state is considered an exception since the facilitation of delusional *maṣlaḥa* means suspending the verses of the Qurʾan and sunna, which are the cornerstones of Islamic law. In exploring the concept of 'exception', Carl Schmitt states that '[S]overeign is he who decides on the exception'.[3] Hence, by issuing a fatwa based on delusional *maṣlaḥa*, the jurist becomes 'sovereign'. Furthermore, in reality, a jurist does not issue this fatwa by his own will; rather it is the enforcement of the capitalist market system that leads jurists to issue such a fatwa based on delusional *maṣlaḥa*. Consequently, we can argue that it is capitalism and its unceasing demand rather than shariʿa scholars that remains sovereign over Islamic law and IFIs in such a state of exception.

The hegemony of the capitalist financial system over the Islamic financial sector is very strong, as the accelerated convergence of IFIs towards conventional institutions in terms of product and services during the last decade shows. Shariʿa scholars are not eligible to prevent this convergence even though they are the authority that renders 'Islamic' identity to IFIs. This can be explained mainly through the three important transformations have taken place in *iftāʾ* (the act of issuing a legal opinion in Islamic law) institution from pre-modern to modern period, which are: (i) embeddedness of shariʿa scholars into the modern financial system, whether it is Islamic or not; (ii) change in the source of legitimacy of shariʿa scholars; and (iii) the relative complexity of the modern period compared to pre-modern period. Due to such transformations, we witness that the existence of shariʿa governance or shariʿa boards (SBs) in modern IFIs is insufficient to challenge the hegemony of the capitalist system.

This chapter, therefore, aims to offer a potential way out of this hegemony, at least a way to moderate the outcomes of the observed convergence, which is expressed as a 'social failure' in bringing the existing IFIs closer to the initial aspirations.[4] As a potential solution, this study suggests a civil society-based regulatory mechanism to evaluate the shariʿa compliance of the products and services of IFIs. Civil society refers to the organisations and institutions besides government and business. In this civil society-based regulatory mechanism, the

2 Schmitt, *Political Theology*, 6.
3 Schmitt, *Political Theology*, 6.
4 Asutay, 'Conceptualising and Locating the Social Failure of Islamic Finance', 100–109.

establishment of non-profit organisations composed of scholars from various disciplines, including shariʿa scholars, political scientists, economists, etc., is necessary. Moreover, to minimise the influence of politics and business, invited scholars should be independent, to overcome conflicts of interest.

Such a regulatory mechanism does not substitute but complements the role of shariʿa scholars, which should go beyond the binary opposition of *ḥalāl*/*ḥarām* or permissible/impermissible and implement a fuzzy logic approach to articulate the morality of shariʿa in IFIs' everyday practices. In other words, rather than deciding whether a certain product is *ḥalāl* or *ḥarām*, this mechanism should mainly aim to decide to what degree a certain product or service is compatible with the morality of shariʿa in various dimensions, such as environment, employee-employer relationship, production process, etc. Such labelling as 'suitable for vegetarians' or 'fair trade', for instance, are examples of binary dichotomies, whereas the energy efficiency rating of houses on a scale of 1–100 is an example of the fuzzy logic approach.

Furthermore, as the scholars in these organisations are not expected to possess the aforementioned shortcomings of the shariʿa scholars in IFIs, this measure is expected to be less influenced by competition among the commercial banks. Additionally, the number of these rating institutions should not be limited to a few, as this might also create a hegemony of these institutions. Instead, as is the case in the *ḥalāl* certificate industry, multiple rating organisations with their set of criteria, respected and independent scholars and transparently displayed indices could help to disseminate the power.

The rest of the chapter consists of six sections, including this introduction and a conclusion. In the next section, we explore the concept of sovereignty and analyse the cause of the state of exception in both Western context and Islamic law. In section 3, we explain *maṣlaḥa* and its utilisation by various scholars in the history of Islamic law. In section 4, we analyse *maṣlaḥa* in modern times and how it is employed to decide a state of exception. In section 5, we offer and discuss a potential way out of the hegemony of the capitalist market system through utilisation of a fuzzy logic approach. Finally, we present the concluding remarks.

2 Sovereign and Exception

In this study, as stated above, we argue that the sovereign over IFIs is the capitalist market system. This is evidenced by the fact that it has the power of deciding an exception in shariʿa compliance in the construction process of the products and services as well as institutional forms.

While the theory of sovereignty has a long tradition in Western literature, it is mostly affiliated with political power. The concept of sovereignty, as a modern theory, is first defined by Jean Bodin in the sixteenth century. However, the notion of the sovereign is used in former periods without implying a political power in terms of its modern meaning.[5] Bodin defines sovereignty in the later Latin edition as '[T]he supreme power over citizens and subjects, unrestrained by law'. This supreme power, according to Bodin, is absolute. It means sovereignty is completely free from the constraint of law and is not held subject to any condition or limitation. It is only limited by laws of God, of nature and nations. Bodin's theory of supreme power laid the foundation of the seventeenth- and eighteenth-century absolutism.[6]

In the following centuries, the concept of sovereignty was theorised further by various scholars. In the seventeenth century, for instance, Hobbes suggested a theory of sovereignty in his book, *Leviathan*, in which he proposed a social contract and placed insecurity and fear at the centre of the covenant, which creates sovereignty.[7] With this social contract, people transfer their rights to the sovereign and authorise it, since the sovereign must have absolute authority to govern effectively.[8] As a response to Bodin and Hobbes' sovereignty theories, John Locke's new theory proposed the community as a source of sovereignty, in which the government merely plays the role of legitimate executor of this sovereignty. Responsibilities of this government, Locke argues, consist of the protection of life, liberty, and property. In the eighteenth century, Jean-Jacques Rousseau proposed another social contract, a contract that transferred sovereignty from the state to the community, to the 'people'. According to his theory of social contract, everybody makes a contract with everybody, so, 'everybody becomes a ruler and ruled at the same time'.[9] In order to become a member of the state, people give up their natural liberty. In this way, they place a legal limitation on governmental power instead of a moral limitation. Consequently, the individual wills combine to form the general will and in such a setting, popular assembly represents the sovereign will, while government acts solely as an executive agent.[10]

Contrary to the seventeenth and eighteenth century, where an omnipotent lawgiver was identified with a personal factor of the rule, in the nineteenth

5 Handler, 'Towards the Sociology of Sovereignty', 425.
6 Merriam, *History of the Theory of Sovereignty since Rousseau*, 8.
7 Nagan and Haddad, 'Sovereignty in Theory and Practice', 443–444.
8 Nagan and Haddad, 'Sovereignty in Theory and Practice', 444.
9 János Rapcsák, 'Sovereignty—Past and Present', 33.
10 Willis, 'The Doctrine of Sovereignty Under the United States Constitution', 439.

and twentieth centuries the personal element disappeared from the concept of sovereignty. As a result of such political transformation leading to democratic legitimacy and division of power, 'power must be checked by the power', and consequently, 'sovereignty of law should replace the sovereignty of men', leading to the split of political power.[11] According to Austin, for instance, sovereignty vested neither in the ruler, as Bodin claimed, nor in the people, as popular sovereignty suggested. Austin defined positive law as sorts of command that stem from a political superior, and claimed that this political superior is the sovereign.[12]

As for the definition of sovereignty according to Islam, Ahmad[13] argued that, in Islam, sovereignty belongs to Allah and it is His Authority alone that should be recognised as the foundation and articulation of sovereignty, even from a legal perspective. While political science only considers the sovereignty of people in the world, in Islam, the sovereignty of Allah is at the centre of life: He governs and controls everybody. Ahmad[14] also asserts that, being the only sovereign in Islam, Allah is also the real Legislator, and His Law (Qur'an) cannot be altered by any human, although analogy (*qiyās*), interpretation (*ijtihād*), and consensus of community (*ijmāʿ*) can be utilised to respond to new situations that do not have an explicit solution in the Qur'an and the sunna.

As Ahmad[15] argues, shariʿa, or as Hallaq[16] would state, the morality of shariʿa, is at the centre of everyday life and shapes it, including but not limited to the matters related to the law and finance. This is because even the scope and extent of exceptions are determined by shariʿa. In an attempt to elaborate on the concept of exception further, it is important to define it first. Schmitt characterises an exception as 'a case of extreme peril, a danger to the existence of the state, or the like'.[17] Schmitt further claims that the sovereign decrees whether there is an extreme emergency or not, and if there is such a situation he decides how to handle it.[18]

As for the causes of exception, Agamben divides the Western states into two categories based on how a state of exception is situated in legal tradition:[19] the first group embodies the state of exception in the text of the constitution, such

11 Schmitt, Introduction, xiii.
12 Willis, 'The Doctrine of Sovereignty Under the United States Constitution', 440.
13 Ahmad, 'Sovereignty in Islam', 244.
14 Ahmad, 'Sovereignty in Islam', 249–253.
15 Ahmad, 'Sovereignty in Islam', 245.
16 Hallaq, *The Impossible State*, 12.
17 Schmitt, Introduction, 6.
18 Schmitt, Introduction, 6–7.
19 Agamben, *State of Exception*, 9–10.

as France and Germany, and second group does not include the state of exception into the constitution, such as Italy, Switzerland, England, and the United States.[20] In both groups, whether the state of exception is explicitly defined by the constitution or not, after the state of exception has been decided, the constitution was suspended. So it is important to determine the cause of the exception. Agamben states that the basis of the state of exception, therefore the cause of the exception, is a *necessity*.[21] An ancient maxim, *necessity has no law*, is the source of state of exception. This maxim can be explained by two different meanings: 'necessity does not recognise any law' and 'necessity creates its own law'.[22] In both meanings, necessity can be considered as the foundation for a state of exception.

In the medieval world, the theory of necessity was considered as a theory of exception that led to merely releasing one particular case from the obligation of law, not to the suspension of law. Gratian, in his *Dectrum*, mentions such cases twice and, due to supreme necessity, he allows acting against the law.[23] Therefore, necessity is neither a source of law nor suspends the law but only release a specific case from the literal application of the law. Therefore, in medieval times, suspension of law for the common good out of necessity was a foreign idea. Conversely to the medieval world, in modern times, the state of exception is inclined to be embodied in law and has gained an identity as a state of law.[24] Agamben criticises writers who consider the nature of necessity as an objective situation for being naive and claims that necessity requires subjective judgement, whereby deciding the necessity (exception) as the crucial point.[25] That is the reason Schmitt[26] advocates that it is the sovereign who decides what 'the exception' is and how to act in 'the state of exception'.[27] As for Islamic law, such a state of exception is both embodied in the textual sources of shariʿa (Qurʾan and sunna) in the form of legal licenses and left as a space for *ijtihād* of shariʿa scholars based on the objectives of shariʿa to go beyond the legal licences. *Maṣlaḥa*, or public utility, in this regard, is utilised to respond to emergent cases to internalise new circumstances. Such an understanding of *maṣlaḥa* is defended by prominent scholars such as al-Ghazālī, al-Rāzī and al-Shāṭibī, among others.

20 Agamben, *State of Exception*, 10.
21 Agamben, *State of Exception*, 16.
22 Agamben, *State of Exception*, 24.
23 Agamben, *State of Exception*, 24.
24 Agamben, *State of Exception*, 26.
25 Agamben, *State of Exception*, 29–30.
26 Schmitt, Introduction, 5.
27 Schmitt, Introduction, 6–7.

The theory of *maṣlaḥa* suggested by al-Ṭūfī, on the other hand, approves the disregarding of scriptural rulings in the case of a contradiction with *maṣlaḥa*, which remains as a minority view in the course of Islamic history until the twentieth century. However, Jamāladdīn al-Qāsimī published the *risāla* of al-Ṭūfī to bring him to the agenda in 1906, which is followed by Rashīd Riḍā's *risāla* in al-Manār.[28] The idea was to introduce the method of al-Ṭūfī as an answer to the modern problems of life. As a result of this method, jurists would not be restricted by Islamic law. Consequently, *maṣlaḥa*, as an independent source of law, might be employed to judge on new circumstances, if it is required. Furthermore, when the ties between the concept of *maṣlaḥa* and textual rulings is severed by accepting a situation as *maṣlaḥa* even if it is contrary to textual rulings, *maṣlaḥa* is rendered as a subjective concept. On the other hand, in the theory of *maṣlaḥa*, jurists such as al-Ghazālī, al-Rāzī and al-Qarāfī, the concept of *maṣlaḥa* is originated from the textual evidence implying a more objective nature.

If we consider *maṣlaḥa* as an objective concept and the definition of '*maṣlaḥa*' is decided in the light of textual evidences, which necessarily means that there should not be any contradiction between the *maṣlaḥa* and the Qur'an or sunna, then we may conclude that the sovereign (who decides what is *maṣlaḥa*) is Allah and He is alone. On the other hand, if we follow al-Ṭūfī, and his modern followers, who consider *maṣlaḥa* as an independent source of law and admit the possibility of conflict between a *maṣlaḥa* and textual evidences, we must accept *maṣlaḥa* as a subjective concept and let the jurists decide what is *maṣlaḥa* and accept their judgement as a valid ruling, even if it is contrary to the scriptural rulings. In this case, we have to announce these jurists, who decide what is *maṣlaḥa* for the public good, is the sovereign, because they are the one who decide on the exception, which means Islamic law should be suspended due to contradiction with *maṣlaḥa*, and they can give a ruling without the constraint of Islamic law. Furthermore, we claim that jurists do not decide which circumstances constitute the *maṣlaḥa* based on their own opinions. This implies that, for example, in the case of a market economy, the enforcement of capitalism leads jurists to determine the concept of the *maṣlaḥa* in economic and financial matters.

In the next section, we will define the concept of *maṣlaḥa* and discuss the examples of how it is used by early scholars such as al-Ghazālī and al-Shāṭibī. To explain further, two examples regarding the modern practice of *maṣlaḥa* in

---

28 Kayadibi, 'al-Ṭūfī Centred Approach to Al-Maṣlaḥah Al-Mursalah (Public Interest) in Islamic Law', 72.

Islamic finance are presented to demonstrate as to how *maṣlaḥa*'s subjective nature is exploited, leading to the declaration of 'capitalism' as a sovereign.

3 Maṣlaḥa in Early Times

Since the early periods of law in Muslim history, the concept of *maṣlaḥa* is considered as a legitimate principle and applied on issuing a fatwa, even though it is referred to with different terms.[29] We can trace the roots of the concept of *maṣlaḥa* back to the Companions of the Prophet. While the establishment of prison and issuance of currency are examples for which there is no evidence from the Qur'an or sunna, such practices, along with others, are implemented by the Companions to ensure human welfare and the welfare of the society. Founders of the four schools of law, especially Imam Malik's legal opinions, stress the concept of *maṣlaḥa*. For this reason, some authorities claim that Imam Malik is the first jurist to use the concept of *maṣlaḥa* as a practice without referring to the term *maṣlaḥa*. For instance, Imam Malik validated the payment of blood money in currency instead of camels, which was the ruling during the time of Prophet Muḥammad and Abū Bakr. He claimed that the camel was mostly used in rural areas where wealth is not held in currency and allowed people to pay blood money in terms of their principal medium of exchange for the sake of accommodating people's interest.[30]

Abū Ḥanīfa, the founder of Ḥanafite school, employed *istiḥsān* for adaptability to social needs or public necessity such as validating to ask a tailor to sew clothes. Because according to analogy or *qiyās*, it is not supposed to be valid due to the possibility of an error in the final product. Al-Shāfiʿī, the founder of the Shāfiʿī school, on the other hand, rejected the use of *istiḥsān* due to lack of its basis in the main sources and its arbitrary nature. This implies that if *maṣlaḥa* (or *istiḥsān*) has grounds in main sources, he would have accepted utilising it in decision making. According to Muṣṭafā Zayd's work, *al-Maṣlaḥa*, Aḥmad ibn Ḥanbal, the founder of Ḥanbalī school, used *maṣlaḥa* as an authoritative source in his rulings, such as the death penalty for the spies who cause harm to the Muslim community.[31]

In terms of intellectual and legal historical work, we may find the initial discussions of the *maṣlaḥa* in the book of Juwaynī (d. 419/1028), al-Burhān. In his

29 Qomariyah, 'Al-Ghazālī's Theory of Munāsaba in the Context of the Adaptability of Islamic Law', 13–37.

30 Qomariyah, 'Al-Ghazālī's Theory of Munāsaba', 19–20.

31 Qomariyah, 'Al-Ghazālī's Theory of Munāsaba', 25–26.

book, Juwaynī attempted to give the first descriptions and divisions regarding *maṣlaḥa*, albeit they are not complete. We also observe that he did not mention all subjects related to *maṣlaḥa*.[32]

3.1 *al-Ghazālī and al-Rāzī on Maṣlaḥa*

al-Ghazālī (1058–1111) defines *maṣlaḥa* according to its lexical meaning: 'bringing a cause of benefit or avoiding a cause of harm'. But this definition of *maṣlaḥa* is oriented towards the purpose of human beings, which, therefore, is not used in the discussion of 'authoritativeness' (*ḥujjiyya*). According to al-Ghazālī, as a legal term, *maṣlaḥa* means the preservation of the purposes of the *Shariʿa*. In other words, what constitutes *maṣlaḥa* is not defined according to people's desire and expectation but on the basis of the will of Allah.[33] Therefore, according to al-Ghazālī, *maṣlaḥa* is not a completely subjective concept that depends on people's will, but more of an objective concept derived from textual evidence.

Al-Ghazālī describes the objectives of shariʿa as protecting religion (*dīn*), life (*nafs*), intellect (*ʿaql*), progeny (*nasl*), property (*mulkiyya*). He further categorises these purposes based on their effect on attaining *maṣlaḥa* or avoiding harm into three categories: necessities (*ḍarūriyyāt*), needs (*ḥājiyyāt*) and embellishment (*taḥsīniyyāt*). According to al-Ghazālī, a *maṣlaḥa* under the category of needs or embellishment has to be associated with textual evidence; otherwise, it has no legitimacy. On the other hand, if a case falls under necessity, it can be ruled based on a *maṣlaḥa* albeit it is not supported by textual evidence. However, to issue such a fatwa, the jurist has to be sure of three things: necessity, certainty, and universality, implying that it should be relevant to all Muslims not just a specific group of Muslims. If one of these three preconditions does not hold, then the jurist cannot judge on the basis of *maṣlaḥa*, according to al-Ghazālī.[34]

After a century, al-Rāzī (d. 606/1210) wrote *al-Maḥṣūl* in legal theory, in which he combined al-Ghazālī's *al-Muṣṭasfā* and Abū'l-Ḥusayn al-Baṣrī's *al-Muʿtamad*. Regarding definitions and categories of the theory of *maṣlaḥa*, al-Rāzī follows al-Ghazālī. However, he widens both and presents more detail about controversial matters by providing a well-defined notion of *maṣlaḥa* and places it under the methodology of legal analogy,[35] and hence brought a particular methodological understanding to the debate and confusion.

---

32 Duman, 'Imam Gazzali'nin Maṣlaḥat Dusuncesine Katkilari', 11.

33 Duman, 'Imam Gazzali'nin Maṣlaḥat Dusuncesine Katkilari', 14.

34 Duman, 'Imam Gazzali'nin Maṣlaḥat Dusuncesine Katkilari', 17.

35 Opwis, *Maṣlaḥa: An Intellectual History of a Core Concept in Islamic Legal Theory*, 71–116.

3.2 *al-Qarāfī on Maṣlaḥa*

al-Qarāfī (d. 684/1285), as he stated in his book, closely follows al-Rāzī's *al-Maḥṣūl* in his discussion on the concept of *maṣlaḥa*. In consideration of the *maṣlaḥa*, he adopts two paths: the first path is the path of al-Rāzī by integrating *maṣlaḥa* into the legal analogy. He employs suitability (*munāsaba*) in the determination of *ratio legis* (*ʿilla*) and defines it in the same way al-Ghazālī and al-Rāzī did. In the second path, he utilises *maṣlaḥa* to derive new rulings and further expand application areas of it such as legal licence and legal precept. Contrary to al-Rāzī, al-Qarāfī also uses the principle of *maṣlaḥa* for blocking means or eliminating pretexts to unlawful ends.[36] This implies that al-Qarāfī does not only follow al-Rāzī and al-Ghazālī in the integration of *maṣlaḥa* into legal analogy but further develops the theory of *maṣlaḥa* by considering it as a legal precept (*qawāʿid*) and employs it to derive new rulings for changing circumstances.

Legal precepts are norms and legal maxims which are extracted from the sources of the law. In the process of deriving laws by the means of legal precepts, no reference is made to the primary textual sources; rather, general legal precepts are formulated on the basis of those sources. On the contrary, the methodology of legal analogy derives the ruling for the new case directly from the sources of law. According to al-Qarāfī, attaining *maṣlaḥa* and avoiding harm is one of the legal precepts extracted from the scriptural texts.[37] In addition, al-Qarāfī, following the work of al-Rāzī, also adopts the formal interpretation of *maṣlaḥa* to provide a tangible criterion to defend *maṣlaḥa* against the subjectivity of interpretations and abuse.[38]

3.3 *al-Ṭūfī on Maṣlaḥa*

al-Ṭūfī's views regarding legal theory and theology have not received much attention until modern times, when his theory of *maṣlaḥa* has become the centre of interest,[39] when he presented his controversial ideas about *maṣlaḥa* in his commentary to Nawawī's forty hadiths. When he commented on the hadith that 'harm is neither inflicted nor reciprocated in Islam', he argued that *maṣlaḥa* is a superior indicant of law compared to the scriptural texts (the Qur'an and the sunna) and *ijmāʿ* or consensus. In the case of a contradiction beween these sources and *maṣlaḥa*, *maṣlaḥa* is preferred over the texts and

36 Opwis, *Maṣlaḥa*, 131–136.
37 Opwis, *Maṣlaḥa*, 135.
38 Opwis, *Maṣlaḥa*, 142–144.
39 Opwis, *Maṣlaḥa*, 194.

consensus by employing *takhṣīṣ* (particularisation) and *bayān* (clarification).[40] He derives from the hadith stating that 'no harm should be inflicted', an affirmative meaning that '*maṣlaḥa* shall be safeguarded'.[41]

al-Ṭūfī elaborates his theory by considering possible cases. If all the primary sources, the Qur'an, the sunna, consensus, and safeguarding *maṣlaḥa* agree, then ruling is given according to all of these sources. However, if any of the three indicants (the Qur'an, the sunna, and *ijmāʿ*) diverges from safeguarding *maṣlaḥa*, then safeguarding *maṣlaḥa* is given priority. al-Ṭūfī, therefore, advocates that *maṣlaḥa* can be utilised as an independent source of law.

It should be noted that unlike al-Ghazālī and al-Rāzī, al-Ṭūfī does not employ his theory of *maṣlaḥa* through legal analogy; rather, his position can be applied to all cases except acts of worship and fixed ordinances, since it is a universal indicant. Moreover, it has priority over text and consensus, if they do not safeguard *maṣlaḥa*.[42] Although al-Ṭūfī presents evidence from the Qur'an and the sunna to support his theory of *maṣlaḥa*, he does not provide a concrete criterion to measure it. Thus, in a specific case, a ruling based on *maṣlaḥa* is a subjective decision.[43]

3.4 *al-Shāṭibī on Maṣlaḥa*

al-Shāṭibī (d. 790/1388) suggests a new epistemic foundation for legal theory, namely, inductive corroboration, as he places his theory in comprehensive inductive surveys instead of multiple transmitted reports or Qur'anic verses. According to al-Shāṭibī, to reach a certain premise, one has to conduct a broad inductive survey of a large amount of probable evidence that shares a common element. As a result of this survey, we can attain the foundations of shariʿa, namely universality (*kulliyyāt*). Every universal consists of particulars (*juzʾiyyāt*) and each of them affirms one meaning of that universal. Accordingly, five fundamental universals (life, property, progeny, mind, and religion) are examples of such an inductive survey that are not mentioned in the text specifically. Authoritativeness (*ḥujjiyya*) of public interest is also attained through the method of inductive corroboration.[44]

As Opwis stated, al-Shāṭibī advocates that the notion that the objective of the shariʿa is to protect *maṣlaḥa* of the people.[45] Similar to al-Ghazālī, he

40 Kayadibi, 'Al-Ṭūfī Centred Approach', 78–79.
41 Opwis, *An Intellectual History*, 198.
42 Opwis, *An Intellectual History*, 199.
43 Opwis, *An Intellectual History*, 217.
44 Hallaq, *A History of Islamic Legal Theories*, 166.
45 Opwis, *An Intellectual History*, 261–268.

divides *maqāṣid* (objectives) into three categories, namely necessity, need, and embellishment. As mentioned before, al-Ghazālī suggested that they consist of five universal principles, religion (*dīn*), life (*nafs*), intellect (*ʿaql*), progeny (*nasl*), and property (*mulkiyya*). Every level further includes supplementary and complementary elements. Moreover, al-Shāṭibī claims that all these categories (necessity, need, and embellishment) are interrelated, which suggests that, for instance, need is complementary for necessity.

According to Opwis, in al-Shāṭibī's theory, *maṣlaḥa* is a universal concept, which leads him to attest that attaining *maṣlaḥa* and avoiding *mafsada* is not due to human beings' *maṣlaḥa* in this world but to hereafter expectation. Al-Shāṭibī argues that in this world, *maṣlaḥa* does not exist in its pure form but that things are a mixture of *maṣlaḥa* and *mafsada* in different ratios.[46] In addition, due to the changing and particular nature of personal interests, we cannot employ personal interests in the decision process of what constitutes *maṣlaḥa* and *mafsada*. Hence, in the process of deciding what *maṣlaḥa* is, the human intellect is incapable of deciding without the guidance of the law, since 'the law intends to properly arrange the *maṣlaḥa* of this world in order to enable thereby those of the Hereafter'.[47]

Regarding the knowledge of the intention of the Lawgiver, al-Shāṭibī follows a middle path where he rejects both extremes. At one extreme, *Ẓāhirī* group advocates that the intention of the Lawgiver is hidden from us unless he revealed His intention. At another extreme, there are two groups; one of them is *Bāṭinīs*, who claim His intention can be grasped only through the inner meaning of the texts, not by the obvious meaning of them. The other group is gives priority to legal theory over the texts. They defend that to grasp the intention of the Lawgiver meaning that attention should be given to the theoretical meaning of a word. Accordingly, if it differs from the text, theoretical meaning gains precedence. Jurists like al-Ṭūfī, who considers that safeguarding *maṣlaḥa* should have priority over texts, are an example of this group. Al-Shāṭibī, on the other hand, maintains the view that meaning should be considered with revealed texts and textual rulings should be applied considering the meanings they have.[48]

46 Opwis, *An Intellectual History*, 272.
47 Opwis, *An Intellectual History*, 273.
48 Opwis, *An Intellectual History*, 338–339.

4 Maṣlaḥa in Modern Times

As discussed above, scholars utilised the concept of *maṣlaḥa* within the boundaries of shariʿa, and in line with its moral principles. We can even argue that the utilisation of *maṣlaḥa* has been a tool to realise the morality of *Shariʿa* in everyday practice, since it leads to *maṣlaḥa* both in this world and hereafter. However, as Hallaq[49] claims, Muslim individuals live in a world that is constructed by a different worldview. As a result, modern life has brought many issues and challenges for Muslim identity, for which there is no easy solution within Islamic law that can solve the conflicts between the two worldviews, Islamic and modern. As a result, various reformist groups emerged to respond to the challenges of modern life from an intellectual perspective. 'Religious utilitarianism' is one such group, which utilises *maṣlaḥa* as their central concept in legal theory.

As part of the reformist movement, Rashid Rida (d. 1354/1935) is considered one of the pioneer names and adheres to the theory of *maṣlaḥa* developed by al-Ṭūfī and al-Shāṭibī, who prioritised the concepts of 'necessity' and 'interest', which traditionally has limited use. Other important figures such as 'Abd al-Wahhāb Khallāf, 'Allāl al-Fāsī and Ḥasan al-Turābī also embraced this particular school. The effects of this utilitarianism in the religio-legal interpretation of Islamic norms in relation to IFIs can be observed in many spheres of life. The high influence of *maṣlaḥa* can be noticed particularly regarding the financial transactions in which shariʿa scholars can be very liberal,[50] while at the same time, abstaining from the utilisation of *maṣlaḥa* in other spheres, such as regarding social or personal issues.

We argue that jurists in the field of Islamic finance sometimes issue rulings on the basis of delusional *maṣlaḥa* even though it contradicts with scriptural texts. Since these texts are God's commands, jurists who make their judgements based on delusional *maṣlaḥa* decide to nullify God's commands. This very judgement constitutes the exception in the shariʿa since the ruling based on *delusional maṣlaḥa* means scriptural texts (the Qurʾan and sunna) are inadequate to provide a solution for the case at hand, and an exception should be decided for the case to solve the problem. Hence, following Schmitt, we argue that the one who decides the exception is the sovereign. Thus, a ruling based on *delusional maṣlaḥa* announces these jurists as the sovereign through the authority of deciding exception in the law. On the other hand, we can observe

---

49 Hallaq, *The Impossible State*, 3.
50 Shaharuddin, 'The Bayʿ Al-ʿInah Controversy in Malaysian Islamic Banking', 508.

in the Islamic banking industry that shari'a scholars are not necessarily willing to issue rulings based on *delusional maṣlaḥa*, but they are obliged to issue such rulings due to the compulsion of the market system and financialised economy, as Islamic banks consider themselves in competition with conventional banks, and therefore, they feel that they must be on a par with them. Since conventional banks operate within neoclassical norms such as efficiency, maximisation, and low transaction cost, as a consequence, Islamic banks act with a compulsion that they have to essentialise efficiency as defined by neoclassical economists to sustain their growth. However, theoretically there is an important distinction between Islamic and conventional banks in operational terms: 'Islamic bank' financing and operations have to be approved by shari'a scholars for their shari'a compliancy. Thus, in return, in reality, shari'a scholars approve contracts and operations that are constructed with neoclassical norms of efficiency, effectiveness, optimisation, etc. These are the areas where *delusional maṣlaḥa* is utilised by shari'a scholars, as Islamic norms defines a moral economy beyond the neo-classical definition of what economy and finance is.[51] Consequently, it can be argued that it is capitalism and its unceasing demands that makes the market system sovereign over Islamic ontology through the agency of shari'a scholars in relation to Islamic banking. In order to articulate the argument through an example, the following section focuses on organised *tawarruq*, an emergent popular Islamic financial instrument, which is considered controversial in terms of shari'a compliance, while in the following section, two further examples are presented to demonstrate the utilisation of delusional *maṣlaḥa* to operate in line with the principles of the capitalist market system.

4.1 *Organised* Tawarruq *as an Exception*

Organised *tawarruq* is a modified version of classical *tawarruq*, which is now commonly used in Islamic banking operations. Classical *tawarruq* is employed to obtain cash, especially for short-term needs. In terms of operating mechanism, in this financial transaction, firstly, the *mutawarriq* or seeker of cash purchases a commodity from a seller on deferred payment. In the next step, *mutawarriq* sells this commodity in the market on cash for a lower price to a third party.[52] Although utilisation of classical *tawarruq* has been a topic of debate

51 Asutay, 'A Political Economy Approach to Islamic Economics', 14.

52 Dusuki, 'Can Bursa Malaysia's Suq Al-Sila' (Commodity Murabahah House) Resolve the Controversy Over Tawarruq?', 3.

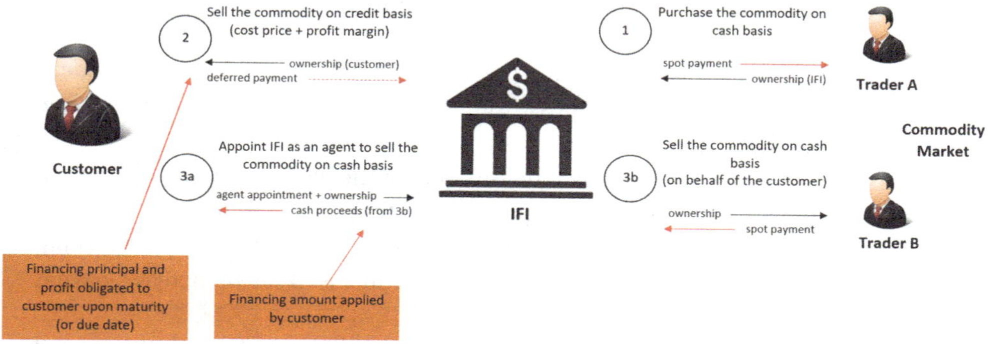

FIGURE 2.1 Working mechanism of organised *tawarruq*
GHAZĀLĪ, 'TAWARRUQ IN MALAYSIAN FINANCING SYSTEM', 70

by jurists due to its substance, which is considered an interest-like instrument despite its form-compliancy, organised *tawarruq* as practised by Islamic banks was constructed in a more controversial structure to increase the efficiency and decrease the transaction cost in attaining short-term liquidity for the clients. The most important difference between classical and organised *tawarruq* is the removal of *mustawriq*'s or the seeker of cash's involvement in the process and transferring intermediary steps to an Islamic bank. In order to construct such an efficient and low-transaction cost instrument, an exception, which is the delegation system, is transformed into a norm. Thus, organised *tawarruq* has become a norm rather than the exception, as it is, as a structure, heavily utilised by Islamic banks in most jurisdictions.

As a frequently used financial instrument, organised *tawarruq* is, hence, used by Islamic banks to facilitate and overcome the liquidity needs of businesses, financial institutions as well as individuals. The working mechanism of organised *tawarruq*, as presented above, is depicted in Figure 2.1.

To contextualise the discussion, it should be noted that in terms of shariʿa permissibility of organised *tawarruq*, the OIC's International Council of Fiqh Academy (ICFA) in Mecca ruled organised *tawarruq* as impermissible in 2009.[53] The reasons behind such prohibition are due to the differences between classical and organised *tawarruq*:[54]

(i) The commitment by the seller in the contract of *tawarruq* by proxy to sell the commodity to another buyer or to line up a buyer makes it similar to

53 Dar and Azmi, *Global Islamic Finance Report 2016*, 305.
54 Dar and Azmi, *Global Islamic Finance Report 2016*, 299.

the prohibited *ʿīna*, whether the commitment is explicitly stipulated or is merely customary practice.

(ii) This practice leads in many cases to a violation of the shariʿa requirement that a buyer must take possession of a commodity in order for any sale after that to be valid.

(iii) The reality of this transaction is based on the bank providing cash financing with an increase to the party called the *mustawriq* through purchase and sales transactions it conducts, which are, in most cases, pure formalities. The aim of the bank from this procedure is to get an increase in what it gave in the way of financing.

ICFA's ruling against the prohibition of organised *tawarruq* has deeply affected the Islamic finance industry, which was aiming to expand this facilitatory financial instrument. As a response to the prohibition of organised *tawarruq* by ICFA, as reported by Khnifer,[55] a group of shariʿa scholars occupying seats at Islamic banks' boards, led by Nizam Yaquby, opposed and rejected this prohibition, as they appealed to the principle of *maṣlaḥa* to legitimise the use of organised *tawarruq*. They advocated the utilisation of organised *tawarruq* due to its facilitation in providing short-term liquidity as a backbone of the IFIs and suggested that it should be permissible based on 'social usefulness or social needs of the Islamic *umma*'.[56] In an interview with Reuters in 2009, a prominent shariʿa scholar defended the use of organised *tawarruq* on the basis of lower transaction costs.[57] Yaquby argued that carrying out the process of selling the assets through a bank would help minimise the transaction cost, and also asked: 'How can shariʿa allow something which is burdensome on a person … and not allow something which is organised and well done, and this man who is in dire need for cash will not suffer a lot?' On the other hand, due to the controversial nature of organised *tawarruq*, some Islamic banks started to avoid it in countries[58] such as Oman or use it without advertising, while Malaysia has been using it openly and extensively. As the available data evidence, in Malaysia the use of organised *tawarruq* has increased by 104% from 2014 to 2016.[59]

Although there are other shariʿa-compliant alternatives for organised *tawarruq* that have not been declared impermissible by ICFA, they are not considered

55 Khnifer, 'Maṣlaḥah and the Permissibility of Organized Tawarruq', 7.

56 Khnifer, 'Maṣlaḥah and the Permissibility of Organized Tawarruq', 7.

57 Islamic Finance Resource, 'Organized Tawarruq Is Permissible: Sheikh Nizam Yaquby'. https://ifresource.com/2009/07/23/organized-tawarruq-is-permissible-sheikh-nizam-yaquby/ (accessed 6 September 2016).

58 Parker, 'Are More and More Islamic Banks Shunning Tawarruq?' Accessed 10 September 2016. https://www.arabnews.com/node/324553.

59 Bank Negara Malaysia, 'The Financial Stability and Payment Systems Report 2016', 91.

as efficient as organised *tawarruq* and riskier, such as *salam*.[60] However, the essential issue is that the financial function of organised *tawarruq* is similar to interest-based borrowing transactions,[61] which is also the cornerstone of a capitalist market economy. Hence, Islamic banks, under the pressure of the capitalist market system feel that they have to utilise organised *tawarruq* to overcome the short-term liquidity needs of their clients and, as a consequence, in responding to the needs of Islamic banks, as a facilitation function, shariʿa scholars feel obliged to announce organised *tawarruq* as legitimate based on '*delusional maṣlaḥa*', even if it is not in the boundaries of Islamic law. Thus, the sources of the motivation to use organised *tawarruq* are necessitated by the capitalist operation of the system rather than an Islamic Moral Economy (IME),[62] which essentialises asset-based financing. Thus, the permissibility of organised *tawarruq* should be considered as an exception in this process of shariʿa compliance conducted by the members of shariʿa boards, which has become a norm, as the practice indicates.

Such a reality brings about the issue of sovereignty in the process of shariʿa compliance. Recalling the above discussion in which Schmitt claims that the sovereign is the one who decides on the exception and its announcement as an exception, we witness that the exception turns into the default state and the sovereign changes the old constitution with a new one through exceptions. However, among others, Ahmad[63] argues that God is the only Sovereign in Islam; no other authority has the privilege of deciding exception. Thus, modern applications within the Islamic spheres indicate asymmetry in the substance while form-based compliance is assured, as in the case of Islamic banking operations.

It is well known that through the Qur'an and sunna, God draws the boundaries of the shariʿa. All the rulings, including necessity and *maṣlaḥa*, are given within these limits. In spite of this fact, as in the case of organised *tawarruq*, following Ṭūfī, some modern jurists have attempted to transcend these boundaries by nullifying some part of the scriptural texts and the objectives of shariʿa in the quest to respond to modern problems by using *maṣlaḥa* principle as an

60 Khan, 'Why Tawarruq Needs To Go—AAOIFI and the OIC Fiqh Academy: Divergence or Agreement?', 20.

61 Siddiqi, 'Islamic Banking and Finance in Theory and Practice: A Survey of State of the Art', 16.

62 For further details of IME, please refer to Asutay, 'Conceptualising and Locating the Social Failure of Islamic Finance', 94–97.

63 Ahmad, 'Sovereignty in Islam', 244.

excuse, albeit none of the pre-modern jurists with the exception of Ṭūfī understood *maṣlaḥa* principle in that way.

We can easily trace the effect of this way of reasoning on Islamic banks, which operate under the capitalist market system. Since the capitalist economy favours risk-minimising instruments, such as an interest-based loan, it therefore forces Islamic banks to employ instruments that are the least risky. If risk-free (or least risky) instruments cannot be derived within the boundaries of shariʿa, shariʿa scholars are expected, under market hegemony, to announce an exception and produce a risk-free or less-risky product based on *delusional maṣlaḥa*. Such products are not generated due to the lack of alternatives, but rather a capitalist market system does not allow any other alternatives to be utilised as Islamic banks aim to be efficient and competitive.

As can be seen, the prevailing system enforces Islamic banks and shariʿa scholars to engineer products that fit the nature of capitalism. In other words, in substantiating its hegemonic nature by not allowing any other practice beyond its own in the economic and financial sphere, the hegemonic nature of capitalism subjugates its own operating system on the shariʿa determined Islamic financial instruments whereby 'new forms' of Islamic financial instruments are generated. It should be noted that the announcement of such an exception, as in the case of organised *tawarruq*, sometimes is not as temporary a solution as it should be but becomes a default practice,[64] which is supported by the Malaysian data provided above. In evidencing this, as reported by Hassan,[65] a member of the shariʿa Advisory Board of Bank Negara Malaysia (the Central Bank of Malaysia) stated that the Islamic finance instruments, which derived through *maṣlaḥa* or necessity, continue to be employed even after there is no longer need for it:

> Some people say we are liberal. I will say that, before any decision is made, there is a thorough study of the particular issue. We might prefer certain views to others and, in certain circumstances, the bank can go for the exception but the bank is given a time limit for that. However, sometimes the exception has become the default.

Thus, as the statement of this particular shariʿa scholar indicates, 'exception' in shariʿa has become the default in Islamic finance and its operation with the

64 Hassan, 'An Empirical Investigation into the Role, Independence and Effectiveness of Shariʿa Boards in the Malaysian Islamic Banking Industry', 357.

65 Hassan, 'An Empirical Investigation', 357.

blessing of the shariʿa scholars. In this, as the above data show, organised *tawarruq*, in becoming a norm, has displaced other financing instruments, which implies its 'normality' and 'commonality' in existing Islamic financial practices.

In view of such a paradigmatic change, a question might arise concerning the role and status of shariʿa scholars in IFIs: if shariʿa scholars have the power to provide shariʿa legitimacy for IFIs, why are they unable to prevent the utilisation of (delusional) *maṣlaḥa* or other exceptional instruments in the observed convergence towards conventional financial systems? Although we explored the reasons for this failure in detail in another work,[66] it is useful to share a summary of the findings in the next section, as the issue relates to the transformation that has occurred in the role and status of shariʿa scholars and the source of their legitimacy.

4.2 *Transformation of the Role and Status of Shariʿa Scholars*

In our analysis of the role and status of shariʿa scholars in pre-modern and modern periods, we located three main transformations regarding the role and status of shariʿa scholars that are responsible for the emergence of delusional *maṣlaḥa*-based practices becoming norms in IFIs.

Firstly, in the pre-modern period, shariʿa scholars were absorbed into society, as society provided their legitimacy, whereas shariʿa scholars in modern SBs integrate into the Islamic banking sector more due to the nature of their profession compared to their position in society. Behind such a transformation, there also lies the influence of capitalist ideology on education, urbanisation, and city structure and other institutions of modernity, in the sense of modernity as a way of life, project, and social formation, which hinders the integration of shariʿa scholars into society and creates deviations. In other words, some shariʿa scholars in SBs have become embedded in the modern financial system and internalised the rules and principles of capitalism as a result of the process they have gone through in modern society (particularly the education system) by accepting the realism as a methodological positioning. We can observe traces of such capitalist embeddedness in the fatwa-giving process of such scholars, who essentialise the principles of capitalism such as efficiency, maximisation, low-transaction cost, and shareholder value to justify their rulings and prioritise them in the case of a contradiction between Islamic law and these principles. This can be evidenced by the practice of organised *tawarruq*, among other practices, in IFIs despite the resolution of the ICFA.

66 Sencal, 'Essays on the Shariʿa Governance System in Islamic Banks: Disclosure Performance of Shariʿa Boards and Historical Evolution of the Roles of Shariʿa Scholars', 153–179.

Secondly, in the pre-modern period, shariʿa scholars attained their 'civil leader' status through their deep knowledge of shariʿa, sustaining an exemplary way of life and having an embedded relationship with society, which bestowed upon them the power to negotiate on behalf of people with the elite-ruling class individually rather than as a class of 'learned people'. In other words, in the pre-modern period, jurist-consults attained their status individually, which could not easily be replaced by another scholar. Therefore, being local leaders and scholars, they were considered one of the main stakeholders constraining the negotiating power of the ruling authority. However, the negotiating power of the shariʿa scholars in SBs, compared to the pre-modern period, has lessened, since shariʿa scholars in SBs attain their source of legitimacy by being appointed to a specific SB and by being paid by the respective IFIs rather than deriving their negotiation power directly from the society. In other words, due to change in the social formation and social structure, leading to a new social contract beyond the influence of shariʿa scholars, they have lost the negotiating power and therefore have become exogenous 'variables' and 'units' within the existing governance system, including IFIs, implying that causality in the power relations has shifted in favour of IFIs. This asymmetricity, hence, leads to inadequate negotiating power with top-level management in IFIs for members of SBs. Unlike pre-modern periods, members of SBs attain their legitimacy by directing, monitoring, and supervising the operations of the IFIs by being appointed by the board of directors of an IFI as a member of SB, and by being salaried by a respective IFI, not due to their role and status in the society. This situation makes members of SBs replaceable without any disruption, even maybe without the notice of any stakeholders. This is because customers usually do not seek information regarding members of SBs since, for them, the existence of an SB is sufficient condition for an IFI's shariʿa compliance. Consequently, this transformation in the source of legitimacy of jurist-consults, as well as the lack of awareness about the composition of SBs by the demand side in the modern IFIs, diminishes the negotiating power of members of SB with top-level management and prevents the articulation of the claims for Islamic authenticity in a robust manner.

Thirdly, the complexity of society and the everyday practices of people has changed drastically compared to the pre-modern era in the Muslim world. In the pre-modern period, market exchanges and their expected outcomes, as well as the transaction structures, were simpler. Moreover, since 'man's economy, as a rule, is submerged in his social relationships',[67] jurist-consults were

67 Polanyi, *The Great Transformation*, 48.

aware of the content of these exchanges. On the other hand, capitalism has produced complex and interdependent products and services. Especially due to globalisation, impacts of economic and financial decisions are not limited to within a certain border but might have a synchronised effect in the global markets. Therefore, while foreseeing the consequences of legal rulings was easier during the pre-modern period and could be undertaken by individual scholars, the interdependent and complex nature of the modern world obliges shariʿa scholars to work in collaboration with other disciplines such as sociology, economics, politics, etc. Thus, while confirmation from a shariʿa scholar for a certain product or service is a necessary condition to fulfil the form or compliance with the scriptural text, it is not sufficient condition to achieve the objectives of shariʿa. The realisation of the objectives of the shariʿa requires the collaboration and approval of other disciplines as well as developing the capacity to foresee the long- and short-run outcomes of the decisions in society. This is crucial in attaining an Islamically required comprehensive and holistic approach.

As a consequence, as explained by Asutay,[68] the hegemonic nature of pragmatism as a methodological position should be considered as a reason for the observed divergence. Due to being embedded in a market economy, some shariʿa circles and professionals in IFIs relegate the entire task and process to 'moving capital' with Islamic metaphors by ignoring the substance and moral implications of the form-based compliance. Therefore, delusional *maṣlaḥa* becomes a norm to lead such a pragmatic approach to facilitate the decision-making process by relegating the main objective to 'moving capital with Islamic metaphors'.

These three main transformations between the pre-modern and modern period make shariʿa scholars very vulnerable against the hegemony of the capitalist market system and its sovereignty. In the next section, we offer a potential way out of the hegemony of the capitalist market system, at least to moderate the outcomes of the operations of existing IFIs through the utilisation of a fuzzy logic approach with the objective of moderating the consequences of the market system on IFI practices.

68 Asutay, 'Islamic Political Economy: Critical Perspectives on the Emergence of a New Paradigm', 18.

5 A Fuzzy Logic Perspective: A Way Forward

As discussed in the previous section, there are three main obstacles preventing contemporary shariʿa scholarship from realising the objectives of shariʿa as members of SBs, namely embeddedness of shariʿa scholars in capitalist market systems, lack of negotiating power relative to the pre-modern period, and the necessity of interdisciplinary collaboration due to the complexity of products and services in the modern period. These obstacles make the approval of SBs on IFIs' shariʿa compliance without elaborating and substantiating the compliance unreliable. Although there are solutions proposed to increase the independence of shariʿa scholars and make shariʿa governance more effective, they are still within the institutional logics of the capitalist market system or state bureaucracy. Establishing a central shariʿa board at the national level, for instance, to supervise and supersede the firm-level SBs is an articulation of state bureaucracy, and efforts to centralise shariʿa governance further that would deliver the same consequence as such national institutions would sustain the institutional logic of the existing system rather than questioning it for alternative solutions.

As an alternative solution, this study suggests a civil-society-based regulatory mechanism to evaluate the shariʿa compliance of the products and services of IFIs. This proposed regulatory mechanism does not substitute but complements the role of SBs. This regularity system should go beyond the binary opposition of *ḥalāl/ḥarām* or permissible/impermissible and implement a fuzzy logic approach towards the morality of shariʿa. In other words, rather than deciding whether a certain product is *ḥalāl* or *ḥarām*, this mechanism should go beyond that dichotomy and aim to decide to what degree a certain product or service is compatible with the morality of shariʿa by considering various stakeholders currently kept beyond the decision frame, such as environment, employee-employer relationship, production process, etc. Labelling such as 'suitable for vegetarians' or 'fair trade', for instance, are examples of binary dichotomies whereas energy efficiency rating of houses on a scale of 1–100 is an example of the fuzzy logic approach. As for IFIs, in addition to determining whether a product or service is *ḥalāl* (with a binary approach), we can also measure its fulfilment of certain dimensions of the morality of shariʿa with a fuzzy logic approach to evaluate to what degree it is compatible with the morality of shariʿa by going beyond the *ḥalāl/ḥarām* dichotomy. For example, a product can be deemed *ḥalāl* through the *fiqhī* process, but with a fuzzy logic approach when it is rated in terms of fulfilling the morality of shariʿa expectations, its substantive morality score could be anything between 0% to 100%, which also responds to the current debate on shariʿa-complaint Islamic finance vs Islam based finance,[69] as the latter refers to 100% compliance. Such a rating could give those investors seeking predominance of the morality of shariʿa in their financial and economic transactions an opportunity to go beyond the initial *ḥalāl* sphere to the *taḥsīniyyāt* or embellishment sphere in essentialising aspirations of the morality of shariʿa. Hence, such an arrangement can go beyond the confinement of the term and definition of shariʿa compliance by giving individuals the choice of the extent of *ḥalālness* that they can be comfortable with.

Such a regulatory mechanism has two superiorities over the existing SB-driven shariʿa governance mechanism. Firstly, a civil-society-based mechanism would convert the negotiating process from top-level management vs SB into IFIs vs stakeholders. This shift would help to solve the first two obstacles, namely embeddedness and lack of negotiation power, in particular. In the first case, the conflict between top-level management and SB would be minimum, since both groups are driven with similar institutional logics, namely capitalism, which produces conformist behaviour of shariʿa scholars towards the expectations of top-level management, which is mostly profit-maximisation oriented demands. In the second case, although SB resists the demands of top-level management to realise the morality of a shariʿa or IME-oriented outcome, due to lack of negotiating power, they are forced to settle for a moderate solution. These two cases are specific to IFIs in which top-level management prioritise the profit over the implementation of the morality of shariʿa. If the opposite is the case, namely harmony with the top-level management, then SB should be able to implement the morality of shariʿa apart from the complex cases where interdisciplinary collaboration becomes a necessity. By shifting the regularity mechanism for shariʿa governance partly to the civil society, the issue no longer becomes only to get the approval of the SB on a certain product or service in terms of permissibility but requires going beyond that and convincing the civil society that shariʿa compliance is genuine by disclosing the relevant information related to the dimensions of the morality of shariʿa. Therefore, the shariʿa compliance is no longer a binary decision of *ḥalāl/ḥarām* but also, after it is approved as *ḥalāl*, to what degree it is compliant with the morality of shariʿa by considering the consequences of the *ḥalāl* process, as in the current practice shariʿa scholars only utilises the 'intentionalist' approach in their decision-making.[70] The utilisation of such a civil-society-based mechanism, therefore, solves the obstacles of the embeddedness of shariʿa scholars and

69 Asutay, 'Conceptualising and Locating the Social Failure of Islamic Finance', 100–109.

70 Asutay, 'Islamic Political Economy: Critical Perspectives on the Emergence of a New Paradigm', 1–23.

lack of the negotiating power, since the IFIs must convince the stakeholders also rather than shariʿa scholars alone. Considering the impact of civil society on the emergence of ethical finance in the West, the importance of civil society in shaping the nature of IFIs should be considered a viable process.

The second aspect mainly solves the third obstacle, which is the complex nature of products and services in IFIs. Even if embeddedness and lack of negotiating power is not a problem for shariʿa scholars regarding the realisation of the objectives of shariʿa, the complexity of the products and services and necessity of interdisciplinary collaboration in such cases might lead to an obstacle. A civil-society-based regularity mechanism would be instrumental in such a case by evaluating the product or service in various dimensions of the morality of shariʿa, such as environmental or social impact, by using the information provided by the IFI. In such a mechanism, the information provided by IFIs would be used as an input to evaluate the degree of compliance with IME for the products and services approved by SB as permissible. Based on the input, civil society organisations would have the opportunity of providing a score on a scale of 1–100 regarding IME in projects such as ZamZam Tower (the major hotel and business centre in Makkah opposite to the Ka'bah financed by *suqūq*) or other *suqūq* projects. Such a rating process would also have an impact on pricing and compensate for the cost of fulfilling IME requirements, which would further encourage IFIs and investors to comply with a higher score of IME. This type of encouragement is especially important, since, in the absence of such a feedback mechanism on higher compliance of IME and compensation in exchange for the efforts of IFIs, there would be no incentive for an IFI to implement IME. In a similar manner to Gresham law, which states that 'bad money drives out good money', having the same face values, namely being 'ḥalāl' or permissible, IFIs with higher compliance of IME would be driven out of the market. Fuzzy logic based civil society evaluation mechanism, therefore, would provide a unique value for each product or service in line with their score, in compliance with IME. While shariʿa-compliant products and services with a low IME score would find customers, who are only concerned with the form of shariʿa, the product and services with higher IME scores would be compensated and survive in the market as well.

In such an arrangement, it is not expected that every IFI would aim for a high score on the scale since every range within the scale of 1–100 would have a certain market share. However, this mechanism would provide an opportunity to open a niche market for those who aim to invest or do business with IFIs which achieve a high score regarding IME compliance. After the emergence of such a market, it would also be the responsibility of civil society to promote and extend the share of stakeholders who aim for a higher score. We can term such an effort IME inclusiveness or augmentation since the goal is to convince people to require IME features to be present in IFIs' operation through expecting a higher score.

As mentioned above, the proposed process resembles the process that led to the emergence of 'ethical investing' or 'socially responsible investment', which represents the market responses to the demands emerging from civil society for their finances to be invested in 'ethically acceptable and social impact areas'. The successful expansion of such investing areas is an indication of the power of civil society but also indicates the flexibility of the market system for making additional inroads through market segmentation. Furthermore, since, 'the newly emerging consumption practices create opportunities for imagining and expressing new forms of religious identities, both collectively and privately',[71] such segmentation as explained above through fuzzy logic will serve the expectations of 'further morally inclined Muslim individuals'. Thus, the power of civil society can overrule the imposed shari'a hegemony and further democratise Islamic finance. Such a process might also help to overcome the observed shari'a arbitrage.[72]

It is also important to recall the *ḥisba* (market regulation body through examining the moral consequences of market) experiment in the Muslim world as part of the civil society, an articulation of the 'brotherhood' or 'guild' system in the Ottoman business environment (the *ahilik* system), that can provide authentic examples to develop new structures to essentialise Islamic normativeness and substantive morality of Islam in economy, finance, and business.

This study, however, acknowledges the difficulties and limits of a civil-society-based regularity mechanism based on fuzzy logic. First and foremost, the disclosure practices of IFIs regarding the details of the products and services that is required as input to a potential IME index is insufficient, as indicated by the *maqāṣid al-sharīʿa* (the higher objective of shari'a being human well-being) performance of IFIs.[73] Therefore, it requires state involvement to enhance the level of disclosure. Secondly, dimensions and potential index

---

71 Sandıkcı, 'Religion and the Marketplace: Constructing the 'New' Muslim Consumer', 15.

72 al-Gamal, 'Mutuality as an Antidote to Rent-Seeking Shariah Arbitrage in IslamicFinance', 194.

73 Aksak and Asutay, 'The Maqāṣid and the Empirics: Has Islamic Finance Fulfilled Its Promise?', 197–214; Asutay and Harningtyas, 'Developing Maqāṣid Al-Shari'a Index to Evaluate Social Performance of Islamic Banks', 13–55; Mergaliev at al., 'Higher Ethical Objective (*Maqasid al-Shari'ah*) Augmented Framework for Islamic Banks: Assessing the Ethical Performance and Exploring its Determinants', 7–23; Mohamada et al., 'Determinants of Maqāṣid Al-Shari'a-Based Performance Measurement Practices', 58–69.

items should be developed in line with IME. Considering that such theoretical studies attract less attention, this might be a challenging task to achieve. Nevertheless, studies related to the construction of *maqāṣid*-index might be a good starting point to develop an IME index. Furthermore, such a civil-society-based approach can also lead to 'the clash between opposing moral frameworks' among Muslims, leading to a lack of consensus in deciding dimensions and potential index items.[74] Nevertheless, if these competing frameworks do not prioritise the capitalist principles over the foundational aspects of objectives of shariʿa, such competition becomes fruitful in providing diversity similar to the schools of thought in *fiqh*, which has traditionally prevailed in the Muslim world over many centuries. Thirdly, such a civil-society-based regulatory mechanism requires a certain degree of awareness on the demand side, which is necessary to sustain IME -compliant products and services in the market and compensate for their additional expenses in providing such a product and services. Demand for sustainable products and services, organic food, and fair trade suggests that such a demand for IME-based products and services is not unlikely but requires effort to raise awareness.

Despite these limitations, however, it is important to strive to realise the morality of shariʿa or IME in a decentralised manner and maybe with several alternative IME-based rating mechanisms to bring the IFIs and other financial institutions closer to the initial aspirations of IME. This is crucial to provide and sustain a human-centred development path by going beyond economic growth obsession so that *falāḥ* or salvation could be achieved and *iḥsān* or beneficence, as objectives of individuals in Islam, can be attempted in this world, which constitutes the objective of being *khalīfa* (the viceregency) of Allah in this world.

6 Conclusion

At the beginning of the twentieth century, the reintroduction of al-Ṭūfī's approach to the *maṣlaḥa* by reformist scholars such as Jamāladdīn al-Qāsimī and Rashid Rida has led to the birth of a new method for the solution of modern problems, namely delusional *maṣlaḥa*, particularly in the case of facilitation of Islamic finance. The most important feature of delusional *maṣlaḥa* is that it can be contrary to the verses of the Qur'an or the sayings of the Prophet Muḥammad, but as long as jurists consider this solution as a *maṣlaḥa* or pub-

74 Sandıkcı, 'Religion and Everyday Consumption Ethics: A Moral Economy Approach', 14.

lic utility, it is considered valid, as such a fatwa is rendered on emerged issues. Since these sources of Islam are God's commands, jurists whose judgement is based on delusional *maṣlaḥa* decide when to nullify God's commands. This very judgement constitutes the exception in the shariʿa since the ruling based on delusional *maṣlaḥa* means that scriptural sources (the Qur'an and the sunna) are inadequate to provide a solution for the case at hand, and an exception should be decided for the case to solve the problem. Organised *tawarruq*, which is utilised by most of the Islamic banks on the ground of delusional *maṣlaḥa* as part of Islamic financial expansion, is a good example of such an instrument, albeit it is announced as prohibited by ICFA. Some of the shariʿa scholars appeal to the delusional *maṣlaḥa* principle and defend it with the claim that lower transaction cost by means of the organised *tawarruq* is for the public good.

Following Schmitt, we claim that the one who has the power to decide the exception is the sovereign. Consequently, a ruling based on delusional *maṣlaḥa* pronounces these jurists to be the sovereign through the authority of deciding exceptions to the law. On the other hand, we can observe in the Islamic finance sector that shariʿa scholars do not always willingly issue rulings based on delusional *maṣlaḥa*. But they are obliged to issue such rulings due to the compulsion of the capitalist market system, since Islamic banks operate in a capitalist system, even though they are 'Islamic financial institutions'. Capitalism imposes its own principles, such as the importance of low transaction costs and efficiency, on these institutions. But to announce these financial institutions as 'Islamic', shariʿa scholars have to approve these operations. This point is where delusional *maṣlaḥa* is utilised by shariʿa scholars. Hence, we claim that it is capitalism rather than the shariʿa scholars who are declared sovereign over Islamic ontology in relation to Islamic financial institutions.

In proposing a potential way out of this hegemony, we argue that a civil-society-based fuzzy logic approach might be utilised to open a space for the products and services that fulfil the objectives of shariʿa. This can be achieved by going beyond the *ḥalāl*/*ḥarām* dichotomy and examining the products and services from the perspective of their fulfilment of the various dimensions of the morality of shariʿa, articulated as the objectives of shariʿa. Rated independently by the civil-society-created institutions, this mechanism might help IFIs to inform stakeholders about the shariʿa-based nature of their products and services rather than remaining at the shariʿa compliance level. It is important to note that this mechanism is not a substitute for the shariʿa governance of IFIs at a firm level but a complementary feature. In this way, the institutions with a mission to implement the morality of shariʿa might open a niche market for themselves, since they will be able to differentiate their products and services from those institutions that only strive to achieve shariʿa compliance at a minimum level while following the principles of the capitalist market system.

Considering that the twenty-first century provides us with expanded and faster communication channels, along with tools to examine big data, two challenges might be overcome relatively easier in the following years. First, it will be easier to access and analyse the information provided by the companies through formal (e.g., company reports) and informal channels (e.g., advertisements and social media). Particularly tools such as blockchains powered by artificial intelligence should facilitate the collection of the required information to differentiate the products and services of competitive companies. This accessibility is not limited to large enterprises but includes small and medium-sized enterprises. Second, the diminishing transaction cost of communication year by year helps small and medium-sized enterprises to offer a variety of products and services, including those that fulfil the objectives of shariʿa. These enterprises will no longer be limited to small areas but can convey their products and services to a wider market and become part of the niche market of shariʿa-based products and services. Such developments can support companies in differentiating their products and services as shariʿa-based and provide the necessary information to compensate for the additional cost that imposes. Furthermore, due to such developments in the communications field, promoting the distinguishing features of these products and services and reaching out to potential customers should be cheaper and easier in future.

Importantly, Muslim customers have been moving into new sphere where Islamic ethicality has gained a new dimension beyond shariʿa compliance. As part of gaining confidence in Islamic identity, the awareness of consequences of Islamic finance and halal markets beyond the fatwas of shariʿa scholars has been making important inroads into Muslim economic, financial, and consumption behaviour. On the one hand, are 'Generation M, namely young Muslims changing the world',[75] with such critical awareness and, on the other hand, the market system, by moving into sustainability discourse and practice, has been redefining Islamic finance and business, as is seen in the emergence of ethical, socially responsible, impact investing and green *sukuk* movements within Islamic spheres.[76] Decentralised decision-making processes through

75 Janmohamed, *Generation M: Young Muslims Changing the World*, 5–37.

76 Moghul, *A Socially Responsible Islamic Finance: Character and the Common Good*, 39–81; Zamir and Mirakhor, *Ethical Dimensions of Islamic Finance: Theory and Practice*, 103–134; Aassouli et al., *Green Sukuk, Energy Poverty, and Climate Change: A Roadmap for Sub-Saharan Africa, 12–16; Richardson*, 'Responsible finance Sukuk—Can They Bring Societal Value to a Value-Neutral Market?', 398–425.

increased social media presence has been helping the emergence of virtual civil societies that can help the fuzzy logic theory to work in relation to Muslim consumption patterns and endogenisation of essentially Islamic norms rather than form-based and market-crafted shariʿa compliance.

Bibliography

Aassouli, Dalal, Mehmet Asutay, Mahmoud Mohieldin, and Tochukwu Chiara Nwokike. 2018. 'Green Sukuk, Energy Poverty, and Climate Change: A Roadmap for Sub-Saharan Africa'. World Bank Policy Research Working Paper No. 8680, 18 December.

Agamben, Giorgio. 2005. *State of Exception*. Chicago: University of Chicago Press.

Ahmad, Ilyas. 1958. 'Sovereignty in Islam'. *Pakistan Horizon* 11, no. 4: 244–257.

Aksak, Ercument, and Mehmet Asutay. 2015. 'The Maqāṣid and the Empirics: Has Islamic Finance Fulfilled Its Promise?' In *Islamic Finance: Political Economy, Values and Innovations*, edited by Mehmet Asutay and Abdullah Turkistani, 187–220. Berlin: Gerlach.

Al-Būṭī, Ramaḍān. 2005. *Ḍawābiṭ al-Maṣlaḥa fī al-Sharīʿa al-Islāmiyya*. Damascus: Risāla Publishers.

Al-Gamal, Mahmoud A. 2007. 'Mutuality as an antidote to rent-seeking Shariah arbitrage in Islamic finance'. *Thunderbird International Business Review* 49, no. 2: 187–202.

Asutay, Mehmet. 2007. 'A Political Economy Approach to Islamic Economics: Systemic Understanding for an Alternative Economic System'. *Kyoto Bulletin of Islamic Area Studies* 1, no. 2: 3–18.

Asutay, Mehmet. 2012. 'Conceptualising and Locating the Social Failure of Islamic Finance: Aspirations of Islamic Moral Economy vs. the Realities of Islamic Finance'. *Asian and African Area Studies* 11, no. 2: 93–113. https://doi.org/citeulike-article-id:13936380.

Asutay, Mehmet. 2018. 'Islamic Political Economy: Critical Perspectives on the Emergence of a New Paradigm'. Durham Centre for Islamic Economics and Finance Working Paper, Durham University Business School, Durham, UK.

Asutay, Mehmet, and Astrid Fionna Harningtyas. 2015. 'Developing Maqāṣid Al-Shariʿa Index to Evaluate Social Performance of Islamic Banks: A Conceptual and Empirical Attempt'. *International Journal of Islamic Economics and Finance Studies* 1, no. 1: 5–64.

Bank Negara Malaysia. 2017. The Financial Stability and Payment Systems Report 2016. Kuala Lumpur: Bank Negara.

Dar, Humayun and Nursofiza Azmi, ed. 2016. *Global Islamic Finance Report 2016: Islamic Financial Policy*.

Duman, Soner. 2011. 'Imam Gazzali'nin Maṣlaḥat Dusuncesine Katkilari'. *Islam Hukuku Arastirmalari Dergisi* 18: 9–32.

Dusuki, Asyraf Wajdi. 2010. 'Can Bursa Malaysia's Suq Al-Sila' (Commodity Murabahah House) Resolve the Controversy Over Tawarruq?' *ISRA Research Papers*, no. 10: 1–26.

Ghazālī, Nasrun Bin Mohamad. 2014. 'Tawarruq in Malaysian Financing System: A Case Study on Commodity Murabahah Product at Maybank Islamic Berhad'. PhD thesis., University of Malaya.

Hallaq, Wael. 2012. *The Impossible State: Islam, Politics, and Modernity's Moral Predicament*. New York. Columbia University Press.

Hallaq, Wael. 1999. *A History of Islamic Legal Theories: An Introduction to Sunni Usul Al-Fiqh*. Cambridge: Cambridge University Press.

Handler, Benjamin. 1936. 'Towards the Sociology of Sovereignty'. *Canadian Journal of Economics and Political Science/Revue Canadienne de Economiques et Science Politique* 2, no. 3: 424–430.

Hassan, Ahmad Fahmi. 2012. 'An Empirical Investigation Into The Role, Independence And Effectiveness Of Shari'a Boards in the Malaysian Islamic Banking Industry'. PhD thesis. Cardiff University.

Iqbal, Zamir, and Abbas Mirakhor. 2017. *Ethical dimensions of Islamic finance: Theory and Practice*. New York: Palgrave.

Islamic Finance Resource. 2016. 'Organized Tawarruq Is Permissible: Sheikh Nizam Yaquby'. Accessed September 6, 2016. https://ifresource.com/2009/07/23/organized-tawarruq-is-permissible-sheikh-nizam-yaquby/.

Janmohamed, Shelina. 2016. *Generation M: Young Muslims Changing the World*. London: I.B. Tauris.

Kayadibi, Saim. 2007. 'Al-Ṭūfī Centred Approach to Al-Maṣlaḥah Al-Mursalah (Public Interest) in Islamic Law'. *Islam Hukuku Arastirmalari Dergisi* 9: 71–96.

Khan, Salman H. 2009. 'Why Tawarruq Needs To Go—AAOIFI and the OIC Fiqh Academy: Divergence or Agreement?' *Islamic Finance News*, September.

Khnifer, Mohammed. 2010. 'Maṣlaḥah and the Permissibility of Organized Tawarruq'. *Opalesque Islamic Finance Intelligence* 668, no. 8: 1–23.

Mergaliyev, Arman, Mehmet Asutay, Alija Avdukic, and Yusuf Karbhari. 2019. 'Higher Ethical Objective (Maqasid al-Shari'ah) Augmented Framework for Islamic Banks: Assessing Ethical Performance and Exploring its Determinants'. *Journal of Business Ethics*: 1–38.

Merriam, Charles Edward. 2001. 'History of the Theory of Sovereignty since Rousseau' [electronic resource]. Batoche.

Moghul, Umar F. 2017. *A Socially Responsible Islamic Finance: Character and the Common Good*. New York: Palgrave.

Mohamada, Muslim Har Sani, Muhammad Ahmar Alic, and Ros Aniza Mohd Sharif. 2016. 'Determinants of Maqāṣid Al-Shari'a-Based Performance Measurement Practices: The Case of Malaysian Islamic Banks'. *International Journal of Economics, Management and Accounting* 24, no. 1: 49–81.

Nagan, Winston P., and Aitza M. Haddad. 2011. 'Sovereignty in Theory and Practice'. *San Diego Int'l LJ* 13: 429.

Opwis, Felicitas M.M. 2001. 'Maṣlaḥa: An Intellectual History of a Core Concept in Islamic Legal Theory'. PhD thesis. Yale University.

Parker, Mushtak. 2001. 'Are More and More Islamic Banks Shunning Tawarruq?' *Arabnews*, 2009.

Polanyi, Karl. 2001. *The Great Transformation*. Boston: Beacon.

Qomariyah, Siti. 1994. 'Al-Ghazālī's Theory of Munāsaba in the Context of the Adaptability of Islamic Law'. PhD thesis, McGill University.

Rapcsák, János. 1998. 'Sovereignty—Past and Present'. *Társadalom És Gazdaság Közép-És Kelet-Európában/Society and Economy in Central and Eastern Europe* 20, no. 1: 28–44.

Richardson, Edana. 2019. 'Responsible Finance Sukuk—Can They Bring Societal Value to a Value-Neutral Market?' *Capital Markets Law Journal* 14, no. 3: 394–428.

Sandıkcı, Özlem. 2018. 'Religion and the Marketplace: Constructing the 'New' Muslim Consumer'. *Religion* 48, no. 3: 453–473.

Sandıkcı, Özlem. 2020. 'Religion and Everyday Consumption Ethics: A Moral Economy Approach'. *Journal of Business Ethics*: 1–17.

Schmitt, Carl. 2005. *Political Theology: Four Chapters on the Concept of Sovereignty*. Chicago: University of Chicago Press.

Sencal, Harun. 2017. 'Essays on the Shariʿa Governance System in Islamic Banks: Disclosure Performance of Shariʿa Boards and Historical Evolution of the Roles of Shariʿa Scholars'. PhD thesis. Durham University.

Shaharuddin, Amir. 2012. 'The Bayʿ al-ʿInah Controversy in Malaysian Islamic Banking'. *Arab Law Quarterly* 26, no. 4: 499–511.

Siddiqi, Mohammad N. 2006. 'Islamic Banking and Finance in Theory and Practice: A Survey of State of the Art'. *Islamic Economic Studies* 13, no. 2: 1–48.

Willis, Hugh Evander. 1929. 'The Doctrine of Sovereignty Under the United States Constitution'. *Virginia Law Review* 15, no. 5: 437–475.

CHAPTER 3

Halal Practices at the Dawn of Southeast Asian Modernity: Some Cases of Halal Fatwa in *al-Manār* in the Beginning of the Twentieth Century

Jajat Burhanudin

> As for the king himself it is true that he became a Muslim inasmuch as he gave up worshiping idols and eating pork; but apart from that he did not alter a single one of his heathen habits.[1]

•••

> Having been defeated in a battle of power, the ruler addressed the *'ālim*, 'I will comply [to convert to Islam]', although ugh he asked for a little more time in order to finish [eating] pork.[2]

∴

For the majority of Muslims nowadays, the points in the above quotations are taken for granted. No one questions the quoted statements, which have strong foundation in the Qur'an. Eating pork, the habit the Malay rulers had to abandon as they converted to Islam, is too obvious to become the issue of halal. For this discussion, the quotations reveal the legal notion that associates halal practice to not eating pork. As the quoted Malay texts relate, it became the essence of traditional practices of food consumption, where halal and non-halal (*ḥarām*) was a simple matter. As a result, the issue of halal hardly emerged in pre-modern times. Not only did almost all Muslims resolutely avoid eating pork—otherwise they would be regarded as non-Muslims—but the food they consumed was traditionally home-produced and -made, and therefore was not something to be concerned about.

---

1 Teeuw and Wyatt, *Hikayat Patani*, 152.

2 *Salasilah Kutai*, quoted from Jones, 'Ten Conversion Myths from Indonesia', 147–148.

 | DOI:10.1163/9789004459236_004

In Southeast Asia, the halal issue began to arise in the early twentieth century, when the Muslims of the regions encountered the impact of modern developments introduced by the colonial government. It was the initial question concerning legal practice, so far as can be documented. Notwithstanding, for the reasons elucidated below, the issue of halal did not deal with food-consumption. As will be shown, it was mostly concerned with the legal status of modern devices and materials that were newly invented and started to influence Muslims' socio-religious lives.

Muslims' perception of and trust in modernity and newness seem to have constituted the main reason for the rise of the halal issue. In fact, it was the same thing that occurred in Indonesia in the 1970s. The establishment of food-producing industries served as the main factor behind the rising halal issue that began to be concerned with food consumption.[3] Possibly strengthened by anti-Chinese sentiment, some Muslim groups questioned the process of food-making, claiming that it was contaminated by non-halal ingredients.

Recently, this halal issue has heightened as the encounter with modernity intensifies. The subjects of concern also broadened, to include such fields as finance,[4] hospitality, and tourism,[5] as well as dating among youth.[6] With due regard to any difference, the rise of the halal issue in the three subjects mentioned denotes the fact that, for Muslims of today, the main concern is a way of being Islamic in the increasingly modern cities with urban and Westernised life-styles and facilities.

This article presents a historical study on the halal issue in Southeast Asia in the early twentieth century, which was documented in the requests for fatwas (legal opinions) by Southeast Asian Muslims to Cairo-based journal *al-Manār*. Appearing first in 1898, *al-Manār* held an important role in the establishment of Islamic communication between Southeast Asia and Egypt. In this particular context, the journal provided its readers with a space to have contact and dialogue with reformist Cairo 'ulama' (Muslim scholars, sing. *'ālim*). Under the editorship of Rashīd Riḍā (1865–1935), the journal facilitated requests for fatwas from Muslims in Southeast Asia and elsewhere in the world.

3 Mudzhar, Fatwa of the Council of Indonesian Ulama: a Study of Islamic Legal Thought in Indonesia 1975–1988, 96–101.

4 Hayat, Den Butter, and Kock, 'Halal Certification for Financial Products: A Transaction Cost Perspective', 601–613.

5 Hall and Prayag 2020.

6 Ali et al., 'Halal, Dating: Changing Relationship Attitudes and Experiences among Young British Muslims', 775–792.

Taking the requests for fatwas as the primary sources, this article discusses three important points. The first one is concerned with identifying what Muslims in Southeast Asia thought particularly necessary to determine their legal status, whether or not they were religiously permitted. This point is to look at the legal concept of halal that prevailed among Southeast Asian Muslims of the period. The second one deals with the social-intellectual profile of the Muslims who requested for fatwas from the journal; those who were exposed to the journal *al-Manār* and to reform ideas of Cairo ʿulamaʾ. The last point is the substance of the fatwas issued by Rashīd Riḍā and the way the fatwas were disseminated to a wider audience among Muslims in Southeast Asia. With this point, the impact of fatwas in Muslims' religious ideas and practices will be examined.

Before we come to the above points of discussion, some explanations on the fatwas of nineteenth-century Southeast Asia are important in this regard. These will serve as a traditional background to enrich our understanding on fatwas in *al-Manār* that dealt with modern aspects of Islam and Muslims' affairs.

1 Fatwa Collections of Nineteenth-Century Southeast Asia

Turning to the points of argument in the beginning of this article, it should be kept in mind that modernity emerged as the prime element of fatwas in *al-Manār*. Their appearance was very much related to the modern milieu of cities, in which the fatwa seekers lived and engaged in their socio-cultural and religious dynamics. Arguably, similar issues can hardly be found in the fatwa collections of the pre-modern period, where the elements and impact of modernity did not exist yet. For this, a close look at two fatwa collections of nineteenth-century Southeast Asia is of special importance. These two fatwa collections are *Muhimmat al-Nafāʾis* (hereafter referred to as *Muhimmat*) and *al-Fatāwā al-Faṭāniya* (hereafter referred to as *al-Fatāwā*) by Ahmad ibn Muhammad Zain al-Fatani (1856–1906).

As regards the *Muhimmat*, this text has the complete title *Muhimmat al-Nafāʾis fī Bayān Asʾila al-Ḥadīth* (The Precious Gems Dealing with the Explanation of Questions about Current Topics). Lithographed in Mecca in 1892, *Muhimmat* contains 130 fatwas, the majority of which were issued by Aḥmad ibn Zainī Daḥlān, the *mufti* of Shafiʾite school of law (1871–1886) and the great *ʿālim* of Mecca of the period. He had strong connection with Indonesia, mainly through the *ḥajj* contingent from the country and the Muslims living permanently in Mecca (the Jawa) for Islamic learning. Because of his position, many

Indonesians came to him to request fatwas and Islamic guidance to solve many issues current in the life of Indonesian Muslims in the latter part of the nineteenth century.[7]

What is of special importance is the subjects the fatwas addressed; they were various in nature, ranging from doctrinal themes to practised forms of Islam laden with local elements of Muslim culture in the Dutch East Indies. Of the doctrinal themes, the *ḥajj*-related rituals and activities formed a leading issue. The questions were raised by *mustaftī* among the pilgrims who came to Mecca for the *ḥajj*; others point to intellectual matters, such as the position of certain scholarly work (*kitāb*) in Islamic learning. Inquiries related to local practices of Islam included the following examples: circumcision (*sunat*); the burial of placenta (*ari-ari*); beating a drum (*bedug*) to announce praying times; the system of inheritance and family affairs; and many other examples which are ethnographic in nature and are deep-seated in Muslim traditions in Indonesia and Southeast Asia. In addition, the *Muhimmat* also contains fatwas that deal with issues pertaining to Dutch colonialism in the Indies, as was formulated in such language as *kaum kafir Olanda* (infidel Dutch people), *hakim kafir* (infidel ruler), and other questions related to the way the Acehnese should behave to the Dutch during the Aceh war.[8]

In other words, the issues included in the fatwas of *Muhimmat* were of topical interest to the Indonesian Muslims in the latter part of the nineteenth century, both in Mecca (the Jawa) and in the Indies. The *Muhimmat* functioned as a medium through which the dialogue between, and the transmission of, Meccan-based Islamic ideas to the Indies can be observed. Next to the *kitāb* and the 'ulama' who had graduated from the Holy City, the *Muhimmat* evidenced the crucial role of Mecca, described by Snouck Hurgronje as 'the heart of the religious life of the East-Indian Archipelago'.[9] As such, the *Muhimmat* is therefore, as Kaptein asserts, to be regarded 'as a perfect reflection of the nature and level of traditionalist Islamic thinking in the period'.[10]

Next to the *Muhimmat*, another fatwa collection in Mecca from the same period was *al-Fatāwā al-Faṭāniya* (The Legal Opinions from Patani). As already noted, *al-Fatāwā* was composed by a leading *'ālim* of Patani background, Ahmad ibn Muhammad Zain al-Fatani. In Patani-Malay intellectual tradition, he had a central position after Shaykh Da'ud al-Fatani, the father of

7 Kaptein 1997; see also his article, 'Meccan *Fatwa* from the End of the Nineteenth Century on Indonesian Affairs', 141–159.

8 Kaptein, *The Muhimmat*, 9–14.

9 Hurgronje, *Mekka in the Latter Part of the 19th Century*, 291.

10 Kaptein, *The Muhimmat*, 15.

Patani 'ulama', leading him to be described as 'the most influential and versatile of the long line of Patani scholars'.[11] Born in Kampung Jambu, Yaring, Patani in the southern part of Thailand today, Ahmad came from a family of 'ulama'. His father, Muhammad Zain, was the brother of Shaykh Da'ud al-Fatani, the doyen of Patani religious elites, who made major contribution to the dynamics of Islam in Thai-Malaysia border areas and Southeast Asia more broadly.[12]

Like other 'ulama' of the period, Ahmad pursued his further Islamic studies in Mecca. Sadly, not much is known about his learning experiences in the Holy City, except he was once said to have studied medicine with a famous Indian scholar Shaykh 'Abdu al-Rahīm al-Kabūlī, and wrote a work on this subject, *Ṭibb al-Aḥsān fi Ṭibb al-Iḥsān* (The Better Medicine in the Treatment for Beneficence). From Mecca, he went to Cairo to study for some time at al-Azhar, but again his studying in Cairo is not well documented. His name began to appear in 1884 as he was entrusted as a supervisor of the Turkish government printing press in Mecca for the Malay section.[13] With this position, the Patani *'ālim* held a central role in the printing activities of the works of Patani and Malay 'ulama'.

In the closing decades of the nineteenth century, the intellectual picture of Ahmad became apparent as he established his career as an 'ālim in Mecca, writing *kitāb* and teaching mainly Malay-speaking Jawi students. He is reported to have written a few works, namely *Farīda al-Farā'id fī 'Ilm al-Aqā'id* (The Precious Gem of Gems in the Science of Creeds), which discusses Islamic theology, *Abniya al-Asmā' wa al-'Af'āl* (The Structure of Nouns and Verbs), on Arabic grammar, and *Bahja al-Mubtadīn wa farḥa al-Mujtadīn* (The Joy of the Beginners and the Pleasure of Those who Seek Answers), on Islamic doctrines (*uṣūl al-dīn*) and *fiqh*, concerning both religious obligation and social issues. Among his students who later emerged as Muslim leaders in their countries of origin were Nik Mahmud bin Nik Ismail (who became Chief Minister of Kelantan), Haji Ibrahim (Grand Mufti of Kelantan), Shaykh Mahmud Sa'id (Senior Mufti of Negeri Sembilan), Khatib Jabar (Maharaja Imam of Sambas, Kalimantan), Haji Muhammad Salih (Grand Qadi in Cambodia), and many others who became religious teachers of *pondok* in Patani and Malaysia.[14] To be mentioned here is Muhammad Yusuf, better known as Tok Kenali (1868–1933). He was the

11 Matheson and Hooker, 'Jawi Literature in Patani: The Maintenance of an Islamic Tradition', 28.

12 Bradley, 2016.

13 Hurgronje, *Mekka*, 286.

14 Matheson and Hooker, 'Jawi Literature', 28–30.

'ālim behind the establishment of Majlis Ugama dan Adat Istiadat Melayu in Kelantan in 1915, and was engaged in teaching activities in his *pondok* as well as in writing in the journal *Pengasoh*.[15]

Much more importantly, Ahmad was elevated as a *mufti* for Southeast Asian Muslims, both in Mecca and in their respective countries. This position contributed to strengthening his network with mainly Patani and Malay people and Southeast Asian Muslim at large. The fatwas he issued, in reference to many questions he received, which were on various issues, were collected in the aforementioned *al-Fatāwā al-Faṭāniya*. This text was possibly lithographed for the first time in Singapore in 1907/1908, but that lithographic version is no longer extant. The extant copies that are still available, especially in Patani and Malaysia, are based on the editions printed by Matba'ah al-Kamaliyah in Kota Bharu, Kelantan in 1936 and the one by Matba'ah Patani Press in 1957.[16]

Looking at the issues in *al-Fatāwā*, Ahmad devoted his opinions to subjects being currently debated in mainly Malay regions of Southeast Asia. In addition to Muslims in Patani and Malay kingdoms in northern part of Malaysia today, especially Kelantan, *al-Fatāwā* frequently mentions the Muslims of Cambodia. They formed one important segment of the fatwa seekers, who asked Ahmad to provide them with Islamic opinions and guidance. The subjects that were dealt with in *al-Fatāwā* consisted of many aspects, ranging from theology (such as the questions on the attributes of God), ritual practices (on praying-related topics), religious alms (*zakāt*), system of inheritance (*farā'id*), marriage and divorce (*nikāḥ* and *ṭalāq*), economic transaction (*mu'āmala*), and social relation among Muslims and with non-Muslims. The last point refers especially to the experience of Muslims in Cambodia.

The above subjects were dealt with on the basis of strong knowledge of both Islamic doctrines and culture of local people of Southeast Asia. Besides being concerned with the socio-political affairs of Patani society under the power of Siam, in his *al-Fatāwā* Ahmad seems to have been in line with the rising trend of Islamic discourses in Patani and Southeast Asia of the period, where the interest in *fiqh*-related issues was rising, surpassing previous interest in *uṣūl al-dīn* and *tasawwuf*.[17] Both the requests and the fatwas issued were in accord with so-called traditional Islamic thinking, as is the case with the *Muhimmat*. In fact, the above trend of discourse also developed in Java and the Indies, to

---

15 Salleh, 'To' Kenali: His Life and Influence', in *Kelantan: Religion and Politics in a Malay State*, 85–100; al-Ahmadi, 1983.

16 Abdullah, 'Introduction', 1–10; Matheson and Hooker, 'Jawi Literature', 30.

17 Matheson and Hooker, 'Jawi Literature', 41.

which *al-Muhimmat* addressed its fatwas, as reflected in the subjects studied in *pesantren* Islamic learning.[18]

As such, both *Muhimmat* and *al-Fatāwā* represent the Islamic discourse of nineteenth-century Southeast Asia, where traditional Islam was well established. As a result, nothing touching on modernity emerged in the two fatwa collections that differed from the fatwas in *al-Manār* in terms of either the issues raised or language and expressions employed, as will be discussed, which reflect the modernist and reformist discourses of Islam. To be noted in this respect is the halal fatwa on food consumption. Based on the reading of both *Muhimmat* and *al-Fatāwā*, it is evident that no such issue as halal could be found in either text. The issue of halal was related to the legal status of those of new modern invention emerged only in the reformist groups of Muslims in the modern cities of Southeast Asia, as will be shown below.

2 Southeast Asia-Cairo: New Network and Transmission

In the closing decades of the nineteenth century, al-Azhar in Cairo emerged as a scholarly destination, gradually replacing Mecca as the heart of Islamic development in Southeast Asia. The Jawa of Mecca pioneered the network with Cairo. They started taking Cairo as a scholarly destination, although Mecca remained highly respected due to its longstanding intellectual network with Southeast Asian Muslims and central place in Islamic ritual life. The journal *al-Manār* held a pivotal role in this changing attitude of the Jawa. The journal, with its message of Islamic reformism, caught the attention of the Jawa in Mecca and stimulated in some of them a great deal of interest in the reformism of Cairo.

Of the Jawa of Mecca, the experience of Thaher Djalaluddin is important to note. Born on 7 November 1869 in Bukittinggi, West Sumatra, Thaher Djalaluddin came from a leading 'ulama' family of Minangkabau. He was a maternal relative of Ahmad Khatib, a leading Jawi *'ālim* in Mecca of the period. He took Thaher with him to Mecca in 1880 to study Islam. Under Ahmad Khatib's leadership, Thaher Djalaluddin lived in Mecca as a member of the Jawa, witnessing the changing orientation of Islamic learning that began to consider the importance of Cairo. Therefore, of the Jawa in Mecca he was of the first generation to become interested in the Islamic reformism of Cairo. After having spent fif-

18 Burhanudin, 'Islamic Knowledge, Authority and Political Power: The 'ulama in Colonial Indonesia', 86.

teen years in Mecca, in 1895 he moved to al-Azhar to complete his studies in astronomy (*'ilm al-falk*). It was during his four-year study period in al-Azhar, as a resident of the Jawa boarding house (*riwāq al-jāwī*) that Thaher Djalaluddin was directly exposed to the reformist ideas of Muḥammad 'Abduh and Rashīd Riḍā.[19] This Cairo experience greatly contributed to his future career as an editor of the reformist Singapore journal *al-Imam* in 1906.

In addition, the growing interest in Cairo was also reflected by the rising number of requests for fatwas (*istiftā'*) addressed to Rashīd Riḍā in *al-Manār*.[20] This not only marked the declining number of *istiftā'* to the Meccan 'ulama', but also signalled the establishment of an intensive dialogue between Southeast Asian Islam and al-Azhar in Cairo. Here, the journal *al-Manār* had a crucial role. It became a new source of religious authority, which then paved the way for the advancement of Islamic reformism in Southeast Asia. In this respect, it has to be emphasised that *al-Manār* facilitated an individual reading and interpretation of the Islamic doctrines. As a form of Islamic print culture, the journal not only introduced Islamic reformist ideas in 'synthesized and easily digestible form',[21] but also created the space that made it possible for Southeast Asian Muslims to gain access to Islamic teaching beyond the realm of the traditional master-student transmission process.[22]

This was especially the case with the experience of the Jawa of Mecca. They were at the hub of the traditional mode of Islamic learning, in which submissive obedience to the master formed a core element. Yet, with the rise of printed materials like the journal *al-Manār*, they were provided with opportunities to make contact with the reformist ideas of Cairo. In terms of requests for fatwa, the experience of Basyuni Imran is a good example. He represented the rising trend among the Jawa who began searching for new religious authority. *Al-Manār* of Cairo emerged as the medium to which he addressed his request for fatwa, which in turn led him to be one of the Southeast Asian fatwa seekers (*mustaftīs*) who engaged with and contributed to the transmission of Islamic reformism in Southeast Asia.

---

19 Laffan, *Islamic Nationhood and Colonial Indonesia: The* Umma *Below the Wind*, 129; Othman, 'The Middle Eastern Influence on the Development of Religious and Political Thought in Malay Society, 1880–1940', 227.

20 Bluhm, 'A Preliminary Statement on the Dialogue between the Reform Magazine *al-Manar* and the Malayo-Indonesian World', 35–42; Abaza, 'Southeast Asia and the Middle East: *Al-Manār* and Islamic Modernity', 93–111.

21 Bluhm, '*Al-Manar* and Ahmad Soorkattie: Links in the Chain of Transmission of Muhammad 'Abduh's Ideas to the Malay-Speaking World', 298.

22 Burhanudin, 'Aspiring for Islamic Reform: Southeast Asian Requests for *Fatwas* in *al-Manar*', 14.

Born in Sambas, Kalimantan, on 16 October 1885, Basyuni Imran (Muhammad Bashuni bin Muhammad 'Imran) came from a family of leading 'ulama'. His father, Muhammad Imran, was *Maharaja Imam* (the highest religious official) in the Malay sultanate of Sambas in Borneo.[23] After finishing his basic schooling (*volk-school*) and religious education (Qur'anic recital and Arabic language), he went to Mecca (about 1901) to perform the pilgrimage and to continue his studies. Like most of the Jawi students in the Hijaz, he began with studying Arabic, and went on to learn various branches of Islamic knowledge. He spent almost five years studying in Mecca under the mentorship of mainly the Jawi 'ulama' Umar al-Sumbawi, Uthman al-Sarawaki, and Ahmad Khatib. In 1906, at the request of his father, he returned to Sambas.[24]

During his five-year study abroad, Basyuni Imran became acquainted with Islamic reformism. Through the journal *al-Manār*, he learned about the ideas of Muḥammad 'Abduh and Rashīd Riḍā. After returning to Sambas, he subscribed to the journal and began corresponding with Rashīd Riḍā, requesting fatwa on various subjects. In a later biographical account, Basyuni said that he found in *al-Manār* 'pure knowledge of religion based on the Qur'an and the sunna of the Prophet'.[25] This connection was deepened in 1910 when he travelled to Cairo with his brother Ahmad Fawzi, and his friend Ahmad Sa'ud. All three enrolled at a new school established by Rashīd Riḍā, *Dār al-Da'wa wa al-Irshād*. Basyuni Imran seems to have remained there until his father died in 1913, as he returned to Sambas to take over his father's position as Imam.[26]

After that, Basyuni Imran never returned to Cairo. Yet, his connection with Islamic reform remained strong. He continued sending requests for fatwas to Rashīd Riḍā, leading him to become one of the leading Southeast Asian *mustaftīs* in the journal *al-Manār*.[27] He posed questions dealing with various subjects on Islam and Muslims, especially in the changing Dutch East Indies. Basyuni Imran was concerned with the core of the Islamic intellectual debates of the early twentieth century. He sent questions about the state of Indonesian Islam and of Muslims in the world in general,[28] stating his desire to discover factors that caused the Muslims, particularly in the Indies and Southeast Asia at large, to be stuck in the conditions of relative decadence and backwardness.

---

23 van Bruinessen, 'Basyuni 'Imran' 26; Pijper, *Beberapa Studi tentang Sejarah Islam di Indonesia, 1900–1950*, 142.

24 van Bruinessen, 'Basyuni 'Imran', 26; Pijper, *Beberapa Studi*, 142–143.

25 Pijper, *Beberapa Studi*, 143.

26 Laffan, *Islamic Nationhood*, 138, 255 n. 18.

27 Burhanudin, 'Aspiring', 15.

28 *al-Manar* 31 (1930), 347–349; Bluhm, 'A Preliminary', 40–41.

He was eager to know why the Europeans, the Americans, and the Japanese had achieved their position of dominance over the Muslims. In this light, Imran inspired a Syrian scholar, Amīr Shakib Arslān (1869–1946), to write a book on the subject entitled 'Why Have Muslims Fallen Behind While Others Have Progressed?'.[29]

The experience of Basyuni Imran is only one example of the Jawa in changing Mecca. Many other Jawi students engaged in the requests for fatwas to Rashīd Riḍā in *al-Manār*. Abd al-Hafiz al-Jawi is one of them. Recognising the poor condition of Indies Muslims just as Imran had depicted in his *istiftā'*, Abd al-Hafiz then asked *al-Manār* to become more involved in fostering progress and unity amongst the Indonesian Muslims. Here, he mentioned that submissiveness to the Dutch, superstition, and rigid conservatism were the main woes to combat because they were responsible for the backwardness of the Muslims.[30] More than that, some Jawi students of Mecca also were involved in disseminating Islamic reformism to their countries of origin.

As a result, this spurred more requests for fatwas sent to *al-Manār* from Muslims in Southeast Asia. Based on readings of the fatwa column of the journal,[31] it is possible to include in the list of *mustaftī* of *al-Manār* the Arab residents in Southeast Asia. They formed one other important category that made Cairo a new source of religious authority. Like the reformist section of the Jawa represented by Basyuni Imran, it appears that the Arabs' requests for fatwas to *al-Manār* arose alongside their efforts to cope with the changing Southeast Asia. The Arabs—of which the Hadrami formed a majority—emerged as one of the leading communities to engage in striving for the progress (*kemajuan*) of their own community. In the Indies, the establishment of modern organisations, the Jamiyat Khayr in around 1905 and al-Irsyad in 1915, are evidence of their movement of awakening (*nahḍa*).[32]

In the early twentieth century, the Indies Arabs were keenly aware of Islamic reformism and modern developments in Egypt. Cairo became one of the main destinations for educating children, especially for the upper-class community, *sayyid*.[33] This rising new religious orientation among the Arabs formed one of the most important factors in the extension of the existing Southeast Asia-Middle East network of scholarly interaction with Egypt. Just as for the reform-

29 Hourani, *Arabic Thought in the Liberal Age 1798–1939*, 223–224.
30 *al-Manar* 12 (1912), 929–937.
31 Burhanudin, 'Aspiring', 14–17.
32 Mandal, 1994; Mobini-Kesheh 1999.
33 Mandal, 'Finding Their Place: A History of the Arabs in Java under Dutch Rule, 1800–1924', 146.

ist section of the Jawa in Mecca, so too for the Indies Arabs. *Al-Manār* came to be regarded as a source of authority to which requests for fatwas were addressed.[34] As can be identified either by their use of the title *sayyid* or by their clan names, Arabs were one important category included in *al-Manār*'s Southeast Asian *mustaftī*.

Here, Hashim Bin Thahir (Muhammad bin Hashim bin Thahir, 1882–1960) is noteworthy. Although not much is known about his life, Bin Tahir was one of the Arabs most intensely engaged in sending requests for fatwa to *al-Manār*. He was the editor of the first Arabic periodical in the Indies, *al-Bashar*, first published in Palembang in 1914. In 1915, he and his press moved to Batavia where he took charge of the Jamiyyat Khayr school. He later became a teacher at the Shamil al-Hud school in Pekalongan and the Hadramaut school in Surabaya.[35] By the 1920s, he had become the patron of a lodge for Southeast Asian students in Cairo, where he once delivered a speech in which he encouraged Indonesians to embrace the positive benefits of modern education in Cairo, as well as the new schools run by the Dutch colonial government.[36]

To be added to the list of *mustaftī* were the Muslims in Southeast Asia who were exposed to reformist ideas of Cairo. Here, the experience of Abdullah Ahmad in Padang, West Sumatra, is a good example. He was the editor of the reform journal *al-Munir* of Padang, which involved not only in requesting fatwas from *al-Manār*, but also disseminating them to the Indonesian and Southeast Asian readers. He gained access to the Islamic reformism of *al-Manār* that was circulated in the Indies, despite allegedly having been banned by the Dutch.[37] The journal *al-Manār* contributed to the rise of a new socio-religious sphere in which Islamic reformism constituted the main aspect of the emerging public discourse. This can be explained by the fact that the reformist message of *al-Manār* had a strong impact in primarily urban communities, where the idea of progress—which *al-Manār* promoted—was the main theme of the discourse. *Al-Manār* contributed to laying down a strong foundation for the subsequent development of the Islamic reformist movement in Indonesia.[38]

---

34 Mandal, 'Finding', 143.

35 Mobini-Kesheh, *The Hadrami*, 239.

36 Schmidt, *Through the Legation Window, 1876–1926: Four Essays on Dutch, Dutch-Indian and Ottoman History*, 82; Meulen, *Don't You Hear the Thunder?: A Dutchman's Life Story*, 79–80.

37 Azra, 'The Transmission of *al-Manar*'s Reformism to the Malay-Indonesian World: The Cases of *al-Imam* and *al-Munir*', 80–81.

38 Azra, 'The Transmission', 81; Fogg, 'The Influence of Muhammad 'Abduh in Indonesia: Speech given by Hamka (Haji Abdul Malik Karim Amrullah) when receiving doctorate Honoris Causa from al-Azhar University, Cairo', 125–156.

It was partly due to the spread of *al-Manār* that Cairo increasingly became a leading centre of both religious authority and Islamic learning. This process strengthened as the number of Southeast Asian students in Cairo increased, which culminated in the 1920s when they formed a distinct Jawi community and stayed in a special place for students from Southeast Asia. Alongside the rise of incomes resulting from the boom in rubber prices in Malaya and coffee in Sumatra as well as general economic improvement in Southeast Asia,[39] there appeared substantial numbers of Muslims who could afford to send their children to Cairo. Hence, the number of Jawa in Cairo increased considerably, which led them to establish a well-organised association, the Jamiah Setia Pelajar (The Loyal Association of Students) in 1912 and then the Jam'iyya al-Khayriyya al-Talaba al-Azhariyya al-Jawiyya (The Welfare Association of Jawi Students of al-Azhar) in 1922. The latter association, with the Minangkabau Janan Tayyib as its first president (1922–1926), became an important forum for the Jawa of Cairo. As its name reveals, this association was concerned with providing welfare services for the Jawa, primarily to improve their living in the *riwāq al-jāwī*.[40]

3 Fatwa Requests to *al-Manār*

As already stated, the desire to have an Islamic explanation for the modernity that Muslims encountered, in terms of both newly invented materials and urban life-style, became a major part of the social and intellectual discourses of Southeast Asian Islam in the early twentieth century. This desire was reflected in the fatwa requests to *al-Manār* regarding food consumption as well as the permissibility of modern inventions and life-style. The request dealt with the issue of making a new way of life that was increasingly urban and modern in nature while remaining Islamic.[41]

In terms of halal issues regarding food, there appeared two fatwa requests, one of which was concerned with drinking beer and wine. It was requested by a Hadrami, Sayyid Aqil bin Uthman bin Yahya, from Kupang in West Timor. Having lived in an area where Christians formed the majority, in a heterogeneous neighbourhood, Sayyid Aqil most likely witnessed the habit of non-Muslims to drink alcohol, in particular beer and wine. As a Muslim, this practice became

39 Roff, *The Origins of Malay Nationalism*, 88; Taufik Abdullah, *School and Politics: The Kaum Muda Movement in West Sumatra*, 141.

40 Abdullah, *School and Politics*, 140; Othman, 'The Middle Eastern', 231.

41 Burhanudin, 'Aspiring', 17–21.

his concern. Yet what is of special importance is the fact that his request for a fatwa deals primarily with the substance of the drinks his Christian brothers consumed. He asked from what ingredients they were made and whether they could be categorised as medicine.[42] Instead of asking the legal status of beer and wine, it seems that he tried to find a reason that the Muslims might perhaps be allowed to drink these beverages. This last point is most likely also in reference to the argument that came up on the basis of new scientific discoveries in medicine at the period, whereby the European technology of the microscope could help transform alcohol into a treatment for certain diseases.

The way Sayyid Aqil posed his question was not without good reason. Like many other Hadramis in the Dutch East Indies, he most likely belonged to the growing urban life-style at the turn of the century, where practices such as drinking alcohol became common.[43] It is known that most of the Arabs in the Indies lived in the very centre of the cities, due in part to the Dutch colonial policy, which put them—together with the Chinese and Indians as 'Foreign Orientals' (*vreemde oosterlingen*)—in special geographic zones the Dutch arranged in the cities for close supervision.[44] In the early twentieth century, as the urban centres grew thanks to the Dutch 'Ethical policy' of modernisation, the urban life-style also advanced. And this life-style was even more common in such Christian-dominated areas as Kupang in West Timor. Thus, an Arab like Sayyid Aqil was very much exposed to non-Muslim practices in the city. On the one hand, he was familiar with the Christian habit of drinking but on the other he realised his status as a Muslim. It was the feeling that was clearly expressed in his fatwa request to *al-Manār*, in which he asked if there were any halal ingredients in the beer and wine that would permit the Muslims to consume them.

Another fatwa request related to food consumption was sent by Salim Munji in Surabaya, East Java. In contrast to the previous one which dealt with the possibly halal status of beverages' ingredients, this request was concerned with external factors associated with food. To be more precise, the fatwa seeker asked whether Muslims were permitted to eat food offered by someone committed to *ribā* (usury) in his business, which is forbidden in Islam.[45] Nothing is known about the fatwa seeker, but he is clearly concerned with the need to make sure that the food the Muslims consume should be halal, in terms of

---

42 *al-Manar* 10 (1907), 46–47.
43 Padmo, 'Perkembangan Sosial-Ekonomi Pribumi', 227.
44 Jonge, 1997.
45 *al-Manar* 29 (1929), 593.

both its materials and its association with something else forbidden (*haram*). It is evident that Salim Munji was not sure about the legal status of food that belonged to someone who was committed to sinful business; he seemed to fear that the food was bought with forbidden money (*uang haram*), or was made from ingredients coming from unlawful sources of income.

As such, the above fatwa request appears to demonstrate not only caution in religious attitude—possibly in reference to his personal experience—but also advanced thought on the halal issue. The substance of his fatwa request is reminiscent of a well-known postulate in Islamic jurisprudence (*uṣūl al-fiqh*), stating that to determine legal status (halal or non-halal) of a certain thing (including food), the way and the process by which the thing is made should be considered. In this particular case, it is the money from *ribā* practice that is taken by the fatwa seeker to be the reason for questioning the halal status of the food. Thus, this request strongly indicates the religious inclination of its *mustaftī*, who tried to avoid consuming anything non-halal in terms of food and beverage. This is possibly in reference to a cautious mode of Islamic attitude and practice, which is formulated in Islamic jurisprudence in the following postulate: 'should there be halal and haram together, haram must be the champion'. Therefore, it is much better, for him, not to consume food that is deemed to have relation with non-halal elements.

In addition, the above fact also gives us a strong hint that the fatwa seeker belonged to an educated group of Indonesian Muslims that was well exposed to the Islamic tradition of learning. The postulates of Islamic jurisprudence just mentioned can be found in the religious books studied in *pesantren*, Islamic institutions of learning with strong historical roots in Indonesian society and culture.[46] These texts include, for instance, *Fatḥ al-Mu'īn*, by Indian scholar Zayn al-Dīn al-Mālibārī, and *al-Ashbāh wa al-Naẓā'ir fī al-Furū'*, by Jalāl al-Dīn al-Suyūtī. These two *kitāb* were widely used as important sources of *pesantren* learning and therefore were popular in Indonesia.[47]

Belonging to the educated class in the city of Surabaya, a Muslim like Salim Munji, as was Sayyid Aqil of Kupang discussed above, was exposed to the emerging urban life-styles. Therefore, Salim Munji's fatwa request also dealt with a new form of gambling in the city, a public lottery. He asked if Muslims are permitted to buy lottery tickets, a practice that began to grow among people in cities like Surabaya in this period.[48] The two fatwa requests were formulated in reference to the newly encountered phenomena in the cities, in which

46 Dhofier, 1982.
47 Bruinessen, 'Kitab kuning: Books in Arabic Script Used in the Pesantren Milieu', 247, 251.
48 *al-Manar* 29 (1929), 593.

some modern aspects of life began to emerge. The fatwa seekers tried to uphold Islamic principles in the increasingly 'non-Islamic' milieu of the Western-styled mode of living.

We can see that modernity-based issues were prominent in fatwa requests to *al-Manār*. These appeared as the main issues Southeast Asian Muslims were concerned with in their questions to the editor of this Cairo-based journal, next to the issue of food consumption just delineated. As discussed in previous work,[49] they also questioned the newly-invented devices that had started to influence Muslims' socio-religious life. One of the fatwa requests to explain here concerned the legal status of using a gramophone for broadcasting a recitation of the Qur'an. It is the question posed by Hasan bin Alwi bin Shihab from Singapore. He asked if the record on which a recitation is recorded should be regarded like the holy text, *muṣḥaf*, in which case Muslims must be in a state of ritual purity when handling it. However, the underlying problem here related to supposedly 'non-Islamic' activities attached to the gramophone, as it was widely-used, mainly by Westerners, for entertainment purposes in cafes, where people listened to music while they drank alcohol.[50]

Also important to expound is the fatwa request posed by the aforementioned Basyuni Imran from Sambas. His question concerned representation of the body. In 1908, he sent a request for a fatwa to the editor of *al-Manār*, asking the legal status of painting and photography and the difference between these two forms of art.[51] This question was most likely in relation to the arrival of photography in the Indies in the early twentieth century—alongside the programme by the Dutch to collect photographic representation of this country[52]—which began to change perceptions of the representation of the body. In the last point of his question, Basyuni Imran seemingly expressed the new voice of mainly urban Muslims who wished to differentiate photography from painting, especially of living creatures, which is religiously forbidden. With this, it was hoped that photography was allowed (halal), so that the Muslims could enjoy the products of this new technology.

A related question was raised by Muhammad bin Hashim bin Thahir in Malang, East Java. Again taking the growing urban life-style in the Indies as the backdrop, he asked the legal status of watching movies that had started to become an increasingly common practice of Indonesian people, includ-

49 Burhanudin, 'Aspiring', 17–21.
50 *al-Manar* 10 (1907), 439.
51 *al-Manar* 11 (1908), 772.
52 Strassler, 2010.

ing the Muslims, in the early twentieth century.[53] Since the 1900s, thanks to the coming of recording technology introduced by the Western enterprises, the people already enjoyed what was locally called as *gambar idoep* (moving pictures). Provided by the rising entertainment companies of the time—such as Nederlandsche Bioscoop Maatschaapij, American Biograph, and American Animatograph—the number of people who watched moving pictures increasingly grew in Batavia and then the Indies more widely.[54] Therefore, due in part to his personal experience as well, Muhammad bin Hashim sent his question with great expectation that the *'ālim* Rashīd Riḍā would issue a fatwa concerning this matter, which was described as to have made the Muslims, and himself, anxious.[55]

In addition to the above subjects, other issue Southeast Asian Muslims were concerned with the wearing of Western dress. The question was posed by Abdullah Ahmad, a leading reformist *'ālim* of West Sumatra, as already noted above. In 1911, Abdullah Ahmad sent a fatwa request to *al-Manār* raising the dress-related topic, which was debated among the 'ulama' of West Sumatra. He asked the Cairo *'ālim* Rashīd Riḍā to clarify the statements on dress by the traditionalist 'ulama', known locally as *kaum tua* (old generation), who regarded those who wore Western clothes, as well as those who were behind them—the reformist 'ulama' (locally called *kaum muda* or young generation), to which group Abdullah Ahmad belonged—as sinful and even against Islam. Without specifying what kind of dress the Muslims were allowed to wear or not, the 'ulama' of *kaum tua* claimed that wearing Western dress was forbidden, based on a hadith saying that those who imitate a certain group of people (in this case the Westerners) belong to them.[56]

Still in this topic, one other point Abdullah Ahmad noted in his fatwa request was about the legality (or permissibility) of donning brimmed hats and neckties by Muslims. Again this question was posed as a response to a fatwa by local 'ulama' who stated that they were forbidden, with the reason that hats and neckties were worn by the European (and Turkish) people. With this request, it appears that Abdullah Ahmad tried to obtain religious support from a Cairo *'ālim* with high reputation in the increasingly prominent centre of Islamic learning in the Middle East in the early twentieth century. As an *'ālim* of *kaum muda* group, he was of the opinion that wearing of European clothes was permissible for Muslims, because Islam does not determine detailed aspects of

53 *al-Manar* 12 (1909), 270.
54 Biran, 'Film di Masa Kolonial', 271–272.
55 *al-Manar* 12 (1909), 270.
56 *al-Manar* 14 (1911), 669.

dress, such as style and colour. In this case, Abdullah Ahmad had support from the Cairo *'ālim* Rashīd Riḍā through his fatwa, on the basis of which he argued against the claim of *kaum tua* 'ulama' in a debate on dress.[57] In this respect, Abdullah Ahmad represented the increasing number of urban Muslims of West Sumatra who began to adopt the Western style of dressing.

The experience of Abdullah Ahmad, as those of other fatwa seekers already discussed, points to intensive encounters with modernity in Indies cities like Padang, his home town, in West Sumatra. In this city, not only did he have close contact with new elites who had graduated from modern schools, including those of al-Azhar in Cairo, Egypt, which came to be the backbone of *kaum muda* movement with the spirit of progress (*kemajuan*),[58] but he also witnessed the increasing influence of European ideas and culture on Muslims' socio-religious life. As a result, in his fatwa request just noted, Abdullah Ahmad also pointed to what might be called modernity-based issues, such as the legal status of making paintings and hanging paintings or pictures on the wall of a house, which were also raised by Basyuni Imran, and of listening to music.[59]

From the above discussion, it is clear that modernity constituted one leading dimension of the fatwas in *al-Manār*. Modernity became the main issue the fatwas addressed. This should be understood from the fact that the journal *al-Manār* was designed to be the channel for the dissemination of Islamic reformism, which arose as a response to the advancement of modern ideas and movement. In the case of Southeast Asia, therefore, besides dealing with new inventions the Muslims encountered in the cities, the requests for fatwas to *al-Manār* voiced the urgent need to reform Islamic ideas and practices, as well as Muslim leadership.[60]

4 Halal Fatwa Disseminated: A Few Examples

Now we come to the discussion on the way the fatwas in *al-Manār* reached their audiences in Southeast Asia. Besides being for the personal interest of its seeker and for journal readers, there were fatwa which came to be public knowledge and caught the attention of local press in Southeast Asia. In this respect,

57 Kaptein, 'Southeast Asian Debates and Middle Eastern Inspiration: European Dress in Minangkabau at the Beginning of the Twentieth Century', 176–195; Dijk, 'Sarongs, Jubbahs, and Trousers: Appearance as a Means of Distinction and Discrimination', 39–84.

58 Abdullah, *School and Politics*, 10–11.

59 *al-Manar* 14 (1911), 670.

60 Burhanudin, 'Aspiring', 21–26.

there were two journals that emerged as the channels for the dissemination of Islamic reform to Southeast Asia and took the journal *al-Manār* as the sources of their contents, *al-Imam* in Singapore (1906–1908) and *al-Munir* in Padang, West Sumatra (1911–1916). As I will show below, these two journals published certain contents of *al-Manār*, including fatwas on Islamic affairs in Southeast Asia.

As the first reform journal to appear in Southeast Asia, *al-Imam* made clear reference to *al-Manār*. First published in Singapore in 1906, *al-Imam* was directed to disseminate the Cairo-based Islamic reform ideas to Southeast Asia, taking *al-Manār* as both its model and its source. *Al-Imam* published many articles or the like that had originally been published in *al-Manār*, including the Malay translation of a work by an Egyptian Nationalist Muṣṭafā Kāmil, *al-Shams al-Mushriqa* (1904), which appeared as an article in the journal with the title 'Matahari Memancar' (The Rising Sun),[61] as well as the *Tafsir al-Manār* by Rashīd Riḍā.[62] It is noteworthy that *al-Imam* allocated special space for a fatwa column, *tanya-jawab*, in which *al-Imam* made frequent quotations from *al-Manār*. To mention only one example, *al-Imam* obviously followed *al-Manār* in answering a request for fatwa concerning the Sufi brotherhood (*tarekat*) of Naqsabandiyah. In this case, *al-Imam* stated that 'as already explained in our partner, the journal *al-Manār* in Egypt', the Muslim practice of the brotherhood should be based on Islamic law. *Al-Imam* then stressed that 'there is no doubt in the legal explanation *al-Manār* already made on this subject'.[63]

Yet, one thing should be stated that, as far as the issue of food consumption is concerned, it seems that it did not appear in the Southeast Asian Islamic media of the period. It is perhaps because the issue of food was not sensitive enough for the Muslims of Southeast Asia of the time, to the extent that it went unnoticed in the media. No mention was made on this issue in either *al-Imam* or *al-Munir*. Likewise, no public debates were held to discuss the subject. The issue of dress, however, was different. The journal *al-Munir*, under the editorship of Abdullah Ahmad, covered the topic. Taking *al-Manār* as its source, *al-Munir* published a fatwa by Rashīd Riḍā that had been issued through the Cairo journal mentioned.

As already explained, *al-Manār* received fatwa requests from Abdullah Ahmad in Padang, one of which concerned a debated issue of dress. And one of the reasons for his request was a fatwa by local 'ulama' of West Sumatra that forbade wearing European dress, as part of their anti-Christian Dutch attitude.

---

61 *al-Imam* (2, 1907); Laffan, *Islamic Nationhood*, 160–165.
62 *al-Imam* (3, 1908); Burhanudin, 'Islamic Knowledge', 180–182.
63 *al-Imam* (5, 1908).

The answer of Rashīd Riḍā in *al-Manār* became the source for Abdullah Ahmad to issue a *fatwā* on a similar topic of dress in *al-Munir*. In one edition of the same year (17, 1911), *al-Munir* published a fatwa that was the same in substance as that in *al-Manār*, stating that Islam does not have a particular mode of dress nor particular styles of wearing dress with the exception of the specific ritual of *iḥrām* during *ḥajj* and *'umra*, even though those who do not wear the ritual dress of *iḥrām* are not classified as non-believers. With this example, *al-Munir* made *al-Manār* of Cairo the foundation of its fatwa for dealing with disputed religious subjects in West Sumatra. Abdullah Ahmad admitted that the fatwa of 'the 'ulama' of Egypt with their journal' (*ulama Mesir dan Majalah mereka itu*) was to be the source of his fatwa in *al-Munir*.[64]

Again, although it does not belong to the halal issue, another example of *al-Munir*'s use of and reference to the fatwa in *al-Manār* should be mentioned here. It was the fatwa that dealt with the issue of moving some parts of the body as a sign for something was about to happen in a certain individual's life. This question was sent by Mahmud bin Shaikh Muhammad Idris in Tilatang, Bukittinggi, West Sumatra.[65] The answer to this question was delivered in the next edition of this journal, in which quotation was taken from *al-Manār*. To the journal *al-Munir*, so the editor wrote, 'it is a priority to present the answer [to this question] made by the journal *al-Manār* on the same issue'. Again following *al-Manār*, this journal stated that there is no relation at all between moving certain parts of the body with the nature and the characters of certain individuals, as well as their life in the future.[66] Thus, as on the issue of dress, *al-Munir* referred to *al-Manār* as a source of its issuing fatwa, strongly indicating its active engagement in the transmission of Islamic reform to the Indies in the early twentieth century.

With the above examples, it is clear that a new form of Islamic legal practice began to emerge in Southeast Asia in the early twentieth century. The fatwa given through printed media, as one important aspect of legal practice, became increasingly common among Muslim leaders. The printed media, which grew considerably in the early twentieth century, provided the mainly urban Muslims in the cities with new facilities and arena in the fields of religion, including in legal practice. While the 'ulama' of *pesantren* continued acting as *muftī* for mainly rural Muslims in the country areas, where oral tradition of fatwa giving still existed, urban Muslims started to shift their practices to new Muslim leaders who arose out of modernity. As argued, the rising use of

64 *al-Munir* 17 (1911).
65 *al-Munir* 12 (1913).
66 *al-Munir* 13 (1913).

print and electronic media have been credited as having contributed to the rise of the Islamic public sphere, in which the 'ulama' appear as only one of many Muslims who could speak for Islam.[67] The role of 'ulama' as the sole maker of contemporary Islam has ended, affirming the opinion that the rise of the public sphere is an inherent part of the modernity.[68]

In the experience of Indonesia, the above condition is expressed in the case of *Islam Bergerak*, one of the newspapers published by Hadji Misbach, a leading Muslim activist of the radical wing of the Sarekat Islam movement. In one of its editions, the newspaper published a question from a reader asking the legal status of eating pork if he or she was facing starvation and could not find any other food.[69] Regardless of the fatwa issued, this is one example of the way the Indies Muslims of the period asked for religious opinions. Looking at the journals and newspapers of the time, there often existed a specific column for fatwa giving—commonly referred to as *'tanya jawab'* (question and answer)—providing their readers with the opportunity to send questions to the editors to receive an explanation on certain issues, ranging from those concerning religious practices to sophisticated subjects of theology and philosophy.

Indeed, one salient feature to appear with the printing press is the changing mode of presenting Islam. The journals and newspapers represented a radical departure from the tradition of writing *kitāb*. In addition to their use of the Malay language, the journals and newspapers—especially those published after *al-Imam* and *al-Munir*—used Latin script (*rumi*), which had been associated with the Dutch. The cited example of *Islam Bergerak* represented an increasing shift in the seeking of fatwa, where the question was sent to the newspaper and the fatwa seeker invited the editor of the newspaper to give a religious explanation. This was one of the essences of the aforementioned changing Islamic legal practices in early twentieth-century Indonesia and Southeast Asia.

5 Closing Remarks

From the above discussions, we can see that the traditional legal practices of Muslims in Southeast Asia had a simple formulation concerning the issue

67 Robinson, 'Technology and Religious Change: Islam and the Impact of Print', 254.

68 Taylor, 1992.

69 *Islam Bergerak* (10 June 1917).

of halal in food consumption. The boundary between halal and non-halal is very modest, following what the Qur'an says, as for instance in the quotations at the beginning of this article. And that formed the basic picture of Islamic legal practice during the pre-modern period, when the elements and the influence of modernity did not yet exist within the communities. The two fatwa collections of nineteenth-century Southeast Asia provide us with strong evidence of the mentioned legal practice, where questions on the legality of foods were not found. For the Muslims of the period, halal was not the issue to be concerned with. The food they consumed was homemade in nature, and its production was under their control. The issues the Muslims were concerned with pointed to the way socio-political affairs among the Muslims of the time were in accord with Islamic teachings as formulated by the 'ulama'.

The issue of halal began to emerge in the early twentieth century, as the impact of modernity increasingly grew in the cities of Southeast Asia. Yet, as already discussed above, the issue was not concerned much on food-consumption. Reading the fatwas in *al-Manār*, it is clear that requests for fatwa to the Cairo *'ālim* Rashīd Riḍā did not pay much attention to the issue of halal food. Rather, they dealt mainly with the significance of new inventions arising out of modernity for Muslims' socio-religious life. The questions were concerned primarily with way the Muslims handled new developments that started coming into their life, such as the use of gramophones, the making of paintings and photographs, the wearing of European dress, and the like. In this respect, the meaning of halal broadened, in the sense that it included the legal status (permissibility) of these newly invented materials.

With this fact, it is argued that modernity appeared as the prime factor behind the rise of fatwa requests on the halal issues to the journal *al-Manār*. No similar question, therefore, could be found in the fatwa collections of the nineteenth century. Modernity-related issues constituted the main points Southeast Asian Muslims highlighted in their questions to the Cairo *'ālim* mentioned, representing a new trend of the Islamic development in Southeast Asia, where modernity, coupled with Islamic reformism, formed the core subject of public discourse. Also, the questions to *al-Manār* indicated the changing Islamic legal practices in the area, in that they become increasingly modern in both substance and language expression, which continued to grow in the following decades of the twentieth century.

One important point must be highlighted here; that the condition of modernity was responsible for the rise of feeling unfamiliar, even uncertain, with new devices and facilities, as well as urban life-style, in the increasingly Westernised milieu of Southeast Asian cities. This feeling appeared as an important factor behind the rise of Muslims' concern on the halal issue of new inventions and food consumption. In such conditions, turning to Islam became more common among Muslims, which led them to be more pious in socio-religious attitudes and behaviour.

This condition remains intact, even much stronger, in contemporary developments of Islam in Southeast Asia. The growth of modern food industries, mostly run by non-Muslim businessmen and framed in non-Islamic brands, has strengthened the feeling of uncertainty among Muslims. As a result, the call to make life more Islamic has intensified, as expressed in the rising will to define as halal not only food but also many other goods and services, which is extending and deepening the earlier trend seen in early twentieth-century fatwas.

Bibliography

Periodicals

al-Imam, Singapore (1906–1909).

al-Manār, Cairo (1898–1936).

al-Munir, Padang (1911–1916).

Islam Bergerak, Solo (1917–1923).

Books and Articles

Abaza, Mona. 1998. 'Southeast Asia and the Middle East: *Al-Manār* and Islamic Modernity'. In *Mediterranean to the China Sea: Miscellaneous Notes*, edited by Claude Guillot, Denys Lombard, and Roderich Ptak, 93–111. Wiesbaden: Harrassowitz Verlag.

Abdullah, Taufik. 1971. *School and Politics: The Kaum Muda Movement in West Sumatra*. Ithaca: Modern Indonesian Project Cornell University.

Abdullah, H. Wan Mohd. Shaghir, ed. 1999. *Al-Fatawal Fathaniyah Syeikh Ahmad Al-Fathani*. 3 vols. Kuala Lumpur: Khazanah Fathaniyah.

Ali, Nafhesa et al. 2020. 'Halal Dating: Changing Relationship Attitudes and Experiences among Young British Muslims'. *Sexualities* 23, nos 5–6: 775–792.

Al-Ahmadi, Abdul Rahman. 1983. *Tokoh dan Pokok Pemikiran Tok Kenali*. Kuala Lumpur: Kementerian Kebudayaan Belia dan Sukan Malaysia.

Azra, Azyumardi. 1999. 'The Transmission of *al-Manār*'s Reformism to the Malay-Indonesian World: the Cases of *al-Imam* and *al-Munir*'. *Studia Islamika* 6, no. 3: 79–111.

Biran, H. Misbah Yusa. 2012. 'Film di Masa Kolonial'. In *Indonesia dalam Arus Sejarah* vol. 5, edited by Taufik Abdullah and A.B. Lapian, 269–293. Jakarta: Ichtiar Baru van Hoeve.

Bluhm, Jutta E. 1983. 'A Preliminary Statement on the Dialogue between the Reform Magazine *al-Manār* and the Malayo-Indonesian World'. *Indonesia Circle* 32: 35–42.

Bluhm, Jutta E. 1997. '*Al-Manār* and Ahmad Soorkattie: Links in the Chain of Transmission of Muhammad 'Abduh's Ideas to the Malay-Speaking World'. In *Islam: Essays on Scripture, Thought and Society: A Festschrift in Honour of Anthony Johns*, edited by P.G. Riddell and A.D. Street, 295–308. Leiden: Brill.

Bradley, Francis R. 2016. *Forging Islamic Power and Place: The Legacy of Shaykh Da'ud 'Abd Allah al-Fatani in Mecca and Southeast Asia.* Honolulu: University of Hawaii Press.

Bruinessen, Martin van. 1990. 'Kitab kuning: Books in Arabic Script Used in the Pesantren Milieu', *Bijdragen to de Taal-, Land-, en Volkenkunde* 146, no. 2: 226–269.

Bruinessen, Martin van. 1992. 'Basyuni 'Imran'. In *Dictionnaire Biographique des Savants et Grandes Figures du Monde Musulman Peripherique du XIX Siecle a Nos Jours*, edited by Marc Gaborieau et al., 26–28. Paris: EHESS.

Burhanudin, Jajat. 2005. 'Aspiring for Islamic Reform: Southeast Asian Requests for *Fatwas* in *al-Manār*'. *Islamic Law and Society* 12, no. 1: 9–26.

Burhanudin, Jajat. 2007. 'Islamic Knowledge, Authority and Political Power: The Ulama in Colonial Indonesia'. PhD thesis. Leiden University, The Netherlands.

Dhofier, Zamakhsyari. 1982. *Tradisi Pesantren: Studi tentang Pandangan Hidup Kyai.* Jakarta: LP3ES.

Dijk, Kees van. 1997. 'Sarongs, Jubbahs, and Trousers: Appearance as a Means of Distinction and Discrimination'. In *Outward Appearances: Dressing State and Society in Indonesia*, edited by Schulte Nordholt, 39–84. Leiden: KITLV.

Fogg, Kevin. trans. and ed. 2015. 'The Influence of Muhammad 'Abduh in Indonesia: Speech Given by Hamka (Haji Abdul Malik Karim Amrullah) When Receiving Doctorate Honoris Causa from al-Azhar University, Cairo'. *Afkaruna: Indonesian Interdisciplinary Journal of Islamic Studies* 11, no. 2: 125–156.

Hall, C. Michael and Girish Prayag, eds. 2020. *The Routledge Handbook of Halal Hospitality and Islamic Tourism.* New York: Routledge.

Hayat, Raphie, Frank Den Butter, and Udo Kock. 2013. 'Halal Certification for Financial Products: A Transaction Cost Perspective', *Journal of Busines Ethics* 117, no. 3: 601–613.

Hourani, Albert. 1984. *Arabic Thought in the Liberal Age 1798–1939.* Cambridge: Cambridge University Press.

Jones, Russel. 1979. 'Ten Conversion Myths from Indonesia'. In *Conversion to Islam*, edited by Nehemia Levtzion. London: Methuen.

Jonge, Huub de. 1997. 'Dutch Colonial Policy Pertaining to Hadrami Imigrants'. In *Hadrami Traders, Scholars and Statements in the Ocean, 1750s–1960s*, edited by Ulrike Freitag and William G. Clarence-Smith. Leiden, New York and Köln: Brill.

Kaptein, N.J.G. 1995. 'Meccan *Fatwa* from the End of the Nineteenth Century on Indonesian Affairs'. *Studia Islamika* 2, no. 4: 141–160.

Kaptein, N.J.G. 1997. *The Muhimmat al-Nafa'is: A Bilingual Meccan Fatwa Collection for Indonesian Muslims from the End of the Nineteenth Century.* Jakarta: INIS.

Kaptein, N.J.G. 2009. 'Southeast Asian Debates and Middle Eastern Inspiration: European Dress in Minangkabau at the Beginning of the Twentieth Century'. In *Southeast Asian and the Middle East: Islam, Movement, and the* Longue Duree, edited by Eric Tagliacozzo, 176–195. Stanford: Stanford University Press.

Laffan, Michael F. 2003. *Islamic Nationhood and Colonial Indonesia: The* Umma *Below the Wind*. London and New York: Rutledge and Curzon.

Mandal, Sumit Kumar 1994. 'Finding their Place: A History of the Arabs in Java under Dutch Rule, 1800–1924'. PhD dissertation. Columbia University.

Matheson, Virginia and M.B. Hooker. 1998. 'Jawi Literature in Patani: The Maintenance of an Islamic Tradition', *JMBRAS* 61, no. 1: 1–86.

Meulen, van der. 1981. *Don't You Hear the Thunder?: A Dutchman's Life Story*. Leiden: Brill.

Mobini-Kesheh, Natalie. 1999. *The Hadrami Awakening: Community and Identity in the Netherlands East Indies, 1900–1942*. Ithaca: Southeast East Asian Program Cornell University.

Mudzhar, M. Atho. 1993. *Fatwa of the Council of Indonesian Ulama: a Study of Islamic Legal Thought in Indonesia 1975–1988*. Jakarta: INIS.

Othman, Mohammad R. 1994. 'The Middle Eastern Influence on the Development of Religious and Political Thought in Malay Society, 1880–1940'. PhD dissertation. University of Edinburgh.

Padmo, Soegijanto. 2012. 'Perkembangan Sosial-Ekonomi Pribumi'. In *Indonesia dalam Arus Sejarah vol. 5*, edited by Taufik Abdullah and A.B. Lapian, 192–231. Jakarta: Ichtiar Baru van Hoeve.

Pijper, G.F. 1984. *Beberapa Studi tentang Sejarah Islam di Indonesia, 1900–1950*. Jakarta: UI-Pres.

Robinson, Francis. 1993. 'Technology and Religious Change: Islam and the Impact of Print'. *Modern Asian Studies* 27, no. 1: 229–351.

Roff, William R. 1967. *The Origins of Malay Nationalism*. New Haven and London: Yale University Press.

Salleh, Abdullah al-Qadir. 1975. 'To' Kenali: His Life and Influence'. In *Kelantan: Religion and Politics in a Malay State*, edited by W. Roff, Kuala Lumpur: Oxford University Press.

Schmidt, Jan. 1992. *Through the Legation Window, 1876–1926: Four Essays on Dutch, Dutch-Indian and Ottoman history*. Istanbul: Nederlands Historisch-Archaoelogisch Instituut te Istanbul.

Snouck Hurgronje, C. 1931. *Mekka in the Latter Part of the 19th Century*. Leiden: E.J. Brill.

Strassler, Karen. 2010. *Refracted Visions: Popular Photography and National Identity in Java*. Durham, NC: Duke University Press.

Taylor, Charles. 1992. 'Modernity and the Rise of Public Sphere'. In *The Tanner Lectures on Human Values*, edited by Grethe B. Peterson. Stanford: Stanford University.

Teeuw, A and David K. Wyatt. eds. 1970. *Hikayat Patani*. Leiden: KITLV Press.

CHAPTER 4

Halal Issues, *Ijtihād*, and Fatwa-Making in Indonesia and Malaysia

Syafiq Hasyim

1 Introduction

Indonesia and Malaysia are the two largest Muslim countries in Southeast Asia that pay a great attention to the growing scale of halal issues. Both countries are fertile soil for the development of halal industry, as can be seen from the prevalence of halal restaurants, cafes, supermarkets, tourism, and manufacturing and many others. The increasing trend of halal lifestyle is not only visible in urban settings, but also in rural areas in both Indonesia and Malaysia.[1] Halal lifestyle in both countries has transformed from private to official and public domains in the last two decades, as can be seen in the institutionalisation of halal through the legislation of halal law. At the level of Muslim communities, the increasing awareness of the Muslim public of the importance of halal is visible in the daily attitude of Muslim consumers in using lawfulness and unlawfulness as a main consideration in deciding to buy or not to buy products. Simply speaking, halal consumers will not consume food sold by vendors that did not gain a halal certificate although what they are selling is actually not necessarily non-halal.[2] It seems that this tendency will remain more visible in the future of both countries. This is evident from some states' policies in both countries that support a halal lifestyle as well as industry.[3]

1 Talib, Chin, and Abdul Hamid, 2018; Rachman and Syamsuddin, 'Halal Industry in Indonesia: The Role of Sharia Financial Institutions in Driving Industrial and Halal Ecosystem', 35–58.

2 This case has happened to Solaria restaurants. These restaurants can be found in many malls and public places throughout Indonesia. The Indonesian Muslims judge these restaurants as non-halal restaurants because they did not get a halal certification from MUI.

3 Amalia, Sosianika, and Suhartanto, 'Indonesian Millennials' Halal Food Purchasing: Merely a Habit?', 1185–1198; see also Rachman and Syamsuddin, 'Halal Industry in Indonesia: The Role of Sharia Financial Institutions in Driving Industrial and Halal Ecosystem', 35–58 and Ab Talib, Ai Chin, and Abdul Hamid, 2018.

 | DOI:10.1163/9789004459236_005

The rapid expansion of halal sectors not only needs a dynamic response from political and economic standpoints, but also a religious point of view. The massive flow of various products from either domestic or international companies to Indonesia and Malaysia is not only the matter of economic production but, importantly, a matter of religion. For some groups of Muslims, knowing the lawfulness of such products is the most important issue. This is why *ijtihād* and fatwa-making on halal issues are relevant. The objects of halal certification are, for instance, not limited to only consumable products such as food, drink, cosmetics, and medicines but also to other important aspects of human life such tourism,[4] shariʿa hotels, and manufactured goods such as refrigerators and kitchen appliances.[5] All these things need response from *ijtihād* and fatwa-making that can provide answers for problematic issues faced by the Muslim communities of both countries.

This chapter aims to investigate *ijtihād* and fatwa-making on halal issues in Indonesia and Malaysia. It portrays how *ijtihād* and fatwa-making are implemented for issuing halal fatwas in both countries. This investigation, therefore, includes the discussion of *ijtihād* and fatwa-making in the classical texts of Islam as well as in the modern notion of *ijtihād* promoted by modern Muslim scholars. The chapter also pays attention to the institutionalisation of halal in Indonesia and Malaysia by looking at the roles of Majelis Ulama Indonesia (MUI, the Council of Indonesia Ulama) and Jabatan Kemajuan Islam Malaysia (JAKIM, Department of Islamic Development). It includes, for the case of Indonesia, the legislation of State Law No. 33/2014 on Halal Product Assurance, which creates a state-owned halal institution, Badan Penyelenggara Jaminan Produk Halal (BPJPH, State Agency of Halal Product Assurance). For the case of Malaysia, this section pays attention to the role of JAKIM and also halal authority at the Malaysian state level.[6] Discussions on the concept of *ijtihād* at the discursive and praxis level are also taken into consideration in this chapter. Last but not least, the chapter elaborates the principles of Islamic legal jurisprudence and also Islamic legal theory used in the process of *ijtihād* and fatwa-making on halal issues in Indonesia and Malaysia.

The chapter argues that the model of *ijtihād* and fatwa-making is closely related to the size of the halal market. Modern industry needs more flexibility in obtaining a response from the process of *ijtihād* and fatwa-making. With

---

4 https://www.thestar.com.my/news/nation/2018/09/06/ministry-to-push-for-multibillion-dollar-halal-tourism, accessed 1 November 2019.

5 https://sharianews.com/posts/kulkas-bersertifikasi-halal-ini-tanggapan-warganet, accessed 1 November 2019.

6 I mention JAKIM and JAIN because Malaysia is federalist.

the austere method of *ijtihād* and fatwa-making such as strict adherence to the Shāfiʿī school of Islamic law, crucial issues emerging from the unlimited number of products and the limited space of the halal market are not simple matters to overcome. Both Indonesia and Malaysia are struggling to become international halal hubs and the success of this is not only connected to market-aspects like promotion and producing a good quality of goods but also to the support of religion, such as supportive halal fatwas.

This chapter is written on the basis of library research. I have conducted several interviews on halal issues with the members of Fatwa Commission of MUI in Jakarta, halal entrepreneurs, academician and also observers. For the case of Malaysia, I rely on written sources found either in published books, journal articles, or online sources. All the gathered information based on primary and secondary sources is seen from the combined perspectives of Islamic law, Islamic legal theory, and social sciences. In this regard, the combined perspectives are not only used to highlight but also to critically explain the increasing phenomenon of halal lifestyle and also the considerable amount of policy that has been introduced in Indonesia and Malaysia as well as how *ijtihād* gives response to these issues. On the basis of the gathered data, this chapter finally produces a multi-disciplinary analysis on the halal issue on one hand and *ijtihād* and its application in Indonesia and Malaysia on the other.

2 The Halal Issue in Academic Discussion

Academic studies and research on halal issues at global level as well as at the regional level as in Indonesia and Malaysia have started to flourish in the last two decades. Most studies of halal issues in Indonesia and Malaysia are related to the role of MUI for the context of Indonesia and on the role of JAKIM for the context of Malaysia in undertaking halal certification. Elsewhere, I have stated that halal certification is part of simultaneous agenda of shariatisation of Indonesia—inclusion of shariʿa in the legal and public sphere—which is conducted by MUI.[7] Tim Lindsay looks at the role of MUI in monopolising Indonesian Islam through Islamic economy, especially halal economy.[8] As the largest Muslim country with a large potential market, Indonesia has

7 Hasyim, 2014; Hasyim, 'Fatwas and Democracy: Majelis Ulama Indonesia (MUI, Indonesian Ulema Council) and Rising Conservatism in Indonesian Islam', 21–35.

8 Lindsey, "Monopolising Islam? The Indonesian Ulama Council and State Regulation of the 'Islamic Economy'", 253–274.

prepared for established halal governance.[9] In relation to *ijtihād* on the halal issue, Nadirsyah Hosen, in his article, 'Hilal and Halal: How to Manage Islamic Pluralism in Indonesia?',[10] outlines aspects of *ijtihād* on halal issues. Hosen discusses a different stance between the Ḥanafī school of Islamic law and the Shāfiʿī school of Islamic law in determining the legal status of goods. The Ḥanafī school of Islamic law agrees the use of *istiḥāla* while the Shāfiʿī school of Islamic law disagrees.

In the context of Malaysia, Johan Fischer describes the behaviour of the Malaysian Muslim middle class in the tradition of consumption.[11] Fischer tries to examine the interface between the invocation of Islam—reflected by the closeness of Malaysian middle-class families to mosques—and the practice of consumption among them—reflected by their closeness to malls and centres of shopping. Fischer observes the Malaysian practice of halal and the use of halal to promote Malay Muslim and ethnic identity by referring to the Malaysian diaspora in London.[12] His observation covers both Malaysians in Malaysia and the Malaysian diaspora in London in practising and asserting halal that he describes as frontier. However, neither of his books pay special attention to the process of *ijtihād* in declaring halal. In addition, many studies on the *ijtihād* method on halal issues in Malaysia are written by Malaysian scholars themselves, using both Malaysian and English languages, published variously in their international and local journals. Norhidayah Pauzi, Saadan Man and Syed Mohd Jeffri Bin Syed Jaafar compared the role of fatwa and fatwa-makers on halal in Indonesia and Malaysia. Socially and politically speaking, Indonesia and Malaysia are different and therefore this difference also reflects the difference in halal fatwa in both countries. They state that Malaysia tends to adhere more strictly to the Shāfiʿī school of Islamic law while Indonesia remains open to the thinking of other *madhāhib*, although the majority groups of Indonesian Islam follow the Shāfiʿī school of Islamic law as well. In the case of halal fatwa, based on their study, Indonesia accepts Ḥanafī and Mālikī schools of Islamic law.[13]

I aim to enrich discussion on halal issues by looking at the model of *ijtihād* and fatwa-making on halal in both countries. I see the importance of this

---

9 Hidaefi and Jaswir, 'Halal Governance in Indonesia: Theory, Current Practices and Related Issues', 89–116.

10 Hosen, 'Hilal and Halal: How to Manage Islamic Pluralism in Indonesia?', 1–18.

11 Fischer, 2011; LPPOM, 2011.

12 Fischer, 2011.

13 Pauzi, Man, and Syed Jaafar, 'Analisis Perbandingan Fatwa Indonesia dan Malaysia: Kajian Terhadap Isu-Isu Halal yang Terpilih', 1–16.

topic because *ijtihād* and fatwa-making play a dynamic role in developing halal issues both in fulfilling religiosity and Islamic lifestyle as well as affecting the economy in Indonesia and Malaysia. This chapter also wants to indicate how *ijtihād* and fatwa-making—part of religion—negotiate and bargain with the development of market, lifestyle, and state policy.

2.1 Ijtihād *and Fatwa-Making in Indonesia and Malaysia*

Mohammad Hashim Kamali states that *ijtihād* and fatwa are two concepts of Islamic law that are often used interchangeably.[14] Wael Hallaq also states that that *ijtihād* and fatwa-making are interchangeably employed in the discourse of many classical ʿulama', such as Abu Ḥusayn al-Baṣrī, Abu Muḥammad al-Juwaynī, Imam Ḥaramyn al-Juwaynī, and al-Ghazālī.[15] al-Ghazālī, for instance, asked for a *muftī* to practice *ijtihād* in fatwa-making.[16] In this regard, al-Ghazālī places *ijtihād* and fatwa-making at an intersection. Al-Qaraḍāwī states that *ijtihād* in the current situation is implemented in three forms; scientific research (*baḥth al-ʿilm*), Islamic legislation (*taqnīn*), and legal opinion (fatwa).[17] Finally, I should say that this chapter follows the use of *ijtihād* and fatwa-making as interchangeable.

Ijtihād and fatwa-making are integral parts of halal concerns in Indonesia and Malaysia. Both MUI and JAKIM are halal authorities engaged in the principle of *ijtihād* (deductive-Islamic legal reasoning) and fatwa-making individually or collectively. Based on this, discussion of the model of *ijtihād* and fatwa-making on halal issues seems to be very important because of the prevalence of halal issues in modern life. *Ijtihād* and fatwa-making provide a way for Muslim people to contextualise shariʿa with developments in daily life of Muslims. The use of *ijtihād* and fatwa-making is evident for the function of Islam in our daily life.[18] *Ijtihād* and fatwa-making are tools for Muslims to help their religion survive in the challenge of modern world. In this context, the door of *ijtihād* has never been closed—as assumed by many European Western scholars[19] and also traditionalist ʿulama' in both Indonesia and Malaysia—but it continues in the different forms of *ijtihād* up to the current situation.

Wael B. Hallaq states that classical and modern Muslim scholars propose various definitions of *ijtihād*.[20] Classical Muslim scholars like al-Ghazālī define

---

14 Kamali, *Shari'ah Law: An Introduction*, 162.
15 Hallaq, 'Ifta' and Ijtihad in Sunni Legal Theory: A Development Account', 34–35.
16 Hallaq, 'Ifta' and Ijtihad in Sunni Legal Theory: A Development Account', 35.
17 al-Qaradawi, 1994.
18 Alharbi, *Democracy in Islamic and International Law*, 203.
19 Feener, *Muslim Legal Thought in Modern Indonesia*, 24.
20 Hallaq, 'Was the Gate of Ijtihād Closed?', 3–41.

ijtihād as a serious effort of *mujtahid*—someone who conducts *ijtihād*—to gain knowledge of God's law (*aḥkām al-shārʿīa*). al-Shāṭibī understood *ijtihād* as taking advantage of a situation to produce knowledge (certain knowledge) and preconceptions (*al-ẓan*) on Islamic legal rulings. Ibn Ḥazm defines *ijtihād* as an effort to come to a ruling on particular issues that are based on the Qur'an and Sunna (the tradition of the Prophet Muhammad). Abdul Hamid Abu Sulayman states that *ijtihād* represents 'a systematic endeavor that requires ongoing effort and commitment'.[21] From this definition, *ijtihād* is a continuous process that is not limited by time and space. Said Shabbar emphasises the role of *umma* as the regulator of *ijtihād*.[22]

Based on all the definitions, it can be stated that *ijtihād* is 'a measure of individual effort in arriving at legal decisions for cases in which no clear textual ruling was evident'.[23] In the context of halal issues, although most halal objects have clear textual evidence (*qaṭʿiyya*) in the Qur'an and Sunna, *ijtihād* remains necessary. This argument is based on the agreed opinion of the majority of Muslim jurists, who say that *ijtihād* can be conducted for either *qaṭʿiyya* or *ẓanniya*. It is said that '*ann al-aḥkām al-thābita bi ijtihād minhā ma huwa qaṭʿiyyun wa minhā ma huwa ẓanniyun*' (the Islamic ruling which is resulted from ijtihad can be either in the form of clear textual evidence or in the form of unclear textual evidence).[24] To conclude, conducting *ijtihād* at its various forms and levels is unavoidable in the context of the prolific development of halal issues in Indonesia and Malaysia.

In a general overview, most Indonesian and Malaysian Muslim scholars of Islamic law and Islamic legal theory conduct *ijtihād* and fatwa-making on the basis of the Shāfiʿī school of Islamic law. Indonesian Muslim scholars are more open to the four *maḏhabs* than those of Malaysia.[25] In the Shāfiʿī tradition, *ijtihād fī al-maḏhab* is commonly allowed. In this model of *ijtihād*, the Shāfiʿī 'ulama' do not directly take legal rulings or opinions from the Qur'an and Sunna, but rather collect and select them from the books of *fiqh* written by their predecessors. Michael Feener states that the historical fact behind the prevalent use of *ijtihād fī al-maḏhab* is that most Muslim communities in Southeast Asia focus more on the teaching of *fiqh* (Islamic legal jurisprudence).[26] As a

21 Shabbar, *Ijtihad and Renewal*, 84.
22 Shabbar, *Ijtihad and Renewal*, 79.
23 Feener, *Muslim Legal Thought in Modern Indonesia*, 25.
24 al-Zubaydi, *Ijtihād Fī Manāṭ al-Hukm al-Shar'ī: Dirāsah Ta'ṣīliyyah Taṭbīqiyyah*, 31.
25 Pauzi, Man, and Syed Jaafar, 'Analisis Perbandingan Fatwa Indonesia Dan Malaysia: Kajian Terhadap Isu-Isu Halal Yang Terpilih', 1–16.
26 Feener, *Muslim Legal Thought in Modern Indonesia*, 25.

consequence of this, they tend to study *furūʿ* (the branch ruling) rather than *uṣūl* (the principle ruling), where the latter is close to the implementation of independent *ijtihād* (*ijtihād mustaqil*).[27]

How is the notion of *ijtihād* contested and implemented in the current contexts of Indonesia and Malaysia? The traditionalist majority Muslim groups of Indonesia that are mostly represented by NU do not allow *ijtihād* but, rather, *istinbāṭ*, because Nahdlatul Ulama (NU) follows the opinion that *ijtihād* was displaced in the third century of Hijra.[28] For NU, differently from *ijtihād*, *istinbāṭ* (the derivation of rules for novel legal cases) is conducted and refers to the four schools of Islamic law, although at the practical level the use of the Shāfiʿī school of Islamic law retains its priority among other schools of Islamic law. Since that era, NU has insisted that the current generation of Muslims only have the authority to conduct *istinbāṭ al-aḥkām*, which sits below *ijtihād*. NU recognises the *ijtihād* of the second and third generations of *mujtahids* (*ijthād fī al-madhab*), but not for the *ijtihād* of current Muslim scholars. After the third generations, activity in deducing Islamic legal status from the primary sources of Islam is called *istinbāṭ al-aḥkām*. Some conservative-traditionalist Muslim scholars of NU even disagree with the use of *istinbāṭ al-aḥkām* because this level is still very high for the current cohort of Muslim scholars. Instead of *istinbāṭ al-aḥkām*, they employ the concepts of *tarjīḥ* (opting for one legal opinion), *taḥqīq* (ascertaining meaning from a particular case of text), and *taqrīr* (abstracting legal evidence from the circumstances and conditions surrounding it).[29] Therefore, an authoritative institution within NU responsible for conducting *istinbāṭ al-aḥkām* is called *Bahsul Masa'il* (the investigation of problems), meaning to discuss problems (*masā'il*) based on the works of classical Muslim scholars, not based on their direct study of the Qur'an and sunna.

Unlike NU, Muhammadiyah does not see the authoritative *ijtihād* of previous classical Muslim scholars as a reason to close off the opportunity for current Muslim scholars to conduct *ijtihād*. Muhammadiyah allows not only the name but also the activity of *ijtihād*. Muhammadiyah, claiming to be a reformist Islamic organisation, follows an argument that the door of *ijtihād* is never closed. In the Muhammadiyah model of *ijtihād*, the *mujtahids* of this organisation try to refer to the Qur'an and Sunna because they do not fol-

27 Feener, *Muslim Legal Thought in Modern Indonesia*, 25.

28 Burhanuddin, *Islam Dalam Arus Sejarah Indonesia*, 433.

29 Mallat, *The Renewal of Islamic Law: Muhammad Baqer As-Sadr, Najaf and the Shi'i International*, 125.

low *maḏāhib*. The primary sources of Islam are the Qur'an and *Sunna al-Maqbūla*.[30] However, in their fatwa books, it is very common to find the opinions of classical 'ulama' quoted.[31]

Although NU believes that the door of *ijtihād* is closed for current scholars, the *Bahsul Masa'il* forum of NU is not trapped in issuing conservative fatwas. Many NU fatwas are compatible with the modern way of life.[32] Although Muhammadiyah considers that the *ijtihād* door is open, this is often translated into the form of Islamic purification.[33] This can happen because the overarching idea about returning to the Qur'an and Sunna can be easily twisted into purifying the reading of the Qur'an and Sunna.

MUI offers a middle way on *ijtihād*. Like NU, MUI can accept the system of *maḏāhib* on one hand and, like Muhammadiyah, the open door of *ijtihād* on the other hand. This can be seen in some MUI fatwas that are based on the Qur'an and Sunna and also on the opinions of *maḏāhib* Muslim scholars. In the context of halal issues, the *ijtihād* model of MUI to some extent goes beyond both NU and Muhammadiyah. MUI has established a special institution that handles halal issues, while Nahdlatul Ulama and Muhammadiyah are not interested in this matter up to now. It is true that NU has tried to establish a particular institution that is commissioned to undertake halal certification, but this attempt appeared to end after the first certification, given to the Solaria restaurant.[34] Muhammadiyah, as the second largest Muslim organisation, does not consider it importany to have a halal body. In this regard, Muhammadiyah places its whole expectation for halal control to MUI. Based on this, it is understandable that MUI has dominated the process of halal certification in Indonesia during the last thirty years because the two largest Muslim organisations have had no interest in this matter.

In the Malaysian context, halal issues are clearer, as the system (the Shāfiʿī school of Islamic law) is adopted. In the official website of Pejabat Mufti Wilayah Persekutuan (Department of Mufti of Federation), one term used for

30 Majelis Tarjih dan Tajdid Pimpinan Pusat Muhammadiyah, *Himpunan Putusan Tarjih Muhammadiyah*, vii.

31 Majelis Tarjih dan Tajdid Pimpinan Pusat Muhammadiyah, *Himpunan Putusan Tarjih Muhammadiyah*, vii; Alimatul Qibtiyah, 'Pengakuan Ulama dan Isu Perempuan di Majlis Tarjih dan Tajdid Muhammadiyah', 193–211.

32 Zahro, 2004.

33 Azra, 'Islamic Thought: Theory, Concept and Doctrine in the Context of Southeast Asian Islam', 15; Peacock, 2017.

34 See https://www.nu.or.id/post/read/48830/pbnu-berikan-sertifikasi-halal-untuk-restoran-solaria, accessed 6 September 2019.

ijtihād is *istinbāṭ* (deriving legal rule or opinion).[35] Malaysia can be described as a Shāfiʿī country[36] because the Shāfiʿī school of Islamic law is used in all the fatwa councils of 14 states.[37] In the context of Malaysia, shariʿa law means the Shāfiʿī school of Islamic or also Islamic law taken from Māliki, Ḥanafi, and Ḥanbali schools of Islamic law agreed by the supreme head of the Malaysia kings.[38] Interestingly, Malaysia does not have the prevalence of Islamic civil society organisations that Indonesia has that are also responsible for *ijtihād* and fatwa-making. The absence of these organisations makes Malaysia stronger in having one opinion about the various schools of Islamic law.

The *ijtihād* process of Malaysian fatwa councils at its various levels, after receiving a request for fatwa from a fatwa seeker, begins with conducting a careful investigation into the collection of *qawl muʿtamad* (prevailing views) within the scope of the Shāfiʿī school of Islam law. When the observed prevailing opinions are already known but do not conform to public interest (*maṣlaḥa*), then the *muftis* are given right to follow the *qawl muʿtamad* of different schools of Islam law. However, if all *qawl muʿtamad*s indicated are against public interest thenthe *mufti* could practice their own *ijtihād*. From this, it is obvious that the Malaysia fatwa councils begin their own *ijtihād* when all the prevailing opinions cannot fulfil public interest. Interestingly, *maṣlaḥa* in the context of Malaysian *ijtihād* is well considered. This circumstance is different from the context of Indonesian *ijtihād*, in which *maṣlaḥa* is rarely used as a legal reason and argument.

How is collective *ijtihād* implemented in the halal issues? Historically, *ijtihād* is individually managed by an individual qualified Muslim scholar. A collective *ijtihād* means *ijtihād* is carried out by more than one *mujtahid*. Since the early history of Islamic law, there had been no institutionalisation of *ijtihād* because it is the private affair of Muslim jurists.[39] Based on this, the collective *ijtihād* and fatwa-making are, therefore, modern phenomena. Muhammad Qasim Zaman associates collective *ijtihād* with the notion of unclosed door of *ijtihād*. Modern

35 http://muftiwp.gov.my/ms/pengenalan/bahagian/fatwa/unit-buhuth, accessed 21 November 2018. This website consists of many information on fatwa issued by National Fatwa Council of Malaysia.

36 Pauzi, Man, and Syed Jaafar, 'Analisis Perbandingan Fatwa Indonesia dan Malaysia: Kajian Terhadap Isu-Isu Halal Yang Terpilih', 4.

37 Mehmood, Chisthi, and Mughal, 'Islamic Concept of Fatwa, Practice of Fatwa in Malaysia and Pakistan: The Relevant of Malaysian Fatwa Model for Legal System of Pakistan', 48.

38 Pauzi, Man, and Syed Jaafar, 'Analisis Perbandingan Fatwa Indonesia dan Malaysia', 5.

39 Kamali, *Shari'ah Law: An Introduction*, 163; Zaman, *Modern Islamic Thought in a Radical Age: Religious Authority and Internal Criticism*, 93.

jurists can continue to conduct *ijtihād* in the form of collective *ijtihād*.[40] Modern Muslim scholars, like Rashīd Riḍā (d. 1935) and Muhammad Iqbal (d. 1938), who tried to associate the legislative assembly with their capacity to undertake collective *ijtihād*.[41] Dār al-Iftā' (House of Fatwa, Egypt), Majma' al-Buhūth al-Islāmiyya (Islamic Research Academy, Azhar University), and Majma' al-Fiqh al-Islāmiyy (Fiqh Research Academy) are examples of collective *ijtihād* institutionalisation.[42]

Based on the previous explanation, both MUI and JAKIM can be described as sites of collective *ijtihād*. MUI and JAKIM invite many *mujtahid*s, fatwa-makers and experts to get involved in deciding a fatwa. When pork lard was identified, in such products, for instance, as Dancow by the research of Tri Soesanto from the University of Brawijaya, Malang, East Java in 1988,[43] Suharto asked the MUI to conduct further investigation into the case. Since this first investigation, the Fatwa Commission of MUI has been aware of their lack of expertise on this issue. To investigate pork lard in such a product was not easy for them. The Fatwa Commission needed help from scientists to validate delicate issues of food fusion with chemical goods extracted, for instance, from pigs. The illicit goods are often invisible and therefore need laboratorial investigation that should be done by those who are trained and knowledgeable in sciences. The scientists are given specific responsibility to investigate the purity of food, drink, medicines, and cosmetics. They bring the result of their empirical investigation to the *mufti*s of MUI, grouped in the Fatwa Commission, and then if there is no question and objection from the *mufti*s and they can issue a fatwa based on the scientific findings. This applies not only to halal issues but also shari'a economic lifestyle, such as financial and economic issues. This practice continues to date.

JAKIM also involves many Muslim scholars in *ijtihād* or fatwa-making.[44] The element of collective *ijtihād* in the Malaysian fatwa is evident from the composition of fatwa institutions. In the National Fatwa Council of Malaysia (NFC) there is a chairman, a secretary, and also representative *mufti* from 14 states. Besides that, the NFC also involves five experts on shari'a and one expert on law.[45] Their fatwas are issued either by the National Fatwa Council of Malay-

40 Zaman, *Modern Islamic Thought in a Radical Age*, 92.

41 Zaman, *Modern Islamic Thought in a Radical Age*, 92.

42 Zaman, *Modern Islamic Thought in a Radical Age*, 93.

43 The result of this research was published in Canopy Bulletin 1988; see also En-Chieh Chao's chapter in this volume.

44 Man, 'Patterns of Contemporary Ijtihād in Malaysia: Analysis on Fatwas of Malaysian National Fatwa Council', 106.

45 Man, 'Patterns of Contemporary Ijtihād in Malaysia', 106.

sia or by the State-Level Fatwa Councils in the form of their state fatwa. The involvement of experts outside Islamic experts is evidence of a collective *ijtihād* in Malaysia. It is often said that the result of Malaysian *ijtihād* should be valid not only in the view of religion but also in the view of scientific knowledge and this can be achieved through the adoption of collective *ijtihād*.

2.2 *The Institutionalisation of Halal Fatwa in Indonesia and Malaysia*

This section attempts to explain the history of fatwa institutionalisation in Indonesia and Malaysia. In Indonesia, *ijtihād* and halal fatwas have become the main task of MUI. MUI, although it is a non-state institution, has been issuing fatwas on halal as well as halal certificates since the 1990s. The JAKIM is an official institution in Malaysia that has issued fatwas on halal since the 1970s.

Historically speaking, the use of the fatwa has been recognised since the colonial era in both Indonesian and Malaysian contexts. In that era, the Muslim communities in both nations asked for a fatwa either from local or international muftis. Nico Kaptein states that the Dutch colonial government recognised the use of Islam as the law of Muslim people in the Netherlands East Indies. Because most of the population in the Netherlands East Indies were Muslims, therefore the Dutch administrators categorised Islamic law as indigenous law.[46] From this time, many classical books were used as the curriculum for the Dutch colonial educational institutions.[47] Kaptein concludes that the fatwa became a unifying factor of Muslims in the Netherlands East Indies.[48]

In the post-colonial era, by constitution, Indonesia became neither a theocratic nor a secular state. Indonesia is referred to as a Pancasila state.[49] Being a Pancasila state means that the state and society of Indonesia believe in five ideological principles, of which 'believe in one God' is the first principle. Based on this, Indonesia has no obligation to follow a particular religion, but some values of religions from Islam, Christianity, Hinduism, Buddhism, and Confucianism can be adopted into state law as long as it is done through national legislative process and not aimed at establishing a theocratic state. As a non-theocratic state, Indonesia, unlike Malaysia, has no an official fatwa body. In the context of Indonesia, fatwas can be issued by Islamic civil society organisations like NU, Muhammadiyah, and MUI. As a consequence, their fatwas are not legally binding for Muslim communities in Indonesia because they are not issued by Indonesia's lawmakers. NU (established in 1926 and the first largest Muslim

46 Kaptein, 'Fatwas as a Unifying Factor in Indonesia History', 76.
47 Kaptein, 'Fatwas as a Unifying Factor in Indonesia History', 76.
48 Kaptein, 'Fatwas as a Unifying Factor in Indonesia History', 77.
49 Darmaputera, 1988; Intan, 2006; Faisal Ismail, 1995.

organisation in Indonesia), has a fatwa commission called Lembaga Bahsul Masa'il (LBM).[50] The LBM is responsible for issuing Islamic legal opinion asked for by both Nahdliyyin and non-Nahdliyyin. Muhammadiyah (established in 1912 and the second largest Islamic organisation) also has its own fatwa division called Lembaga Tarjih Muhammadiyah (LTM), whose task is to prepare fatwas for Muhammadiyah or non-Muhammadiyah members who are seeking fatwas.[51] Persis (Persatuan Islam, established in 1923 and the third largest Muslim organisation), has its own fatwa institution called Majelis Hisbah.[52] The task of Majelis Hisbah is to issue fatwas and Islamic recommendations (*tawṣiyya*). From this, we can say that almost all Muslim organisations in Indonesia have their own fatwa division[53] but all the fatwas issued by these Islamic organisations are not legally binding for their followers.

In 1975, under the sponsorship of Suharto, MUI was established.[54] The aims of establishing this 'ulama' organisation was to mediate dialogue between the state on one hand and the other existing Muslim organisations on the other hand, regarding shared Islamic issues and nation-state. Although Islamic organisations like NU, Muhammadiyah, Persis, and many others were already established, Suharto needed one voice that represented the Islamic organisations to communicate with the state. Early on, NU, as the largest Muslim organisation, seemed to be reluctant to agree on the Suharto proposal for the establishment of MUI.[55] For NU, the establishment of MUI indicated that Suharto did not trust existing Muslim organisations. The establishment of MUI prompted more polarisation among *umma* and Muslim organisations.[56]

However, the political interests of the regime and some 'ulama' in Indonesia finally agreed for the establishment of MUI. Since its establishment in 1975, although the Suharto regime was confident in the face of the Muslim groups, MUI was not formed as an official fatwa body of Indonesia. When some people wanted MUI to be created as a state fatwa-giving body, this proposal was rejected by Suharto and also by some groups of Indonesian 'ulama'. This refusal was based on two considerations. First, formulating MUI as the state fatwa-giving body means that MUI was not independent from state interest, while the ideal of position of 'ulama' was expected to be independent from any intervention,

50 Zahro, 2004.

51 Qibtiyah, 'Pengakuan Ulama Dan Isu Perempuan Di Majlis Tarjih Dan Tajdid Muhammadiyah', 193–211.

52 Federspiel, 2009.

53 Federspiel, 2009.

54 Mudzhar, 1993; Adams, 2004; Hasyim, 2011.

55 Personal conversation with Masdar F. Mas'udi, Jakarta, 2011.

56 Personal conversation with Masdar F. Mas'udi, Jakarta, 2011.

even from the state. Another reason was that a state *mufti* implies a connotative sign as if the state of Indonesia has adopted a system of political Islam like Egypt, Saudi, and other Middle East countries. Ultimately, the establishment of MUI was agreed to as we see it now and one of its responsibilities is to issue halal fatwas in Indonesia. From the 1990s to 2019, this responsibility remains voluntarily undertaken by LPPOM-MUI, but since Indonesia fully enacted State Law No. 33/2014 in 17 October 2019, halal issues have been taken over by BPJPH.

The history of Malaysia legal system is different from that of Indonesia. During the Sultanate era in the thirteenth century Malaysia used various forms of Islamic law.[57] The arrival of Europeans to the Malay world in the sixteenth century created colonies.[58] The presence of so many mainland Europeans and the British changed the legal landscape of Malaysia. The implementation of Islamic law in its various form slowly started to change to the secular law introduced by the British colonists. There are two levels of legal system in Malaysia's post-colonial era, the Federal level and the state level. Islamic law is found in the state level because the Constitution of Malaysia stipulates that Islam is a matter for the states, not the federation. However, the Federation can adopt an institution that occurs in the tradition of Islam. This is evident in the case of institutionalisation of fatwa.

The institutionalisation of fatwa in the Malaysian context has a long history, starting with the sultanate era of Malaysia. The sultans of Malay usually had *mufti* (individual or collective), as was the case in Kelantan in the 1830s.[59] Sultan Muhammad I of Kelantan, for instance, asked Sheikh Abdul Halim to be his *mufti*.[60] In Malaysia's post-colonial era, the establishment of fatwa institution gained legitimacy from the Federal Constitution of this country, making Islam a state matter. It means that states of Malaysia have rights to accommodate everything applying to shari'a aspiration and doctrine into public and legal sphere of this country, including regulating on halal, which is based on Islamic fatwa. Malaysia has 14 states and on the basis of the Federal Constitution all these states have the right to appoint *mufti* or fatwa-issuing institutions. The remit of the appointed *mufti* is only to take care of religious affairs of state (*negeri*). Those who appoint *mufti* or fatwa-giving institutions are the rulers of states. The appointed *mufti* of such a state usually works under state institutions that have different names from one state to another.

57 Shuaib, 'The Islamic Legal System in Malaysia', 87.

58 Shuaib, 'The Islamic Legal System in Malaysia', 87.

59 Abd. Rahman, 'Sejarah Dan Perkembangan Instititusi Fatwa Di Negeri Kelantan', 185–210; Azman Ab Rahman et al., 2008.

60 Abd. Rahman, 'Sejarah Dan Perkembangan Instititusi Fatwa Di Negeri Kelantan', 188.

On the basis of above explanation, we can see that the history of fatwa institutionalisation in Malaysia is centred in the hands of rulers. In the history of modern Malaysia, fatwa institutionalisation begins from the establishment of Majlis Kebangsaan bagi Hal Ehwal Ugama Islam Malaysia (National Council for Islamic Affairs (MKI)) in 1970. From 1970 to 1980, the MKI organised 20 meetings that discussed Islamic affairs. Y.A.B. Tun Abdul Razak bin Dato' Hussein (1922–1976) considered that the development of Islam in Malaysia was flourishing, therefore it needed more complete and organised administration on Islamic affairs. In 1974, the Federal government upgraded the MKI into a higher status, as Bahagian Ugama (Section of Religion), part of the office of Prime Minister of Malaysia. The Federal government commissioned Majlis Agama Islam under the responsibility of Kementerian Wilayah Persekutuan (Ministry of Federation). Because of its wider responsibility, in 1985, Bahagian Ugama (Religious Divison) became Bahagian Hal Ehwal Islam (BAHEIS) (Islam Affairs Division). The task of BAHEIS, which remained under the office of Prime Minister of Malaysia, was to plan and accelerate law and administration on matters of Islam. This institution assured the implementation of Islamic programmes such as *daʿwa* and other activities at central government level. Due to the increasingly complex development of Islamic affairs, in 1997 the BAHEIS was transformed into JAKIM (Jawatan Kemajuan Islam Malaysia or Department of Islamic Development Malaysia). There are three objectives of the JAKIM establishment: first, to assure the spread of Islam into the wider society; secondly, to build authoritative leadership and to create well-trained, skilful, dedicated, and useful management; and thirdly, to produce a management system that is based on the values and ethics of Islam.

Although the establishment of National Fatwa Council of Malaysia (Federal level of fatwa institution, Jawatankuasa Fatwa Majlis Kebangsaan Bagi Hal Ehwal Ugama Islam Malaysia) was prior to the establishment of JAKIM, it works under the coordination of JAKIM. The federal government of Malaysia regulates halal issues and therefore JAKIM plays a key role, and fatwa on halal refers to fatwas of National Fatwa Council of Malaysia. The constitution of the Malaysian government on halal refers to 'Akta Perintah Perihal Dagangan 2011 and Perintah Perihal Dagangan 2011'. Both acts regulate the criteria of halal and *ḥarām*. Halal food or goods are described as such when they contain no materials prohibited for consumption in Islam and when animals have been slaughtered in line with shariʿa and fatwa prescription. The act also states that halal food or goods should be free from impure materials that are based on shariʿa and fatwa.

The overall institutional management of halal in Malaysia is organised and administered under JAKIM at the Federal government level and under JAIN (Jabatan Agama Islam Negeri, State Department of Islam) at the state government level. Both authorities establish procedures and systems on halal administration, audit, and certification. Both JAKIM and JAIN have rights to enforce the implementation of halal acts. Both have established inspector (*ḥisba*) positions that work to observe and detect the violation of halal acts. On the theological side, the *ḥisba* establishment is aimed at commanding right and forbidding wrong, especially in the use of the halal logo in the public market. The misuse of the halal logo is crucial issue in Malaysia. From 2012 to 2014, for instance, there were indications of 63 violations of the 2011 act on halal by producers.[61] The institutionalisation of *ḥisba* can happen in Malaysia because it is recognised in the history of Islam and Malaysia applies some part of Islam in its positive law.

2.3 *The Mechanism of* Ijtihād *and Fatwa-Making of* MUI *and* JAKIM

In Indonesia, *ijtihād* and fatwa-making on halal matters are conducted by MUI. Prior to the establishment of Badan Penyelenggara Jaminan Produk Halal (BPJPH, National Agency of Halal Product Assurance), MUI issued halal certificates. Since 17 October 2019, with the full enactment of State Law No. 33/2014, BPJPH is fully responsible for the issuance of halal certification and MUI retains the function of *ijtihād* and fatwa-issuer. This section describes the role of MUI in *ijtihād* and fatwa-making before the enactment of State Law No. 33/2014. The process started from collecting and receiving the request of fatwa (*istiftāʾ*) from fatwa seekers (*mustaftī*), who could be government, private companies, or individuals on halal related issues. Then, the Fatwa Commission of MUI brought this *istiftāʾ* to their regular meeting (fatwa-issuance or *ijtihād*). In this process of *ijtihād*, the Fatwa Commission needed information on requested issues of halal from food auditors, who have the special task of investigating the material contents of such products and goods. The food auditors were under the coordination of LPPOM-MUI. The list of material contents provided by the food auditors was then discussed by the Fatwa Commission. The Fatwa Commission also recruited non-shariʿa experts as panel members in the process of fatwa-making. To conclude there are three elements that reflect the use of collective *ijtihād* principle in the fatwa-making of MUI in halal issues: the presence of shariʿa experts (*mufti*); the presence of non-shariʿa experts; and the presence of food auditors as data investigators.

In conducting *ijtihād* and fatwa-making, MUI required three important steps. First, each fatwa should have a basic foundation from the Qurʾan and *sunna muʿtabara*[62] and not contradict public welfare (Indonesian: *kemasla-*

61 Nasohah and Mokhtar, 'Konsep Amar Ma'ruf Nahi Munkar dalam Pematuhan Halal', 144.

62 The meaning of sunna mu'tabara is sunna that can be used as a legal argument. There are

hatan umat). Secondly, fatwa should not contradict *ijmāʿ* (ʿulamaʾ consensus), *qiyās muʿtabar* (analogy), of other *dalil*s (indicators or textual sources) like *istiḥsān, masāliḥ mursala* and *sadd al-dharīʿa*. Thirdly, prior to issuing a fatwa the opinions of classical *madhāhib* and those who have expertise were invited in the fatwa-making meeting.[63] MUI called the first and second steps a form of *ijtihād inshāʾī*, which refers to the three foundation of *ijtihād* (Qur'an, sunna, and consensus). In the Sunni tradition, the domain of *ijtihād inshāʾī* belongs to the founders of *madhāhib* like Mālik, Ḥanafī, Shāfiʿī, and Ibn Ḥanbal. The third step, then, is called *ijtihād intiqāʾī* because it refers to the thoughts of the *madhāhib*. In this regard, the *ijtihād intiqāʾī* uses *muqārana* (comparative) approach among different four schools of Islamic law.[64] MUI stated that fatwa should have basic legal foundation from the consensus of previous ʿulamaʾ. When there is no *ijmāʿ* encountered concerning such fatwa, fatwa still cannot challenge the ʿulamaʾ consensus. MUI understood that *ijmāʿ* is very authoritative, absolute, and universal.[65] In this regard, the MUI *ijtihād* was at the level of *ijtihād intiqāʾī*.

How was a halal fatwa issued by MUI at the practical level? There were several steps that should be taken into consideration before issuing halal fatwa. First, MUI provided the halal auditor of LPPOM with information on the category of unlawful goods from the perspective of shariʿa, especially regarding *ḥarām li-dhātihi* (unlawful in itself) and *ḥarām li-ghayri dhātihi* (unlawful because of other's influence). Second, the halal auditors of LPPOM visited companies that had requested halal certificates. This could involve more than one visit. Third, the halal auditors undertook laboratory investigation on the product. The result of the laboratory investigation was submitted to the Fatwa Commission. Finally, the Fatwa Commission issued a fatwa.[66]

How is *ijtihād* is conducted to issue halal fatwa in Malaysia? The authority for halal in Malaysia is given to three bodies: JAKIM at the Federal level; MAIN (Majlis Agama Islam Negeri: State Council of Islamic Affairs); or JAIN (Jabatan Agama Islam Negeri: State Department of Islamic Affairs) at the state level. In the context of Malaysia's JAKIM and MAIN or JAIN, a fatwa on halal is issued by the Pengesahan Halal Malaysia (Malaysia Halal Legalisation Panel) of these organisations. This panel comprises seven members; chairman, sec-

different level of sunna and not all sunna can be used as legal argument, see MUI, *Himpunan Fatwa MUI Sejak 1975*, 15.

63 MUI, *Himpunan Fatwa MUI Sejak 1975*, 14.

64 MUI, *Himpunan Fatwa MUI Sejak 1975*, 16.

65 MUI, *Himpunan Fatwa MUI Sejak 1975*, 16.

66 MUI, *Himpunan Fatwa MUI Sejak 1975*, 21.

retary, two experts on shari'a law, at least one expert on technical issues, and at least two other members. The Panel in this regard is very strong, which means their decision is *mu'tamad* (ultimate). The decision issued by the Panel consists of six categories: pass; conditional pass; KIV (Keep In View); unsuccessful; re-audit; and cancel application.[67]

Fatwa institutions in Malaysia either at federal or state level do not conduct *ijtihād inshā'ī*.[68] The fatwa-makers in Malaysia follow the *madhab qawlī* of Shāfi'ī school of Islamic law, which refers to the classical *fiqh* of the *taqlid* era.[69] They do not refer directly to the Qur'an and Sunna or to the Shāfi'ī Islamic legal theory, but to the products of *madhab*. Apart from following the products of the Shāfi'ī school of Islamic law, the Malaysian *ijtihād* follows views or opinions issued by fatwa institutions at the state level.[70]

2.4 *Islamic Legal Maxims and Principles of Islamic Legal Theory*

Based on the previous explanation on *ijtihād*, the classical books of *fiqh* and *usūl al-fiqh* (Islamic legal theory) are fundamental sources, after the Qur'an and sunna, in conducting *ijtihād* and fatwa-issuing in both Indonesia and Malaysia. The following section is devoted to elaborating some principles of Islamic legal maxims (*qawā'id fiqhiyya*) and *uṣūl al-fiqh* used by MUI and JAKIM as arguments in their *ijtihād* and fatwa-making on halal.

2.4.1 Istiḥāla and Istihlāk

Because of its inclination to the Shāfi'ī tradition, MUI disagrees with the use of *taṭhīr* (purification or the process of cleaning) method, a concept that was introduced by the *madhāhibs* of *fiqh* concerning the method of cleaning. In the tradition of Islamic legal jurisprudence there are two concepts discovered in the context of *taṭhīr*,[71] *istiḥāla* and *istihlāk*. Both concepts are well recognised among the Indonesian and Malaysian fatwa authorities and Muslim scholars. *Istiḥāla* means the transformation of one material into another through chemical intervention (processing). The Māliki and Ḥanafī schools of Islamic law, which are not popularly practiced in Indonesia and Malaysia, allow the use of

67 JAKIM, *Manual Procedure for Malaysia Halal Certfication*, 61.

68 Abdul Rahim, Ismail, and Mohd Dahlal, 'Ijtihad Dalam Institusi Fatwa Di Malaysia: Satu Analisis', 201.

69 Abdul Rahim, Ismail, and Mohd Dahlal, 'Ijtihad Dalam Institusi Fatwa Di Malaysia: Satu Analisis', 201.

70 Abdul Rahim, Ismail, and Mohd Dahlal, 'Ijtihad Dalam Institusi Fatwa Di Malaysia: Satu Analisis', 202.

71 Personal conversation with Hasanuddin, the member of Fatwa Commission of MUI, Jakarta, 2018.

istiḥāla. Both *madhāhib* agree that everything that changes from the status of *ḥarām* to the status of *ḥalāl* resulting from the process of *istiḥāla* is lawful.

MUI's rejection of the concept of *istiḥāla* is evident in its view on gelatine. MUI has its own definition on this matter. MUI considered that gelatine extracted from pigs—which has already changed from lawful to unlawful—cannot be justified as part of *istiḥāla*.[72] MUI has stated that gelatine extracted from pork is considered *ḥarām* because its material origin is taken from unlawful material. In this regard, MUI understood that the change of gelatine is different from the change of wine to vinegar. This understanding is against the result of the World Halal Conference in Kuwait that declared gelatine as halal because it is the product of *istiḥāla*. In addition, Amidhan (former MUI chairman) stated that most of Indonesian 'ulama' understand that pork is not permitted and the use of all materials extracted from pork is also not permitted. In this regard, the Indonesian 'ulama' rejected the concept of *istiḥāla* to be applied as the method of *ijtihād* in halal issues. Ma'ruf Amin stated that, in principle, 'we at MUI cannot accept the legal maxim of *istiḥāla* for any kind of products that remain benefiting pork. It means that pork, although it has already changed to a different form, its legal status remains unlawful'. In arguing this, Ma'ruf Amin refers to al-Baqarah, 2:173 and al-Mā'idah, 5:3.[73]

Another Islamic legal argument used by MUI to refuse the method of *istiḥalah* is related to the principle of *intifā*ʿ. MUI followed the opinion of 'ulama' that *istiḥāla* is a process by design or intention and anything that intentionally benefits from pig or unlawful materials is unlawful in Islam. In this regard, MUI held to three hadiths as the basis of its argument. First, a hadith narrated from Abū Hurayrah that the Messenger of God said: 'Actually God has prohibited wine and its selling, carrion and its selling, and pork and its selling' (narrated by Abū Dawud). Second, a hadith narrated from Jābir bin 'Abdillāh, who heard that the Messenger of God said in the year of the Mecca occupation when the Prophet Muḥammad was in Mecca: 'Actually God has prohibited selling wine, carrion, pork and sculpture.' Someone asked: 'Messenger of God, is the sale of carrion allowed because it can be used to paint a boat and to lubricate skin and to fuel oil-lamps?' The Prophet Muḥammad answered: 'It is not allowed; the fat of car-

72 Lukmanul Hakim, Director of LPPOM MUI issued this argument in his dissertation defense at Islamic University of Europe, Rotterdam, *An Islamic and Scientific Perspective on Istihalah*, 1 April 2015. See https://www.hidayatullah.com/berita/nasional/read/2015/05/04/69119/bahas-istihalah-direktur-lppom-raih-cum-laude-dari-iue.html, accessed 20 November 2018.

73 http://www.ḥalālmui.org/mui14/index.php/main/detil_page/8/22688, accessed 20 November 2018.

rion is unlawful.' Then the Prophet Muḥammad said again: 'God condemns, or may God condemn the Jewish community, surely God has banned the fat of carrion and then he changed its form into oil and then they sale it and eat the result of sale.'[74] From several mentioned hadiths above, getting any benefit (*intifā'*) from parts or materials prohibited in Islam is unlawful. In this regard, MUI in Indonesia followed the Shāfi'īte school of Islamic law.[75] An example of this case is Rubella vaccines that use s pork-extracted enzyme in processing. This trypsin is actually already *taṭhīr* (no evidence of impurity in the final stage of empirical investigation) in its Islamic legal ruling, but MUI still considers it as *ḥarām*, unless under an emergency situation (*ḍarūra*). According to MUI, the concept of *taṭhīr* does not follow the tradition of Prophet Muhammad (sunna). Maulana Hasanuddin (a member of MUI Fatwa Commission) argued that what would be produced by the process of *taṭhīr* is not purely *taṭhīr* but remains fused with *najs* (impurity).

In the Muzakarah of National Fatwa Council 26, 7–9 March 1990 the Malaysian fatwa authorities also rejected the use of *istiḥāla*. Any food, drink, or any other material resulting from the process of *istiḥala* that used chemical material from pork are unlawful. The Muzakarah gave an example that the production of cheese that used chemical material from pork remains unlawful. Cheese is lawful if its production uses chemical material from trees and vegetables. In 1999, the Muzakarah of National Fatwa Council of Malaysia decided that biotechnology that produced food, drink etc. that used pork DNA was also not permissible in Islam even if in the end process the pork DNA was no longer detectable. In 2006, the Muzakarah of National Fatwa Council discussed the Islamic legal status of consuming fish that had been intentionally fed with unlawful or impure food. The Muzakarah also declared the unlawfulness of consuming fish that was intentionally nurtured in an impure environment. A similar legal decision was the unlawfulness of consuming *jallalah*, fish that ate unlawful food. This legal opinion is applied by the almost all fatwa councils of Malaysia at the state level.

Interestingly, the *ijtihād* and fatwa issuing on halal employed by both Indonesian and Malaysia fatwa authorities in terms of *istīḥala* places them in opposition to the broader position of international 'ulama' in the Middle East. Wahbah al-Zuḥaylī, for instance, agrees with the use of *istiḥala* in the *ijtihād* on halal issues. Zuḥaylī has said that although gelatine that is derived from pork DNA (Deoxyribonucleic acid) that is used because of *istīḥala* is lawful. Soap,

---

74 The hadith was narrated by Bukhari dan Muslim.

75 See http://www.halalmui.org/mui14/index.php/main/detil_page/8/22688 last retrieved 21 November 2018.

cheese, cosmetics, and medicine that are the products of *istiḥala* are lawfully used and consumed.[76] Similarly, the opinion of Yūsuf al-Qaraḍāwī is also to accept the use of *istiḥāla*. It means that all food that are produced through the process of *istiḥāla* are permissible for Muslim consumption.[77]

The Indonesian fatwa authority also rejects the use of *istihlāk*, which literally means dilution or assimilation, for most cases of food, drink, medicine, and cosmetics. One way of describing the concept of *istihlāk* is a small quantity of impurity or unlawful material is mixed with a larger quantity of purity eradicates the small quality of impurity, as indicated by the change in its taste, smell, and colour. The Indonesian fatwa authorities also tend to reject the use of *istihlāk*. In this regard, again, the Shāfiʿī principle has a strong influence on Indonesian fatwa authorities. In the view of the Shāfiʿī school of Islamic law, for a mixture of impure (*najs*) and pure material, the impurity should be removed when possible. If the impurity is not in a concrete and solid form, such as fluids, and it cannot be taken out because it already contaminates the purity of water, for instance, the water is regarded as *ḥarām*. The Indonesian fatwa authority follows this principle in issuing fatwas on drink, perfumes, and many other products that apply a zero tolerance to alcohol. This can be seen in the MUI fatwa about the mixture of impurity and purity since the 1980s. In the fatwa, there are three points: first, all food and drink that are clearly mixed with unlawful and impure materials are unlawful; second, for all food and drinks that are suspected to have been mixed with unlawful and impure materials, it is recommended to avoid them; third, regarding unclear or doubtful fusion with unlawful and impure materials, MUI asks the state authority to follow up with a laboratory investigation to determine its Islamic legal status.[78] It can be defined, in short, as an extremely small dilution of the lawful into a larger size of the unlawful.

In the classical literature on *fiqh*, the perception of Muslim jurists on this matter is also divided into those who accept and those who do not accept. Muslim jurists who agree with the use of *istiḥāla* usually agree with the use of *istihlāk* because the latter is understood as the variant of the former. In this regard, the Ḥanafi school of Islamic law is in the position of allowing the use of *istihlāk*. Ibn Taymiyyah (inclining to the Ḥanbali school of Islamic law) agrees with the use of *istihlāk*. An illustration given by Ibn Taymiyyah, when wine is mixed with water and the taste, colour, and smell of wine is no longer detected and then the resulting liquid is consumed by someone, that person

76 al-Zuḥaylī, *al-Fiqh al-Islāmī wa Adillatuh*, 100.
77 al-Qarāḍāwī, *al-Halāl wa al-Harām fī al-Islām*, 62.
78 MUI, *Himpunan Fatwa MUI Sejak 1975*, 607.

cannot be said to have been drinking wine, but water.[79] This perception of this group seems now to be very much applied by Muslims in Middle East countries and also by Muslims who are living in the West. Yūsuf al-Qaradāwī states this about expanding the spirit of *taysīr* (making easier, not creating a burden).[80] al-Qaradāwī's opinion is actually directed to the Muslim community who live in Western countries. This is part of *fiqh al-'aqalliya*, which al-Qaradāwī promotes.[81]

The Malaysian fatwa authorities sometimes take a flexible position in accepting *istihlāk*. This can be seen in some cases; for instance, the use of the cochineal insect as an additive colour in food. The reason given is that the content of the additive colour is under 0.003 to 0.006 %. The Malaysian fatwa authorities also allow the use of insignificant flavouring alcohol, but the alcohol should not be extracted from wine.[82] On the basis of the above explanation, it can be concluded here that both Indonesian and Malaysian models of *ijtihād* produce a stricter criteria of halal than the general model of *ijtihād* in the Middle East.

2.4.2 Ḍarūra and Sadd al-dharīʿa

The use of *ḍarūra* (emergency) is a kind of safety valve for cases for which a precedent cannot be found in Islamic legal reasoning to determine their lawfulness. The Indonesian fatwa authority defines emergency situations, as illustrated in classical Islamic law, as a situation where, if we do not consume the unlawful food we will die. The limit of emergency here, then, is the threat of death. In an emergency situation, Islam allows the consumption of unlawful goods as a means of survival, as mentioned in the Islamic legal maxim, *al-ḍarūrāt tubīḥ al-maḥḍūrāt*, during emergencies the prohibited is allowed. In this regard, Rubella vaccines still using pork-extracted enzymes are allowed by MUI not because the enzyme itself is already clear from impurity but rather because of emergency reasons. The Malaysian fatwa authorities also define similar criteria of *ḍarūra* as does the Indonesian fatwa authority. Because of this, Malaysian fatwa authorities tolerate the use of gelatine in pharmaceutical products in many cases. In the Muzakarah VIII 1984, the National Fatwa Council of Malaysia decided that the use of gelatine for medicine is lawful because of

79 Ibn Taymiyyah, *Majmū' al-Fatāwā Ibn Taymiyyah*, 308–310.

80 al-Qaradāwī, *Taysīr al-Fiqh li al-Muslim al-Mu'āṣir fī Daw'i al-Qur'ān wa al-Sunna*, 17–19.

81 Warren, *Yusuf al-Qaradawi, his Interlocutors, and the Articulation, Transmission and Reconstruction of the Fiqh Tradition in the Qatar-Context*, 54.

82 Abdullah, Suhaimi, and Mohd Noer, 'Konsep Istihalah dan Istihlak pada Makanan dan Barang Gunaan', 87.

ḍarūra argument unless a replacement material has already been found, which makes its use unlawful. On the basis of this, the emergency argument differs greatly from the use of *istiḥāla*. The *ḍarūra* argument needs further processes of inquiry and research on the materials replacing pork and the use of *istiḥāla* argument is not.

Sadd al-dharīʿa means to prevent something from happening that could result in negative impacts in the future. Besides other Islamic legal reasons, MUI also refers the concept of *sadd al-dharīʿa* as a way of determining fatwas on lawfulness. MUI argues that we should prohibit the production of wine, beer, and many alcoholic drinks because MUI wants to protect humans from the negative impact of these drinks. The Malaysian fatwa authorities also use the argument of *sadd al-dharīʿa* in many cases on halal issues. In the case of Menactra vaccine, this vaccine is used to protect children under the age of 9 months from meningococcal disease. The Muzakarah Fatwa Kebangsaan of Malaysia decided to allow the use of this vaccine in order to prevent disability.

2.4.3 Iḥtiyāṭ Wājiba

Although the method of *ijtihād* and fatwa-making embraced by the fatwa authorities of Indonesia and Malaysia try to be open to other *madḥāhib*, but, at the practical level, the Shāfiʿī school of Islamic remains dominant for resolving halal issues. MUI for instance consistently adheres to *iḥtīyāṭ* (precaution) and *aḥyaṭ* (most precaution).[83] Both concepts are claimed by MUI as first having been introduced and used in the Shāfiʿī tradition. The JAKIM also follows the Shāfiʿī school of Islam law in its state law on halal, which can be seen in Perintah Perihal Dagangan (2011), which defines halal in the perspective of Shāfiʿī maḏhab. In this regard, JAKIM also follows *iḥtiyāṭ* as can be seen in their rejection of the use of *istiḥāla*.[84]

The concept of *iḥtiyāṭ* is used in the Shāfiʿī tradition as well as other *madhāhib*. However, the fatwa authorities in Indonesia and Malaysia tend to follow the Shāfiʿī concept of *iḥtiyāṭ*. MUI, in addition, proposes not only employing *iḥtiyāṭ* but also *aḥyāṭ*. Conceptually speaking *iḥtiyāṭ* is used by Muslim jurists to explain the importance of considering precautions in the practice of Islam in daily life. Among Muslim jurists, embracing *iḥtiyāṭ* is a choice, but many suggest it is obligatory (*iḥtiyāṭ wājiba*). For the case of halal, the principle of *iḥtiyāṭ* held by both Indonesian and Malaysian fatwa councils is

---

83 Personal conversation with Arwani, the member of Fatwa Commission of MUI, Jakarta, 2018.

84 A more elaboration on *istiḥalāh* is discussed in next part of this chapter.

iḥtiyāṭ wājiba (obligatory precaution). Here, technically speaking, *iḥtiyāṭ* functions a guiding principle of Islamic legal theory to prevent us from falling into *shubha*. *Shubha*, which is literally translated a 'doubtful', ultimately means 'a position between lawful and unlawful'. Although *shubha* can lead to benefits, it cannot be applied to all instances.[85] The use of *iḥtiyāṭ* from the perspective of Islamic legal theoreticians can help prevent us from falling into *shubha*. This is very important because the status of *shubha* often has an impact on goods, food, drink, and other products.

The majority of Muslim jurists who follow the Ḥanafī, Māliki, Shāfiʿī, and Ḥanbali schools of Islamic law tend to see *iḥtiyāṭ* as the instrument of *ijtihād* for the affairs of *furūʿ* (branches of Islamic law). Although they employ *iḥtiyāṭ*, however, many of them allow the use of *istiḥāla*, which is assumed by the Shāfiʿī followers to be a sign of carelessness.[86] The Ḥanafī and Māliki schools are obvious examples of this case. For both, *madhāhib* is considered quite flexible and not strict in determining halal. Sufi groups such as al-Ghazālī, Ibn Qayyim, al-Shawkānī, and many others are well known for adopting the concept of *iḥtiyāṭ* for the daily lives of Muslims.

How do the Indonesian and Malaysian halal authorities implement the use of *iḥtiyāṭ* in their *ijtihād*? Both of them state that all food, drink, medicines, and cosmetics that have possibly been contaminated by impurity (*najs*) should be considered as *ḥarām*. There is no tolerance in this matter. The variety of *iḥtiyāṭ* discourse, which is richly discussed in the classical literatures of Islamic legal jurisprudence and Islamic legal theory, does not make them waver from the Shāfiʿī concept of *iḥtiyāṭ*. Therefore, for instance, MUI and JAKIM do not want to take the risk of legalising the status of halal resulting from *istiḥāla* methods.[87] Specifically, MUI absolutely rejects the status of lawfulness because of the *istihlāk* process, although in some cases JAKIM tolerates *istihlāk*.[88]

---

85 Nyazee, *Outlines of Islamic Jurisprudence*, 151; Ann, Hossein, and Hosen, *Modern Perspectives on Islamic Law*, 234.

86 Personal conversation with Hasanuddin, the member of Fatwa Commission of MUI, Jakarta, 2018.

87 It can be defined as a total mutation from *ḥarām* to *ḥalāl* because of chemical substance and process. In this regard, the original taste, smell and colour should also totally change.

88 This is from *halaka*, meaning dilution. *Istihlāk* literally means extreme dilution, putting the unlawful material into the lawful material that the substance of unlawful material is no longer noticeable. The example of *istihlāk* is the mixture of urine in the lawful lake water, in this regard, overriding the halal ingredients.

2.4.4 al-Aṣl fī al-Ashyā' al-Ibāḥa

Public debates on the principle *al-aṣl fī al-ashyā' al-ibāḥa* (the origin of such thing is lawful) appeared in the public sphere when the lawmakers of Indonesia started to discuss the importance of Indonesia having a state law on halal during 2013 and 2014. The debates focused on whether the state law should focus on declaring the lawfulness or unlawfulness of goods. Where lawfulness is agreed, halal certification should be issued, and where unlawfulness is agreed then an certificate of unlawfulness should be issued. Many Indonesian Muslim scholars of Islamic legal theory and Islamic law criticised MUI for focusing more on unlawfulness than lawfulness. This discussion is driven by a legal maxim that is popular among the Shāfiʿī followers, 'al-aṣl fī al-ashyā' al-ibāha ḥattā yadulla al-dalīl ʿalā al-taḥrīm', meaning, the initial legal status of everything is allowed until there is an evidence that indicates its prohibition. Instead of listing the unlawful products, MUI prefers to shortlist lawful products that are technically not different from one to another. According to MUI, this legal maxim principle cannot be used as a legal argument for prioritising the certification of unlawfulness over that of lawfulness.[89] In fact, since the 1990s MUI has administered halal investigation and certification through LPPOM. In 2014, the lawmaker of Indonesia agreed to legislate State Law No. 33/2014 on Halal Product Assurance.

In the Malaysian context, debates about this Islamic legal maxim are rare because the government of Malaysia has powerful authority in the institutionalisation of halal. Differing from the experience of Indonesia, halal certification in Malaysia is imposed by the government. In this context, the fatwa authorities in Malaysia—at both Federal and state level—agree to prioritise the certification of lawfulness over the certification of unlawfulness.

3 Concluding Remarks

An overall result of *ijtihād* and fatwa-making methods from both Indonesian and Malaysian fatwa authorities is the strictness of halal criteria that is applied to food, drink, cosmetics, and medicines. Both Indonesia and Malaysia employ zero tolerance on the use of *ḥarām* ingredients—they reject all such ingredients as impure. The stricter criteria of halal resulting from the strict model of *ijtihād* can, of course, have an impact on the halal market. The Malaysian context—more experienced in global markets—seems to be fine with this

89 Interview with Maulana Hasanuddin, Vice Chairman of MUI Fatwa Commission, at UIN Jakarta, October 2018.

method of *ijtihād*. The problem with the market is not about being strict or not strict, but the certainty of halal regulation enforcement. The halal market, as other markets, will have certain flexibility.

The stricter *ijtihād* of halal adopted in both Indonesia and Malaysia reflects loyalty to the textual reading of the sources of Islamic law on one hand, but it also indicates ignorance of new findings in sciences and technology related to bio-technological and chemical issues and other new scientific findings. If we absorb the spirit of *ijtihād*, we should be open to new possibilities. Following the Shāfiʿī school of Islam law, in this regard, probably prevents a possible fusion between shariʿa and science and technology and this is not in line with the spirit of *ijtihād* and sciences, which always develop and look for innovation.

The domination of state-related agencies in *ijtihād*—in both Indonesian and Malaysian contexts are represented by MUI and JAKIM—establishes an Islamic legal certainty for the market on one side, but can create danger for democracy on the other. The centralisation of *ijtihād* tends to denigrate the principle of legal pluralism, which is highly respected in the tradition of Islamic legal jurisprudence and legal theory. Indonesia and Malaysia are both countries that promote diversity and pluralism—something that runs counter to the state's monopoly on fatwas regarding halal issues.

Both Indonesia and Malaysian fatwa authorities should enrich the perspective of their fatwa-issuers. They should be introduced and exposed to new findings in sciences and technology as well as social sciences. Establishing oneself in the global halal market necessitates a global vision on *ijtihād* on halal issues. The strict criteria of halal on the basis of loyalty to a particular school of Islamic law should be accompanied by an understanding of who ultimately will derive benefit from the halal certification process. More open and flexible *ijtihād* methods are not only needed in the future, but would also provides public benefits for all stakeholders.

Bibliography

Ab Rahman, Azman, Zahari Mahad Musa, Nik Salida Suhaila Nik Saleh, and Adel M. Abdul Aziz. 2008. *Biografi Mufti-Mufti Malaysia*. Negeri Sembilan: Universiti Sains Islam Malaysia.

Ab Talib, Mohammed Syazwan, Thoo Ai Chin, and Abubakar Abdul Hamid, eds. 2018. *Halal Food Certification and Business Performance in Malaysia*. Singapore: Patridge Publishing.

Abd. Rahman, Noer Naemah. 2004. 'Sejarah dan Perkembangan Instititusi Fatwa di Negeri Kelantan'. *Jurnal Usuludin* 19: 185–210.

Abdul Rahim, Rahimin Affandi, Paizah Ismail, and Nor Hayati Mohd Dahlal. 2009. 'Ijtihad dalam Institusi Fatwa di Malaysia: Satu Analisis'. *Shariah Journal* 17, no. 1: 195–222.

Abdullah, Jafri, Rahman Suhaimi, and Zaidah Mohd Noer. 2011. 'Konsep Istihalah dan Istihlak pada Makanan dan Barang Gunaan'. *Jurnal Penyelidikan Islam* 24: 71–92.

Adams, Wahiduddin. 2004. *Pola Penyerapan Fatwa Majelis Ulama Indonesia (MUI) dalam Peraturan Perundang-Undangan 1975–1997*. Jakarta: Departemen Agama.

Alharbi, Ibrhaim S. 2011. *Democracy in Islamic and International Law*. Washington: Author House.

Ali Hidaefi, Fahmi, and Irwandi Jaswir. 2019. 'Halal Governance in Indonesia: Theory, Current Practices and Related Issues'. *Journal of Islamic Monetary Economics and Finance* 5, no. 1: 89–116.

Amalia, Fatya Alty, Adila Sosianika, and Dwi Suhartanto. 2020. 'Indonesian Millennials' Halal Food Purchasing: Merely a Habit?'. *British Food Journal* 122, no. 4: 1185–1198.

Ann, Black, Esmaeili Hossein, and Nadirsyah Hosen, eds. 2013. *Modern Perspectives on Islamic Law*. Cheltenham & Northhampton: Edward Elgar Publishing.

Azra, Azyumardi. 2005. 'Islamic Thought: Theory, Concept and Doctrine in the Context of Southeast Asian Islam'. In *Islam in Southeast Asia, Political, Social and Strategic Challenges for the 21st Century*, edited by K.S. Nathan and Mohammad Hashim Kamali, 3–21. Singapore: ISEAS.

Burhanuddin, Jajat. 2017. *Islam Dalam Arus Sejarah Indonesia*. Jakarta: Kencana.

Chibli, Mallat. 2004. *The Renewal of Islamic Law: Muhammad Baqer As-Sadr, Najaf and the Shi'i International*. Edinburgh & Cambridge: Cambridge University Press.

Darmaputera, Eka. 1988. *Pancasila and the Search for Identity and Modernity in Indonesian Society: A Cultural and Ethical Analysis*. Leiden & Boston: Brill.

Federspiel, Howard M. 2009. *Persatuan Islam: Islamic Reform in Twentieth Century Indonesia*. Singapore: Equinox Publishing.

Feener, R. Michael. 2011. *Muslim Legal Thought in Modern Indonesia*. Cambridge: Cambridge University Press.

Fischer, Johan. 2011. *The Halal Frontier: Muslim Consumers in a Globalized Market*. New York: Palgrave Macmillan.

Hallaq, Wael B. 2005. 'Ifta' and Ijtihad in Sunni Legal Theory: A Development Account'. In *Islamic Legal Interpretation, Muftis and Their Fatwas*, edited by Muhammad Khalid Masud, Brinkley Messick, and David S. Powers. Oxford & New York: Oxford University Press.

Hallaq, Wael B. 1984. 'Was the Gate of Ijtihad Closed?' *International Journal of Middle East Studies* 16, no. 1: 3–41.

Hasyim, Syafiq. 2014. 'Council of Indonesian Ulama (Majelis Ulama Indonesia, MUI) and Its Role in the Shariatisation of Indonesia'. PhD Thesis. Free University.

Hasyim, Syafiq. 2020. 'Fatwas and Democracy: Majelis Ulama Indonesia (MUI, Indone-

sian Ulema Council) and Rising Conservatism in Indonesian Islam'. *TRaNS: Trans-Regional and -National Studies of Southeast Asia* 8, no. 1: 21–35.
Hasyim, Syafiq. 2011. 'The Council of Indonesian Ulama (Majelis Ulama Indonesia, MUI) and Religious Freedom'. Bangkok: IRASEC.
Hosen, Nadirsyah. 2012. 'Hilal and Halal: How to Manage Islamic Pluralism in Indonesia?' *Asian Journal of Comparative Law* 7: 1–18.
Ibn Dhakir al-Zubaydi, Balqasam. 2014. *Ijtihād fī Manāṭ al-Hukm al-Shar'i: Dirāsah Ta'ṣīliyyah Taṭbīqiyyah*. London: Takwin.
Ibn Taymiyyah. 2005. *Majmū' al-Fatāwā Ibn Taymiyyah*. 3rd edition. Vol. 21. al-Manṣūrah: Dar al-Wafā'.
Intan, Benyamin Fleming. 2006. *Public Religion And the Pancasila-Based State of Indonesia: An Ethical And Sociological Analysis*. New York: Peter Lang.
Ismail, Faisal. 1995. 'Islam, Politics and Ideology in Indonesia: A Study of the Process of Muslim Acceptance on the Pancasila'. Unpublished PhD thesis. McGill University.
JAKIM. 2014. *Manual Procedure for Malaysia Halal Certfication*. Selangor: Firdaus Press.
Kamali, Mohammad Hashim. 2008. *Shari'ah Law: An Introduction*. Oxford: One World.
Kaptein, Nico J.G. 2005. 'Fatwas as a Unifying Factor in Indonesia History'. In *Islam in the Era of Globalization: Muslim Attitudes Towards Modernity and Identity*, edited by Johan H. Mueleman, 72–79. London & New York: Routledge Curzon.
Lindsey, Tim. 2012. 'Monopolising Islam? The Indonesian Ulama Council and State Regulation of the "Islamic Economy"'. *Bulletin of Indonesian Economic Studies* 48, no. 2: 253–274.
LPPOM. 2011. *Indonesia Halal Directory 2001*. Jakarta: LP-POM MUI.
Majelis Tarjih dan Tajdid Pimpinan Pusat Muhammadiyah. 2018. *Himpunan Putusan Tarjih Muhammadiyah*. Yogyakarta: Suara Muhammadiyah.
Man, Saadan. 2014. 'Patterns of Contemporary Ijtihad in Malaysia: Analysis on Fatwas of Malaysian National Fatwa Council'. *International Journal of Social Science & Human Behavior Study* 1, no. 3: 104–107.
Mehmood, Muhammad Ifzal, Siddiq Ali Chisthi, and Muhammad Junaid Mughal. 2015. 'Islamic Concept of Fatwa, Practice of Fatwa in Malaysia and Pakistan: The Relevant of Malaysian Fatwa Model for Legal System of Pakistan'. *International Research Journal of Social Sciences* 4, no. 9: 46–51.
Mudzhar, Muhammad Atho. 1993. *Fatwa of the Council of Indonesian Ulama: A Study of Islamic Legal Thought in Indonesia 1975–1988*. Jakarta: INIS.
MUI. 2011. *Himpunan Fatwa MUI Sejak 1975*. Jakarta: Erlangga.
Nasohah, Zaini bin, and Majidah binti Mokhtar. 2016. 'Konsep Amar Ma'ruf Nahi Munkar Dalam Pematuhan Halal'. *Jurnal Penyelidikan Islam*: 132–147.
Nyazee, Imran. 2010. *Outlines of Islamic Jurisprudence*. Islamabad: Advanced Legal Studies Institute.
Pauzi, Nurhidayah, Saadan man, and Syed Mohd. Jeffri Bin Syed Jaafar. 2018. 'Analisis

Perbandingan Fatwa Indonesia Dan Malaysia: Kajian Terhadap Isu-Isu Halal Yang Terpilih'. *Journal of Fatwa Management and Research* 13, no. 1 (July): 1–16.

Peacock, J.L. 2017. *Purifying the Faith: The Muhammadijah Movement in Indonesian Islam*. North Carolina: University of North Carolina Press.

al-Qarāḍāwī, Yūsuf. 1994. *al-Ijtihād al-Mu'āṣir Bayna al-Inḍibāṭ wa al-Infirāṭ*. Cairo: Dār al-Tawzī'.

al-Qarāḍāwī, Yūsuf. 2001. *Taysīr al-Fiqh li al-Muslim al-Mu'āṣir fī Daw'i al-Qur'ān wa al-Sunna*. Beirut: Resalah Publisher.

al-Qarāḍāwī, Yūsuf. 2012. *al-Halāl wa al-Harām fī al-Islām*. Cairo: Dār al-Kutub al-Miṣriyyah.

Qibtiyah, Alimatul. 2018. 'Pengakuan Ulama dan Isu Perempuan di Majlis Tarjih dan Tajdid Muhammadiyah'. In *Demokratisasi Fatwa, Diskursus, Teori dan Praktik*, edited by Syafiq Hasyim and Fahmi Syahirul Alam, 193–211. Jakarta: ICIP.

Rachman, M. Aulia, and Syamsuddin. 2019. 'Halal Industry in Indonesia: The Role of Sharia Financial Institutions in Driving Industrial and Halal Ecosystem'. *Al-Iqtishad* 11, no. 1: 35–58.

Shabbar, Said. 2017. *Ijtihad and Renewal*. London & Washington: The International Institute of Islamic Thought.

Shuaib, Farid S. 2012. 'The Islamic Legal System in Malaysia'. *Pacific Rim Law and Policy Journal* 21, no. 1: 85–113.

Warren, David H. 2014. *Yusuf al-Qaradawi, his Interlocutors, and the Articulation, Transmission and Reconstruction of the Fiqh Tradition in the Qatar-Context*. PhD Thesis. University of Manchester.

Zahro, Ahmad. 2004. *Tradisi Intelektual NU: Lajnah Bahtsul Masa'il, 1926–1999*. Yogyakarta: PT LKiS Pelangi Aksara.

Zaman, Muhammad Qasim. 2012. *Modern Islamic Thought in a Radical Age: Religious Authority and Internal Criticism*. New York: Cambridge University Press.

al-Zuḥaylī, Wahbah. 1997. *al-Fiqh al-Islāmī wa Adillatuh*. vol. 1. Damascus: Dār al-Fikr.

CHAPTER 5

Developing the Halal Market: China's Opportunity to Strengthen MENA Ties and Address Uighur/Hui Issues

Zaynab El Bernoussi

1 Introduction

China has the largest Muslim community in East Asia, and this represents an advantage to tie in the country to the world's Muslim community. Exploiting such an advantage is consistent with China's stance on developing and expanding economic and trade links with an increasing number of regions in the world, including the region of the Middle East and North Africa (MENA), with its substantial energy resources and need for infrastructure building. With the global shock of COVID-19, China's ambition for more international cooperation has continued. The deafening silence from the MENA governments on the US act on protecting the rights of Uighurs, effective on 17 June 2020, is telltale of the China-MENA dynamic because the silence suggests that these governments leave aside the marking feature of their identity, i.e. solidarity with Muslim communities, for the sake of avoiding ruffling China's feathers. In the same way, no MENA country has taken a stance regarding Hong Kong's extradition law, also passed in summer 2020. MENA holds a significant portion of the halal market, estimated at $1.6 trillion, in its total. President Xi Jinping's extensive visits to the region in 2016 heavily supported this stance. The One Belt, One Road (OBOR) plan, unveiled in 2013, now called the Belt Road Initiative (BRI), is a mega policy developed in Beijing and facilitated by Chinese funding that supports integrating the world economy, including the MENA. MENA countries are also now taking China more seriously than they used to (particularly the conservative and US-supporting Gulf) because of their increasing need to become its trading partners.

China is using its local Muslim communities to strengthen diplomatic ties with the Muslim world at large, but this is an opportunity that also carries a threat because China has 'good' Muslims and 'bad' Muslims. The 'good' Muslims are the Hui Muslims in the inland regions, and Yinchuan city of Ningxia in particular. The Chinese government built a Disney-like 'Muslim Park' there, where tourists are invited to see a picture-perfect lifestyle of Muslim Chinese in har-

 | DOI:10.1163/9789004459236_006

mony with the state. The Hui speak local Mandarin and Putonghua and are related to the Han, unlike the Uighur who have Turkic origin. The latter are considered the 'bad' Muslims. This hierarchy of Sino-Muslim relations within China continues to be adopted by the state as a mechanism to manage these communities.[1]

How the Chinese government deals with Uighur people also has the potential to sever Chinese relations with Muslim countries or normalise arbitrary repression of dissident groups. The demands of the Uighur include more space and freedom of religious practices, and ethnic autonomy, which can be limited under an atheist regime like China's. I argue here in an effort to stabilise the Uighur threat, greater access to state-provided halal products is much needed in China. However, there has been great controversy about Chinese halal labeling as 'fake'. For their halal labeling, many Chinese Muslims have greater trust in imported products from Malaysia, Singapore, Indonesia, and beyond than local Chinese halal products. This prompts us to question the reasons behind the negative reputation of the Chinese halal label: does the Chinese state lack the resources to deliver a trustworthy halal label? Or is such a negative reputation a sign of a lack of normalised religious practices in China at the state level because of its atheist nature? The two questions ought to be investigated. The method used for this article is a review of relevant literature and analysis of secondary sources on relations between MENA countries and China since the establishment of communist China. The approach here is to focus on select sources of information to understand the China-MENA economic tie in what concerns the halal industry, and some of its political implications. Particular attention is also paid to data on trade volumes in the last decades between MENA countries and China, as they reflect both the China's growing energy needs and an increasing detachment of MENA countries from Western powers. In this chapter I focus on both Uighur and Hui communities, even though the Uighur's consumption is relatively marginal to halal issues in the Chinese market compared to the Hui. A major part of Uighur consumption is nuts harvested in Xinjiang and Nang, and the bread and lamb that is locally produced and thus more controlled by the Uighurs themselves. However, compared to the Hui, the Uighur's connection to halal issues is much more politicised.

1 Friedrichs, 'Sino-Muslim Relations: the Han, the Hui, and the Uyghurs', 55–79.

2 Brief Literature Review on MENA Ties to China

In the premodern era, the Silk Road was a turning point for the expansion of world trade and constituted a major era of economic and cultural ties between China and MENA. After the obsolescence of the Silk Road and the development of maritime roads mostly controlled by European powers, China's role as an economic power declined and its ties with MENA dwindled. After the communist takeover, China joined the *cri de cœur* from nations of the Third World and rallied with the efforts of the Non-Aligned Movement, which revived its relations with MENA. Recently, China's ties with MENA are again expanding for two main reasons: 1) China has developed capabilities that can help with infrastructure building in the region and; 2) MENA represents a large market that China can integrate into further. Of course, MENA is a diverse region, with different kinds of economy (labour intensive, labour poor, resource intensive, resource poor), but such diversity in factors of production and resources helps in the greater project of expanding the world market that China can tap into.

The MENA region counts several enduring political conflicts that have attracted international attention and intervention, but China has kept a non-interventionist approach to those conflicts, which is a stark difference with other major political powers. China has its own Muslim communities and, among them the Uighur have voiced independentist claims that alienated them from central power.[2] Because of their lack of support for Uighurs as a Muslim minority in a communist state, MENA countries have shown an inconsistency in their stance towards solidarity with Muslim communities. One of the key reasons for this lack of consistent support is that Muslim countries often prefer to turn a blind eye to some of the Chinese state's treatments of Muslim communities so as not to jeopardise their economic ties with China and also to uphold a non-interventionist stance that supports sovereignty.

The Chinese government has recently shown efforts to improve its ties with MENA countries and has boasted that the Chinese cultural diversity includes Muslim identities. With the retracting of Western powers in the region as economic and political partners, China has been gaining their lost terrain. China adopts a quasi-mediation diplomacy, in which it defends its commercial, political, and diplomatic interests rather than focusing solely on security and stra-

2 Rudelson, *Oasis Identities: Uyghur Nationalism along China's Silk Road*, 6; Cesaro, 'Consuming Identities: Food and Resistance among the Uyghur in Contemporary Xinjiang', 225–238; Friedrichs, 'Sino-Muslim Relations: the Han, the Hui, and the Uyghurs', 55–79.

tegic interests.[3] Data on MENA imports from China also show that the MENA market has become of increasingly higher value to China as consumer goods imports dropped from 74.4 per cent to 30.5 per cent and machinery and equipment imports rose from 22.7 per cent to 49.4 per cent in the period between 1993 and 2018.[4] Much of the literature that examines the Chinese relation to the MENA focuses on China's pragmatic economic interests in the region.[5] However, such descriptions of China's pragmatic interests in the MENA region fall short in being convincing concerning the continuing prospects of these ties. Indeed, if economic interests are the sole driving force of this relationship, such interests can be easily withdrawn in an economic downturn. My argument in this chapter is that a Chinese alliance with MENA presents many gains for both parties but needs to become permanent to build a relationship of trust between the two collaborators. Investigating how to make a permanent connection between MENA and China has been overlooked in the relevant literature for the simple reason that the rapid developments in this relation show a swift growth of economic ties, which overshadows other considerations. One important consideration is the prospect of dwindling economic ties in the future in case of a downturn in growth in either China or MENA, which is also more likely with the COVID-19 global health crisis. In the current context of trade wars, heightened by the global pandemic, a rise of populist discourses and economic precarity, it is important for a growing superpower like China to establish a new managerial power based on creating cultural ties and deepening trust. Food practices and habits are important components of cultural identities and can help build intercommunal trust.[6]

---

3 Sun and Zoubir, 'China's Participation in Conflict Resolution in the Middle East and North Africa: A Case of Quasi-Mediation Diplomacy?', 224–243.

4 'MENA Product Import Product Share China 1993–2018', *The World Bank*.

5 Sun and Zoubir 'China's response to the revolts in the Arab World: A Case of Pragmatic Diplomacy', 2–20; Sun and Zoubir 'China's Economic Diplomacy towards the Arab Countries: Challenges Ahead?' 903–921; Sun and Zoubir, 'China's Participation in Conflict Resolution in the Middle East and North Africa', 224–243; Zambelis, 'Xinjiang Crackdown and Changing Perceptions of China in the Islamic World', 4–8; Dorsey, 'China and the Middle East: Venturing into the Maelstrom', 1–14.

6 Cesaro, 'Consuming Identities: Food and Resistance among the Uyghur in Contemporary Xinjiang', 225–238.

3 From Communist Beginnings in China to the Reform Era

The rise of the Communists in China came after an extreme economic decline that culminated in the weak stances of the Kuomintang Republicans vis-à-vis Western powers in the post-empire era. Over the last two centuries, China has moved from being the dominant economic power to being a marginal economic power, and back to recovering its economic strength. Even with the takeover of the Communists in 1949, the Chinese economic performance stagnated for over two decades to dismal levels. It is only starting in the Reform era, beginning in the 1970s with Deng Xiaoping, that the economic recovery started. The Reform era was also one of opening China to the rest of the world. China re-established diplomatic relations with the United States and established several Special Economic Zones (SEZs), in which the laws of the communist economy were relaxed. The SEZs were China's response to the imperative of global trade in the neoliberal era. The SEZs are also the first prototype mechanism of China's state capitalism, which has recently been promoted as the Beijing Consensus to dethrone the infamous Washington Consensus as a major development paradigm targeting the Global South.

Since the establishment of the Communist state, China has also endorsed strong anti-imperialist stances. Even if in its early Communist era China was more inward- than outward-looking, a few Chinese officials were vocal about the benefits of international relations. Among them, Zhou Enlai joined his voice to that of the Non-Aligned Movement (NAM) and became the charismatic diplomatic face of China.[7] Gamal Abdel Nasser, a major promoter of the NAM, grew close to Zhou Enlai, marking the first notable leadership ties between China and MENA in the modern post-colonial era.

After Zhou Enlai lost his popularity with Chinese Communist party (although he did not lose it among the Chinese people) and his death in 1976, the budding Sino-Arab relation of the postcolonial era waned for most of the Reform era. At that time, there was little political Sino-Muslim relation. Even the oil crises of the time prompted little reaction from China as it had not yet grown enough economically to be significantly disturbed by these events. The intensification of political repression for the sake of economic growth of the Reform era had particularly targeted the rebellious Uighur people, who simultaneously increased their religious pilgrimages to Mecca in Saudi Arabia.[8] This

7 Prashad. *The Darker Nations: A Biography of the Short-Lived Third World*, 36–37.
8 Friederichs, 'Sino-Muslim Relations: the Han, the Hui, and the Uyghurs', 55–79.

further sustained the increasing religiosity of the Uighur people, starting with their modern nationalist uprisings in the nineteenth century.[9]

Among the repressions suffered by the Uighur people was limitation on religious practice. Among the many regulations targeting the religious practices in the Uighur community, the lack of regulations regarding shariʿa-compliant food has been more easily circumvented by Uighur people, as food practices are more private. Food even became the weapon of resistance of Uighur communities in China and the space of religious expression.[10] For instance, fasting or refraining from purchasing pork are Muslim practices that the Uighur have been able to do without direct confrontation with Chinese state authorities. Sourcing one's own food to ensure its compliance with Muslim standards for food consumption has also been somewhat possible for Uighur communities. However, in the accelerated neoliberal drive of the 1980s and the further opening of China to trade, growing socio-economic inequalities have particularly disadvantaged the Uighur. The precarious living conditions of many Uighur people have complicated their autonomy in freely choosing food sources.[11] However, it is important to note that crises are inherent to capitalist development, and this causes further power distancing and inequalities.[12] Such crises occur even with the model of state capitalism in China and worsen the precarious conditions for communities like the Uighurs.

Regarding how the particular state repression of the Uighur was received in MENA, there is little evidence of much attention from MENA towards China to begin with. Up to the 1990s, China was peripheral to the interests of MENA, which have been more closely tied to the Western part of the world, mostly Europe and the United States.

4 The 1990s and the Eve of 9/11

In 1993, Ahmed Asmat Abdel-Meguid, Secretary General of the Arab League, visited Beijing and opened the League's first office in China. This opening signalled an increased interest from the Arab world vis-à-vis China. The Chinese

9 Friederichs, 'Sino-Muslim Relations: the Han, the Hui, and the Uyghurs', 55–79.

10 Cesaro, 'Consuming Identities: Food and Resistance among the Uyghur in Contemporary Xinjiang', 225–238.

11 Smith, ''Making Culture Matter': Symbolic, Spatial and Social Boundaries between Uyghurs and Han Chinese', 153–174; Miao, 'Sinicisation vs. Arabisation: Online Narratives of Islamophobia in China', 1–15.

12 Streeck, 'How Will Capitalism End?', 35–64.

government returned the favour and President Jiang Zemin became the first Chinese leader to visit the League during his trip to Egypt in 1996. The 1990s witnessed the continuation of reform efforts through which China's economy continued to grow. This Chinese economic growth attracted the attention of increasingly more countries, including those of the MENA region. After the Tiananmen incidents of 1989, which further affirmed the authoritarian nature of reforms, and up to the early 2000s, China rose to power not only as a trade giant but also as a diplomatic agent of non-intervention and supporter of the supremacy of national sovereignty.[13] Chinese diplomatic stances since then have not changed much and have further attracted the attention of leaders from the MENA region worried about Western military intervention and appeased by Chinese support for national sovereignty.

Internally, Hui Chinese continued to be a low threat to authorities, whereas the Uighur Chinese started reinforcing contemporary Uighur national identity in relation to Xinjiang's growing Han Chinese population.[14] The growing interaction between Han and Uighur, caused by the general demographic growth, catalysed the already existing tensions between the Uighur people and Chinese authorities. This increasing direct interaction was accompanied by socio-economic inequalities between Uighur and Han communities in which the Uighur people saw themselves as purposefully marginalised by the state and grew even more dissatisfied with the Chinese state.

Despite intensified repression of Uighur Chinese by the state in the 1990s,[15] there was an officialisation of the relationship between the Arab League and China in that same period. Back then, the Arab League played a more significant role as a front of solidarity in the region. For instance, the Arab League Boycott of Israel that led to banning Coca-Cola from the Arab world between 1977 and 1991 attested to such solidarity and created and opportunity for a boycott-abiding company like Pepsi to grow significantly in the Arab world ever since.[16] Another example of the sensitivities of the Muslim market is the 1997 row that broke with Nike when it commercialised shoes with a logo that looked like the Arabic word for God. To avoid a sales ban in the Muslim world, Nike had to recall all shoes, issue a public apology, and donate $50,000 to an Islamic

13 Since joining the United Nations Security Council in 1971, the People's Republic of China has been conservative in its position, consistently vetoing military intervention.

14 Smith, '"Making Culture Matter"', 153–174.

15 Many arrests and executions constituted the outcome of the 'Strike Hard' campaign launched by Beijing to halt violence and disturbances in the Xinjiang region. One of the notable triggers to such a campaign was the Urumqi bus bombing in Chinese New Year celebrations in 1992; Castets, 'The Uyghurs in Xinjiang—The Malaise Grows', 1–19.

16 Alserhan, *The Principles of Islamic Marketing*, 44.

Elementary School in the United States.[17] These two examples show the importance of abiding by the designated norms of Muslim markets that China has observed as the rest of the world. Even with these examples, China was not yet dissuaded from blocking the halal market to Muslim Chinese, which did not send a positive image to the MENA countries. China continued to mistrust its local Muslim population, and particularly the Uighur community. Part of the reason for such mistrust at the time was simply a lack of resources to keep up with the needs of a rising economic power that had witnessed a demographic upsurge. Another part of the reason for the continued mistrust was again the very nature of the atheist communist state in which the blossoming of religious freedom is inherently constrained. By the end of the era of rising Chinese power (1989–2002), Chinese officials started for the first time to talk about Chinese legislation regarding the halal market. China and MENA international relations can be studied using a wider picture, but this chapter focuses mostly on Uighur issues and their impact on such relations.

5 From the War on Terror Up to Today

In the aftermath of 9/11, US President George W. Bush's call for the War on Terror has rallied many countries in the world in an intensified fight against Islamic radicalism, including China, which also targeted the Uighur community in particular. Since the Reform era and the sacrifice of political freedoms in China for the sake of economic growth, the Uighur people have borne the brunt of the Chinese state repression apparatus. This had the effect of pushing many Uighur Chinese to further radicalise, achieving the reverse effect intended by the Chinese state. Even before 9/11, many Uighur people had left China to migrate to countries that were friendlier and more tolerant towards Muslims. Uighurs also looked for countries that would not extradite them to Chinese authorities and Afghanistan was, therefore, a destination of choice. After 9/11, several Uighur men were captured by US, Afghan, and Pakistani authorities, wrongly condemned as terrorists, and sent to Guantanamo Bay Detention Camp.[18] Chinese authorities had little concern for righting the wrongs done to the Uighur people and were more concerned with pressuring countries that refused to extradite so-called Uighur outlaws.

---

17 Alserhan, *The Principles of Islamic Marketing*, 44.
18 Wayne, 'Inside China's War on Terrorism', 249–261.

Later in the post-9/11 era, the discourse of the War on Terror started to lose attention and new priorities emerged, such as recovering from one of the largest global financial crises of human history in 2007–2008, which is again a priority for 2021 and afterwards, due to the global pandemic. While most of the Western part of the world was suffering a financial panic in 2007, China's economic strengthening was further revealed and is likely to make China achieve a relatively better recovery from of the pandemic's impact compared to other parts of the world, due to Chinese domestic demand.[19] Indeed, China started promoting the revival of the New Silk Road, One Belt, One Road (OBOR), more recently called the Belt Road Initiative (BRI), to centralise its role in expanding the global economy. BRI pushes for trade to strengthen the global network of countries. Of course, many countries have reservations about the veracity of the good intentions behind BRI. Among these countries, India has been particularly vocal about its reservations on BRI, due to its mistrust of China since the 1962 border war. India has even launched Project Mausam, its BRI equivalent, on a much smaller scale, to strengthen trade ties with its neighbours. Unlike the case for China, India's attempt to have Mausam inscribed on a UNESCO world heritage list did not succeed.

With the eruption of the Arab Spring, China expressed concern over military intervention, which was consistent with its usual diplomatic stances. However, the cautious reactions from China about the Arab Spring events also had the effect of challenging Chinese plans and ambitions to become an assertive global political power, while also unveiling Chinese concerns about implications for its own system.

Hong Kong has been China's experimental laboratory in terms of its dealing with the needs of the growing Muslim market. In one year in Hong Kong, the number of certified halal restaurants tripled, and the Hong Kong Tourism Board reported a 20 per cent growth of visitors from the MENA, which surpassed that of the mainland.[20] The Wanchai neighbourhood in Hong Kong is a particular Mecca for halal food, with several options for Uighur cuisine, which is particularly liked by Hong Kong residents.[21] However, despite the efforts seen in Hong Kong to accommodate the halal market, China is still lagging behind in the region.

---

19 Crossley and Yao, 'China's Economy Rebounds after Steep Slump, Weak Demand, US Tensions raise Risks', *Reuters Business News*, July 16, 2020.

20 Hayoun. 'Can China Make Its Cuisine—and Finance—Friendly to Muslims'?, *Time*, Wednesday, 4 April 2012.

21 O'Connor, *Islam in Hong Kong: Muslims and Everyday Life in China's World City*, 182.

The doubts over China's genuine interest in the halal industry are also spreading beyond its borders through Muslim expatriates who communicate their negative experience to the rest of the world.[22] Quality standards for Muslims when it comes to the nature of the meat consumption are quite unanimously observed.[23]

Again, in this most recent decade, other episodes of major scandals in Islamic markets are examples for China to avoid. Sadia, the Brazilian halal meat giant, was banned from several countries in the Gulf region because of contamination of its halal meats with non-halal meats. Here rests an additional opportunity of a sizeable market that China can take over.

In terms of examples to look up to for China, the development of the halal business in the United States presents a case in point. In the United States, one can now even find halal 'drive-by' certifying bodies that facilitate the process of assessing shariʿa compliance but are usually offering inadequate certification. There is also the recent growth of Green Zabiha, which is meat that is both halal and organic. In many parts of the United States one can have a halal Thanksgiving turkey that is Green Zabiha and ṭayyib, meaning that the slaughtered animal is guaranteed to have had a good life.[24] These examples show that the vibrant consumerist nature of the American market has pushed for even more developments in the halal business. The Halal Advocates of America were founded in 2008 in California by American-born and South-African trained Mufti Shaykh Abdulla Nana to control further and determine the status of the halal industry in the United States.[25] In addition, several Community-Supportive Agriculture (CSA) farms have blossomed all over the country to support halal consumption. There is even a growth of halal veganism, despite pressure to eat meat in Eid Celebrations based on principles of *ʿadl*, meaning justice, and *mīzān*, meaning balance.[26]

The halal market has increasingly endorsed an ecological and environment-friendly ethos that is consistent with the nineteenth Chinese Party Congress commitment to environmental protection and moderation in China.[27] In addition, recent constitutional changes in China have incorporated environmental

22 Ali et al., 'Factors Affecting Halal Meat Purchase Intention: Evidence from International Muslim Students in China', 527–541.

23 Ali et al., 'Factors Affecting Halal Meat Purchase Intention', 527–541.

24 Abdul-Matin, *Green Deen: What Islam Teaches about Protecting the Planet*, 171–179.

25 Abdul-Matin, *Green Deen*, 148.

26 Abdul-Matin, *Green Deen*, 150.

27 El Bernoussi, 'World War C: How the COVID-19 Pandemic Should Teach us to Consume Less and Cooperate More?', *Tribune Libre—RSSI*, 5 August 2020.

protection and can pave the way for more legislation that tackles the environment. Again, China can seize the ecological trend in the halal market as it is already in line with its state policies. Given the continuing dependence on fossil fuels in the MENA region, China can also even trigger a movement promoting renewable energies as alternatives to fossil fuels as a way of advancing an even more shariʿa-compliant market.

In terms of the Chinese state's political relations with its local Muslim communities, the last decade has seen further distancing from the Uighur community. State relations with the Hui, on the other hand, have strengthened even more. In 2016, the Chinese government launched the construction of a giant Muslim park in Yinchuan, Ningxia Hui Autonomous Region. The Chinese government is usually keen to send special guests, particularly from the rich Gulf countries, to visit the site as the shining face of Islam in China.

In terms of marking events in the ongoing degradation of Chinese state relations with the Uighur community of this last few years, 2016 witnessed the ISIS killing of a Chinese hostage. ISIS singled out China as a target for its followers in light of Beijing's ongoing crackdown on Uighurs and Muslims in Xinjiang. Chinese president Xi Jinping suffered considerable criticism for not doing enough to protect Chinese nationals in places like the Middle East and Africa.

China passed a controversial new anti-terrorism law in December 2016 that requires technology firms to help decrypt information but not install security 'back-doors' as initially planned, and allows the military to venture overseas on counter-terror operations. Chinese officials say their country faces a growing threat from militants and separatists especially in its western region of Xinjiang.[28] The law has attracted deep concern in Western capitals, because of concerns that it could violate cybersecurity and human rights such as freedom of speech.[29] China's constraining of Uighurs, once again, is sending a negative message to Muslim countries of the MENA region. The Chinese deputy head of the parliament's criminal law division under the Legislative Affairs Committee responded that China was simply doing what other Western nations already do in asking technology firms to help fight terror.

28 In a major lecture delivered by President Xi Jinping at the nineteenth National Congress of the Communist Party of China on 18 October 2017, entitled 'Secure a Decisive Victory in Building a Moderately Prosperous Society in All Respects and Strive for the Great Success of Socialism with Chinese Characteristics for a New Era', the President listed 'separatist activities, and religious extremist activities' (in page 44 of the script) as major threats to the safeguarding of national security.

29 Blanchard, 'China Passes Controversial Counter-Terrorism Law', *Reuters*, 28 December 2015.

In terms of recent relations between China and MENA, there has been a noticeable rekindling. Several Egyptian leaders visited China and Chinese President Xi Jinping showed particular support to Egypt's President Abdel Fattah al-Sisi. King Mohamed VI of Morocco paid a visit to Beijing in May 2017. Several Saudi Arabian royals have visited China in the last decade.

The Belt Road Initiative (BRI) includes China's New Grand Strategy for the Middle East to foster a peaceful MENA region that will support a strong and stable trade and investment environment. It will also expand markets for Chinese goods and services, and Beijing has already committed hundreds of billions of dollars to this mega policy/project. The BRI offers a mechanism for China to stimulate its economy, which is currently afflicted by slowing growth. But an unstable MENA region stands in the way of all of that. So, Beijing's interest in the MENA countries is now becoming vital to its mega-project for international trade.

China is also having open communication with both the key capitals of the MENA region in conflict, Teheran and Riyadh.[30] BRI could reduce the tensions between the two countries and involve them in more trade to hopefully normalise their relationship and overcome the Shiite-Sunni divide. If such involvement between the two countries is achieved, this would be a major gain for China's involvement in the region, even if its goals are primarily pragmatic. So, in a nutshell, China's involvement in business in the region can help integrate the region economically.[31]

China could also be the single largest beneficiary from US President Donald Trump's retraction from the Iranian nuclear deal, so it stands to reason that Beijing could also benefit from a smaller US footprint elsewhere in the region too. In addition, US retraction necessarily means European retraction as well because of European businesses' dependence on US pressures and US funding.[32]

China has an increasingly healthy relationship with Israel, and it has been able to simultaneously develop robust ties with Israel, particularly related to technology, while also building its presence in the rest of the MENA region. This is consistent with the China's 'no enemies' approach regarding political dealings at the international level.

30 Riyadh and Teheran are the new rivals in the region, when it used to be Riyadh and Cairo in the so called Arab Cold War in the 1950s and19 60s.

31 El Bernoussi, 'China's Civilizational Diplomacy', Politics, *Project Syndicate*, 5 December 2016.

32 France is already divesting from Iran due to US President Trump's retraction from the Iranian Nuclear Deal.

A couple of years ago, in 2013, China invited key players in the Middle East peace process to Beijing for talks. Everyone back then was amused because it was Beijing's first foray into the quagmire that is the Arab-Israeli peace process, yet it seemed to have been a good learning experience for the Chinese.[33] It might look like a huge stretch to move from a Chinese role of peace-making in the MENA region to talking about China's stake in the MENA halal market, but the tie is there. China has a vested interest in developing the MENA region economically and doing that can happen through growing China's share of the halal business both domestically and internationally, in that region. The Gulf portion of the region is particularly dependent on imports of halal food; countries of the Gulf import 78 per cent of their food.[34]

China seeks greater regional integration and dominance, and to date other countries in the Asian region have dominated the halal business. For instance, Penang Port is now a major halal port in Malaysia, following the footsteps of Rotterdam Port, which is considered the largest halal port in which halal traceability and shariʿa-compliant logistics are the most trustworthy.[35] Logistical control and monitoring are essential to the flourishing of the halal market. Sri Lanka is also taking over the halal food industry in the region despite having a dominant Buddhist population.[36]

Negligence in Chinese halal compliance and the lack of regulating bodies explain China's missed opportunity in the halal market. In the past few years, Chinese officials have been more actively calling for national standards on halal food. This comes as a result of numerous scandals that have occurred regarding the complete disregard for upholding halal standards and the resilience of the halal taboo in China.[37] There have also been several cases of counterfeit halal certification that damaged the Chinese reputation in the halal business, but it is also important to note that scandals regarding food quality assurance are pervasive in China beyond the halal market.[38] The idea of a national institution for the halal market in China has been under consideration since

33 El Bernoussi, and Olander. 'China's Risky Power Play in the Arab World', *A China in Africa Podcast*, 25 December 2016, https://www.chinafile.com/library/china-africa-project/chinas-risky-power-play-arab-world (accessed 27 September 2020).

34 Isaura, 'Gulf Countries Import 78% of their Food', *Salaam Gateway*, 27 February 2017.

35 Alserhan, *The Principles of Islamic Marketing*, 104–105.

36 Stewart, 'Muslim–Buddhist Conflict in Contemporary Sri Lanka', 241–260.

37 Erie, 'China's Halal Constitution "Islamic" Legislation Stirs Debate as the PRC Engages the Muslim World', *The Diplomat*, 27 May 2016.

38 Wee Sile, 'Why China wants a bite of the booming halal food market', *CNBC*, November 24, 2015.

2002 and China still lacks legislation regarding halal food.[39] Part of the reason for this delay in legislation is an attempt to postpone a direct confrontation with the Uygur community, the so-called trouble-making actor on the Chinese political scene.[40] It seems that Chinese officials have become accustomed to a strategy of avoidance, or burying their heads in the sand, instead of confronting the problem as a way of solving it.[41] Strategically, China has a lot to gain from dealing with this so-called Uighur problem through clarifying regulation of the halal market. First, it should attempt to gain the trust of halal consumers within and beyond its borders. Then it would gain a tool for controlling its Muslim population. For instance, the British authorities use indicators of halal consumption to accurately determine the number of Muslims living in the country.

There are more than 22 million Muslims in China and some estimate that the Muslim population is up to 40 million.[42] China needs to develop its halal business credentials to benefit from the growing Islamic market. In small Islamic markets, like the one of Singapore, for instance, all their major fast-food chains are 100 per cent halal certified. This is a relatively quick fix that China could start with in promoting its halal market.

The Chinese delaying of national regulation and legislation of the halal market is no longer related to a lack of recourse and resources and may reveal a missed opportunity. Indeed, China has grown even more as an economy and superpower and can thus easily accommodate a trustworthy halal market. This delaying is actually more indicative of a lack of normalised religious practices in China at the state level because of its atheist nature. In the accelerated globalisation wave, even authoritarian countries like China have witnessed increasing demands for individual liberties and freedoms.[43] Therefore, the Chinese state, even if inherently opposed to religious practices, must open a space for religious practices or run the risk of greater popular dissatisfaction and unrest. This delaying is symptomatic of Chinese government policies of avoidance and non-confrontation. Such political behaviour has become a trademark of contemporary Chinese diplomacy, but it is now counteracting China's growing

39 Erie, *China and Islam: The Prophet, the Party, and Law*, 69; Erie, 'Shari'a As Taboo of Modern Law: Halal Food, Islamophobia, and China', 3.

40 Erie, *China and Islam: The Prophet, the Party, and Law*, 2.

41 Erie, ibid, 333.

42 Hernandez and Wu, 'Officials in China Call for National Standards on Halal Food'. *New York Times, Sinosphere*, March 14, 2016.

43 Scholte, *Globalization: A Critical Introduction*, 205.

ambition to become a political power, as more political assertiveness is expected from Chinese officials. Undoubtedly, China needs to become more assertive with taking action in developing the Chinese halal business.

6 Conclusion

The halal market is estimated at $1.6 trillion, which represents an opportunity for China to lead its further integration into the world economy. Over 20 per cent of the world's population embraces Islam: Muslims represent the majority population in over 50 countries, and Islam is the fastest growing religion in the world, according to a 2017 Pew Research Center study that remains undisputed. China counts a significant local Muslim population, but its repressive policy towards Uighurs might limit its credentials as a supporter of the development of the halal market that is needed in its call for integrating the world economy. Indeed, China passed a number of laws in 2019 that concerned the Uighurs in particular, regarding banning the veil and beards, legalising so-called 're-education camps', and adapting Islam to Chinese socialism. This created a global backlash, as many international organisation and states have condemned Chinese policies towards Muslims, and Uighurs in particular. Beijing does not have a clear global strategy regarding halal but adopting such a strategy is likely to support the BRI in its outreach, particularly toward MENA, a region of interest for China as seen with the launch of the Sino-Arab Cooperation Forum (SACF) in 2004. Most Arab states tend to support China in its policy towards the Uighurs;[44] however, this is not necessarily supported by public opinion in these countries. Currently, it is not clear that economic actors in China are targeting the halal market; rather, recent campaigns oppose such a market (such as anti-halal campaigns). Beijing has also pressured countries to return Uighur refugees and denies human rights accusations by the US and EU regarding the 're-education camps' in Xinjiang,[45] which shows that the Uighur issue is a sensitive one for China with the potential to sever diplomatic relations. But China's notable pragmatism as a rising economic and political power shows how even this tumultuous Chinese relation with its Muslim communities and the Muslim world can still be framed in a positive way (particularly the

44 Hassanein, 'Arab States Give China a Pass on Uyghur Crackdown', *The Washington Institute*, 26 August 2019.

45 Maizland, 'China's Repression of Uighurs in Xinjiang', *Council on Foreign Relations*, 9 October 2019.

way in which the 're-education camps' are presented as boarding schools that help local communities and how Islam is compatible with the Party's values).[46]

The growing Muslim market is attracting even non-Muslims, who view such a market as more ethical and sustainable.[47] China's position is not clear regarding this market; however, its BRI and push to integrate the world economy indicate that taking part of the growth of Muslim market is advantageous to China, even more at a time of economic retraction due to COVID-19. The Muslim market also has the potential to become the largest unified market in history, in which a trade giant like China can have a significant gain. The large halal market is also diversified and includes small disposable incomes, looking for reduced prices that are rendered possible by China's economies of scale, and large disposable incomes that target high-end products with more profit margins (particularly in the premium segments in the Gulf), which can also be targeted by Chinese production. In a 2017 study, the Pew Research Center estimated that the Muslim population is by far the fastest growing major religious group for 2015 to 2060. The nature of the halal market and its magnitude represent an opportunity for China to further assert itself as an irreplaceable trading partner but also an increasingly sought-after one in MENA. China is using its local Muslim communities to strengthen the diplomatic ties with the Muslim world at large, including the MENA region. However, this is an opportunity that carries a threat because the Chinese state has a tumultuous relationship with the local Uighur Muslim population. China is also concerned about violence from radical Islamist groups both within and outside its borders. How the Chinese government deals with the Uighur opposition could lead to the severing of Chinese relations with Muslim countries, if we see a return to Arab solidarity and a distancing from the current pragmatic stances most MENA countries adopt. Some of the demands of the Uighur are more space for and freedom of religious practice, which can be limited under the central state's interest in political control over a vast, strategic, and potentially problematic province. In an effort to respond to the needs of the Uighur community, the Chinese state has provided greater access to halal products, as I witnessed in Beijing and Hong Kong. However, there has been great controversy about the Chinese halal labelling as 'fake', which invalidates the efforts of the Chinese state to genuinely cater to the needs of its Muslim population. Many Chinese Muslims have more trust in imported goods from Malaysia, Singapore, Indonesia, and beyond for their halal labelling than local Chinese halal

46 Maizland, 'China's Repression of Uighurs in Xinjiang'.

47 Alserhan, *The Principles of Islamic Marketing*, 59; Sandikci, 'Religion and Everyday Consumption Ethics: A Moral Economy Approach', 1–17.

products, but this comes at a higher cost. Other Chinese Muslims with limited resources would opt for foods manufactured by Hui Muslims with labels of halal certification almost as much as the food imported from other countries with higher halal credentials. Because the imported food has higher prices, the Hui prefer local manufactured food with the guarantee of security and halal certification. Given the magnitude of the halal market, it is in China's interest to gain local trust in its halal production and even become an exporter in this segment. If China develops a trustworthy image as a halal producer, this will serve the local Muslim community and even strengthen ties with the Muslim world, including the MENA region. MENA's substantial energy resources and needs for infrastructure building are attractive to China. President Xi Jinping's visits to the region in 2016 attest to China's interests in the region. These visits also promoted the new Silk Road project to develop trade relations with the MENA countries. The recent US retraction from its role as a peace broker in the MENA region is also an opportunity to bring in a new player. This new role can help China in its growing international political assertiveness. MENA, more than any other region, can propel China both as a leader of the halal market and as a new international political power. Right now, China is still not a major player in the halal market: it has no halal Certification Bodies (HCB) or national authority for its halal market, no halal ports, and it still suffers from distrust of its halal production. Even small Muslim Markets like Singapore and Sri Lanka have been able to capture the potential of halal markets better. This is a missed opportunity for China's ambition to become a greater political and economic power in the international community. With Islamic markets, rules such as limiting *gharār*, meaning risk-taking, promoting *ʿadl*, meaning justice, seeking *mīzān*, meaning balance, hedging against *shak*, meaning doubt, upholding *ḍarūra*, meaning necessity, and emphasising *khilāfa*, meaning humans' deputy role on earth, would be further developed.[48] Such rules promote equity and justice, and this supports a more sustainable economic system. China can benefit from promoting such positive Islamic rules and even adapt them to its needs. Even in Muslim countries, these trends of adapting Islamic rules to state needs have been observed with processes of shariʿa compliance.[49] In addition to the cornerstone principle of *ijtihād*, or independent interpretation, as a trope supporting progress in Islam, there is also insistence on advancing the Muslim community or *umma* and being clever, which leaves an enormous space for developing Islamic markets.[50]

48 Warde, *Islamic Finance in the Global Economy*, 6263; Rabb, *Doubt in Islamic Law*, 184.

49 Rumee, *Sharia Compliant: A User's Guide to Hacking Islamic Law*, 4.

50 Abdul-Matin, *Green Deen*, 185–189.

Acknowledgement

I would like to thank my former research assistant at Al Akhawayn University in Ifrane, Leila El Euldj, for compiling data on trade between the MENA and China, and two anonymous reviewers in 2019 and 2020.

Bibliography

Abdul-Matin, Ibrahim. 2010. *Green Deen: What Islam Teaches about Protecting the Planet*. San Francisco: Berrett-Koehler Publishers.

Ahmed, Rumee. 2018. *Sharia Compliant: A User's Guide to Hacking Islamic Law*. Stanford: Stanford University Press.

Ali, Afzaal, Guo Xiaoling, Mehkar Sherwani, and Adnan Ali. 2017. 'Factors Affecting Halal Meat Purchase Intention: Evidence from International Muslim Students in China'. *British Food Journal* 119, no. 3: 527–541.

Alserhan, Baker Ahmad. 2011. *The Principles of Islamic Marketing*. Surrey: Gower.

Blanchard, Ben. 'China Passes Controversial Counter-Terrorism Law', *Reuters*, December 28, 2015.

Castets, Rémi. 2003. 'The Uyghurs in Xinjiang—The Malaise Grows'. *China Perspectives* 49: 1–19.

Cesaro, Cristina M., 2000. 'Consuming Identities: Food and Resistance among the Uyghur in Contemporary Xinjiang'. *Inner Asia* 2, no. 2: 225–238.

Crossley, Gabriel and Kevin Yao. 'China's Economy Rebounds after Steep Slump, Weak Demand, US Tensions raise Risks', *Reuters Business News*, July 16, 2020. https://www.reuters.com/article/us-china-economy-gdp-idUSKCN24H0AM

Dorsey, James M. 2017. 'China and the Middle East: Venturing into the Maelstrom'. *Asian Journal of Middle Eastern and Islamic Studies* 11, no. 1: 1–14.

El Bernoussi, Zaynab. 'China's Civilizational Diplomacy', Politics, *Project Syndicate*, December 5, 2016. https://www.project-syndicate.org/commentary/china-egypt-global-south-by-zaynab-el-bernoussi-2016-12?barrier=accesspaylog

El Bernoussi, Zaynab, and Eric Olander. 'China's Risky Power Play in the Arab World', *A China in Africa Podcast*, December 25, 2016, https://www.chinafile.com/library/china-africa-project/chinas-risky-power-play-arab-world (accessed 27 October 2020)

El Bernoussi, Zaynab. 'World War C: How the COVID-19 Pandemic Should Teach us to Consume Less and Cooperate More?', *Tribune Libre—RSSI*, August 5, 2020. http://www.rssi-rabat.ma/2020/09/02/world-war-c-how-the-covid-19-pandemic-should-teach-us-to-consume-less-and-cooperate-more/

Erie, Matthew S. 'China's Halal Constitution "Islamic" Legislation Stirs Debate as the PRC Engages the Muslim World', *The Diplomat*, May 27, 2016.

Erie, Matthew S. 2016. *China and Islam: The Prophet, the Party, and Law*. Cambridge: Cambridge University Press.

Erie, Matthew S. 2019 'Shari'a As Taboo of Modern Law: Halal Food, Islamophobia, and China'. *Journal of Law and Religion* 33, no. 3: 390–420.

Friedrichs, Jörg. 2017. 'Sino-Muslim Relations: the Han, the Hui, and the Uyghurs'. *Journal of Muslim Minority Affairs* 37, no. 1: 55–79.

Hassanein, Haisam. 'Arab States Give China a Pass on Uyghur Crackdown', *The Washington Institute*, August 26, 2019. https://www.washingtoninstitute.org/policy-analysis/view/arab-states-give-china-a-pass-on-uyghur-crackdown

Hayoun, Massoud. 'Can China Make Its Cuisine—and Finance—Friendly to Muslims'?, *Time*, April 4, 2012. http://content.time.com/time/world/article/0,8599,2110979,00.html

Hernandez, Javier C. and Adam Wu, 'Officials in China Call for National Standards on Halal Food'. *New York Times, Sinosphere*, March 14, 2016. https://www.nytimes.com/2016/03/15/world/asia/china-halal-food-standards.html

Isaura, Daniel, 'Gulf Countries Import 78% of their Food', *Salaam Gateway*, February 27, 2017.

Maizland, Lindsay. 'China's Repression of Uighurs in Xinjiang', *Council on Foreign Relations*, October 9, 2019. https://www.cfr.org/backgrounder/chinas-repression-uighurs-xinjiang

Miao, Ying. 2020. 'Sinicisation vs. Arabisation: Online Narratives of Islamophobia in China'. *Journal of Contemporary China* 29, no. 125: 748–762.

O'Connor, Paul. 2012. *Islam in Hong Kong: Muslims and Everyday Life in China's World City*. Vol. 1. Hong Kong: Hong Kong University Press.

Prashad, Vijay. 2007. *The Darker Nations: A Biography of the Short-Lived Third World*. New Delhi: Left Word Books.

Rabb, Intisar A. 2014. *Doubt in Islamic Law*. Cambridge: Cambridge University Press.

Rudelson, Justin Jon. 1997. *Oasis Identities: Uyghur Nationalism along China's Silk Road*. New York: Columbia University Press.

Sandikci, Ozlem. 2020. 'Religion and Everyday Consumption Ethics: A Moral Economy Approach'. *Journal of Business Ethics*: 1–17. https://doi.org/10.1007/s10551-019-04422-2.

Scholte, Jan Aart. 2005. *Globalisation: A Critical Introduction*. London, New York: Palgrave Macmillan.

Smith, Joanne N. 2002. ''Making Culture Matter': Symbolic, Spatial and Social Boundaries between Uyghurs and Han Chinese'. *Asian Ethnicity* 3, no. 2: 153–174.

Stewart, James John. 2004. 'Muslim–Buddhist Conflict in Contemporary Sri Lanka'. *South Asia Research* 34, no. 3: 241–260.

Streeck, Wolfgang. 2014. 'How Will Capitalism End?' *New Left Review* 87: 35–64.

Sun, Degang, and Yahia Zoubir. 2014. 'China's response to the revolts in the Arab World: A Case of pragmatic diplomacy'. *Mediterranean Politics* 19, no. 1: 2–20.

Sun, Degang, and Yahia Zoubir. 2015. 'China's Economic Diplomacy towards the Arab Countries: Challenges Ahead?' *Journal of Contemporary China* 24, no. 95: 903–921.

Sun, Degang, and Yahia Zoubir. 2018. 'China's Participation in Conflict Resolution in the Middle East and North Africa: A Case of Quasi-Mediation Diplomacy?' *Journal of Contemporary China* 27, no. 110: 224–243.

Warde, Ibrahim. 2000. *Islamic Finance in the Global Economy*. Edinburgh: Edinburgh University Press.

Wayne, Martin I. 2009. 'Inside China's War on Terrorism'. *Journal of Contemporary China* 18, no. 59: 249–261.

Wee Sile, Aza. 'Why China wants a bite of the booming halal food market', *CNBC*, November 24, 2015. https://www.cnbc.com/2015/08/24/china-wants-a-bite-of-the-booming-halal-food-market.html

Zambelis, Chris. 2009. 'Xinjiang Crackdown and Changing Perceptions of China in the Islamic World'. *China Brief* 9, no. 16: 4–8.

CHAPTER 6

Science, Politics, and Islam: The Other Origin Story of Halal Authentication in Indonesia

En-Chieh Chao

1 The Significance of the Indonesian Case

The Islamic dietary code has been known for centuries but making halal authentication a scientific matter is a very recent phenomenon. In the past, the concept of 'halal food' was not mediated by science and technology as we know it today. In Muslim-majority countries, Muslims acquired meat from butchers and cooks whom they could trust. Wherever Muslims found themselves in the minority, however, they developed a more reflexive consciousness towards food. For example, Muslims in the United States, when facing an absence of halal food, might seek out available kosher food products.[1] In Argentina during the late 1960s, for another instance, Lebanese immigrants launched one of the earliest versions of modern halal-certified labeling (using Arabic calligraphy) to facilitate the sale of trusted halal products locally. None of the practices above envisaged halal labels that required scientific verification. All they required was religious verification, or simply social trust.

Things changed in the late 1970s and onwards. After the Iranian Revolution in 1979, the Islamic Republic demanded that meat imported from other countries be halal. New Zealand and Australia, both major meat-exporting countries, were keen to enter Iran, as the Middle Eastern market could be the answer to their economic crisis after Britain decided to cut down its imports from them. For this to happen, the New Zealand government not only invited Muslim immigrants from Iran and Fiji, but also recruited veterinary scientists. They needed these scientists to prove to the suspicious eyes of 'ulama's that the meat they produced was indeed halal despite using electrical stunning techniques, and to prove that the process also qualified as 'humane slaughter' to meet the demand of new laws regarding animal welfare in New Zealand and

1 Please see https://www.npr.org/sections/codeswitch/2017/10/26/554298738/the-rise-of-halal-cuisine-in-an-age-of-islamophobia (accessed 2019 Oct 9).

 | DOI:10.1163/9789004459236_007

globally. After tremendous efforts put into laboratory experiments by its veterinary scientists, and debates with international Muslim groups, finally New Zealand proudly presented a kind of pre-slaughter stunning that allegedly fulfilled both the criteria of Islamic law and humane slaughter in the early 1990s.[2] At this point, the halal certification was mostly limited to meat products. No one was asking if bread, oil, or chocolate also needed scientific examination to prove their halalness.

It was not until the late 1980s that the idea that manufactured foods required laboratory testing to determine their halal status arose. This development of scientific halal certification of manufactured foods took place on a large scale in Southeast Asia first. By scientific halal certification, I mean the application of scientific knowledge and laboratory technologies dedicated to detecting the presence of non-halal elements in manufacturing procedures of food, drugs, and cosmetics. The leading roles of Malaysia and Indonesia in such development is attested by the fact that it was their halal standards that came to be seen as some of the most authoritative standards by other certifying bodies around the world.[3] The particular importance of Indonesia can also be observed from the fact that its most influential halal certifying body has headed some of the largest global alliances of such groups, namely the World Halal Food Council. Most importantly, the paradigmatic shift in the reception of halal certification that Indonesians have experienced—from everything-is-halal-unless-otherwise-noted to nothing-is-halal-until-certified—is a critical part of the global history of halal awareness and practices.

Hence the intriguing question: how did a country like Indonesia, long seen as a peripheral part of the Islamic world, come to be one of the leading pioneers of modern halal certification? How did the institutionalisation of halal certification start in Indonesia? What are the processes that have transformed halal certification from being something 'unnecessary' (see below) into something obligatory? It should be noted that this chapter is concerned with the change of halal consciousness up to 2014, when halal certification was still voluntary. We stop in 2014 because that year was a turning point, when a new law was passed that made it obligatory for all goods circulated in Indonesia to go through halal certification, starting in October of 2019. Many businesses, knowing that 2019 would come soon, would be compelled to apply for halal certification, or at least start to prepare for the upcoming requirement. The focus of this essay

2 Chao, 'Halal Stunning: A Techno-moral History of Animal Welfare and Islamic Slaughter'.
3 Farouk, 'Advances in the Industrial Production of Halal and Kosher Red Meat'.

is on the 'voluntary' period. As I shall show below, even when it was optional to apply for halal certification, who needed the authentication the most was a political matter, not simply a religious one.

Before I proceed to answer the questions outlined above, I shall say a few more words on the global rise of the desire for certified halal products. I have two goals in laying out this newly flourishing desire. First, I aim to make a stark contrast between the past and the present, so that we do not naturalise the desire for halal certification, as if all Muslims at all times need halal certification and it is simply a matter of raising the awareness. Second, I suggest that a deeper exploration of the historically localised cultural milieu behind the origin story of any given halal certifying institution is necessary. This can contribute to the existing body of related literature that often simplifies the establishment of halal certifying bodies to the formulation of a list of legal regulations or the founding of some organisations. Here I am proposing something else. I suggest that we treat the origin story as a site of political struggle that is shaped by specific socio-cultural contexts where ethno-religious politics is at stake.

2 Remaking Halal Awareness

Nowadays the term 'halal' is increasingly paired with 'market'. It has been estimated that the global Muslim population will increase from 1.6 billion in 2010 to 2.2 billion in 2030, which constitutes more than one quarter of the global population.[4] With the sheer size of Islamic finance and the growing revenue of the halal meat industry, as well as other new halal products such as processed foods, beverages, and cosmetics, the 'halal market' is now described as a market that is even 'larger than China'.[5] The discourse of the expanding halal market seems to assume that all Muslims naturally desire halal products, and with their population growth, the demand will undoubtedly increase.

But desire and demand are never 'natural'. They are culturally produced in specific historical moment. Bergeaud-Blackler has pointed out that such deployment of halal certification for daily products was only recently inven-

4 Grim and Karim, 'The Future of the Global Muslim Population: Projections for 2010–2030'.

5 Anggara, 'Development of Indonesia Halal Agroindustry Global Market in ASEAN: Strategic Assesment', 66.

ted.[6] This is not to say that no Muslim cared about whether food products were halal in the past, or that the discourse of the halal market has made no real impact on the local and global economy already. The point is first and foremost that modern halal certification is different from its predecessors, as briefly alluded to earlier. The recent invention of halal certification aided by scientific methods requires an explanation of just how new halal awareness was aroused in particular historical and local circumstances. In fact, precisely because the halal field is expanding and innovating,[7] more attention needs to be paid to halal enterprises as cultural processes and historical products.

So far, the market discourse advocates, designs, and prescribes ways to help enlarge and enrich the halal market. Some research from business schools is dedicated to this aim.[8] For their goal, it is more convenient to introduce a static view about the meaning of halal, which often neglects the role that complex interactions between religion, politics and technology have played in the rising halal market. What is missing here is a genealogy of how halal awareness was arrived at historically in the local context. After all, halal certification *is* a recent invention, and the long existence of Islamic law itself did not demand its implementation until recently. Hence, we must treat scientific halal certification as a new phenomenon that demands interpretations. In this vein, Bergeaud-Blackler has described the forces of state intervention in creating the

6 Bergeaud-Blackler, 'The Halal Certification Market in Europe and the World: A First Panorama'.

7 http://paper.udn.com/udnpaper/POE0039/320000/web/ (accessed 2019 Aug 30). In 2017, a Global Islamic Economy Report made by Reuters estimated that its value has reached US$ 3.9 trillion, and would climb to US$ 6.5 trillion in 2021. Meanwhile, tourism, fashion, and restaurants that accommodated Muslims' daily needs are all expanding at an impressive rate. Among 57 member countries in the Organization of Islamic Cooperation, the economic growth in Indonesia and Bangladesh is expected to be higher than that of most countries in the Middle East. Please see Rudnyckyj. 'Economy in Practice: Islamic Finance and the Problem of Market Reason'. Southeast Asia seems special. Mastercard has targeted Southeast Asian Muslims to offer a special halal plan. China, Japan, and Korea have also had their share. The largest Japanese bank, Mizubishi, for example, has promoted Islamic bonds and Islamic insurance plans. Taiwanese companies, for another instance, also planned to create a Taiwanese halal zone with world's largest online halal shop platform, Alddinstreet, to further promote Taiwanese products through halal certifications, particularly in Malaysia and Indonesia. These two countries have had world-renowned halal authentication procedures, and Indonesia has another advantage in the size of population as potential customers.

8 Farhan and Andriansyah, 'Factors Affecting Muslim Students Awareness of Halal Products in Yogyakarta, Indonesia'; Rasyid, 'Raising the Awareness of Halal Products among Indonesian Consumers: Issues and Strategies'; Aziz and Chok, 'The Role of Halal Awareness, Halal Certification, and Marketing Components in Determining Halal Purchase Intention among

halal market.[9] Meanwhile, Johan Fischer's works open up horizons for understanding the Malay Muslim middle-class desire for Islamic commodities, the institutionalising power of the state, the branding of halal products, and the emergence of the halal technoscience.[10] While building on the research above, this chapter has a different aim. The focus will be a localised history of the birth of halal certification in Indonesia, which is inseparable from scientific intervention and ethno-religious politics.

3 Notes on Research Methods

The popular origin story of halal certification that is widely circulated in Indonesian society usually has two main components. First, it often accredits Professor Tri Soesanto from Brawijaya University as the hero who pioneered the efforts. Second, it portrays the institutionalisation of halal certification as a natural outcome of the 1988 Lard Scandal. In what follows, however, I shall demonstrate that both components of this origin story are problematic and need to be reconsidered.

The subsequent analysis draws on the data collected from Indonesian magazines and newspapers in the national library in Jakarta and university libraries in Yogyakarta during archival research between 2017 and 2019. I focused primarily on *Kompas*, the most widely circulated newspaper in the country, and *Tempo*, a leading news magazine, as well as using other newspapers as sources when necessary.

The analysis also benefits greatly from interviews with employers of the Food, Drug, and Cosmetics Section of the Indonesian Council of Religious Scholars (LPPOM MUI) in 2015, and with members of the Halal Research Group (HRG) at the nation's prestigious Gajah Mada University (UGM) in 2017. Finally, this research also examines fatwas issued by Majelis Ulama Indonesia (MUI) related to halal matters. Drawing on this variety of data, I focus on the changing political implications of halal issues from 1988 to 2014 in Indonesia.

Non-Muslims in Malaysia: A Structural Equation Modeling Approach'; Awan, Siddiquei, and Haider, 'Factors Affecting Halal Purchase Intention—Evidence from Pakistan's Halal Food Sector'; Batu, Regenstein, and Dogan, 'Gelatin Issues in Halal Food Processing For Muslim Societies'.

9 Bergeaud-Blackler, 'The Halal Certification Market in Europe and the World'.

10 Fischer, 'Religion, Science and Markets'; Fischer, *Islam, Standards, and Technoscience: In Global Halal Zones*.

The approach I adopt in this essay is one of Science and Technology Studies (STS). This is not the place to introduce a variety of STS approaches such as strong programme, actor network theory, and social world theory. Here, suffice it to say that broadly speaking, my approach highlights the salience of socio-cultural contexts in affecting and creating new ways of utilising certain technologies and generating particular knowledge.[11] Further, once well developed, these technologies can in turn influence and reconstitute the techno-moral fabric of the society.

4 The Other Origin Story: When Raising the Halal Issue Was 'Subversive'

The other origin story of the scientific halal certification in Indonesia also goes back to Brawijaya University in East Java, just like the popular origin story. Professor Tri Soesanto from the Department of Food Technology conducted some simple investigations with his students in 1988, concluding that many products on the market might have pork derivatives, especially those that contained gelatine and shortening.[12] It was unclear whether the source of these ingredients was vegetarian or animal-based.[13] The team listed 34 products, including instant noodles, sweet soy sauce, milk formulas, and noodles, as at risk of being non-halal. They presented a reasonable doubt, and did not assert that all these products were haram. The survey was published uneventfully in February 1988 in the school journal *Canopy Bulletin*.[14]

It was six months later that things started to flare up. A tampered-with version of the article published by Tri Soesanto's team was produced that included a fabricated list of 64 products and claimed these products were all

11 Jasanoff and Wynne, 'Science and Decision-making'.

12 Gelatine is derived from collagen taken from animal body parts after an irreversible hydrolysis process, in which hydrolysis reduces original protein fibrils into smaller peptides, resulting in hydrolysed form of collagen. Gelatine serves for supplementary source of protein, bonding agent, clearing of drinks, and others. It can be found in most gummy candy and marshmallows, and in some ice creams and yogurts. Other than food, gelatine is also commonly used in manufacturing drug and vitamin capsules and cosmetics. For more information about gelatine, please see Djagnya, Wang, and Xu, 'Gelatin: A Valuable Protein for Food and Pharmaceutical Industries: Review'. Shortening refers to any fat that is a solid at room temperature, such as lard, and is commonly used in bakery. Conventionally, however, it is rarely applied to refer to butter.

13 *Kompas*, 8 November 1988.

14 *Tempo*, 5 November 1988.

haram. On 13 October of the same year, a newspaper in Surabaya published Tri Soesanto's team's survey.[15] Soon, two newspapers in Jakarta followed. The news quickly created a nationwide panic, leading to accusations that Indomie instant noodles, Colgate toothpaste, certain brands of soap, and ABC sweet soy sauce had all been discovered to be non-halal. Boycotts soon ensued. Within a month, ABC lost 25 per cent of its sales, Bango sweet soy sauce lost 75 per cent, Siong Hoe biscuits went down to one third of its production, and Indomie suffered a 20 per cent to 30 per cent decline in sales.[16] In Palembang, one Indomie factory sent 200 out of 500 workers home.[17] Meanwhile, several companies spent tens of millions of Rupiah putting up new advertisements across the nation, reassuring consumers that their products were really halal.

While being forced to respond to the popular unrest, the government expressed little interest in enlarging state intervention in halal matters. An official from the Ministry of Religious Affairs responded that they could not be responsible for halal labels, because 'we do not have laboratories to conduct examinations'; the Ministry of Health stated that their mission was to ensure health, and as to the question of the halalness of products, people should ask the Ministry of Religious Affairs; finally, the spokesman of the Food and Drug Sector under the Ministry of Health concurred, saying that their job was to observe 'the microbiological condition', not the halal condition, and that it was simply unnecessary to label anything halal, because what was needed was simply the warning label 'contains pork' on specific products, which was already required by law.[18] In other words, no government apparatus at the time was thinking about a standardisation of halal certification. In fact, the Indonesian Council of Religious Scholars, or MUI, insisted at the time that before a product was proved haram, it should be considered halal.

Before I proceed to demonstrate MUI's stance at that time, a few words are needed to clarify the nature of MUI. The MUI was established in 1975 as a semi-state-sponsored institution. From the New Order regime's perspective, the major reason to form the MUI was to unify several major, often opposing, Muslim organisations in Indonesia. With representatives from all the important Muslim organisations, MUI was a product of Suharto's authoritarian regime,

15 Tri Soesanto repeatedly clarified that the result was not out of 'research' but only a 'survey' (*Kompas*, 10 November 1988).
16 *Kompas*, 9 November 1988.
17 *Kompas*, 9 November 1988.
18 *Tempo*, 2 November 1988.

at least in terms of its form and inception. This is certainly not to say that MUI does not have its own voice. In fact, among all the fatwas that MUI have issued, while some justify government policies, others run against them.[19] Many scholars see MUI as a major force of religious conservatism, while others have evaluated the more nuanced effects of MUI's influence in the democratising era.[20] Due to the limits of this chapter, it would be an impossible task to make a fair assessment of the relationship between MUI and different regimes, let alone that between different MUI leaders and different political groups. Thus, in this chapter I will restrict my discussion about MUI to its role as an internally heterogeneous but, in effect, a singular and powerful actor in the shifts of halal awareness in Indonesia.

Back to November of 1988: there were numerous news articles about the Lard Scandal, and often the head of the fatwa committee of the MUI, Professor Dr H. Ibrahim Husen, was interviewed. Ibrahim's response was consistent for several months. Take a frontpage story in *Kompas* for example.

> 'The Indonesian Council of Religious Scholars holds the opinion that, what was found regarding certain food materials that contained derivatives from pork recently was still accusations that were not yet proved with certainty (*tuduhan yang belum dibuktikan dengan pasti*). Therefore, the previous ruling still applies to the aforementioned foods, namely what was halal was halal and so forth, until there is certainty that comes to light ...
>
> Before there is the result of research that can prove that these products mentioned contain lard, according to the Indonesian Council of Religious Scholars in line with the teachings of Islam, the ruling remains halal because earlier on [they were] indeed halal. If the result of research states that they contain lard, then it will be clear that the ruling must be haram', emphasised Ibrahim.[21]

The quote from Professor Ibrahim may seem rather unconventional, since all Muslim religious scholars know that other than halal and haram, there is the category of *mushtabihāt*, or doubtful things. Although scholars differ in their

---

19 Hosen, 'Behind the Scenes: Fatwas of Majelis Ulama Indonesia (1975–1998)'; Ichwan. ''Ulamā', State and Politics: Majelis Ulama Indonesia After Suharto'.

20 Ichwan, 'Towards a Puritanical Moderate Islam: The Majelis Ulama Indonesia and the Politics of Religious Orthodoxy'.

21 *Kompas*, 8 November 1998.

opinions about the status of doubtful things, certainly these problematised products in question should fall into this category. But Professor Ibrahim had good reasons for saying otherwise. He had personally met with President Suharto and all the ministers of related ministries, especially Ministry of Health, which was in charge of labelling manufactured foods. The Minister of Health at the time reassured the public that everything that was officially registered was halal, except those that contained pork and they were already required to have 'contains pork' captions or pictures of a pig. Also, the suspected Dancow milk powder had just been proved by the laboratory test run by the Bureau of Drugs and Food to be free of lard. Backed by these developments, Professor Ibrahim had good reasons to assert that 'everything remains halal unless proved otherwise', not to mention he was probably asked by the president to help appease the upset citizens.

To sum up, the mentality about halalness among government officials and even the MUI leaders at the time was rather different from the mentality surrounding institutionalised halal certification we are familiar with today. With the latter, one cannot claim to be halal without the authentication first. Yet back in 1988, everything could be considered halal, unless it was noted or proven otherwise. In fact, the title of the frontpage news above was simply 'Halal, before it was certain to contain lard'.

But it was not merely that the government and religious scholars wished society to calm down. The government was also enraged about the controversy. Stability was the key thing that the New Order regime took pride in, and anything that dared to tamper with stability should be punished, or at least admonished. Indeed, President Suharto ordered the Attorney General, Soekarton Marmosoedjono, to step up investigations to get to the bottom of the lard allegations. While Soekarton noted that a third party had tampered with the results of Professor Soesanto's survey, which was disseminated without the author's knowledge, the Attorney General was still hard on the food scientist. On 18 November 1988, an anonymous editorial opinion in *Kompas* responded to Soekarton's intention to investigate Tri Soesanto on the basis of the latter's recklessness or negligence (*keteledoran*) and implied that this was a political intervention into the academic freedom of research and publication. Attorney General Soekarton went so far as to suggest that Tri Soesanto might have had problematic motivations.

> Soekarton also said the professor deserves to be held partly responsible for the affair, especially since his academic qualification lends credence to the survey and is bound to stir unrest in the general community. The attorney general said, 'A person who willingly creates and publicises such

> an issue can be categorised as subversive', and added that the newspapers which first brought the issue to public attention are also being investigated.[22]

The official opinions about Tri Soesanto's research in 1988 thus ranged from reassuring the public that things were under control to criminalising the event as unnecessarily disturbing the peaceful society. The Attorney General even went so far as to say that because Professor Tri Soesanto had produced such a potentially 'subversive' report, he might have to be held partially responsible for the social unrest.

Despite the government's efforts to appease troubled citizens and to restore the society to normal life, there was no turning back after the sheer scale of the mass panic and economic loss. Several consumer groups called for state intervention into the regulation of halal labels, and several parliament members also hoped that MUI and the Foundation of Consumers' Institution (Yayasan Lembaga Konsumen) could have their own laboratory.[23] Indeed, the situation pushed the New Order regime to take other measures. Suharto's government soon sought help from MUI, who in turn sought help from Bogor Institute of Agriculture (IPB), the nation's premiere university. Together, they established the Food, Drug, and Cosmetics Section of MUI (LPPOM MUI) in 1989 to tackle the halal problem by institutionalising halal certification. This was the first attempt to incorporate scientists, full-time technicians, and laboratory experiments into the references for the issuing of fatwa with regard to the question of halal authenticity.

The major lesson learned here is that the origin story is more complicated than is often presented in Indonesian society. As mentioned before, the popular origin story of halal certification often credits Tri Soesanto as the hero who pioneered the discovery of the need for halal authentication, and usually portrays the institutionalisation of halal certification as a natural outcome of the 1988 Lard Scandal. So far, it should be clear that both views are anachronistic and oversimplified. In fact, even after 1989, when LPPOM was established, the general public's opinions about the necessity of halal certification was still quite inconsistent. As I will demonstrate below, it turns out that some food companies need halal certification more than others. While some companies are assumed to be halal, others are often doubted, and this has much to do with ethno-religious politics.

---

22 UCA News, 30 November 1988.

23 *Kompas*, 8 November 1988.

5 Halal Certification and Ethnic Politics: Some Need it More Than Others

The 1988 Lard Scandal was by no means the first of its kind in the country. Historically, rumours of supposedly halal food being adulterated with lard occurred periodically. While modern food technology has to a greater degree mystified the source of mass-produced food products and potentially made accusations of adulteration all the more plausible, the targets of rumours of 'hidden pork' were almost always highly selective.

In the wake of the 1988 Lard Scandal, the companies that were most vulnerable were those run by Chinese Indonesians, non-Muslims, and foreigners. The aforementioned products that were boycotted, such as ABC sweetened soy sauce, Bango, and Indomie, were owned by Chinese Indonesians, whereas Siong Hoe biscuits were owned by a Singaporean company, with a name that signaled its Chinessness. Even Professor Tri Soesanto himself displayed this inclination to suspect the Chinese in daily life in his problematised survey published in the *Canopy Bulletin* on the campus of Brawijaya University:

> Materials that were accused of being haram were perhaps found ... as an unintended consequence, for example the residue of alcohol of fruits that were left over-ripe, or the cooking tools in Chinese restaurants that were contaminated by pork and other things (*alat masak di restauran Cina yang tercemar daging babi dan lain-lain*).[24]

To the readers of Professor Tri Soesanto, it seemed obvious that Chinese restaurants, which were found everywhere across the country, often provided non-halal food.

The ethno-religious politics implicated in the Lard Scandal meant that the association of the Chinese with lard could be easily extended from Chinese restaurants to Chinese-owned factories. As a professor of economics at University of Indonesia, Rhenald Kasali, commented:

> The pork scandal (1988) indicates that, the victims of rumors are usually certain target groups (usually those who are considered as powerful corporations, dominated by non-pribumi and non-Islamic entrepreneurs), who always rank at the top of the problematic list.[25]

---

24 *Canopy Bulletin*, January 1988, cited in Kasali, *Sembilan Fenomena Bisnis*, 176. The issue of Canopy Bulletin is currently missing, according to several friends at Brawijaya University. After years of searching, to this day I have not found the original copy.

25 Kasali, *Sembilan Fenomena Bisnis*, 25.

It should be noted that in Indonesia, the term 'non-pribumi' almost always means Chinese Indonesians.

After MUI started to issue officially recognised halal labels, many international fast-food companies such as McDonald's and KFC immediately applied for and obtained the halal certificate. Indeed, large transnational corporations' restaurants were often smeared as having haram ingredients. They are more vulnerable to rumours than are *pribumi* restaurants, just like Chinese Indonesian-owned enterprises. Under these circumstances, it is unsurprising that the most popular instant noodle brand in the nation, Indomie, also signed up for halal certification soon after LPPOM launched its certification service. Indomie is owned by PT Sanmaru Food Manufacturing, a Chinese-Indonesian-owned conglomerate. Its share in the market currently is as high as 70 per cent, and it is also sold in Asia, America, Australia, Europe, Africa, and the Middle East. Currently, all Indomie products have the halal label from MUI, and every single item goes through LPPOM's certification. One auditor and researcher from LPPOM told me that halal certification was a matter of national security, and Chinese-owned brands, more than other general brands, were eager to obtain halal certification to protect themselves from suspicion. One of the auditors made a serious comment:

> Even a simple sms [text message] carrying a rumor that certain products contain lard can stir up panic among the general public. People would blame the owner of the product, to the point that even the boss of the factory could be killed.[26]

This view was echoing what was thought of back in 1988. Addressing the danger of 'lard rumours', the Minister of Coordinating Ministry for Political, Legal, and Security Affairs, Sudomo, warned the public that it was possible there might be riots and chaos in the consequences of the Lard Scandal. He said:

> If seen from the widespread influence of the consequence of the news story, it's likely that they [the extreme right and extreme left] aim to create chaos, for example by encouraging people to burn factories and things like that.[27]

26 Field notes, 3 August 2015.

27 *Kompas*, 9 November 1988.

From this perspective, halal certification has come to be seen as a tool to prevent potential ethno-religious conflict and socio-economic unrest. Although one may be tempted to think that ethno-religious conflict was the primary cause of the need for certification, it is perhaps more accurate to say that multiple factors, including scientific investigation, authoritarian politics, and ethno-religious tension altogether lead to such a development.

To sum up, the 1988 scandal did not immediately bring about the institutionalisation of halal certification. After all, we should remember that in 1988, when the pork scandal happened, Professor Tri Soesanto was accused of negligence or even subversion, and the government was merely responding to consumer rights groups by inviting religious scholars and scientists to reach a solution to the halal problem. It did not immediately initiate the standardisation of halal labelling until several years later. In fact, even when LPPOM was initially established, in 1989, most Muslim-owned companies were reluctant to apply for a halal label. Their reasoning was that they and their customers knew that their products had always been halal, so why should they pay LPPOM to tell them what they already knew? In parallel, in the scientific field, the head of LPPOM, Professor Aisjah Girindra, told the press that LPPOM's work was looked down upon and considered unnecessary, if not ridiculous, by fellow scientists.[28] It almost seemed that halal certification was only needed by the colossal corporations and foreign companies such as KFC or Indomie so that they would not have to fear periodically being smeared and boycotted. In short, halal certification was in practice only popular among some sectors of the market, ethno-religiously marked, and it remained so for years.

6 Religious Authority with Scientific Knowledge: Further Politicisation

The relatively low status of halal certification was transformed, however, by the Ajinomoto case in September 2000. Ajinomoto is a Japanese company that controls one third of the world MSG (monosodium glutamate) market, and one of its largest consumers is Indonesia. The Ajinomoto branch in East Java had already obtained halal certification from MUI through the LPPOM examination. Yet, when the company wished to renew the certificate in 2000, LPPOM discovered that Ajinomoto had changed its manufacturing process since obtain-

28 *Republika*, 19 December 2008.

ing halal certification. In the production process of MSG, the previous enzyme was replaced with a less costly enzyme, bacto soytone. An investigation of bacto soytone ensued.

A few words should be said here about what MSG is and how it was produced in our case. MSG is a seasoning commonly used in East Asia, Southeast Asia, and other parts of the world where one can find restaurants run by immigrants from the abovementioned areas. Its appearance is white and crystalline. Its function is to enhance the flavour of foods.

In the case of Ajinomoto produced in East Java, the process of producing MSG, according to Mochammad and Kes,[29] can be summarised into three stages, as outlined below.

1) At the beginning of the production of MSG, the soybean protein is used as the material. The major process of this stage is a hydrolysis process. In this process, a porcine enzyme is used to break down the protein of soybean into shorter peptides. The enzyme used in this stage was derived from pig pancreas. The result is bacto soytone, a medium for cultivating bacteria.
2) In the next stage, which is separate from the first stage, bacto soytone is used as a medium in which to grow bacteria that will later be used for the fermentation that is needed for making MSG. Once the bacteria are grown enough on the bacto soytone medium, they are moved to the following stage.
3) The final stage utilises a liquid medium to multiply the bacteria grown in the second stage. Usually the bacteria are corynebacterium glutamicum (previously known as brevibacterium lactofermentum). The multiplied bacteria are then incorporated into the fermentation process in order to produce glutamic acid. Later soda (sodium carbonate/Na_2CO_3) is added to neutralise, purify and crystalise the result, which is MSG.

In sum, we can say that the first stage is creating the medium to produce bacteria, the second stage is to grow the bacteria needed for the next stage, and the third stage includes the multiplication of bacteria and the fermentation process that produces MSG. The porcine enzyme only appears in the first stage and only serves as a catalyst to facilitate the hydrolysis.

Now if we see this process from a molecular perspective, the porcine enzyme does not become part of the molecular structure of bacto soytone. Put in another way, laboratory tests would not detect any traces of pork DNA within the MSG. Yet, this is merely a molecular perspective, based on seeing things as bounded entities that are defined by their molecular structure.

29 Mochammad and Kes, 'Proses Produksi MSG (Monosodium Glutamat)', 2011.

Now, be it the cultivation of bacteria or the production of MSG, these are things that could not have possibly been covered by centuries-old legal texts. This is a new terrain for religious scholars. Indeed, one must recall that in the 1995 Fiqh Medical Seminar in Kuwait, the World Health Organization, medical scientists, and Islamic jurists were brought together to address modern medical issues from an Islamic perspective. They recommended that gelatine used for medical purposes, such as capsules, should be permitted. The justification is through the principle of *istihāla*, or transformation. This refers to the process that turns the unclean material into clean material, and therefore turns prohibited things into things permissible by the shariʿa.

It is commonly thought that the Shafi'i school, to which most Indonesian Muslim scholars belong, holds a more negative view on the extension of *istihāla* to new examples beyond those that already existed in legal texts, and thus might be expected to disagree with the 1995 recommendation. Yet, MUI do not only follow one school of thought, but instead use different ones for different cases.[30] Meanwhile, MUI does not make the process of their reasoning transparent, and their method is also not consistent.[31] According to Hosen, when MUI issue a fatwa, sometimes they cite directly from the Qur'an and hadith; other times they give only secondary texts as the reason for their ruling. Occasionally, they do not give any reasons at all.

So, in a most rigorous sense, it was quite difficult to foresee what method and which school of law MUI would choose to make its ruling on Ajinomoto's MSG production method. If we judge from the most relevant fatwa, the 1980 fatwa about contamination, there is nothing about the production of manufactured materials specifically stated.

Finally, on 16 December 2000, the fatwa committee of MUI issued its conclusion. The fatwa starts as follows:

> It was discovered that the manufacturing process [of the Ajinomoto factory in Mojokerto, East Java] between June, 1999 and November, 2000 has used bacto soytone as a catalyzer (*bahan penolong*), and the production of bacto soytone has involved elements (*unsur*) including a kind of enzyme derived from pig.

---

30 Ni'am, *Metodologi Penetapan Fatwa Majelis Ulama Indonesia: Penggunaan Prinsip Pencegahan dalam Fatwa*; Hosen, 'Behind the Scenes: Fatwas of Majelis Ulama Indonesia (1975–1998)'.

31 Hosen, 'Behind the Scenes: Fatwas of Majelis Ulama Indonesia (1975–1998)'.

It seems clear that the members of the fatwa committee knew well that bacto soytone itself was produced through a kind of enzyme that was made from pork derivatives. The fatwa then lists nine reminders and five points, as well as four applications. Reminders No. 1 to No. 3 listed al-Quran 2:168, 173, 5:3, 6:145, 7:157 and the hadith regarding the status of unclear matters as *syubhat*.[32] Reminder No. 4 states that according to *ijmāʿ* ('ulama' consensus) every element that belongs to or is derived from pigs and pork is essentially unclean (*najis*). No. 7 points out that back in June of 1980, MUI had issued a fatwa specifying that all food and beverage adulterated by unclean materials was haram.[33]

It is only in Point 1 that the fatwa explains the process of LPPOM's on-site auditing, in which they found 'the original material poly peptone was replaced with bacto soytone (which contains pork enzyme) without reporting to LPPOM'. Point 2 briefly describes the fatwa meeting on 25 November, and Point 3 documents the visit of fatwa committee members to the factory in Mojokerto on 4 December, as well as that another meeting that was held on 9 December, in which they concluded that 'in order to cultivate bacteria for the subsequent production of MSG, the adulteration (*percampuran*) of gelatin, bacteria and the medium bacto soytone (which contains pork enzyme) took place'. The fatwa continues its list of applications:

> No. 1, The seasoning product (MSG) from Ajinomoto Indonesia, which utilises bacto soytone in the process of its production (*dalam proses produksinya*), is haram.
> No. 2, Whoever in the Islamic community consumed the MSG without knowing this should not feel guilty.
> No. 3, The Islamic community should be cautious in consuming any products that are suspected or forbidden by religion.
> No. 4, This decision is effective starting from 16 December 2000, or Islamic Year of 1421 Ramadan, and confirms that if in the future that this decision is wrong, it will be improved with all the knowledge available.

---

32 The term *syubhat* refers to the duty of the Muslim leaders or judges to seek the doubt (in Arabic *shubha*) before implementing any verdict.

33 Reminder No. 7 also mentions that MUI had issued another ruling in September of 1994, which specified that pigs and all their derivatives are haram. However, so far I have not been able to find the actual content of the fatwa. This fatwa was not included in the Halal Directory published by LPPOM MUI in 2015, where all of the 27 fatwas related to food, cosmetics, and drugs were compiled. Nor was it included anywhere else, except in this 2000 fatwa.

This fatwa is, to the best of my knowledge, the first time that MUI directly commented on the contamination *in the whole manufacturing process of a product.*

There were different opinions, of course. Many scientists, including a leading expert in detecting oil adulteration and an expert in detecting DNA fragments of meat species, both working at UGM, believed that the problematised MSG was halal, because there was absolutely no pork in it. In a plain language, it contains no trace of porcine DNA. In 2000, many scientists took the same stance. But this time, their opinion did not count. After all, the fact that the MSG in question did not contain any porcine material was already known to MUI, and the head of LPPOM, Aisjah Girindra, also commented to the press that while she knew that the MSG did not contain any pork, she respected the decision of the fatwa committee of MUI. So, it was definitely not out of confusion about the process of production, or out of ignorance, that the committee reached its conclusion.

More importantly, the static structure of something is never the only criterion on which to judge whether it is halal or not. The problem of contamination is always a dynamic process, which cannot be reduced to any static structure alone. The real question was, rather, how to judge contamination found in an indirect place (that is, far from the end product) both physically and chemically, such as in the position of the catalyst for bacteria growth needed for the production. This was a question that MUI scholars had not practiced their ijitihad and collectively dwelled on before.

After MUI's fatwa committee decided that the reformulated MSG was not halal and the decision was made public, national outrage and protests ensued in all major cities. The comment of Abdurrahman Wahid, the President of Indonesia then, only made the situation worse. Wahid told the press that based on his understanding of related laboratory research, the MSG of Ajinomoto was halal. Most media were unsympathetic to Wahid. Some accused the president of confusing the public, and the head of Jakarta police department clearly stated that the police would only follow MUI's judgement in order to help take subsequent actions.[34]

The issue was the cover story of *Tempo* magazine in January 2001. The government finally ordered the company to recall 3,000 tons of MSG, and the factory in East Java was temporarily closed until the company obtained a new halal certification. Five to six high-ranking managers of the company were held in custody by the police, and prosecutors initially asked for one of them to be sentenced to five years in prison for fraudulent advertising.

---

34 *Kompas*, 10 January 1989.

Ajinomoto completely cooperated with this decision and replaced the bacto soytone immediately. In February of 2001, after another on-site audit, MUI issued another fatwa. This fatwa's wording is virtually identical to the first one, except the last part, in which it specifies that the chemical components of the production process are different, and that now the enzyme is changed back to its original formulation. Ajinomoto MSG was halal again.

7 Halal Authentication and National Politics

The case of Ajinomoto MSG did not happen in a vacuum. Its political context should be addressed. The case took place during the presidency of Abdurrahman Wahid (1999–2001), a time period that Van Klinken characterises as the peak of mass ethno-religious violence in several provinces within the country[35] and Jacques Bertrand calls the 'critical juncture' after the fall of Suharto.[36] This was a difficult period when Indonesia's transition to democracy from three-decade authoritarian regime was complicated by a deep financial crisis as well as the institutional inheritance of the previous regime.

From the very beginning, Wahid's presidency was a result of negotiations between different Muslim parties, secular nationalist parties, the military, and other powerful figures from the former regime. Wahid was a Muslim democrat and a controversial figure for his theories about the merits of a secularised democracy for his country. He was an erudite religious scholar, a *ulama besar* or great Islamic leader, but also 'a most unlikely president' born from an 'unlikely coalition' that pushed him into the presidency.[37]

From the first months, Wahid's administration faced pressure from a hostile legislature dominated by individuals closely associated with New Order regime. Worse yet, Wahid became estranged from Megawati, the most important leader from the secular nationalist party PDI-P in the parliament, irritated the military, and disappointed numerous Muslim leaders with his conciliatory stance towards Israel. His frequent reshuffling of cabinet positions in an attempt to foster reform frustrated even his supporters. His relationship with parliament broke down, and hostile accusations of corruption against his administration followed. As soon as all the allegations had been dismissed for lack of evidence, the anti-Wahid campaign shifted the focus from corruption to incompetence.

---

35 Van Klinken, *Communal Violence and Democratisation in Indonesia: Small Town Wars*, 2007.

36 Bertrand, *Nationalism and Ethnic Conflict in Indonesia*, 2004.

37 Barton, 'Indonesia's Difficult Transition and President Abdurrahman Wahid', 273–274.

And for some observers, including Wahid himself, Ajinomoto was itself a part of the anti-Wahid campaign.[38] Indeed, some political analysis suspected that the leak of the originally internal fatwa and the subsequent social unrest were all instigated to undermine Wahid's presidency. Wahid had had some conflicts with other MUI leaders, including those from NU, the very same organisation that Wahid had led for decades. While it is certainly plausible that some of the actions leading to the Ajinomoto scandal were connected to attempts to undermine Wahid, I do not have the kind of data to prove this is the case.

Whether the conspiracy theory was true or not, it does not affect the fact that a paradigm shift had occurred in the aftermath of the Ajinomoto Case. Hence, regardless of the actual causes behind the way that the case was disclosed, at least five socio-political effects can be observed:

1. In terms of religious authority, LPPOM and MUI had, perhaps unexpectedly, gained unprecedented legitimacy to determine whether a product was halal or not. In fact, MUI's decision was more important than President Wahid's opinion that the MSG in question was halal. This means that a greater degree of institutionalisation of the ruling of halalness has triumphed over the diverse nature of different opinions among religious scholars.
2. The religious authority that MUI acquired has direct economic consequences. The development of the Ajinomoto case has made it clear that any multinational corporation, especially those selling popular items, need the examination of LPPOM and the final approval of MUI in order to claim their halalness. Otherwise, a company could face financial loss or even legal prosecution.
3. In the realm of public knowledge, the case made the public more aware of the whole procedure of certification. Even after a product obtains halal certification, the certificate is only valid for two years and is subject to reexamination if it is to be renewed. Regular application and consistent compliance to the halal regulation is required, and this is ensured by auditing.
4. Halal authentication was further politicised and subject to further regulation. The case became a pretext for later attempts at legislating the Halal Act, the first of which took place in 2006. The negotiations among parliament members were mostly not open to the public, and as late as 2011, most of the factions within the parliament disapproved of a Halal Act that

38 See *Kompas*, 10 January 1989.

would make halal certification an obligation for all products in Indonesia. Yet, perhaps shockingly to many, in 2014 the Act was passed, and it appeared that the disagreement among members of the parliament was about who should be in charge of the new halal assurance system (the government or MUI), no longer whether the Act was necessary.

5. Finally, a paradigmatic shift in the semiotics of halal labelling took place. At least theoretically, no item should claim to be halal unless certified and regularly examined. The situation was a stark contrast with that of 12 years earlier, when MUI held the opinion that before an item was found haram, it should be considered halal.

In sum, legitimacy now is on the side of halal certification, although some anti-halal sentiments can be felt among Muslims, and especially among the non-Muslim population. More and more companies apply for certificates from LPPOM. From 2005 to 2011 MUI has already issued 5,896 certificates. The desire to obtain halal certificates for daily products has grown steadily. In 2014 alone, MUI issued 68,576 certificates.[39] In 2018 the number jumped to 204,222. This should be the consequence of the new law that takes effect in 2019.

In order to deal with the large amount of applications, LPPOM started to operate its own office and laboratory independently in 2012. Well before 2014, any convenience store in Indonesia would have a collection of hundreds of products labelled Halal and MUI. This situation is remarkably different from the one in the late 1980s, when Professor Tri Soesanto published his report. When Soesanto died in 2011, he was remembered by the newspaper *Republika* as a pioneer of halal certification, who combined religion and science. The once 'subversive' scientist was now an insightful 'ulama'.[40]

8 Tentative Conclusion

The neo-conservative turn of Indonesia is now a commonplace on global media. This certainly concerns many, but it should not be seen as the only factor for the institutionalisation of halal certification and the Halal Act. As the other origin story demonstrated above, the process is an outcome of historical contingencies and of complicated negotiations among multiple actors. The birth of scientific halal certification and its further institutionalisation is a complex

39 Please see http://www.halalmui.org/mui14/index.php/main/go_to_section/59/1368/page/1 last retrieved 8 August 2019.

40 *Republika*, 1 December 2011.

response to a series of food scandals, new food technology, long-term ethno-religious tensions, and religious authority in unprecedented domain, as well as parliamentary politics. Neither a natural Muslim desire nor simply rising religious conservatism, halal authentication in Indonesia is always already a socio-material process in which technoscience and ethno-religious politics have played an important role.

Acknowledgement

This chapter is part of my research project funded by Taiwan's Ministry of Science and Technology. I owe much gratitude to Pak Ni'am from MUI, as well as Ibu Muti, Ibu Tizza, and Pak Heryani from LPPOM MUI. I am grateful for the help of Pak Abdul, Pak Yuny, and Ibu Endang from UGM. Many thanks go to my research assistant Tsung Jen Hung and Syuan-Li Renn for collecting and organising the research data. Special thanks to two anonymous reviewers in 2019 and another anonymous reviewer in 2020 for their advice.

Bibliography

Anggara, Fajar Surya Ari. 2017. 'Development of Indonesia Halal Agroindustry Global Market in ASEAN: Strategic Assesment'. *Al Tijarah* 3, no. 1: 65–78.

Awan, Hayat M., Ahmad Nabeel Siddiquei, and Zeeshan Haider. 2015. 'Factors Affecting Halal Purchase Intention—Evidence from Pakistan's Halal Food Sector'. *Management Research Review* 38, no. 6: 640–660.

Aziz, Yuhanis Abdul, and Nyen Vui Chok. 2013. 'The Role of Halal Awareness, Halal Certification, and Marketing Components in Determining Halal Purchase Intention among Non-Muslims in Malaysia: A Structural Equation Modeling Approach'. *Journal of International Food & Agribusiness Marketing* 25, no. 1: 1–23.

Barton, Greg. 2001. 'Indonesia's Difficult Transition and President Abdurrahman Wahid'. *Pacifica Review: Peace, Security & Global Change* 13, no. 3: 273–281.

Batu, Ali, Joe M. Regenstein, And Ismail Sait Dogan. 2015. 'Gelatin Issues in Halal Food Processing for Muslim Societies'. *Electronic Turkish Studies* 10, no. 14.

Bergeaud-Blackler, Florence. 2015. 'The Halal Certification Market in Europe and the World: A First Panorama'. In *Halal Matters: Islam, Politics, and Markets in Global Perspectives*, edited by Florence Bergeaud-Blackler, Johan Fischer, and John Lever, 105–126. London & New York: Routledge.

Bertrand, Jacques. 2004. *Nationalism and Ethnic Conflict in Indonesia*. Cambridge: Cambridge University Press.

Chao, En-Chieh. 2018. 'Halal Stunning: A Techno-moral History of Animal Welfare and

Islamic Slaughter'. *Taiwanese Journal for Studies of Science, Technology and Medicine* 26: 7–54 [趙恩潔. 2018. '清真的電擊: 關於動物福利與伊斯蘭屠宰的一段道德技術史'. 科技醫療與社會, no. 26: 7–54].
Djagnya, Kodjo Boady, Zhang Wang, and Shiying Xu. 2010. 'Gelatin: A Valuable Protein for Food and Pharmaceutical Industries: Review'. *Critical Reviews in Food Science and Nutrition* 41, no. 6: 481–492.
Farhan, Fikri and Yuli Andriansyah. 2016. 'Factors Affecting Muslim Students Awareness of Halal Products in Yogyakarta, Indonesia'. *International Review of Management and Marketing* 6, no. 4S: 27–31.
Farouk, Mustafa M. 2013. 'Advances in the Industrial Production of Halal and Kosher Red Meat'. *Meat Science* 95, no. 4: 805–820.
Fischer, Johan. 2008. 'Religion, Science and Markets'. *EMBO Reports* 9, no. 9: 828–831.
Fischer, Johan. 2015. *Islam, Standards, and Technoscience: In Global Halal Zones*. London: Routledge.
Grim, Brian J. and Mehtab S. Karim. 2011. 'The Future of the Global Muslim Population: Projections for 2010–2030'. Washington DC: Pew Research Center.
Hosen, Nadirsyah. 2004. 'Behind the Scenes: Fatwas of Majelis Ulama Indonesia (1975–1998)'. *Journal of Islamic Studies* 15, no. 2: 147–179.
Ichwan, Moch Nur. 2005. ''Ulamā', State and Politics: Majelis Ulama Indonesia After Suharto'. *Islamic Law and Society* 12, no. 1: 45–72.
Ichwan, Moch Nur. 2013. 'Towards a Puritanical Moderate Islam: The Majelis Ulama Indonesia and the Politics of Religious Orthodoxy'. In *Contemporary Developments in Indonesian Islam: Explaining the 'Conservative Turn'*, edited by Martin van Bruinessen, 60–104. Singapore: ISEAS.
Jasanoff Sheila, Wynne Brian. 1998. 'Science and Decision-making'. In *Human Choice and Climate Change: Vol. 1, the Social Framework*, edited by Rayner S. Malone, 1–87. Columbus: Battelle Press.
Rasyid, Tengku Harunur. 2010. 'Raising the Awareness of Halal Products among Indonesian Consumers: Issues and Strategies'. *Indonesian Journal of Agricultural Economics* 1, no. 1: no page numbers.
Rudnyckyj, Daromir. 2014. 'Economy in Practice: Islamic Finance and the Problem of Market Reason'. *American Ethnologist* 41, no. 1: 110–127.
Van Klinken, Gerry. 2007. *Communal Violence and Democratisation in Indonesia: Small Town Wars*. London: Routledge.

Indonesian Language References

Kasali, Rhenald. 1997. *Sembilan Fenomena Bisnis*. Gramedia Pustaka Utama.
Kasali, Rhenald. 2013. *Re-Code Your Change DNA*. Gramedia Pustaka Utama.
Ni'am, Soleh, Asrorun. 2016. *Metodologi Penetapan Fatwa Majelis Ulama Indonesia: Penggunaan Prinsip Pencegahan dalam Fatwa*. Jakarta: Emir.

Newspapers/News Magazines/Web Contents

Mochammad Agus Krisno Budiyanto, and Dr M. Kes. in Kajian Mikrobiologi Industri. 2011. 'Proses Produksi MSG (Monosodium Glutamat)'. *Pondok Ilmu* (blog), 2011 January 7, available at https://aguskrisnoblog.wordpress.com/2011/01/07/proses-produksi-msg-monosodium-glutamat/ (accessed 2019 July 14).

PART 2

Halal Certification: New Interpretations in Critical Perspective

CHAPTER 7

Halal Certification, Standards, and Their Ramifications in Belgium

Ayang Utriza Yakin

1 Introduction

Contrary to the practice in Muslim majority countries, where halal certification is closely associated with state institutions in charge of religious affairs,[1] in Muslim minority countries it is governed by private organisations commonly referred to as halal certification bodies (HCBs). Prior to the global expansion of the halal market in recent decades, Muslim importers simply demanded that European countries complied with shariʿa law and set up specific Islamic processes in their factories.[2] Today, HCBs play a central role in halal certification, both locally and regionally. Accordingly, one needs to study HCBs closely, because they are as much a blind spot in understanding halal itself as they are a key to the development of the halal system in a Muslim minority context.[3]

In this chapter I focus on HCBs in Belgium, addressing issues of certification and standards, their ramifications, and the neglect of the pluriversality of halal and of Islamic religious authority in a non-Muslim country. To date, there have been few studies of HCB in Belgium,[4] let alone of halal standards and cer-

1 In Malaysia and Singapore, the State institutions, through JAKIM (Jabatan Kemajuan Islam Malaysia) in 1982 and MUIS (Majelis Ugama Islam Singapura) in 1978, have taken on the role of halal certification since its inception, while in Indonesia since 1989 LPPOM-MUI (Lembaga Pengkajian-Pangan, Obat-Obatan, dan Kosmetika, Majelis Ulama Indonesia) has had special status as a non-governmental body (receiving government funding). However, based on Law No. 33/2014 on Halal Products Guarantees, the certification process in Indonesia is organised by the State. These countries have certified, standardised, and bureaucratised halal production, trade, and consumption: Fischer, *Islam, Standards, and Technoscience in Global Halal Zones*, 13–14.

2 Bergeaud-Blackler, 'The Halal Certification Market in Europe and the World: A First Panorama', 105–107.

3 Bergeaud-Blackler, *Le Marché Halal ou l'invention d'une tradition*, 245.

4 Felice Dassetto presented very briefly some halal certification bodies in Belgium, *L'iris et le croissant: Bruxelles et l'Islam au défi de la co-inclusion*, 111–118, while Bergeaud-Blackler did not even mention Belgium as a country where HCBs exist in her chapter on the halal certi-

 | DOI:10.1163/9789004459236_008

tification and their consequences. The scholarly literature has only focused on halal/ritual slaughtering in Belgium and its legal aspect, on halal meat production, quality control and marketing, and on the motives and factors regarding the consumption of halal food/products.[5] I will fill this gap by exploring how halal has been continually normalised and standardised through modern rationality and certification practices that have arguably used halal as a means of regulating the everyday lives of Muslims.[6]

Certification is the provision by an independent body or third party, through an assessment or audit, of a written assurance that the product, service, or system in question meets specific requirements.[7] For several reasons, halal certification is the most significant transformation in the halal market over the last two decades, since around the year 2000. First, a range of food scandals boosted calls for certification and led to the introduction of proper certification.[8] Second, industries need to understand halal norms in order to make

fication market in Europe, Bergeaud-Blackler, 'The Halal Certification Market in Europe and the World: A First Panorama', 105–126.

5 Panafit, *Quand le droit écrit l'Islam: lintégration juridique de l'Islam en Belgique*, 1999; Bonne and Verbeke, 'Muslim consumer's motivations towards meat consumption in Belgium: qualitative exploratory insights from means-end chain analysis', 2006; Bonne, 'Halal Meat Consumption Decision-Making among Muslim Consumers in Belgium', 2007; Bazgour, 'Etude du marché de la viande halal en Belgique', 2007; Bonne and Verbeke, 'Muslim Consumer Trust in Halal Meat Status and Control in Belgium', 2008; Bonne, Vermeir, and Verbeke, 'Impact of Religion on Halal Meat Consumption Decision Making in Belgium', 2008; Bernard and Bergeaud-Blackler, *Comprendre le Halal*, 2010; Torrekens, 'L'introduction du halal dans les écoles communales: entre visibilité de l'islam, reconnaissance et "neutralité" de l'espace public', 2012; Laroussi, 'Le marché du halal en Belgique', 2012; Verbeke, Rutsaert, Bonne, and Vermeir, 'Credence Quality Coordination and Consumers' Willingness-to-pay for Certified Halal Labeled Meat', 2013; Aboutayeb, 'Ethnomarketing et la marché halal en Belgique: quelle est la perception du consommateur belge non-musulman vis-à-vis du produit halal?', 2013; Velarde et al., 'Religious Slaughtering: Evaluation of Current Practices in Selected Countries' 2014; Torrekens, *Belgo-Marocains, Belgo-Turcs: (auto-portrait) de nos concitoyens*, 2015; Sekkat, 'Potential and Analysis of the Halal Meat Chain in Belgium', 2015; Istasse, 'Green Halal: à la recherché d' un halal éthique', 2015; Yakin and Rahmani, *"Halal Food Consumption among the Indonesian Muslim Minority in Belgium,"* 2018.

6 I am influenced by the concept of *Dia-ethnoghraphy* from Paul Rabinow (1996) that is: 'to investigate about the invention of 'new' techniques, practices, sites, objects, and subjects and to reflect on how 'new' these things actually were'.

7 https://www.iso.org/certification.html, (accessed 28 March 2019).

8 The increased awareness of halal products and the necessity of halal certification and its logos on every product in Indonesia pertained to the issue of pork derivative in some food products in the mid-1980s and the *adjinomoto* affairs in the early 1990s. Since then, the halal certification label from the MUI has been 'almost' compulsory for companies and factories to ensure the halalness of product and render it consumable. In the European context, a range of food scandals had recourse to the certification. For instance, Muslims discovered beef meat con-

their products suitable for 'religious' consumers. Third, food and product markets and industries expanded farther and faster in the globalised world. As a result, third-party certification and inspection by HCBs became increasingly important[9] in order to ensure that production, quality, safety, and manufacturing processes conform with appropriate standards.[10]

A standard is a technical document designed to be used as a rule, guideline, or definition. It is a consensus-built, repeatable way of doing something.[11] It is established by a recognised body aimed at achieving the optimum degree of order in a given context.[12] Industries and companies need a standard for compatibility, quality, optimisation, and measurement.[13] Stefan Timmermans and Steven Epstein wrote that 'standards and standardisation aim to render the world equivalent across cultures, times and geography for regulating and organising social life'.[14] Standards and standardisation are clearly linked to modernity.[15] In relation to halal, industrialisation drives the process of standardisation through which halal norms are changed alongside the homogenisation of the capitalist world, the bureaucratisation of modern life, and the processes of rationalisation manifest throughout, all of which are characteristic of modernity.[16] In fact, modernity supplants reason as an overarching norm, legitimising and at the same time dominating political, social, cultural, and scientific symbols, and replacing God and religious leaders with scientific principles. In this context, the natural sciences (quantification and scientific

---

taining pork imported from Germany in the early 2000s, in Anvers, Belgium, in some kebab restaurants claiming to be halal; interview with GvT, Antwerp, 13 May 2017.

9 Lever and Fischer, *Kosher and Halal Business Compliance*, 19.

10 However, according to En-Chieh Chao, in New Zealand, the government worked together with meat scientists, meat merchants, and religious scholars in order to export the first frozen meat to Iran and later to Arab countries. Therefore, for Chao, the mass standardisation had already occurred in the 1990s, but only for meat. The Southeast Asian certification development is different because it is being applied to many different products beyond meat; Chao, 'Halal Stunning: A Techno-Moral History of Animal Welfare and Islamic Slaughter', 7–54 (in Chinese). I thank her for making a summary in English for me.

11 This definition is according to CEN or the European Committee for Standardization, see https://www.cen.eu/work/ENdev/whatisEN/Pages/default.aspx (accessed 15 April 2019).

12 Hatto, *Standards and Standardization Handbook*, 5.

13 Hatto, *Standards and Standardization Handbook*, 5–6.

14 Timmermans and Epstein, 'A World of Standards but not a Standard World: Toward a Sociology of Standards and Standardization', 71.

15 Timmermans and Epstein, 'A World of Standards but not a Standard World', 72.

16 Marx and Engels, *Manifesto of the Communist Party*, 469–500; Weber, *From Max Weber: Essays in Sociology*, ch. 8 on Bureaucracy; Timmermans and Epstein, 'A World of Standards but not a Standard World', 72.

method), philosophy, and the social sciences have pursued standardisation and specialisation as a means of legitimising authority.[17]

Johan Fischer shows that the emergence and expansion of standardisation and certification was built on the successful intersection of Islamic regulations with scientific technologies and global trade.[18] Halal certification is the consequence of halal standards produced essentially by Southeast Asian Muslim countries.[19] The integration of global markets with industry, together with the findings of scientific research, and the approval of religious authorities in Malaysia, Indonesia, Singapore, Brunei, the Philippines, and Thailand have driven the proliferation of halal certification.[20] These standards profoundly influence the global halal market, including in non-Muslim countries like Belgium and across the Western world. Indeed, companies and industries need halal standards because the state, particularly in Europe, does not regulate halal. When the state does not exert any regulation, standards become important; in this case, for halal.[21]

In Islam, full authority belongs to God, and God alone, through the Quran, decides what is halal or not. This authority was delegated to the Prophet Muhammad, who explained more broadly what halal is and listed its categories and criteria in his sayings and traditions (the hadith and Sunna).[22] The Prophet's companions (*ṣahāba*) transmitted their recollection of his words (*hadīth*) and deeds (*sunna*) to the next generation (*tābiʿīn*), who passed it on to the next (*tābiʿ al-tābiʿīn*) and so forth, and whoever learnt what the Prophet said and did acquired religious authority. Those people who owe their authority entirely to their learning came to be known as the 'ulama', the scholars or religious authority.[23] Based on these fundamental Islamic sources (the Quran and hadith), the 'ulama' have the right to interpret and decide what is or is not halal. In fact, the 'ulama' have long been regarded as a religious authority that sets Islamic norms and standards. However, the practice of halal certification by HCBs in Belgium transfers this traditional authority from the 'ulama' to sci-

17 Porter, *Trust in Numbers. The Pursuit of Objectivity in Science and Public Life*, 1995; Shapin and Schaffer, *Leviathan and the Air-Pump. Hobbes, Boyle, and the Experimental Life*, 1985.

18 Fischer, *Islam, Standards, and Technoscience in Global Halal Zones*, 7.

19 Fischer, *Islam, Standards, and Technoscience in Global Halal Zones*, 8; Armanios and Ergene, *Halal Food: A History*, 133, 297, n. 80.

20 Lever and Fischer, *Religion, Regulation, Consumption: Globalising Kosher and Halal Markets*, 7–9; ethnography notes in 2017 with HCBs in Belgium; Armanios and Ergene, *Halal Food: A History*, 133, 297, n. 80.

21 Brunsson and Jacobson, *A World of Standards*, 32.

22 Kadi, 'Authority', 188–190.

23 Crone and Hinds, *God's Caliph: Religious Authority in the First Centuries of Islam*, 1–2.

entists and professionals. In other words, once halal norms are standardised in Muslim majority countries, the associated standards are then appropriated by HCBs in non-Muslim countries, such as Belgium. Afterwards, HCBs modify these standards for their own purposes based on local and regional contexts and interests. Through the halal certification process in Belgium, this practice has gradually transformed religious authority and threatens what I call the pluriversality of halal.

The concept of pluriversality is 'a vision of a world in which many worlds coexist', according Walter D. Mignolo,[24] thus acknowledging all internal diversity and views on halal in Islam and its practice among Muslims. Clearly, there are many definitions, ideas, and opinions of halal that characterise Sunni orthodoxy, and the practices of halal by which Muslims live rely on what they understand to be halal. The pluriversality of halal thus makes it impossible for the state, corporations, companies, and certification bodies to decide what is halal or not, as Mignolo wrote, '[the] pluriverse exists independently of the state and corporation'.[25] Standards and certification consequently threaten the richness of the understanding and practice of halal. The pluriversality of halal refuses standards, certifications, and all forms of intrusion by corporations. At the same time, it respects views and practices that differ from the dominant standards, to prevent a monolithic understanding and practice of halal. In fact, pluriversality defends the right to be different and to live with a diversity of views.[26] Timmermans and Epstein wrote that 'standard and standardisation have specific and unintended consequences of different sorts of standards operating in distinct social domains'.[27] Two of the consequences of standards, through the certification process, are the shift of the religious authority from the 'ulama' to HCBs and the neglect of the diversity of opinions within Sunni orthodoxy and of halal practices among all Muslims.

This study is based on extensive fieldwork in Belgium during 2017–2019, involving in-depth interviews with HCBs,[28] participant observation, and interviews with Imams in Muslim communities and with Muslim organisations. First, I will briefly address Islamic history, the certification of the HCBs in Belgium and their legal aspects. Second, I turn to the issue of the standards/standardisation and certification process by the HCBs, and propose that this should be read as a modern way of harmonising Islamic tradition with national eco-

24 Mignolo, 'Foreword: On Pluriversality and Multipolarity', x.
25 Mignolo, 'Foreword: On Pluriversality and Multipolarity', xii.
26 Mignolo, *The Darker Side of Western Modernity*, 234–235.
27 Timmermans and Epstein, 'A World of Standards but not a Standard World', 70.
28 See Appendix for more about 17 HCBs in Belgium.

nomic interests and international business standards. Finally, I argue that this mode of halal certification has consequences, marginalising the traditional ʿulama' and paving the way for a gradual shift in authority towards HCBs, which become a new authority and also a moral agent. From a Foucauldian perspective,[29] HCBs become an authority that registers, audits, decides, and regulates what is and is not acceptable, what is right or wrong, what is in conformity with norms and standards and what is not. Thus, certification practices deny pluriversal halal opinions in Sunni Islam and the range of halal practices among all Muslims.

2 Islam, Certification, and HCBs in Belgium

Historically, Islam in Belgium is related to the history of Muslim immigration.[30] The presence of Muslims was, in fact, an indirect consequence of the French colonisation of North Africa in 1910,[31] after which Muslims began to arrive 'illegally' in Belgium to take underpaid work in coal mines. Between the two World Wars (1918–1939) they lived in squalid conditions in some of the country's worst housing and poorest communities.[32] No official demographic data exist, but the statistical report of the Turkish council in Antwerp, Ismail Hakki Bey Tevfik, reveals that in 1928 there were 5,751 Muslims within Belgium's total population of 7,874.601.[33] Note that, in the early 1940s, Moroccan (and also Algerian and other African) soldiers fought for Belgium, which supported France against the German Nazi invasion; 2,250 Moroccans died at the Battle of Gembloux on 11–13 May 1940 and all Muslim casualties were buried in the public cemetery of Cortil Noirmont (Chastre).[34]

---

29 Foucault, *Surveiller et Punir: Naissance de la prison*, 229.

30 Dassetto and Bastenier, *L'Islam transplanté: vie et organisation des minorités musulmanes de Belgique*, 1984; Dassetto, *Facettes de l'Islam belge*, 1997; Dassetto, *Migration, sociétés et politiques Belgique, Europe et les nouveaux défis*, 2001, for a thorough explanation about the history of Islam in Belgium, see Torrekens, *Islams de Belgique: Enjeux et Perspective*, 2020.

31 Bousetta and Maréchal, *L'islam et les musulmans en Belgique: Enjeux locaux et cadres de réflexion globaux*, 7.

32 Panafit, *Quand le droit écrit l'Islam: l'intégration juridique de l'Islam en Belgique*, 15; Attar, 'Historique de l'Immigration maghrébine en Belgique', 291–292.

33 This information was published originally in *Der Islam*, 1928, t. 18, pp. 319–320, which was translated from German into French by Professor Yahya Michot, Michot, 'Les musulmans de Belgique en 1928', 33.

34 Attar, 'Historique de l'Immigration maghrébine en Belgique', 293–295; Labarre and François, *Gloire et sacrifices du 2e RTM; Gembloux mai 1940*, 1990.

The situation shifted dramatically after 1945, with immigrants coming from Muslim countries to Belgian soil in a more 'legal' way. At the end of the 1950s, Belgian universities had accepted approximately ten Muslim students. At the same time, Muslim refugees from Albania were given exile status in Belgium.[35] In the 1960s, Belgium opened its borders to immigrants from Muslim countries. On 18 August 1964, Belgium signed a bilateral agreement with Morocco and Turkey, on 7 August 1969 with Tunisia, and finally on 8 January 1970 with Algeria. In fact, Belgium needed more people because of its own ageing population, and this led to the introduction of a family reunification policy.[36] Between 1961 and 1977, 95,000 immigrants arrived from North African countries, the majority Moroccans (80,867), half of whom were women.[37] The data quantifying Belgium's Muslim population shows that in 2002 there were 370,000 Muslims in the country (3.7 per cent of the total population), a figure that had risen to about 450,000 by 2011 (4 per cent).[38] According to sociologist Jan Hertogen, by 2015 Belgium had a Muslim population of 781,887.[39] This huge increase, from around 5,000 in 1928 to almost 800,000 (7 per cent) in 2015, has influenced and accentuated the discourse on Islam and its practices, including halal consumption.

In 1974, Belgium became the first European country after World War II to officially recognise Islam as a religion. Islam was inserted into chapter three of the Law of 4 March 1870 on religion and cults, after Protestantism, Anglicanism, and Judaism,[40] with the later addition of Christian Orthodoxy and Laicism. Immediately after this official recognition of Islam, the Belgian government supported the creation of the Centre for Islam and Culture of Belgium (Centre Islamique et culturel de belgique: CICB) as a 'temporary' official intermediary between Muslim communities and the state. In 1975, the CICB took over the appointment of teachers within Islam.[41] In 1978, the Great Mosque of CICB

35 Renaerts, 'L'historique de l'Islam en Belgique et la problématique de sa reconnaissance', 53.

36 Martiniello and Rea, 'Une brève histoire de l'immigration en Belgique', 17–22; Attar, 'Historique de l'Immigration maghrébine en Belgique', 291–292; Bayar, 'Un aperçu économique de l'immigration turque, in Morelli', 311–328.

37 Attar, 'Historique de l'Immigration maghrébine en Belgique', 291–292, 297.

38 Djelloul and Maréchal, 'Muslims in Western Europe in the late Twentieth Century: Emergence and Transformations in 'Muslim' Revindications and Collective Mobilization Efforts', 87.

39 http://www.sudinfo.be/1580627/article/2016-05-24/781887-musulmans-vivent-en-belgique-decouvrez-la-carte-commune-par-commune (accessed 28 May 2018).

40 Loi du 19 juillet 1974 portant reconnaissance des administrations chargées de la gestion du temporel du culte islamique, *Moniteur belge* 23 August 1974.

41 Sägesser and Torrekens, *La Répresentation de l'Islam*, 7–9.

was inaugurated and in the same year Islamic religion began to be taught in schools by Royal Decree, as a compulsory course for Muslim students.[42] However, from the beginning the question of halal was not among the CICB's priorities, although the inception of halal 'certification',[43] uniquely for meat, was set out by the CICB in the 1970s in an 'informal' way, intended solely to ensure Islamic slaughtering.[44]

Halal consumption and butchers' shops emerged as an 'important subject' in the Muslim community[45] in the 1980s.[46] The question of halal certification in Belgium largely concerns the export of Belgian meat to a Muslim country, where the Islamic method of slaughtering and meat processing must be guaranteed and respected. According to Felice Dassetto, the question arose particularly in Gembloux, where investors from Arab countries had created a state-of-the-art slaughtering facility for the export of Walloon cattle to the Gulf countries.[47] The company was mismanaged and unprofessional. It went bankrupt and the slaughterhouse was dismantled.[48] It seems that this situation continued in the 1990s when the Islamic Association for the Student and Youth of BENELUX (Belgium, the Netherlands, and Luxembourg), in cooperation with an Egyptian businessperson and a Moroccan veterinarian, was asked to 'certify' and to stamp 'halal' using the logo of a halal slaughtering association for a slaughterhouse in Arlon for exports to the Emirates and Kuwait. The Islamic Association stopped cooperating because of a lack of transparency regarding the two individuals concerned.[49] However, the 1970s to 1990s can be defined as the first period of halal certification in Belgium. It was marked by several peculiarities. First, it was driven by international exports, and only to the Arab world. Second, it applied solely to meat products. Third, the 'certific-

42 El Asri and Maréchal, 'Islam belge en mouvement: quelques cadrages de réalités complexes', 11.

43 The term 'certification' here, in the first period (1970s–1990s) does not imply the following of a specific standard with rigid assessment.

44 Interview in French with Dr Abdul Jawwad Ouazzani, head of the halal department at the CICB in 2013–2014, Brussels, 14 February 2017.

45 Interview in French with Mohamed Saïd Guermit, member of the Conseil Supérieur des musulmans de Belgique (CSMB) and President-Founder of the political party Mouvement pour l'Education (MEP), Louvain-la-Neuve, 20 January 2017.

46 Djelloul and Maréchal, 'Muslims in Western Europe in the Late Twentieth Century', 89, 91.

47 Dassetto, *L'Iris et le Croissant*, 114.

48 Until the early 2000s the Islamic slaughterhouse was still active, as attested by AB, interview in French, Louvain-la-Neuve, 13 January 2017.

49 Interview in Arabic with Shaykh Abdulkarim al-Dawoudia, ex-president of the 'Ittihād al-Islāmiyy li al-Ṭalaba wa al-Shabāb', in the 1990s, Brussels, 17 June 2017.

ation' was performed in an 'informal'[50] way, without following any particular standards. Fourth, it was not handled by a professional third party, but merely by the Great Mosque of Brussels or the CICB[51] or an Islamic organisation. Fifth, there was no demand for halal certification for meat from Belgian Muslims at the national level, because they were still able to slaughter cattle and poultry by themselves until the end of the 1980s,[52] when this became prohibited by law.[53]

In Belgium, as in many EU countries, there is no specific legislation on halal matters, and the focus is on animal protection and slaughtering. Religious slaughter (in an Islamic way/halal) is regulated under the Law of 14 August 1986, which deals with animal protection and animal welfare, and prohibits ritual slaughtering by individuals. Ritual slaughtering can only be carried out in slaughterhouses by approved slaughterers. This law was modified by the Law of 4 May 1995 and the Royal Decrees of 13 July 1988 (authorising slaughterhouses to perform ritual slaughtering on Sundays and holidays) and 16 January 1998 (modified by the Royal Decree of 5 October 2006), on the obligation of stunning before slaughtering, except for ritual slaughtering. The situation changed completely when the Flanders[54] and Walloon[55] governments issued a prohibition against slaughter without stunning in 2017.[56] These new regulations modified Articles 3, 15 and 16 in the Law of 14 August 1986 on animal protection. Accord-

50 'Informal' here means it was conducted without any written document explaining the 'certification' process and was organised by an unregistered association.

51 Interview in French with Imam Shaykh Mustafa Kastit, Reponsible for Halal Affairs at the Great Mosque of the CICB 1997–2013, Brussels, 10 March 2017; Djelloul and Maréchal, 'Islam in Belgium', 2017.

52 Interview with Muslims living in Belgium since the early 1970s/early 1980s, in French with MS and BB, in Arabic with MB, Liège, 6 June 2017; in Arabic with IM and AM, in French with KA, Namur, 23 June 2017; in French with YB, Louvain-la-Neuve, 15 February 2017 and 5 May 2017, in Arabic with Abdulkarim al-Daouadi, Brussels, 17 June 2017.

53 However, the practice continued in secret into the 1990s, so they did not need to visit Islamic butchers; interview in Moroccan Arabic with MB, Liège, 6 June 2017.

54 Issued on 7 July 2017 and in force from 1 January 2019, *Moniteur belge/Belgisch Staatsblad*, 18 July 2017.

55 Issued on 18 May 2017 and in force from 1 September 2019, *Moniteur belge/Belgisch Staatsblad*, 1 June 2017.

56 The Wallonia text is as follows: '[…] Lorsque la mise à mort d' animaux fait l' objet de méthodes particulières d' abattage prescrites par des rites religieux, le procédé d' étourdissement doit être réversible et ne peut entraîner la mort de l' animal', while the Flemish text '[…] Als dieren worden geslacht volgens speciale methoden die vereist zijn voor religieuze riten, is de bedwelming omkeerbaar en is de dood van het dier niet het gevolg van de bedwelming'.

ingly, reversible stunning pre-slaughter (head-only stunning, which requires that an animal be bled within 15 to 23 seconds) is mandatory for religious rites.[57]

Halal emerged in public discourse in Belgian media[58] and society[59] only from the early 2000s, for reasons related to both local and global contexts. First, the number of Islamic butchers boomed in Belgium as a consequence of increasing demand from a growing Muslim population[60] and the prohibition against personal ritual slaughtering and slaughtering outside approved slaughterhouses.[61] Second, the Executive of the Belgian Muslims (l'Exécutif des musulmans de Belgique: EMB), created officially in 1996,[62] and active from 1998 as the official representation of Muslims, replaced the CICB.[63] The EMB was considered the principal agent for halal certification,[64] like the CICB, even though this was not its role.[65] In fact, the government advised that 'halal certification' should be handled as a source of income for the EMB,[66] which caused debate in the media. Third, halal issues became a 'trend making news' in Belgium, following the rise of Islamophobia after the 9/11 attack on the

57 The Jewish and Muslim associations pleaded before the Belgian Constitutional Court in Brussels against the decrees of the Walloon and Flemish regions prohibiting slaughter without stunning. The Court of Justice of the European Union has not contested these two decisions so far. The Belgian Constitutional Court submitted a new question to the European Court of Justice a few months ago to rule on this issue. The matter remains ongoing at the time of writing.

58 For instance, the piece entitled 'Les Nouveaux adeptes d'Allah', by Eve-Marie Vaes and Catherine Callico, appeared in *Le Soir*, 5 January 2001, https://www.lesoir.be/art/les-nouveaux-adeptes-d-allah-point-de-vue-a-la-recherch_t-20010105-Z0K3KD.html (accessed 4 March 2018).

59 Interviews with many Belgian Muslims in Brussels, Antwerp, Namur, Liège, Charleroi, Leuven, Brugge, Gent, and Louvain-la-Neuve, during fieldwork in 2017–2018. Furthermore, halal became a topic of daily conversation in Namur only from the 2010s onward; interview in French with KA, on 23 June 2017.

60 See explanation *supra*: on demography.

61 The consequence of the implementation of the Law of 16 August 1986 on the protection of animals and animal welfare.

62 This recognition was formalised by the Royal Decree of 3 July 1996 concerning the Executive of the Belgian Muslims, *Moniteur belge/Belgisch Staatsblad*, 9 July 1996.

63 Sägesser and Torrekens, *La Répresentation de l'Islam*, 13–18.

64 The Muslim communities hope that the EMB will take up a role as a central body for halal certification in Belgium, interview in French, Christine Vrancken, the owner and manager of the online site 'Halal Belgium', in Louvain-la-Neuve, 3 January 2017.

65 Dasetto, *L'Iris et le Croissant*, 115.

66 Interview in French with Salah Echallaoui, the President of EMB (Exécutive des Musulmans de Belgique), Brussels, 24 February 2017; with Saïd Guermit, 20 January 2017.

World Trade Center in New York.[67] The US 'war' against (Islamic) terrorism aroused public curiosity in Belgium to know more about Islam,[68] including the phenomenon of halal. Fourth, the 2000s witnessed the acceptance of standards produced by the Southeast Asian Muslim countries, such as Malaysia, Indonesia, Singapore, Philippines, Thailand, and Brunei, as the expansion of the global halal market pushed companies and enterprises in non-Muslim countries to resort to certification,[69] which led to the mushrooming of HCBs as a third party in Belgium. In fact, the development of halal issues in Belgium is part of the *glocalisation* problem—the dynamic exchange between global and local.[70] The relationship between the local and global contexts is complex and in a constant, active dialogue. Halal certification in Belgium now entered what I call the second period, from the beginning of 2000 up till today. It was marked mainly by the role of the HCB as a third party, working in a professional way and following the required standards of halal certification in order to be transparent and accepted by the market.

Halal certification bodies (HCBs) in Belgium are regulated under the Law of ASBL, or 'association sans but lucrative' (non-profit organisation/NPO), implemented on 27 June 1921, which was modified by the Law of 2 May 2002 (effective 1 January 2006).[71] Hence, HCBs in Belgium have NPO status and are registered legally by the Federal Ministry of Justice (at *moniteur belge/belgisch staatsbladds*) under the Tribunal of Commerce. In 2018, there were approximately 150,247 NPOs in Belgium.[72] The first Article of the ASBL (NPO) Law 1921/2002 states that NPOs should not engage in industrial or commercial operations nor seek to provide their members with material profits. This article is a fundamental change, allowing ASBL/NPOs to engage in commercial activities, such as social entrepreneurship, where part of the profits should be allocated for social

67 Lever and Miele, 'The Growth of Halal Meat Markets in Europe: An Exploration of the Supply Side Theory of Religion', 2012.

68 Interview in French with MB, Namur, 22 June 2017.

69 Fischer, *Islam, Standards, and Technoscience in Global Halal Zones*, 8; Lever and Fischer, *Religion, Regulation, Consumption: Globalising Kosher and Halal Markets*, 7–9: Lever and Fischer, *Kosher and Halal Business Compliance*, 19; Armanios and Ergene, *Halal Food: A History*, 133, 297, n. 80.

70 Robertson, 'Glocalisation: Time-Space and Homogeneity-Heterogeneity', 28–29.

71 The HCB's halal certification is formal, in the sense that these associations are registered legally with the Belgian Ministry of Justice and follow a written document explaining the process of halal certification.

72 *L'Echo*, 8 May 2018, see https://www.lecho.be/economie-politique/belgique/economie/les-asbl-creent-un-nouvel-emploi-sur-deux/10009586.html (accessed 21 April 2019).

purposes. However, the non-profit aspect is undermined by HCBs, which seek profit and the personal enrichment of their members.[73]

During the first period of halal certification in Belgium, from the 1970s to 1990s, certification was granted by the CICB. In the 1970s, it was the referential authority. From the 1980s until the late 1990s, the CICB played an active role in halal certification, mainly regarding meat exports to the Gulf countries.[74] From the beginning of the 2000s, the CICB's role decreased gradually, so that today it has no role at all in halal certification. Three companies remain, but only for certification renewal.[75] This may be explained by the mushrooming of more credible and professional HCBs in the 2000s. When the CICB was replaced by the EMB, there was some discussion by the Ministry of Justice that the EMB could be a source of finance in halal certification, but this failed to materialise.[76] During the second period of halal certification from the early 2000s onwards, the number of HCBs increased rapidly.

About 17 HCBs are found in Belgium (see Appendix), but only a small number of them are active. The majority have simply disappeared from view over time. The following discussion will focus on four key Belgian HCBs: HFCE, Euro-Halal, Halal Expertise, and EIHC,[77] with regard to issues of standardisation, standards, and certification within companies.

3 Standards, Certification, and Their Ramifications

In 2013, the Flemish government estimated that Belgium generated €1.7 billion turnover for halal.[78] This figure, however, is open to question as no official data

73 'The financial aspect of halal certification in Belgium should be transparent', said Karim Chemlal, Vice-President of the Ligue des Musulmans de Belgique (LMB), in French's interview, Brussels, 14 February 2017. I noted that the financial abuse is uniquely by the accredited HCB, notes of ethnography, 2017.

74 According to Shaykh Mustafa Kastit, who oversaw the halal certification of the CICB, during 1997–2013, there were about seven companies certified by the CICB; interview in French, Brussels, 10 March 2017.

75 Interview with Ouazzani, 14 February 2017.

76 Interview with Echallaoui, 24 February 2017. Very recently, the EMB has indicated that it would like to control itself for halal certification, but it needs a legal framework, see https://www.vrt.be/vrtnws/fr/2019/02/12/certificats-halal-lexecutif-des-musulmans-de-belgique-deplore/ (accessed 7 June 2019).

77 I interviewed HALABEL and Ligue des Imams de Belgique. These HCBs are either inactive or undergoing internal restructuring and consolidation, but I might refer to them as well in the discussion.

78 http://www.parishalalexpo.com/belgium-halal-estimated-at-1-7-billion-euros (accessed

on the halal market exist in Belgium, for instance in the period of 2016–2020.[79] We do not know how valuable this market is to the Belgian economy, but the proliferation of HCBs in the 2000s was undoubtedly driven by the new economic opportunities regarding halal, in meeting the needs of Belgian Muslims, and supplying exports to Muslim countries.[80] To achieve this objective, Belgian industries and companies required halal standards that unified a diversity of rules and guidelines, to facilitate the exchange of goods and services across countries both in Europe and worldwide. Obviously, producers benefit from standardisation, as it brings about increased quality and safety and more confidence in the market.[81] In recent years, standards have had a significant impact at the global level, especially in terms of innovation, and they have been critical to the success[82] of halal and other commodities.

In a global context, the first general halal guidelines were published in 1997 by the Codex Alimentarius,[83] which subsequently became the most important formal halal standard, accepted by 165 countries. Of course, there are other official standards in the Muslim world: notably Malaysian Halal Standards (MHS 1500–2000, 1500–2004, and 1500–2009); those issued by the Standards and Meteorology Institute for Islamic Countries of the Organization of Islamic

18 February 2017). Marc Deschamps, responsible for the Halal Club and director-consultant of halal at AWEX (Agence wallonne à l'Exportation et aux invéstissements étrangers/ Wallonie Export-Investment Agency), stated that the total halal market in Wallonia was around €200 million in 2013–2014, with no data after this year (interview in French, Brussels, 7 March 2017).

79 The consultant for the export and international market of the Flemish region, Jan Tirez, from Flanders Investment and Trade (FIT), stated that there are no official data on the value of the halal market to the Flanders region (written interview in English, 24 April 2017). Similarly, there are no data on the halal market in the Brussels-Capital region according to Ghislain Breydel from Brussels Invest and Export (BIE) (interview in French, Brussels, 27 March 2017).

80 See previous explanation of this topic.

81 CEN Compass, The World of European Standards, September 2010, www.cen.eu (accessed 15 April 2019).

82 Schneiderman, *Modern Standardization: Case Studies at the Crossroads of Technology, Economics, and Politices*, 1.

83 CAC/GL 24–1997: this consists of four chapters and approximately 25 articles. The Codex Alimentarius contains international food standards, guidelines, and codes of practice that contribute to the safety, quality, and fairness of this international food trade; see http://www.fao.org/fao-who-codexalimentarius/about-codex/en/#c453333 (accessed 5 May 2019). The Codex Alimentarius Commission (Codex Alimentarius or Codex) was formed in 1962, under the joint sponsorship of two United Nations organisations: the World Health Organization (WHO) and the Food and Agriculture Organization (FAO); Kimbrell, 'What is Codex Alimentarius?', 197–202.

Cooperation (OIC/ SMIIC: 1–2011) and by the Gulf Cooperation Council's (GCC) Standardization Organization (GSO) GSO 05/FDS/2055-1:2014: Halal Products.[84] However, the SMIIC standards from the OIC and the GSO from the GCC are not classed as major standards in the global market. In reality, three Southeast Asian national standards are used by the 150 major third-party halal certifiers around the globe: JAKIM, Malaysian's standard (67), Halal Stock, the Philippines's standard (57),[85] and MUI, Indonesia's standard (32),[86] all of which have become 'informal' world halal standards.

In a regional context, the European Committee for Standardization established the CEN 425/TC-Project Committee—Halal Food in 2013 to create a formal European halal standard, but it was dissolved in 2016. In fact, the Muslim members of the Project Committee and Muslim communities rejected the project because it was overseen by non-Muslims and allowed non-Muslims to certify halal.[87] Accordingly, there is no formal halal standard in Europe to date. As a result of this regional void, the national committee for halal standards in Belgium automatically disbanded. This committee had also been questioned, as it was made up of Muslims and non-Muslims, including representatives of the Belgian NGO of animal rights defenders, GAIA, which was active against halal slaughtering.[88] Because of the absence of a legal framework and of formal halal standards, industries and companies looked to HCBs as a private third party capable of providing halal certification.

HCBs in Belgium are divided into two categories, an accredited HCB, namely the HFCE, and non-accredited HCBs, namely EuroHalal,[89] Halal Expertise, and

84 Armanios and Ergene, *Halal Food: A History*, 138–164.

85 According to FAA, a research fellow working on halal issues in the Philippines, at the Max Planck Institute, this number is not true. In fact, the Halal Stock Philippines' Standard merely copied the JAKIM Malaysian's Standard, informal discussion in Berlin, 4 May 2019.

86 Armanios and Ergene, *Halal Food: A History*, 297, n. 80.

87 Bergeaud-Blackler and Kokoszka, 'La Standardisation du religieux. La norme halal et l'extension du champ de la normalisation', 62–91; Interview with two Belgians members of the CEN: Hakim Azaoum, Louvain-la-Neuve, 21 January 2017, and Iqbal Ahmad Qureshi, Brussels, 20 February 2017.

88 The committee consisted of four Muslims and ten non-Muslims, including Anne De Greef from GAIA (Global Action in the Interest of Animals), Marc Deschamps from AWEX, Hakim Azaoum from HCB 'Halal Expertise', and Koen De Praetere from the halal consultant 'Halal Balancing' (interview in French, with Marc Deschamps, Brussels, 7 March 2017; informal personal information, 13 July 2018 Louvain-la-Neuve, 21 January 2017, and informal discussion, Brussels, 22 22 February 2017, with Hakim Azaoum; interview in English with Iqbal Ahmed Qureshi, Brussels, 20 February 2017).

89 In time, EuroHalal was accredited by the MUIS of Singapore, but this has not been renewed since 2016.

the EIHC. An accredited HCB is recognised by one of the major halal certifiers: JAKIM of Malaysia, MUI of Indonesia, MUIS of Singapore, and the GSO of the Gulf Countries (in the UAE) for exports to these countries. Broadly speaking, if an HCB is accredited by a majority Muslim country such as Indonesia or Malaysia, other countries will accept their exported products,[90] and companies and industries in Belgium therefore choose an HCB according to the export destination country. If they wish to export products to Southeast Asian or Gulf countries, they must choose HFCE. If their products are to be distributed only at the national and regional levels, it is sufficient to go to a non-accredited HCB. The HFCE is supported and backed by the largest HCB in the USA: IFANCA. The clients of IFANCA in Europe go to the HFCE for halal certification. This is why the HFCE has become one of the largest halal certifiers in Europe, based on their assets, capital, number of employees, market, and the like, contrary to the other three Belgian HCBs.

In Belgium, HCBs refer to some halal standards. The HFCE uses all of the major halal standards based on the destination country as requested by companies and industry. These are the Malaysian, Indonesian, Singaporean, Emirati/Gulf, and OIC-SMIIC/Turkey standards. Since this HCB has been accredited by these countries, the HFCE will use the country's standard accordingly. If a product is to be exported to Indonesia, they will use the Indonesian Halal Standard (HAS-MUI 2008), while if to Malaysia, they will use the Malaysian Halal Standard (MAS 1500–2009). If companies wish to export products to other Muslim countries, the HFCE will combine three major standards: the Malaysian, Indonesian, and Emirati/Gulf standards and also use the destination country's standard, if one exists. In the same vein, for exports to non-Muslim countries, the HFCE will use the aforementioned three major standards as guidelines for halal certification.[91]

Halal Expertise uses Malaysian, Indonesian, Singaporean, and Moroccan standards, and the halal Codex Alimentarius,[92] while EuroHalal and EIHC use the HFB's halal standard. They have their own standard, that of the HFB. In 2006, four Belgian HCBs combined to create a single national standardisation process for halal certification. The committee collated and discussed many halal standards from around the world. As principal sources, they used

90 When I conducted research on halal in Japan in 2016, I was informed that if a product had been certified halal by either Indonesia or Malaysia, it could then be exported or imported by Japan.

91 Interview in English, with Iqbal Ahmed Qureshi and Nurita Abubakar Syah, Brussels, 20 February 2017.

92 Interview with Azaoum, Louvain-la-Neuve, 21 January 2017.

the Halal Codex Alimentarius, JAKIM's Malaysian standard, MUIS's Singaporean standard, and the Brunei standard. Ultimately, they created 'le cahier des charges' or the standard of the Halal Federation of Belgium (HFB). It must be understood, however, that the standardisation of halal in Belgium merely entailed compiling many halal major standards from Southeast Asian Muslim countries. This certainly fits the traditional definition of standardisation as: 'a process of constructing uniformity across time and space through the generation of agreed rules'.[93] But the real halal standardisation was according to standards produced by the religious authorities in Indonesia (MUI), Malaysia (JAKIM), and Singapore (MUIS). Once these states and all of the stakeholders had approved their standards, they became a public document. Any institution, organisation, or individual was free to use these standards, including the HCBs in Belgium. In fact, standards are a voluntary, open access document with no charge or license fee for their use, apart from the cost of purchase.[94] Once the halal norms have been standardised in majority Muslim countries, these standards can be used by the HCBs in non-Muslim countries like Belgium. Afterwards, the HCBs can modify these halal standards for their own purposes based on local and regional contexts and interests.

The examination of four Belgian HCBs in regard to compiling several Muslim countries' standards is part of a 'global halal assemblage' phenomenon.[95] 'Global' implies broadly encompassing, seamless, and mobile, while assemblage implies heterogeneous, contingent, unstable, partial, and situated.[96] Even though the standard of the HFB is the result of halal standards assemblage, the standard remains of course a source of authority and an achievement.[97] All HCBs already have a halal standard; they could therefore offer a halal certification process to companies and industries.

The HFCE certifies all product categories, both food and non-food. The food items range from meat, poultry, dairy products, beverages, seafood, cereals, baked goods, confectionary, and food ingredients, to flavourings and seasonings. The non-food items include pharmaceuticals, cosmetics, textiles, accessories, personal care products, and even sanitation chemicals and packaging materials. The HFCE has already certified 700 companies across Europe and more than 10,000 products. The certification fee depends on the scale and size

93 Timmermans and Epstein, 'A World of Standards but not a Standard World', 70–71.

94 Hatto, *Standards and Standardization Handbook*, 7–8.

95 Bergeaud-Blackler, Fischer, and Lever, 'Introduction: Studying the Politics of Global Halal Markets', 10.

96 Collier and Ong, 'Global Assemblage, Anthropological Problems', 12.

97 Timmermans and Epstein, 'A World of Standards but not a Standard World', 70–71.

of the company. Companies in all categories must pay a registration fee when requesting a halal certificate from the HFCE. Upon signing the agreement, the certification process fee for a small enterprise is about €3,000, for a medium enterprise roughly €10.000, and for a big enterprise about €50,000 or more, depending upon the complexity of the ingredients, time required, number of variations, and other factors. The HFCE generates an annual revenue between €2 million[98] and €4 million[99] from this certification.[100]

EuroHalal, Halal Expertise, and the EIHC claim to certify all product categories, but in reality they mainly certify food products. EuroHalal certifies meat and products from the agri-food industry such as beverages, sauces, biscuits, oil, chocolate, cosmetics, the restaurant industry, and catering. They have certified 50 or 60 companies and 700 products. The fee ranges from €700 to about €1,800 and there is no registration fee. They generate an annual revenue of about €25,000 to €50,000.[101] Halal Expertise certifies bakers, sauces, ingredients, meat, cereals, and other items. They have certified about 15–20 companies and 550 products. The fee varies from €750 to €2,400 but in general is €1,500, including the registration and certification process.[102] The EIHC certifies meat, poultry, and other food, and claims to certify cosmetics, transport, and logistics. They have certified around ten companies and 300 products. The fee is between €1,000 and €5,000.[103]

I participated in and observed the halal certification process for sauce[104] and chocolate[105] companies conducted by EuroHalal, and for a cereal company[106]

---

98 According to the Director of the HFCE, Iqbal Ahmed Qureshi, their annual revenue is about €2 million (interview in English, Brussels, 20 February 2017).

99 According to an ex-employee of the HFCE, Mr X, the annual revenue of the HFCE is about €4 million (interview in French, Brussels, 2017). Some rumours that the revenue goes abroad to the owner of the HFCE in the USA to support a life of luxury went viral and the Belgian bank was suspicious about this, note ethnography from anonymous different sources, in 2017–2019.

100 According to the official report of the HFCE submitted to the Commercial Court of Brussels in 2015, it is about €1 million; see *Comptes Annuels en Euros in 2016, BE0827.964.482*, 12 pages.

101 Interview in French, with Gaernaiert, Sebai, El Akili, and Verhaeyen on four different occasions: 21 February 2017; 11 May 2017; 11 October 2018; and 13 December 2018.

102 Interview with Azaoum, 21 January 2017 and informal discussion 22 February 2017.

103 Interview with Salah Eldin, Louvain-la-Neuve, 18 February 2017.

104 Manna Foods NV located at Bijkhoevelaan 24 B, 2110, Wijnegem, Beglium, at the production site for Mahall, Bolognese Sauce, at Schoten, Belgium, 13 December 2018.

105 Neuhaus Chocolate factory, located at Postweg 2, 1602, in Saint-Pieters-Leeuw, Belgium, 11 October 2018.

106 Molens Gyskens, located at Terbekstraat 36, 3580 Beringen, Belgium, on the production site, 22 February 2017.

by Halal Expertise. I was not able to participate in the halal certification of EICH and the HFCE. However, the EICH explained to me in great detail (in a five-hour interview) their certification process for two meat and poultry companies,[107] while the HFCE did not allow me to participate at all, despite several requests; they simply explained their auditing process to me in a three-hour interview at their Brussels office. I briefly summarise my observation below.

The procedures and formalities for halal certification are almost the same for all four HCBs in Belgium under discussion. The process is as follows. A company seeking halal certification contacts an HCB by email or phone to obtain general information. If the company agrees, it will fill out an application form, then submit supporting documents, such as product lists, technical data, an ingredients specification sheet, labels, statements, and process flowcharts, and other production details. If both parties agree to the certification process, a contract is signed. The details of the certification and supervision are confirmed. The on-site audit follows almost exactly the flowchart and procedure of each HCB. Generally, two auditors from the HCB, consisting of one expert in science and technology and one in economics and general affairs, visit the factory. For the most part, the company's production manager welcomes them. An audit of the production facility on the spot is now conducted. One auditor from the HCB delivers a presentation on halal for about 30 minutes. The auditors review and assess the ingredients based on the technical data. The company then answers all of the auditors' questions and shows them the supporting documents. This takes 30–45 minutes. The auditors continue to assess and evaluate the production site: the controlling machines, production line, hygiene, packaging, logistics, transport, and so on. They inspect the factory in detail, accompanied by a production manager. The inspection and auditing of the on-site production takes 30–45 minutes. They then return to the office and exchange some documents, which completes the on-site audit and inspection.

Several weeks later, the team meets at the HCB secretariat; they discuss the audit and write a first report review. The HCB requests samples and extractions from the ingredients and supporting documents from the company. They run their own laboratory tests on these; for instance, for pork-free residuals or DNA pork checks and alcohol-free ingredients. If the company has already provided all the requested documents, the team will verify these. If some issues arise,

107 Teker Bvba, located at Tenbergstraat 3A, 2830, Willebroek, Antwerpen, Belgium and Dekeyzer-Ossaer NV, located at Barnestraat 1, 8680 Koekelare, Belgium. I found these halal meat and poultry products myself at the Belgian convenience stores chain HAPPY 5 in Wavre, during my three years of ethnographic work, 2017–2019.

corrective action will be taken and suggestions offered. If the problem persists, they will determine its nature and offer advice. The committee again discusses the data sheets and audit report internally. If, during these steps, everything is in order, then the HCB committee will deliberate and write a final report. As a final step, the HCB issues a halal certificate. The company pays a fee upon receipt of it, and can then use the HCB logo if they wish.[108] The halal certificate will be renewed annually thereafter. All this process is precisely what John Bowen called the *performative* of halal quality. That is, 'declaring or pronouncing of something as halal (in a form of "halal certificate"), after the procedures dictated by the halal dispositive or mechanism, that involves both procedural demontrations of its search for truth and devices with certain function, have been completed'.[109]

Based on my participation and observation, the 'audit culture' is indeed a new phenomenon within halal practices. It involves carrying out specific procedures that are applicable to all kinds of reckonings, evaluations, and measurements, as part of a bureaucratic process for assessments to be accountable.[110] It emerged and expanded through the HCB's certification process. These certifiers perform on-site audits and inspections in factories.[111] Such systems are a feature of modern societies. To a large extent, halal audit culture is about the cultural and economic authority granted to these auditors, inspectors, and certifiers.[112] In fact, all of the auditors-certifiers have been educated in science, technology, and economics, at various academic levels.[113] Accordingly, they are assumed to be competent.[114] Modernity, whose authority has been based on scientific principles since the Galilean revolution and strengthened by Cartesian logic, has replaced religious authority. The competency and authority of the certifiers and auditors comes from their university training and education.

---

108 The halal logo has a positive impact on selling products: interview with the Sales Manager of MANNA, Johan Brunyseels, Antwerp, 13 May 2017; informal discussion with the Director of EuroHalal, Karim Geirnaert, who explained that the products with halal logo sell better, Antwerpen, 13 December 2018; interview with Abdulwahid Alami, from Alkhayria Belgica, Brussels, 17 February 2017.

109 Bowen, 'Performativité et materialité dans la certification halal', 205–235.

110 Strathern, 'Introduction: New Accountabilities', 1–18.

111 Lever and Fischer, *Religion, Regulation, Consumption: Globalising Kosher and Halal Markets*, 12.

112 Lever and Fischer, *Religion, Regulation, Consumption*, 12–13.

113 Interview with four HCBs on the educational background of certifiers.

114 Bergeaud-Blackler, Fischer, and Lever, 'Introduction: Studying the Politics of Global Halal Markets', 9.

During the on-site auditing and inspection, I observed that no single religious expert or shariʿa board participating in the certification process. During an in-depth interview, two HCBs acknowledged that no religious expert came to audit and inspect a company for halal certification.[115] All of the HCBs stated that religious experts do not understand the auditing process, and that what is needed is scientific competency, which is not the field of religious scholars.[116] Two HCBs even argued that they do not need religious experts because everything is based on standards. If a problem arises that is not mentioned in the standards, they can easily search in books or the Internet, because they also know Islamic teachings even though they are not Imams or religious scholars.[117] Another HCB even stated that it is not necessary to pay religious experts since they do not understand the auditing, inspection, and production process.[118] Furthermore, an auditor from an accredited HCB told me that he had conducted more than 50 audits for both new and renewed halal certification across Europe, and had never been accompanied by a religious scholar.[119] Another auditor confirmed that she had performed many audits and inspections of companies across Europe for halal certification, without a religious scholar in attendance.[120] Although each HCB has a religious board, this is just a formality.[121] My sources say that the minutes of the meeting with their shariʿa committee exist[122] but this too was a mere formality. Moreover, the signature and stamp of the religious committee of each HCB on the halal certificates that they issue did not appear at all.[123]

115 Interview with the HFCE and the EIHC, 2017.
116 Ethnography note, 2017–2018.
117 Ethnography note, 2017.
118 Ethnography note, 2018.
119 The auditor is a male Muslim, HA, living in Germany, who holds a PhD in Science from a German university, (interview in Berlin, 9 June 2017).
120 The auditor is a female Muslim, US, living in Belgium, who holds a PhD in Science from a Dutch university (informal personal discussion both direct and indirect, 16 April 2018 and 2 February 2019).
121 The EuroHalal religious advisors are Prof. Dr Ezzar Hicham, Cheikh Adil Ajattari, and Syaikh Mohamed Fathallah; the HFCE religious boards consisted of Prof. Dr Sofyan Siregar (d. 2017), Syaikh Muhammad Abdullatif, Ustaz Umar Abdurrahman Baktir, and Imam Dicik Nizam; the EICH religious committee was Imam Mohamed Jammouchi and Dr Mohamed Hawari (d. 2015), and the Halal Expertise Shariʿa Committee is Abdelmajid Guetrani and the Imam of the Mosque of El-Ghofrane, in Brussels.
122 Note of the interview, Belgium, 2017.
123 One HCB interviewee explained: 'On n'a pas besoin de la signature et le cachet d'un ouléma dans un contexte industriel et commercial, parce que le certificat, c'est pour la donnée commerciale. Il est inutile de mettre la signature ou le cachet des théologiens [...] Ce n'est pas les théologiens qui livrent un certificat [...] S'il y a une signature ou un

This halal certification process confirms the shift in authority from 'ulama' to the HCBs. Bergeaud-Blackler pointed out that these HCBs, both mercantile and religious, threaten traditional religious authorities[124] by establishing new halal norms in the religious field. Indeed, HCBs have arguably marginalised the role and authority[125] of the traditional 'ulama' as they no longer need any religious experts during the certification. Up until the point at which a halal certificate is issued, they refer to the standard. During the review process before the issuing of a certificate, they do not consult their religious experts. Furthermore, the Belgian Imams explained that to decide whether a product is halal or not, and whether or not it contains alcohol or pork derivatives, a scientifically conducted laboratory test is required.[126] Until this is done, the Belgian 'ulama' cannot say whether a product is halal or haram. Halal certification has, in this sense, diminished traditional Islamic authority,[127] while the process of modern standardisation has neglected the traditional role of 'ulama'.

4 Conclusion: The Shift of Religious Authority and the Threat to Halal Pluriversality

The certification of halal by HCBs through halal standardisation should be read as a modern way of harmonising Islamic tradition, national economic interests, and international business standards. Nevertheless, this standardisation has had consequences. Surprisingly, little attention has been paid to the ramific-

cachet d' un comité des théologiens, c' est pour la formalité. Ils [des oulémas] ne peuvent pas participer [dans le processus de la certification] [...] En sachant que quelque chose qui est très fondamentale dans l' Islam par rapport à d' autres religions, il n'y a pas de hiérarchie. L' islam a voulu un contact entre la personne et le Dieu sans intermédiaire.' Note of the interview, Belgium, 2017.

124 Bergeaud-Blackler, *Le Marché Halal ou l' invention d' une tradition*, 20.

125 For further discussion on authority in Islam, see Hallaq. *Authority, Continuity, and Change in Islamic Law*, 2004.

126 Interview in French with Shaikh Muhammad Galay Ndiaye, Mufti of the Great Mosque of Brussels, Brussels, 14 February 2017; interview in Arabic and French with Shaikh Muhammad Abu Chazin, Imam of the Islamic Centre of Alkhayria Belgica, Brussels, 17 February 2017; interview in Arabic with Shaikh Abdulhadi Suwayf, Imam the Great Mosque of Brussels, Brussels, 21 February 2017; interview in French with Shaikh Mustafa Kastit, Imam of the Centre of Education and Youth Cultures, Brussels, 10 March 2017.

127 Hajib el-Hadjaji, from Association Belge des Professionels Musulmans (ABPM) told me in his interview, 16 16 February 2017, that, 'the religious authority is not enough at all in the halal certification process in Belgium. A professional body should do it'.

ations of this, which includes a shift in religious authority from the traditional 'ulama' to the HCBs, as well as a threat to and suppression of the pluriversality of halal.

The *first* ramification, from a Weberian perspective, is that the halal certification process demonstrates a shift from charismatic authority (in Islam, the 'ulama') to bureaucratic authority, which depends on rationalisation through the HCB.[128] Indeed, in the European context, Islamic religious authority did not exist in the past. Since the 1970s, the 'ulama' has never been institutionally strong. This is why the Belgian HCBs used all of the halal standards that are endorsed and approved by the 'ulama' from Southeast Asia or North Africa. However, once those standards became the guidelines for halal certification it suffices to follow them, and religious authority is no longer needed.

The shift of religious authority from the 'ulama' to HCBs renders the latter the new 'moral agents' in all matters related to halal. I am influenced by Michel Foucault's concept of an 'historical ontology', which involves answering the dialectical interaction between: (1) our relation to **truth** (in this case: halal) through which we constitute ourselves as a subject of knowledge (that is, halal's genealogy in the past); (2) our relation to a field of **power** (halal as a knowledge or science) through which we constitute subjects acting on others (on how we are producing norms, standards, and '**knowledge**' of halal in the present); and (3) our relation to ethics (here the ethics of halal for production and consumption) through which we constitute ourselves as **moral agents** (after producing the knowledge of halal, we become a moral agent, that is to say the halal certification bodies, to control, guide, and dictate what is right and wrong).[129]

Thus the HCB has a new role as a moral agent. In fact, the HCBs have potentially 'the desire of *panoptisme*' in a Foucauldian sense. A panoptic is a prison architecture (imagined by Jeremy Bentham) based on a central tower from which prisoners are monitored by prisoners. Panoptism is a sort of doctrine of the prison, which is designed to ensure total supervision of the prisoners. Foucault wrote: 'the Panopticon, on the other hand, must be understood as a generalisable model of functioning; a way of defining power relations in terms of the everyday life of men'.[130] The HCB, if acting like a panopticon, defines the power relations between enterprises, the *umma*/Muslim community, and

128 See Weber 1946, chapter 8 on Bureaucracy, esp. sub-chapter 9–11 and chapter 9 on 'The Sociology of Charismatic Authority', esp. 245–248.

129 Foucault, 'On the Genealogy of Ethics: An Overview of Work a Progress', 351–352; Foucault, 'What is Enlightenment?', 32–50.

130 Foucault, *Discipline and Punish: The Birth of the Prison*, 205; see original text in *Surveiller et punir: Naissance de la prison*, 206–207.

the state regarding halal that regulates the everyday life of Muslims. We find here the panoptic will of modern systems on halal, which intends to regulate the whole world through a set of norms and standards organised into a system. The HCB serves as a 'panoptic' institution because it is an authority that registers, audits, decides, and regulates what is acceptable or not, what is right and wrong, what is in conformity with the halal standards and what is not.

The *second* ramification is the threat and suppression associated with the pluriversality of halal. An example is the use of alcohol in food ingredients, cosmetics, medicines, and disinfection products. There are many opinions about this in Sunni Islam.[131] Taking only one opinion found in the *fiqh*, and placing it in the standards excludes other opinions outside the standards. The creator of the standards chose only one opinion since the objective is to create uniformity. For example, Halal Expertise's standard refers to JAKIM's Malaysian standard, MUI's Indonesian standard, and the Moroccan standards, all of which allow the use of alcohol in perfume.[132] Belgian Muslims have different views about this. Some allow the use of alcohol, while others forbid it.[133] In an online forum of Belgian Muslims there is much heated discussion, because of their differences over the pros and cons of adding alcohol.[134] Online commerce exists in halal perfume without alcohol,[135] the subject is found in Islamic bookshops,[136] and there is much information in fatwas prohibiting the use of perfume containing alcohol,[137] as well as in numerous books, cassettes, and edited preaching.[138]

In the same vein is the debate about the use of alcohol in mouthwash. The Malaysian standards, according to Halal Expertise, allow mouthwash companies to use unnatural—that is, industrial—alcohol up to 16 per cent in halal

131 al-Zuḥaylī, *al-Fiqh al-Islāmiyy wa Adillatuhu*, v. 6, 160–161; Sābiq, *Fiqh al-Sunna*, 994.

132 Written interview with Azaoum, 6 April 2019. This also applies to the EIHC, which authorises the use of alcohol in cosmetics (interview with Salah Eldin, Louvain-la-Neuve, 18 February 2017).

133 Interview with many Belgian Muslims in Belgium, note ethnography in 2019.

134 https://www.yabiladi.com/forum/alcool-dans-parfum-4-1464533.html (accessed 5 August 2019).

135 https://www.iqrashop.com/Parfum-Aicha-sans-Alcool-30ml-parfums-musc-Bien-etre-p 27042-1__221_293_291.html (accessed 29 July 2019).

136 Many Islamic bookshops in Brussels sell perfume that is halal (without alcohol), note ethnography 2017.

137 https://islamqa.info/fr/answers/9056/le-jugement-de-lusage-des-parfums-contenant-de-lalcool (accessed 30 July 2019).

138 These Islamic products are made in Belgium but sold in mosques in France, Escarnot, *Djihad, C'est arrive près de chez vous*, 2017, ch. 1.

certification,[139] whereas many Muslims avoid using mouthwash containing alcohol on grounds that it is prohibited in Islam.[140] Another example is of Belgian Muslims, mainly from communities of North African origin, who daily use vinegar containing up to 6 per cent alcohol. They claim that this is halal according to Moroccan 'ulama' fatwas based on the hadith of the Prophet, and also that it is natural alcohol.[141] The standards of the Belgian HCBs allow the use of alcohol in vinegar.[142] In this example, both the majority of Belgian Muslims and the HCBs hold the same view. However, for other Muslims, the use of alcohol in vinegar is prohibited.[143] Of course, there is no uniformity in halal either in theory or practice among Sunni Muslims on the use of alcohol, both natural and unnatural.[144]

Nevertheless, it is clear that halal standards and certification oppress the pluriversality of halal practices and neglect the importance of subjective individual and community experiences. Furthermore, the standards and certification of halal are the expression of a broader rejection of the plurality that is inherent in Islam. Halal standards and certification are regarded as a form of cultural oppression[145] against the traditional halal processing of foods and as a suppression of differences in halal in the *fiqh* in Islamic religion. The pluriversality of halal means not simply tolerating difference, but actually understanding the reality of the 'halal lifestyle' that is constituted by many kinds of opinions, practices, and habits, and many ways of interpreting halal and experimenting with consuming and producing it.[146] Halal certification, based on halal standards, is only one of halal's realities in the world, but it should not be

139 Written interview with Azaoum, 6 April 2019.

140 Note ethnography 2018–2019.

141 Interview with many Belgian Muslims in Belgium, note ethnography in 2019.

142 The HFCE, Halal Expertise, EuroHalal, and the EICH relied basically on Southeast Asian Muslim countries' standards (Malaysia, Indonesia, Singapore), which allow vinegar consumption with alcohol (natural).

143 They explained that neither natural and industrial alcohol in vinegar is allowed, even though there is a fatwa based on the hadith of the Prophet. For them, it is uncertain, so it is better to avoid consuming it. Interview with many Belgian Muslims in Belgium, note ethnography in 2019.

144 al-Jazīrī, *Kitāb al-Fiqh 'Alā Madhāhib al-Arba'a*, v. 5, 27; al-Zuḥaylī, *al-Fiqh al-Islāmiyy wa Adillatuhu*, v. 6, 160–161, and for daily practice among Muslims in the Belgian context; interview with el-Hadjaji, 16 February 2017, and with Vrancken, 3 January 2017.

145 I am influenced by the criticism of the standards and standardisation of language as a form of oppression and suppression of differences by Amstrong and Mackenzie, *Standardization, Ideology, and Linguistics*, 5–12.

146 I am influenced by the discussion on pluriverse and pluriversality by Querejazu, 'Encountering the Pluriverse: Looking for Alternatives in Other Words', 3–4.

regarded as superior to other halal practices and experiences found in everyday settings. These opinions, views, and practices should also be recognised and allowed to co-exist with many other ways of experimenting with the halal way of life.

Appendix: Halal Certification Bodies in Belgium

No	Year	HCB			
		The institution	Official address	Status HCB/no registration	Actual status
1	2002	Gestion Halal	–	–	–
2	1/10/2003	the *Islamic Food Council of Europe* (IFCE)	Rue de Verdun 657, Brussels	862.216.667	Non-active
3	7/01/2006	*Halal Control and Certification Belgium* (HCCB)	Rue des Halles, 1, Brussels 1000	0881.522.043	Active
4	07/02/2006	*Service Control Halal* (SCH)	Rue Théodore Verhaegen 50, 1080, Brussels	0879.450.696	Non-active

erson in charge	Birth year	Origin	Official based of HCB	Additional information
	–	–	–	close to the EMB during the presidency of N. Malhajamoum
l Shahbaz Khan	1942	Pakistan	USA	representation of IFANCA in Europe for the period of 2003–2010
ohammad Naeem Shahbaz Khan	1974	Pakistan		
rveen Akhtar	1947	Pakistan		
Lassaad Ben Yaghlane	1965	Tunisia		Owner Radio Arabel & Darul Quran
Mohamed Boulif	1962	Morocco		President of the *EMB* (2003–2005)
Nasreddine Moussaoui	1957	Algeria		
Ismail Batakli	1964	Turkey		
Abdelmajid Mhauci	1967	Morocco		
Jonathan Paul Louis Devos	1979	Belgium		
Mohamed Mouhdad	1981	Morocco		
Souade Touijiri	1980	Morocco		

(*cont.*)

No	Year	HCB			
		The institution	**Official address**	**Status HCB/no registration**	**Actu statu**
5	01/09/2006	*Halal Guarantee*	Av. Louis Bertrand, 102, bte. Do, 1030, Brussels and Rue Albert, 1, 1020 Laeken, Brussels (2015)	883.487.282	Non-activ
6	2007	*European Certification and control of Halal* (ECCH)		NPO was not registered	
7	01/10/2007	*Halal Federation of Belgium* (HFB)	rue de la Victoire, 158, 1060 Brussels	889.055.280	Activ

erson in charge	Birth year	Origin	Official based of HCB	Additional information
. Radouane Bouhlal	1974	Morocco		Chairman of MRAX
. Farid al-Machaoud	1981	Morocco		ex-Spoke Person of LMB and left this HCB in 2007
. Zakaria Kassem Oauli	1968	Morocco		
m. Stephane Renier	1982	Belgium		joined in 2011
. Hassane Lhasnaoue	1981	Morocco		joined in 2011
m. Miranda Vanessa Bonte	1978	Belgium		joined in 2011
. M'rad Dali Fayçal	1952	Tunisia		After the foundation, it splitted into two HCBS: EICH (2007) and Euro-Halal (2008)
rad Dali Fayçal	1952	Tunisia		2007–2013
ohamed Boulif	1962	Morocco		2007–2013
Farid el-Machaoud	1981	Morocco		2007–2013
karia Kassem Ouali	1968	Morocco		joined in 2007
ohamed (Salah) Eldin	1952	Egypt		joined in 2013
rim Geirnaert	1941	Belgium		joined in 2013

(*cont.*)

No	Year	HCB			
		The institution	Official address	Status HCB/no registration	Actua[l] statu[s]
8	13/11/2007	*Comité Théologique Belge du Halal* (CTBH)	rue de Halles, 1, Brussels 1000	0897.935.235	Non-activ[e]
9	19/12/2007	The *European Islamic Halal Certification* (EIHC)	Avenue de la Reine, 7, 1030 Brussels Rue de la Victoire, 158, St. Gilles, Brussels	894.866.174	Activ[e]
10	27/06/2008	*EuroHalal*	Rue de la Victoire 158, 1060 Boulevard Barthélemy, 20, 1000 Brussels	899.386.968	Activ[e]

rson in charge	Birth year	Origin	Official based of HCB	Additional information
ssad Ben Yaghlane	1965	Tunisia		joined in 2013
. Abdallah el-Moudni	1944	Morocco		
. Megahed Hassan Mahmoud	1935	Morocco		
. Abdeslam Senhaji	1944	Morocco		
. Abdallah Fadel	1954	Morocco		
. Yacob Mahi	1965	Morocco		
Mustapha Turki	1962	Tunisia		
Mohamed (Salah) Eldin	1952	Egypt		
M'rad Dali Fayçal	1952	Tunisia		
Brunot Soltan	1970	Belgium		
Vincent Theben	1966	Belgium		left in 2010
ohammed Jamouchi	1961	Marocco		joined in 2010
Karim Geirnaert	1941	Belgium		
M'hamed el-Akili	1961	Morocco		
Roger L. Verheyen	1952	Belgium		joined in 2011
Hakim Azaoum	1970	Morocco		left in 2011
Mjahed Sebai	1969	Morocco		

(*cont.*)

No	Year	HCB			
		The institution	Official address	Status HCB/no registration	Actu statu
11		*Halal Food Council of Europe* (HFCE)	Rue de la Presse, 4, 1001 Brussels	827.964.482	Activ
12	2009	*Certification Officielle Halal Européenne* (COHE)		Non-registered	dis-miss
13	2010	HALABEL		524371275	non-activ (inte nal r struc tura-tion)

rson in charge	Birth year	Origin	Official based of HCB	Additional information
. Mohamed Sadek Nazardin	1942	Malaysia, now in the USA		HFCE is the representation of IFANCA (USA) in Europe
. Zeshan Bin Mohamed Sadek	1968	Malaysia, now in the USA		
. Muhammad Munir Chaudry	1944	USA		
. Iqbal Ahmed Qureshi	1944	India		
ivier Willocx		Belgium		founded by Bruno Bernard in 2009 and cooperation with BECI in 2010, supported by its Director: Olivier Willocx
uno Bernard		Belgium		
sreddin Askrani		Algeria		
cham Bouchama		Morocco	Annecy	registered in Annecy, France
çal Bouchama		Morocco		

(cont.)

No	Year	HCB			
		The institution	Official address	Status HCB/no registration	Actu statu
14	2011	Halal Expertise	rue de l'Obus 70, 1070, Brussels (now they have new office at Avenue Louise, 360, 1050 Brussels)	840.602.196	Activ
15	2015	*Halal Concept* (*European Agency of Halal Certification*)	Avenue Brillat Savarin 76, 1050 Brussels	0643.438.804	Non-activ
16	2015	*La Ligue des Imams de Belgique*	Rue Vanderstraeten 9, 1010, Brussels	non-registered	Non-activ
17	2016	the Halal Food Authority (HFA)	rue du Progrès, 13, 75013 Tournai	0665.748.216	Non-activ

erson in charge	Birth year	Origin	Official based of HCB	Additional information
akim Azaoum	1970	Morocco		It is currently transforming into International Halal Expertise (IHEC-Halal Expertise)
m. Samia Guetrani	1973	Morocco		
. Sadig Mohamed Taher Shlibeek	1969	Morocco		
. Abdelmajid Guetrani	1955	Morocco		
Farid el-Machaoud	1981	Morocco		
m. Aziza Chuitar	1971	Morocco		
m. Latifa el-Ouhabi	1969	Morocco		
eikh Mohamed Toujgani		Morocco		attached to the Mosque of al-Khalil in Brussels
dul Matin Khan		England	London	Representation of the HFA (UK) in EU countries
hamed Saqib		England		

Acknowledgement

The research was funded by the MOVE-IN Louvain Program of the Catholic University of Louvain (co-funded by the Marie-Curie Actions of the EU Commission), 2016–2019. I thank Baudouin Dupret, John Lever, and En-Chieh Chao for their comments of the early draft and anonymous reviewers. This chapter was presented partially at Radboud University Nijmegen in 2017, at the Fifth WOCMES Seville in 2018, and at Indiana University Europe Gateway Berlin in 2019.

Bibliography

Aboutayeb, Badr. 2013. 'Ethnomarketing et la marché halal en Belgique: quelle est la perception du consommateur belge non-musulman vis-à-vis du produit halal?'. Master's Thesis. Louvain School of Management, Université Catholique de Louvain.

al-Jazīrī, 'Abd Raḥmān. 2003. *Kitāb al-Fiqh 'Alā Madzāhib al-Arba'a*. Beirut, Dār al-Kutub al-'Ilmiyyah, vol. 5.

al-Zuḥaylī, Wahbah. 1985. *al-Fiqh al-Islāmiyy wa Adillatuhu*, vol. 7, 2nd ed. Damascus: Dār al-Fikr.

Amstrong, Nigel, and Ian E. Mackenzie. 2013. *Standardization, Ideology, and Linguistics*. London: Palgrave Macmillan.

Armanios, Febe, and Bogac Ergene. 2018. *Halal Food: A History*. Oxford: Oxford University Press.

Attar, Rachida. 1992. 'Historique de l'Immigration maghrébine en Belgique'. In *Histoire des étrangers et de l'immigration en Belgique de la préhistoire à nos jours*, edited by Anne Morelli, 290–310. Bruxelles: Editions Vie Ouvrière.

Bayar, Ali. 1922. 'Un aperçu économique de l'immigration turque, in Anne Morelli'. In *Histoire des étrangers et de l'immigration en Belgique de la préhistoire à nos jours*, edited by Anne Morelli, 311–328. Bruxelles: Editions Vie Ouvrière.

Bazgour, Hanane. 2007. 'Etude du marché de la viande halal en Belgique'. Mémoire en économie, Faculté Universitaire des Sciences Agronomiques de Gembloux.

Bergeaud-Blackler, Florence. 2015. 'The Halal Certification Market in Europe and the World: A First Panorama'. In *Halal Matters: Islam, Politics, and Markets in Global Perspectives*, edited by Florence Bergeaud-Blackler, Johan Fischer, and John Lever, 105–126. London-New York: Routledge.

Bergeaud-Blackler, Florence. 2017. *Le Marché Halal ou l'invention d'une tradition*, Paris: Seuil.

Bergeaud-Blackler, Florence and Valérie Kokoszka. 2017. La Standardisation du religieux. La norme halal et l'extension du champ de la normalisation, *Revue du MAUSS*, no. 49: 62–91.

Bergeaud-Blackler, Florence, Johan Fischer, and John Lever. 2015. 'Introduction: Studying the Politics of Global Halal Markets'. In *Halal Matters: Islam, Politics, and Markets in Global Perspectives*, edited by Florence Bergeaud-Blackler, Johan Fischer, and John Lever, 1–18. London-New York: Routledge.

Bernard, Bruno and Florence Bergeaud-Blackler. 2010. *Comprendre le Halal*. Liège: Edi Pro.

Bonne, Karijn. 2007. 'Halal Meat Consumption Decision-Making among Muslim Consumers in Belgium'. PhD dissertation. Faculteit Bio ingenieurswetenschappen, Universität Gent.

Bonne, Karijn, and Wim Verbeke. 2006. 'Muslim consumer's motivations towards meat consumption in Belgium: qualitative exploratory insights from means-end chain analysis', *Anthropology Food*, 5, May, 2006, pp. 1–17.

Bonne, Karijn and Wim Verbeke. 2008. 'Muslim Consumer Trust in Halal Meat Status and Control in Belgium'. *Meat Science* 79: 113–123.

Bonne, Karijn, Iris Vermeir, and Wim Verbeke. 2008. 'Impact of Religion on Halal Meat Consumption Decision Making in Belgium'. *Journal of International Food and Agribusiness Marketing* 21, no. 1: 5–26.

Bonne, Karijn, Iris Vermeir, Florence Bergeaud-Blackler, and Wim Verbeke. 2007. 'Determinants of Halal Meat Consumption in France', *British Food Journal* 109, no. 5: 367–386.

Bousetta, Hassan and Brigitte Maréchal. 2003. *L'islam et les musulmans en Belgique: Enjeux locaux et cadres de réflexion globaux*. Bruxelles: Foundation Roi Baudouin.

Bowen, John. 2018. 'Performativité et materialité dans la certification halal'. In *Les objets composés*, edited by Nicolas Dodier and Anthony Stavrianakis, 205–235. Raisons Pratiques No. 28, Paris: EHESS.

Brunsson, Nils, and Bengt Jacobson. 2000. *A World of Standards*. Oxford: Oxford University Press.

Chao, En-Chieh. 2018. 'Halal Stunning: A Techno-Moral History of Animal Welfare and Islamic Slaughter'. *Taiwanese Journal for Studies of Science, Technology, and Medicine* 26: 7–54 (in Chinese).

Collier, Stephen J. and Aihwa Ong. 2005. 'Global Assemblage, Anthropological Problems'. In *Global Assemblage: Technology, Politics, and Ethics as Anthropological Problems*, edited by Aihwa Ong and Stephen J. Collier, 3–21. Oxford: Blackwell Publishing, 2005.

Crone, Patricia, and Martin Hinds. 1986. *God's Caliph: Religious Authority in the First Centuries of Islam*. Cambridge: Cambridge University Press.

Dassetto, Felice. 1997. *Facettes de l'Islam belge*. Louvain-la-Neuve: l'Harmattan.

Dassetto, Felice. 2001. *Migration, sociétés et politiques Belgique, Europe et les nouveaux défis*. Louvain-la-Neuve: Academia-Bruylant.

Dassetto, Felice. 2011. *L'iris et le croissant: Bruxelles et l'Islam au défi de la co-inclusion*. Louvain-la-Neuve: Presses Universitaires de Louvain.

Dassetto, Felice and Albert Bastenier. 1984. *L'Islam transplanté: vie et organisation des minorités musulmanes de Belgique*. Anvers: EPO.

Djelloul, Ghaliya and Brigitte, Maréchal. 2017. 'Islam in Belgium'. *In Encyclopaedia of Islam, THREE*, edited by Kate Fleet, Gudrun Krämer, Denis Matringe, John Nawas, and Everet Rowson. Leiden: Brill.

Djelloul, Ghaliya and Brigitte, Maréchal. 2015. 'Muslims in Western Europe in the Late Twentieth Century: Emergence and Transformations in "Muslim" Revindications and Collective Mobilization Efforts'. In *Routledge Handbook of Islam in the West*, edited by Roberto Tottoli, 85–105. Abingdon & New York: Routledge.

El Asri, Farid, and Brigitte Maréchal. 2012. 'Islam belge en mouvement: quelques cadrages de réalités complexes'. In *Islam belge au pluriel*, edited by Brigitte Maréchal and Farid El Asri, 7–47. Louvain-la-Neuve: Presses universitaires de Louvain.

Escarnot, Jean-Manuel. 2017. *Djihad, C'est arrive près de chez vous*. Paris: Robert Laffont.

Fischer, Johan. 2015. *Islam, Standards, and Technoscience in Global Halal Zones*. London & New York: Routledge.

Foucault, Michel. 1975. *Surveiller et Punir: Naissance de la prison*. Paris: Gallimard.

Foucault, Michel. 1984. 'On the Genealogy of Ethics: An Overview of Work a Progress'. In *The Foucoult Reader*, edited by Paul Rabinow, 340–373. New York: Pantheon Book.

Foucault, Michel. 1984. 'What is Enlightenment?'. In *The Foucoult Reader*, edited by Paul Rabinow, 32–50. New York: Pantheon Book.

Foucault, Michel. 1995. *Discipline and Punish: The Birth of the Prison*. Translated by Alan Sheridan. New York: Vintage.

Hallaq, Wael B. 2002. *Authority, Continuity, and Change in Islamic Law*. Cambridge: Cambridge University Press.

Hatto, Peter. 2010. *Standards and Standardization Handbook*. Brussels: Directorate-General for Research Industrial Technologies, European Commission.

Istasse, Manon. 2015. 'Green Halal: à la recherché d'un halal éthique'. In *Les sens du Halal: Une norme dans un marché mondial*, edited by Florence Bergeaud-Blackler, 123–136. Paris: CNRS Editions.

Kadi, Wadad. 2001. 'Authority'. In *Encyclopedia of the Quran*, vol. I, 188–190. Leiden: Brill.

Kimbrell, Eddie. 2000. 'What is Codex Alimentarius?' *AgBioForum* 3, no. 4: 197–202.

Labarre, F., and R. François. 1990. *Gloire et sacrifices du 2e RTM; Gembloux mai 1940*. Gembloux: les éditions de l'Orneau.

Laroussi, Meryem. 2012. 'Le marché du halal en Belgique'. Master's Thesis. Louvain School of Management, Université Catholique de Louvain.

Lever, John and M. Miele. 2012. 'The Growth of Halal Meat Markets in Europe: An Exploration of the Supply Side Theory of Religion'. *Journal of Rural Studies* 28, no. 4: 528–537.

Lever, John and Johan Fischer. 2018. *Kosher and Halal Business Compliance*. London: Routledge.

Lever, John and Johan Fischer. 2018. *Religion, Regulation, Consumption: Globalising Kosher and Halal Markets*. Manchester: Manchester University Press.

Martiniello, Marco and Andrea Rea. 2013. *Une brève histoire de l'immigration en Belgique*. Bruxelles: Fédération Wallonie-Bruxelles.

Marx, Karl and Friedrich Engels. 1978. 'Manifesto of the Communist Party'. In *The Marx-Engels Reader*, edited by R.C. Tucker, 469–500. New York: W.W. Norton.

Michot, Yahya. 1996. 'Les musulmans de Belgique en 1928'. *Le Conseil: Revue du Conseil Supérieur des Musulmans de Belgique*. Bruxelles, Sha'ban 1416/ Janvier, no. 5: 33.

Mignolo, Walter D. 2011. *The Darker Side of Western Modernity*. Durham & London: Duke University Press.

Mignolo, Walter D. 2018. 'Foreword. On Pluriversality and Multipolarity'. In *Constructing the Pluriverse: The Geopolitics of Knowledge*, edited by Bernd Reiter, ix–xv. Durham & London: Duke University Press.

Panafit, Lionel. 1999. *Quand le droit écrit l'Islam: lintégration juridique de l'Islam en Belgique*. Bruxelles: Bruylant.

Porter, Theodore M. 1995. *Trust in Numbers. The Pursuit of Objectivity in Science and Public Life*. Princeton: Princeton University Press.

Querejazu, Amaya. 2016. 'Encountering the Pluriverse: Looking for Alternatives in Other Words'. *Revista Brasileira de Politica Internacionale* 59, no. 2: 1–16.

Rabinow, Paul. 1996. *Essays on the Anthropology of Reasons*. Princeton: Princeton University Press.

Renaerts, Monique. 1998. 'L'historique de l'Islam en Belgique et la problématique de sa reconnaissance'. In *L'islam en Belgique*, edited by Christophe Derenne and Joëlle Kwaschin, 53–70. Bruxelles: Luc Pires.

Robertson, Roland. 1995. 'Glocalisation: Time-Space and Homogeneity-Heterogeneity'. In *Global Modernities*, edited by Mike Featherstone, Scott Lash, and Roland Robertson, 25–44. Sage: London, 1995.

Sābiq, Sayyid. 2004. *Fiqh al-Sunna*. Cairo: Dār al-Hadīs.

Sägesser, Caroline and Corinne Torrekens. 2008. *La Répresentation de l'Islam*. Bruxelles: CRISP, no. 1996–1997: 5–55.

Schneiderman, Ron. 2015. *Modern Standardization: Case Studies at the Crossroads of Technology, Economics, and Politices*. Hoboken: Wiley.

Sekkat, Noor. 2015. 'Potential and Analysis of the Halal Meat Chain in Belgium'. Bachelor's Thesis. Solvay Brussels School of Economics and Management, Brussels.

Shapin, Steven and Simon Schaffer. 1985. *Leviathan and the Air-Pump. Hobbes, Boyle, and the Experimental Life*. Princeton: Princeton University Press.

Strathern, Marilyn. 2000. 'Introduction: New Accountabilities'. In *Audit Cultures Anthropological Studies in Audit, Ethics and the Academy*, edited by Marilyn Strahtern, 1–18. London and New York: Routledge, 2000.

Timmermans, Stefan and Steven Epstein. 2010. 'A World of Standards but not a Standard World: Toward a Sociology of Standards and Standardization'. *Annual Review of Sociology* 36: 69–89.

Torrekens, Corinne. 2012. 'L'introduction du halal dans les écoles communales: entre visibilité de l'islam, reconnaissance et "neutralité" de l'espace public'. In *Polémiques à l'école. Perspectives internationales sur le lien social*, edited by Geoffrey Grandjean and Grégory Piet, 89–103. Paris: Armand Colin.

Torrekens, Corinne. 2012. 'Religion, mosquées, Halal: Une affirmation identitaire?'. In *L'immigration Marocaine en Belgique, mémoires et destinées*, edited by Ahmed Medhoune, Sylvie Lausberg, Marco Martinielleo, and Andrea Rea. Mons: Couleurs Livres.

Torrekens, Corinne. 2015. *Belgo-Marocains, Belgo-Turcs: (auto-portrait) de nos concitoyens*. Bruxelles: Foundation Roi Baudouin.

Torrekens, Corinne. 2020. *Islams de Belgique: Enjeux et Perspective*. Bruxelles: Editions de l'Université de Bruxelles.

Velarde, A., Rodriguez, P., Dalmau, A., Fuentes, C., Llonch, P., von Holleben, K.V., Anil, M.H., Lambooij, J.B., Pleiter, H. Yesildere, T., and Cenci-Coga, B.T. 2014. 'Religious Slaughtering: Evaluation of Current Practices in Selected Countries'. *Meat Science* 96: 278–287.

Verbeke, Wim, Pieter Rutsaert, Karijn Bonne, and Iris Vermeir. 2013. 'Credence quality coordination and consumers' willingness-to-pay for certified halal labeled meat'. *Meat Science* 95: 790–797.

Weber, Max. 1946. *From Max Weber: Essays in Sociology*. Translated by H.H. Gerth and C. Wright Mills. New York: Oxfod University Press.

Yakin, Ayang Utriza and Ima Sri Rahmani, *"Halal Food Consumption among the Indonesian Muslim Minority in Belgium,"* in Research Paper Series, Vol. 5, Institute for Asian Muslim Studies, Waseda University, Tokyo. Proceedings of the International Workshop on "Halal Food Consumption in East and West", March, 2018, pp. 123–150.

Archives

Annexes du Moniteur Belge/Bijlagen bij het Belgisch Staatsblad, 2 March 2006.

Annexes du Moniteur Belge/Bijlagen bij het Belgisch Staatsblad, 6 June 2006.

Annexes du Moniteur Belge/Bijlagen bij het Belgisch Staatsblad, 23 December 2003.

Annexes du Moniteur Belge/Bijlagen bij het Belgisch Staatsblad, 31 March 2008.

Annexes du Moniteur Belge/Bijlagen bij het Belgisch Staatsblad, 7 May 2007.

Annexes du Moniteur Belge/Bijlagen bij het Belgisch Staatsblad, 8 September 2010.

Annexes du Moniteur Belge/Bijlagen bij het Belgisch Staatsblad, 7 December 2011.

Annexes du Moniteur Belge/Bijlagen bij het Belgisch Staatsblad, 7 January 2014.

Annexes du Moniteur Belge/Bijlagen bij het Belgisch Staatsblad, 4 November 2016.

Annexes du Moniteur Belge/Bijlagen bij het Belgisch Staatsblad, 7 December 2015.

Annexes du Moniteur Belge/Bijlagen bij het Belgisch Staatsblad, 8 November 2016.

Annexes du Moniteur Belge/Bijlagen bij het Belgisch Staatsblad, 10 October 2011.
Annexes du Moniteur Belge/Bijlagen bij het Belgisch Staatsblad, 16 May 2013.
Annexes du Moniteur Belge/Bijlagen bij het Belgisch Staatsblad, 11 January 2011.
Annexes du Moniteur Belge/Bijlagen bij het Belgisch Staatsblad, 21 September 2006.
Annexes du Moniteur Belge/Bijlagen bij het Belgisch Staatsblad, 29 August 2011.
Annexes du Moniteur Belge/Bijlagen bij het Belgisch Staatsblad, 22 January 2008.
Annexes du Moniteur Belge/Bijlagen bij het Belgisch Staatsblad, 27 January 2015.
Annexes du Moniteur Belge/Bijlagen bij het Belgisch Staatsblad, 27 January 2015.
Annexes du Moniteur Belge/Bijlagen bij het Belgisch Staatsblad, 31 July 2008.
Annexes du Moniteur Belge/Bijlagen bij het Belgisch Staatsblad, 30 July 2010.
Comptes Annuels en Euros in 2016, BE0827.964.482, 12 pages.
Moniteur belge/Belgisch Staatsblad, 1 June 2017.
Moniteur belge/Belgisch Staatsblad, 18 July 2017.
Moniteur belge/Belgisch Staatsblad, 23 October 1974.
Moniteur belge/Belgisch Staatsblad, 9 July 1996.

News (*Online and Printed*)

http://www.fao.org/fao-who-codexalimentarius/about-codex/en/#c453333.
http://www.parishalalexpo.com/belgium-halal-estimated-at-1-7-billion-euros.
http://www.sudinfo.be/1580627/article/2016-05-24/781887-musulmans-vivent-en-belgique-decouvrez-la-carte-commune-par-commune
https://islamqa.info/fr/answers/9056/le-jugement-de-lusage-des-parfums-contenant-de-lalcool
https://www.7sur7.be/7s7/fr/1502/2010/article/print/detail/1091011/IlyaconfusiondegenresdanslechefdupresidentduMRAX.dhtml
https://www.cen.eu/work/ENdev/whatisEN/Pages/default.aspx
https://www.iqrashop.com/Parfum-Aicha-sans-Alcool-30ml-parfums-musc-Bien-etre-p27042-1__221_293_291.html
https://www.iso.org/certification.html, accessed on 28 march 2019.
https://www.lalibre.be/economie/libre-entreprise/de-la-vodka-et-du-whisky-halal-belges-51b8df83e4b0de6db9c441d9
https://www.saphirnews.com/La-Belgique-lance-sa-norme-halal_a11217.html
https://www.sudinfo.be/art/1393652/article/2015-10-09/le-scandale-du-halal-belge-deux-certificateurs-dans-le-collimateur-de-la-justice.
https://www.vrt.be/vrtnws/fr/2019/02/12/certificats-halal-lexecutif-des-musulmans-de-belgique-deplore/
https://www.yabiladi.com/forum/alcool-dans-parfum-4-1464533.html
https://www.lecho.be/economie-politique/belgique/economie/les-asbl-creent-un-nouvel-emploi-sur-deux/10009586.html
www.cen.eu, accessed online 15 April 2019.

La Dernière Heure-Les Sports, Wednesday 4 August 2010, pp. 2–4.
Le Soir, 17 January 2007, p. 6.
Le Vif, no. 10/6 March 2015, pp. 50–51.
Le Soir, 5 January 2001, 'Les Nouveaux adeptes d' Allah', by Eve-Marie Vaes and Catherine Callico, accessed online 4 March 2018.

Interviews and Informal Discussions (in French, Arabic, English, and Indonesian)

Informal discussion in English with FAA, Berlin, 4 May 2019.
Informal discussion in French with Karim Genaert, the Director of EuroHalal Antwerpen, 13 December 2018.
Informal discussion in Indonesian with US, Leuven and Ghent, 16 April 2018 and 2 February 2019.
Interview in Arabic with IM, Namur, 23 June 2017.
Interview in Arabic with Imam Shaykh Abdulhadi Suwayf, Imam of the Great Mosque of Brussels, in Brussels, 21 February 2017.
Interview in Arabic with Imam Shaykh AD, ex-president of the 'Ittihād al-Islāmiyy li al-Talabah wa al-Shabāb', Brussels, 17 June 2017.
Interview in Arabic with Imam Shaykh MAC, Imam of the Islamic Centre of Alkhayria Belgica, Brussels, 17 February 2017.
Interview in Arabic with Imam Shaykh Mohammad Todjkani, the President of the Ligue des Imams de Belgique, Brussels, 11 January 2017.
Interview in Arabic with MB, Liège, 6 June 2017.
Interview in English with Iqbal Ahmed Qureshi, Brussels, 20 February 2017.
Interview in English with Johan Brunyseels, the Sales Manager of MANNA, Antwerpen, 13 May 2017.
Interview in English with Nurita Abubakar Syah, Brussels, 20 February 2017.
Interview in French with AB, Louvain-la-Neuve, 13 January 2017.
Interview in French with Abdulwahid Alami, lecturer at the Islamic Centre of Alkhayria Belgica, Brussels, 17 February 2017.
Interview in French with AM, Namur, 23 June 2017.
Interview in French with BB, in Liège, 6 June 2017.
Interview in French with Dr. Abdul Jawwad Ouazzani, head of the halal department at the *CICB* 2013/4, Brussels, 14 February 2017.
Interview in French with Dr. Hicham Bouchama, Director of the HALABEL, Louvain-la-Neuve, 8 March 2017.
Interview in French with Ghislain Breydel, Brussels Invest and Export (BIE) of the Region Brussels-Capital, Brussels, 27 March 2017.
Interview in French with Hajib el-Hadjaji, Association Belge des Professionels Musulmans (ABPM), Brussels, 16 February 2017.

Interview in French with Hakim Azaoum, Director of the Halal Expertise, Louvain-la-Neuve and Brussels, 21 January 2017, 22 February 2017, 6 April 2018, and 25 April 2018.
Interview in French with Imam Shaykh Mustafa Kastit, Reponsible of Halal Affairs at the Great Mosque of the CICB 1997–2013 and Imam of the Centre of Education and Youth Cultures, Brussels, 10 March 2017.
Interview in French with Imam Syaikh Muhammad Galay Ndiaye, Mufti of the Great Mosque of Brussels, Brussels, 14 February 2017.
Interview in French with KA, in Namur, 23 June 2017.
Interview in French with Karim Geirnaert, Mjahed Sebae, Mohamed El Akily, and Roger Verheyen, the responsibles of Euro-Halal, Brussels, 21 February 2017, 11 May 2017, 11 October 2018, 13 December 2018, and 30 April 2019.
Interview in French with M. Salah Eldin, Director of the EIHC (European Islamic Halal Council), Louvain-la-Neuve, 18 February 2017.
Interview in French with Marc Deschamps, Director of the Halal Group of AWEX (Agence Wallone à l'exportation et aux Investissement étrangers), Brussels, 7 March 2017 and 13 July 2018.
Interview in French with MB, Namur, 22 June 2017.
Interview in French with Mohamed Saïd Guermit, member of the Conseil Supérieur des musulmans de Belgique (CSMB) and President-Founder of Political Party the 'Mouvement pour l'Education' (MEP), Louvain-la-Neuve, 20 January 2017.
Interview in French with MS, in Liège, 6 June 2017.
Interview in French with Oliver Willocx, Director of the BECI (Brussels Enterprises Commerce and Industry), Brussels, 11 January 2017.
Interview in French with Salah Echallaoui, the President of EMB (Exécutive des Musulmans de Belgique), Brussels, 24 February 2017.
Interview in French with YB, Louvain-la-Neuve, 15 February 2017 and 5 May 2017.
Interview in French, Christine Vrancken, the owner and manager of the online site 'Halal Belgium', Louvain-la-Neuve, 3 January 2017.
Interview in French, with Karim Chemlal, Vice-President of the LBM (Ligue des Musulmans de Belgique), Brussels, 14 February 2017.
interview in Indonesian with GvT, Antwerpen, 13 May 2017.
Interview in Indonesian with HA in Berlin, 9 June 2017.
Written interview in English with Jan Bruffaerts, Flanders Investment and Trade (FIT) of the Region of Flanders, 24 May 2012.
Written interview in French with YM, Belgium, 11 July 2018.

CHAPTER 8

The Italian and Spanish Legal Experiences with Halal Certifying Bodies

Rossella Bottoni

1 The Notion of Halal between Pluralism and Calls for Standardisation

The growth in halal-related scholarly studies reflects the ever-increasing importance of the global halal market,[1] which includes not only food products,[2] but also cosmetics, medicines, financial products,[3] and tourism.[4] Scientific publications have contributed to knowledge on halal industry from the perspective of a wide range of disciplines. Law is no exception. The increase of states' and economic and social actors' interest in halal products results—as with any other human activity—in the need to lay down legal rules to regulate different related aspects. Certification is one of the most debated ones today, as exemplified by the judgement of 26 February 2019 whereby the Court of Justice of the European Union held that the provisions concerned of the European Union law 'must be interpreted as not authorising the placing of the Organic logo of the EU on products derived from animals which have been slaughtered in accordance with religious rites without first being stunned'.[5] Legal studies

1 See, *inter alia*, Lever and Fischer, *Religion, Regulation and Consumption*; Fischer, *The Halal Frontier*.

2 Al-Teinaz et al., *The Halal Food Handbook*; Riaz and Chaudry, *Handbook of Halal Food Production*; Barreiro, 'Halal', 84–92; Fuccillo et al., 'Diritto e religioni nelle scelte alimentari', 21–22.

3 Sandıkcı and Rice, *Handbook of Islamic Marketing*; Amicarelli et al., 'The Influence of Halal Certified Products', 9; Benali, *El crecimiento de la banca y las finanzas islámicas*, 2017; Toselli, *Le diversità convergenti*, 151–161.

4 Hall and Prayag, *The Routledge Handbook of Halal Hospitality and Islamic Tourism*; Biancone et al., 'Halal Tourism', 395–404; Bolifa El Gharbi, et al. 'Razones', 175–185; Carmona Barrero et al., 'La virtualización', 220–225; Cuesta-Valiño et al., 'Sustainable, Smart and Muslim-Friendly', 1778; Halkias et al., 'Halal Products and Services', 1450012-1-1450012-12; Mangano et al., 'Il turismo halal', 57–76; Rasul, 'The Trends', 434–450; Sanchez and Fernandez-Hernandez, 'Mayrit on', 81–93; Zergane, *The Retard of the Positioning*.

5 *Oeuvre d'assistance aux bêtes d'abattoirs* (OABA) *v Ministre de l'Agriculture et de l'Alimentation and Others*, para 52. Text at https://curia.europa.eu (accessed 26 October 2020).

 | DOI:10.1163/9789004459236_009

on halal certification thus offer and will continue to offer a useful perspective to look at the characteristics and developments of the halal market.

This chapter aims to examine halal certifying bodies in Italy and Spain from the legal point of view. The legal perspective does not only provide a method to compare and contrast the two countries but also serves as an approach to address a problem common to many other countries concerned with halal certification, that is, the need to envisage a balance, enshrined in legal rules, between the respect for pluralism and the calls for standardisation.

Pluralism is an intrinsic quality of Islam, which is characterised by national, cultural, language, and even religious differences. A theological and philosophical analysis of the plural character of Islam goes beyond my present purposes. I take pluralism into account as an existing situation that affects the understanding of halal and the legal regulation of halal certification in Muslim-minority countries like Italy and Spain. An example can illustrate this point. A snack-bar manager of Moroccan origin had put stickers with the writing 'halal' (usually translated as 'lawful' or 'permitted') on products that did not contain pork. A customer, a Muslim woman of Pakistani origin, found out that a snack she had bought and eaten contained meat from animals that had been stunned before slaughter, and claimed damages. The judge refused to decide whether 'halal' meant 'no pork' or 'no pork and no stunned animals'.[6] This controversy took place in Amsterdam but could just as well have occurred in Italy or Spain, which have become increasingly concerned with halal certification.

This concern has grown not only to address a specific religious need expressed by an increasing percentage of the resident population, but also to promote economic interests, which have been especially relevant in the times of the recession started by the financial crisis of 2007–2008. Italian and Spanish firms have been encouraged to obtain a halal certificate as a powerful means of expanding into the markets of Muslim-majority countries. Some drawbacks have nonetheless been noted; one of them is the difficulty in interpreting halal standards.[7]

Whereas there is unanimous agreement on some requirements, a split exists over others, including the lawfulness of reversible stunning.[8] The issue of stunning animals before slaughter has monopolised the debate on halal meat. It has been argued that this controversy 'is compromising the probity of halal

6 Havinga, 'Regulating Halal and Kosher Foods', 251.
7 Talib et al., 'Motivations and Limitations', *passim*.
8 Fuseini et al., 'Halal Meat Fraud', 129.

products because it has stood in the way of developing a robust and consensual system of certification'.[9] It should not be neglected that ascertaining halalness requires a 'from-farm-to-fork' approach, thus taking into account aspects like animal welfare on the farm, during transport and lairaging; cleaning and disinfection; materials used during production, including greases and oils; separation of halal and haram substances at all stages of the production process. Contamination of halal food by haram items should be prevented also during storage, display and sale.[10]

For the Italian and Spanish firms interested in obtaining a halal certificate, the choice of one among many different halal certifying bodies means the adoption not only of a specific view on what halal is but also of specific rules and procedures implemented to verify that halal requirements are respected.[11] When these companies obtain a halal certificate in order to export their goods, they have to take into account that products accepted as halal by some countries may be rejected by others, and thus they may have to spend a considerable amount of money and time to repeat the certification procedure for each area of interest.[12] In fact, the marketability of their products also depends on the credibility of the halal body certifying them. Countries like Malaysia, Indonesia, and Singapore have entrusted state agencies with the halal certification process for products in both the domestic and the international market: this is the case of Jabatan Kemajuan Islam Malaysia (JAKIM), Majelis Ulama Indonesia (MUI) and Majlis Ugama Islam Singapura (MUIS). Through the process of accreditation, these agencies may recognise halal certifying bodies in non-Muslim countries, including Italy and Spain, as trustworthy partners that guarantee compliance with the respective halal standards. Italian and Spanish companies, which are subsequently certified by an accredited halal certifying body, may put the halal logo of the certifying body on the package of the exported products. This logo communicates to consumers in a Muslim country that the products concerned are certified consistently with the halal standards issued in that country.[13] However, the halal certificate obtained from a halal certifying body accredited in one country may not be recognised in another.

9 Pointing, John et al., 'Illegal Labelling', 213.

10 Van der Spiegel et al., 'Halal Assurance', 110 and 114; White and Samuel, 'Fairtrade and Halal Food Certification', 389–390; Bonne and Verbeke, 'Religious Values', 40–42.

11 See van der Spiegel et al., 'Halal Assurance', 116; Fuseini et al., 'Halal Meat Fraud', 128.

12 See Toselli, *Le diversità convergenti*, 124–125 and 129.

13 Khan and Haleem, 'Understanding "Halal"', 36.

The above remarks should not be misunderstood. I would like to stress that nowhere in this chapter do I assume that pluralism is something negative, nor do I unconditionally support the need for halal standardisation. There are nonetheless two objective circumstances that should not be neglected. One is the existence of a plurality of Muslim communities, which implies the existence of a plurality of certifying bodies having diverging halal standards. The other is the existence of calls by interested parties and scholars for unified halal standards, in order to make halal production less ambiguous, and to help customers and consumers to choose products that comply with religious requirements. A number of studies have reported on initiatives taken to standardise halal requirements.[14] These include the *General Guidelines for Use of the Term 'Halal'*, adopted in 1997 by the Codex Alimentarius Commission—a joint intergovernmental body of the Food and Agriculture Organization of the United Nations and the World Health Organization, with 188 Member States and one Member Organization (the European Union), working to harmonise international food standards. The guidelines are meant to 'recommend measures to be taken on the use of Halal claims in food labeling', in the awareness 'that there may be minor differences in opinion in the interpretation of lawful and unlawful animals and in the slaughter act, according to the different Islamic Schools of Thought. As such, these general guidelines are subjected to the interpretation of the appropriate authorities of the importing countries.'[15] Overall, they contain very generic definitions, but these are necessarily so: any further specification (be it the authorisation to perform reversible stunning or the prohibition of any form of stunning) ultimately belongs to the competence of religious authorities.[16]

The tension between the need to preserve pluralism—regarded by the European Court of Human Rights (ECtHR) as indissociable from a democratic

---

14 See, *inter alia*, Bergeaud-Blackler, 'Who Owns Halal?', 192–197; Toselli, *Le diversità convergenti*, 129–131; Amicarelli et al., 'The Influence of Halal Certified Products', 13; Kayadibi, 'A Way Forward', 105–116; van der Spiegel et al., 'Halal Assurance', 111–112; Havinga, 'Regulating Halal and Kosher Foods', 252.

15 The text is available at http://www.fao.org/3/Y2770E/y2770e08.htm (accessed 26 October 2020).

16 The expression 'religious authorities' is a standard one and includes anybody who is recognised as such by a religious denomination. The European standards of human rights protection include religious denominations' right to appoint their own religious leaders. See ECtHR, *Serif v. Greece*, application no. 38178/97, 14 December 1999; *Hasan and Chaush v. Bulgaria*, application no. 30985/96, 26 October 2000; *Agga v. Greece*, application nos. 0776/99 and 52912/99, 17 October 2002; *Supreme Holy Council of the Muslim Community v. Bulgaria*, application no. 39023/97, 16 March 2005.

society[17]—and the interest manifested by some social and economic actors in standardisation is the challenge posed to Italy and Spain in the legal regulation of halal certifying bodies.

2 The Legal Regulation of Islam in Italy and Spain and Its Impact on Halal Certification

The legal regulation of Islam in Italy and Spain fits into the interpretative framework elaborated by Silvio Ferrari as the European system of state-religions relationships. European countries are characterised by three common principles as regards the legal regulation of religion: protection of the individual right to religious freedom; respect for religious organisations' autonomy; and the state's selective cooperation with religious organisations.[18] Each of these principles will be examined in the following sections, specifically with regard to their application to halal certification.

2.1 *The Individual Right to Religious Freedom*

Italy and Spain—like other European countries—recognise the individual right to religious freedom. Every individual—citizen or foreigner, professing the majority's religion or a minority one—has the right *inter alia* to manifest their religion or belief, in worship, teaching, practice, and observance under Art. 9 of the European Convention on Human Rights,[19] signed and ratified by both Italy and Spain. According to the ECtHR, the manifestation of one's religion or belief in practice includes 'observing dietary rules'.[20] As highlighted by a great number of studies, religion is a major factor influencing food choices

---

17 ECtHR, *Buscarini and Others v. San Marino*, application no. 24645/94, 18 February 1999, para. 34.

18 Ferrari, 'Islam and the European System', 479–483.

19 Article 9 (freedom of thought, conscience and religion) of the European Convention of Human Rights reads as follows: '1. Everyone has the right to freedom of thought, conscience and religion; this right includes freedom to change his religion or belief and freedom, either alone or in community with others and in public or private, to manifest his religion or belief, in worship, teaching, practice and observance. 2. Freedom to manifest one's religion or beliefs shall be subject only to such limitations as are prescribed by law and are necessary in a democratic society in the interests of public safety, for the protection of public order, health or morals, or for the protection of the rights and freedoms of others'. The text is available at https://www.echr.coe.int/Documents/Convention_ENG.pdf (accessed 26 October 2020).

20 ECtHR, *Jakóbsky v. Poland*, application no. 18429/06, 7 December 2010, para. 45.

and, more broadly, consumer behaviour and attitude.[21] The issue of the respect for the dietary rules prescribed by one's religion or belief has been expressly addressed by Italy's National Bioethics Committee: food differences related to ethnic origins or religious or ideological beliefs deserve protection because they express a person's or a group's identity. This is even more so for dietary rules prescribed by religions or beliefs, whereby individuals manifest their personal and deep adherence to a life and world vision. The integration of differences among cultures must be promoted by avoiding assimilation or separation liable to lead to homogenising undifferentiation and discriminatory marginalisation. The respect for this type of food differences does not generally pose problems of conflict with the fundamental values and principles that must be respected by all members of society.[22] The Committee thus concludes that they may be approached in such a way as to make them a factor of reciprocal enrichment.[23] In this perspective, halal certification can be seen as an effective instrument to protect Muslims' right to religious freedom, by helping them to choose products consistent with their religion-oriented preferences.[24]

2.2 *Respect for Religious Organisations' Autonomy*

This principle 'basically means absence of state intervention in the doctrine and internal organisation of religious communities'.[25] As regards halal certification, this implies that it belongs to Muslim communities to define what halal is and what it is not. Italian and Spanish secular authorities are not directly competent in defining halal. It is worth noting that even in the law of the European Union, to which Italy and Spain belong, there is no legal definition of halal. Art. 5 § 2 of the Treaty on European Union stipulates that '[u]nder the principle of conferral, the Union shall act only within the limits of the competences conferred upon it by the Member states in the Treaties to attain the objectives set

21 See, *inter alia*, Bonne and Verbeke, 'Religious Values', 35–47; Fuccillo, *Il cibo degli dei*; Ceserani, 'Cibo 'religioso' e diritto', 369–384.

22 It should be noted that Italy recognises the right to slaughter animals according to a religious rite, that is, without previous stunning (see Ferrari and Bottoni, *Legislation Regarding Religious Slaughter*, 110–115). Although this practice is controversial, public debate in Italy has not so far been as heated as in other countries, where measures have been adopted to prohibit it (see Bottoni, 'I recenti decreti', 523–558). The same remarks apply to Spain.

23 Italy's National Bioethics Committee, *Alimentazione differenziata e interculturalità*, 2–6. See also Fuccillo et al., 'Diritto e religioni nelle scelte alimentari', 7–15.

24 Baldassarre and Campo, 'Influences of Islamic Culture in Marketing and the Role of Halal Certification', 2015.

25 Ferrari, 'Islam and the European System', 480–481.

out therein. Competences not conferred upon the Union in the Treaties remain with the Member states'. This is the case of the regulation of religion, which remains 'primarily a matter for Member states at national level'.[26] However, as mentioned, Italy's and Spain's internal legal systems refrain from providing a legal definition of halal and leave this issue entirely to private actors (companies and religious authorities).[27]

This situation is consistent with the legal principles prevailing in the European Union space and with the European history of regulation of religion, but it is not necessarily the only possible solution in a legal space where Islam is not the majority's religion. In fact, other Muslim-minority countries have opted for different solutions. Some federated states of the USA have enacted statutes to define what halal is, in order to prevent fraud.[28] However, the constitutional legitimacy of these government-enacted definitions of halal is dubious.[29] It has been argued that these laws breach both the free exercise clause (because consumers may be required to accept as shariʿa-compliant something which they do not regard as such), and the establishment clause (because public authorities interfere with religion).[30] Singapore, as mentioned, has created the Islamic Religious Council, a state department charged with Muslim religious affairs:[31] halal production, space, work processes, trade, and consumption have been standardised and bureaucratised; companies that do not respect such standards are imposed sanctions.[32]

Although secular authorities in Italy and Spain are not *directly* competent in defining halal, they can still *indirectly* regulate it when related aspects concern areas falling within their competence.[33] These are the cases of trademarks and labels, which they are competent to regulate in the pursuit of con-

26 Doe, *Law and Religion in Europe*, 241.

27 On this point see Bergeaud-Blackler, 'The Halal Certification Market', 105–126.

28 Milne, 'Protecting Islam's Garden', 63; Minns, 'Food Fights', 724–729. See also Tirabassi, *Macellazione rituale e certificazione*.

29 The same applies to kosher certification. The first law to protect consumers from kosher fraud was passed as early as 1922 by the State of New York, whose example was later followed by other states (Havinga, 'Regulating Halal and Kosher Foods', 248). The constitutional legitimacy of kosher fraud statutes has also been questioned. See Masoudi, 'Kosher Food Regulation', 667–696; Morgan, 'The Constitutionality', 247–282; Sullivan, 'Are Kosher Food Laws', 201–245; Rosenthal, 'Food For Thought', 951–1013; Greenawalt, 'Religious Law', 785–810; Popovsky, 'The Constitutional Complexity', 75–107.

30 Milne, 'Protecting Islam's Garden', 72–81.

31 Steiner, 'Governing Islam', 1–16.

32 Fischer, 'Branding Halal', 18.

33 For an exhaustive treatment of religious organisations' certification power in the Italian legal system, see Chizzoniti, *Le certificazioni confessionali*.

sumer protection and transparency in commercial relationships. This issue has been regulated also at the European Union level, *inter alia* by Regulation no. 1169/2011 of the European Parliament and of the Council on the provision of food information to consumers.[34] Normative instruments on trademarks—the most distinctive signs linking a producer and the market—and labels—meant to help consumers to make considerate choices by preventing deception[35]—do not concern *specifically* halal certification, but may nonetheless apply *also* to it. The issue at stake, with halal labels as well as with any other labels, is the simplification of complex information, in order to ease identification and influence consumers' behaviour. The existence of a plurality of halal certifying agents (including self-certifying actors) results in a great variety of labels, which leads to uncertainty about halal requirements.[36] For example, halal restaurants and fast food chains advertising their meat as halal generally do not specify whether animals were stunned before slaughter.[37] Despite calls for regulations clarifying the message that a halal label must convey,[38] it has been noted that the heterogeneity of Muslim consumers as well as the complexity of halal food production make the development of an unambiguous labeling system both expensive and unpractical. 'Demands for certification come from quite different sources and expectations vary greatly':[39] Muslim consumers have differing degrees of religiosity and attitudes towards animal welfare and, thus, different expectations about halal food.[40] Also, a greater amount of technical data does not necessarily imply a higher degree of consumer protection. Too much information may indeed be counterproductive and lead to the phenomenon of information overkill.[41] Providing all the required information (guarantee of the quality of a food product, methods

---

34 Regulation (EU) No. 1169/2011 of the European Parliament and of the Council of 25 October 2011 on the provision of food information to consumers, amending Regulations (EC) No. 1924/2006 and (EC) No. 1925/2006 of the European Parliament and of the Council, and repealing Commission Directive 87/250/EEC, Council Directive 90/496/EEC, Commission Directive 1999/10/EC, Directive 2000/13/EC of the European Parliament and of the Council, Commission Directives 2002/67/EC and 2008/5/EC and Commission Regulation (EC) No. 608/2004 Text with EEA relevance, published in the Official Journal of the European Union L 304 of 22 November 2011.

35 Malkawi, 'Food Labeling and Halal Mark', 103.

36 White and Samuel, 'Fairtrade and Halal Food Certification', 394.

37 Fuseini et al., 'Halal Meat Fraud', 130.

38 Rios et al., 'Do Halal Certification Country of Origin and Brand Name Familiarity Matter?', 682.

39 Lever et al., *From the Slaughterhouse to the Consumer*, 77.

40 White and Samuel, 'Fairtrade and Halal Food Certification', 394–396.

41 Savorani, 'Il diritto all'informazione', 597–598.

of productions, procedures of quality assurance, and so on) would probably 'result in a label that is unintelligible, certainly highly confusing, and probably prohibitively expensive to generate. It is even conceivable that such a label would be so large as to dominate or even completely cover the product packaging'.[42]

If Italy's and Spain's legal systems do not provide for a definition of halal, and if their public authorities do not take part in monitoring and enforcing halal standards, how can consumers be guaranteed that a product advertised and sold as halal actually complies with their religious requirements? In case of fraud, Italy and Spain do not apply ad hoc rules specifically approved to regulate halal certification but resort to general rules concerning food mislabelling and aimed at preventing and punishing commercial fraud, including, where this is the case, those prescribed by the Penal Code,[43] irrespective of the religious orientation of the products or actors concerned.[44] It should be stressed that secular authorities may only prosecute fraudulent activities: these are cases of the use of suspect ingredients,[45] and sale of illegally slaughtered animals or of meat unfit for human consumption. Intentional mislabelling of non-halal food products as halal should be understood as either a false declaration of meat species or an omission of present meat species.[46] Pursuant to the principle of the respect for religious organisations' autonomy, secular authorities may not decide whether meat coming from stunned animals is halal or not, as in the above-mentioned case of the snack bar in Amsterdam.

2.3 *States' Selective Cooperation with Religious Organisations*

The third, and last, principle of Silvio Ferrari's European system of state-religions relationships must be framed in the context of the democratic states' attitude to cooperate with all social entities, including those having a religious (or ideological) orientation. Forms of cooperation include public funding and the signing of bilateral agreements between the state and the representative entity of a religious organisation, which thus recognises a number of rights and privileges. Cooperation has a selective character, because rights and privileges

42 White and Samuel, 'Fairtrade and Halal Food Certification', 394.

43 Germanò, 'Informazione alimentare halal', 1–10.

44 This also applies to other European countries. See for example Pointing, 'Strict Liability Food Law', 387–391 as regards the UK.

45 Talib et al., 'Motivations and Limitations', 2666; White and Samuel, 'Fairtrade and Halal Food Certification', 388.

46 See Fuseini et al., 'Halal Meat Fraud', 136–137; Pointing, et al., 'Illegal Labelling', 210.

are not equally recognised for all religious organisations. European states are more prone to collaborate with those regarded as sharing its principles, and less or not at all with those perceived of as alien or hostile to democratic and/or national values.[47]

As regards Italy and Spain specifically, their selective attitude has been aptly described as a three-tier system: the upper tier is represented by the Catholic Church, the most privileged religious organisation; the middle position is occupied by a limited number of religious organisations that have succeeded in obtaining a legal status equal or similar to that of the Catholic Church, through the signing of a bilateral agreement (*intesa* in Italy and *acuerdo* in Spain) between the respective representative entity and the state; the last tier is represented by all the other religious organisations that have not managed or wanted to level up to the status of the privileged religion and, consequently, are defined as 'non-privileged'.[48] Islam in Italy can be placed in the third tier and in Spain in the middle one. This difference might have had an impact on the two countries' different legal experiences with halal certifying bodies.

As mentioned, the Italian government, unlike the Spanish one, has not signed any bilateral agreements with a representative body of Muslim communities. In 1992, Unione delle Comunità Islamiche d'Italia (Union of Islamic Communities of Italy), an organisation reuniting a number of local associations and regarded as promoting a version of Islam influenced by the Muslim Brotherhood's ideology, drafted and presented the text of a bilateral agreement. A few months later, Centro Islamico Culturale d'Italia (Islamic Cultural Centre of Italy)—the Italian expression of the so-called Embassy Islam,[49] linked to the Great Mosque in Rome and to the ambassadors of Sunni Muslim states accredited to Italy or to the Holy See—requested to start negotiations for the signing of a bilateral agreement, without presenting a text. In 1996 and 1998, a draft text was proposed by both Associazione Musulmani Italiani (Italian Muslim Association), which represents Italian Muslims, and Comunità Religiosa Islamica (Islamic Religious Community, hereafter Co.Re.Is.), whose members are mainly converts.[50] The Italian government has never started negotiations with any of them.

The lack of a bilateral agreement has not meant the refusal or uninterest in any form of dialogue or collaboration with Muslim communities. The Italian government has sponsored the promotion of an Islamic consultative body

47 Ferrari, 'Islam and the European System', 482–483.
48 Ferrari and Ibán, *Diritto e religione in Europa*, 43–71.
49 See, *inter alia*, Laurence, 'Muslim Mobilization', *passim*.
50 Aluffi Beck-Peccoz, 'Islam in the European Union: Italy', 184–185.

reuniting the leaders of different organisations, Consulta Islamica (Islamic Council) between 2005 and 2010, and Comitato per l'Islam italiano (Committee for Italian Islam) afterwards.[51] However, this lack marks a difference in treatment from another Italian religious minority, for which the observance of dietary rules and certification are also very important. Under the bilateral agreement with the Union of Italian Jewish Communities, in force since 1989, Jews working in the armed forces, police or similar services (thus excluding those employed in other public offices, as well as in the private sector) have the right to observe Jewish dietary rules upon request and with the assistance of the local Jewish community, without any financial burden on their workplace. In other words, this category of Jews has the right to be provided with kosher food by the relevant Jewish community, which is also in charge with the related expenses[52] (a legal arrangement that further allows public authorities to avoid any concerns about kosher certification). Lacking a bilateral agreement with a Muslim organisation, no similar measure has been taken with regard to Muslims, who are not entitled to the rights recognised to the abovementioned category of Jews.

In Spain, as will be further examined below, a bilateral agreement has been signed between the state and a representative entity of Muslim communities that addresses the issue of a halal trademark. The corresponding bilateral agreement with the Federation of Jewish Communities of Spain also includes a provision on a kosher trademark.[53]

3 Italy's and Spain's Legal Experiences with Halal Certifying Bodies

3.1 *The Trademark Halal Italia and the 2010 Inter-Ministerial Convention*

Trademarks are one of the instruments to which halal certifying bodies resort. In Italy, halal trademarks, like any other trademarks, are regulated by the Industrial Property Code. The term 'halal' may be used freely and may not be monopolised by a single person or organisation. The request to register a trademark

51 Saint-Blancat, 'Italy', 282.

52 Article 7 §1 of the Law no. 101 of 8 March 1989 approving the bilateral agreement signed with the Union of Italian Jewish Communities, published in the Official Gazette of the Italian Republic no. 69 of 23 March 1989.

53 Art. 14 of the Law no. 25/1992 of 10 November 1992 approving the Agreement of Cooperation between the State and the Federation of Jewish Communities of Spain, published in the State Official Gazette no. 272 of 12 November 1992.

bearing only the word 'halal' (without any additional terms or signs) would be rejected because it would have no distinctive character.[54]

Trademarks may be individual or collective. In the former case, the owner of the trademark is the same person as the user. In the latter case, the trademark owner authorises other persons to use it. Collective halal trademarks protect consumers better than individual trademarks. A natural or legal person may register an individual trademark indicating respect for halal dietary rules but no previous control is legally required to verify that this declaration is true. The owner of the individual trademark becomes legally responsible and may be subject to civil or criminal penalties only *ex post*, when a fraud has been proved. By contrast, the owner of a collective halal trademark has the legal obligation *ex ante* to guarantee that the products or services bearing this trademark are shari'a-compliant. Pursuant to Art. 11 §2 of the Industrial Property Code,[55] the request to register a trademark must be accompanied by a copy of the regulation on its use, containing detailed rules on: 1) the characteristics that the products or services must possess in order to bear the trademark; 2) the checks that the trademark owner commits to make, in order to verify that those products or services actually possess such characteristics; 3) the sanctions imposed by the trademark owner on those who are authorised to use the trademark and breach the regulation on its use. A collective halal trademark thus offers more guarantees to consumers, whose trust is strengthened by the envisaged system of checks and sanctions.[56]

The plurality of Muslim organisations in Italy corresponds to a plurality of halal certifying bodies,[57] including private and commercial actors having no clear link to a religious authority.[58] As of May 2018, the database of the Italian Office for Patents and Trademarks reported 20 trademarks including the word

54 Scopel, *Le prescrizioni alimentari*, 11–12; Leonini, 'La certificazione', 145–150, Giuffrida, 'La certificazione di conformità', 103–105; Lojacono, 'La rilevanza dei simboli religiosi', 179–220.

55 Legislative Decree no. 30 of 10 February 2005, *Industrial Property Code, pursuant to Art. 15 of Law no. 273 of 12 December 2002*, published in the Official Gazette of the Italian Republic no. 52 of 4 March 2005, and last modified by the Legislative Decree no. 63 of 11 May 2018.

56 Scopel, *Le prescrizioni alimentari*, 12; Leonini, 'La certificazione del rispetto', 150–154; Giuffrida, 'La certificazione di conformità', 105–109; Lojacono, 'La rilevanza dei simboli religiosi', 168–170.

57 *Inter alia*, see http://www.halalitaly.org, http://www.wha-halal.org, http://www.halalglobal.it
(accessed 26 October 2020). See also Amicarelli et al., 'The Influence of Halal Certified Products', 14.

58 For a discussion of this problem, see Lojacono, 'I marchi', 25–38.

'halal' and seven requests for registration pending.[59] The first request was submitted in 2002 and the related trademark was registered in 2006. Of the 20 registered trademarks, five have been registered by natural persons, and 15 by legal persons. The latter include 12 retail shops and companies, and only three Muslim organisations. The three trademarks clearly linkable to Islamic religious authorities are (in order of registration): 1) Centro Islamico Crema, registered by a Muslim association bearing the same name, and located in the town of Crema, near Milan; 2) Halal Italia, a trademark registered by Co.Re.Is.—as mentioned, an already existing Muslim organisation and active since the 1990s to cater for the general needs of Muslims; 3) Halal International Authority, registered by Halal International Authority Onlus, a body created with the specific purpose of providing halal certification.

The most interesting halal certification experience in Italy is the one related to Halal Italia, which has been the object of the Inter-Ministerial Convention for the Support of the Initiative 'Halal Italia'. This was signed in 2010 in the light of the positive experience of a pilot project on halal certification in the food sector promoted in 2009 by the Region Lombardy, Union Camere Lombardia (the regional union of the Chambers of Commerce of Lombardy) and the Chamber of Commerce of Milan. This project had the two-fold purpose of: a) providing companies with business opportunities in the increasingly important halal market, with about 1.5 billion consumers and a value of over €150 billion; and b) introducing Lombardy's food excellence to the Muslim communities in the Mediterranean area and in the Middle East, and in particular in the United Arab Emirates, which has an important internal market as well as a strategic position for commerce and clearing in the Gulf area. Co.Re.Is was involved as an institutional partner. The project was characterised by three phases: 1) the organisation of a technical seminar in Milan on 20 March 2009 on the opportunities provided by the halal market and the modalities to obtain a halal certificate, which numerous food companies attended; 2) the arrangement of a standard 'certification package', valid three years, for Lombardy's interested companies, and the creation of a technical committee of evaluation at Co.Re.Is concerning all the stages of the production process, from the use of raw materials to the storage of finished goods; 3) the promotion of a mission in Dubai from 23 to 26 May 2009, with a business and at the same time institutional dimension, in order to start the process of recognition of the certificates issued by Co.Re.Is. At the end of the project, the participant companies obtained the halal certificate on the part of Co.Re.Is, consistent with the first

59 See http://www.uibm.gov.it (accessed 18 May 2018).

technical guidelines created in Italy on this matter, which not only specify forbidden materials but also include rules to be followed at all the production stages.[60] The guidelines list forbidden substances and exclude all additives that are not declared on the product label but may contaminate a product or its ingredients. According to the principle of non-contamination, halal substances may not come into contact with haram ones. For this purpose, the guidelines envisage appropriate sanitisation before halal production and separate production lines of incompatible foods or ingredients. They also aim to guarantee the traceability of halal products along the entire supply chain and the periodical training of the staff concerned.[61]

Co.Re.Is submitted its request to register the trademark Halal Italia on 13 May 2009. The trademark was registered on 23 November 2010, but the signing of the Inter-Ministerial Convention took place even before registration, on 30 June. The four signatories were the Ministries of Foreign Affairs, Economic Development, Health, and Agricultural, Food, and Forestry Policies.[62] Interestingly, but not surprisingly, the Convention was not signed by the Ministry of Internal Affairs, which is competent among other things for the regulation of the right to religious freedom and of the relationships between the state and religious organisations. In fact, the Convention has made it clear that its rationale was economic.

The beginning of the text refers to the four ministries' considerations on the need to support the internationalisation of the Italian production system, the protection of the 'made in Italy' labelling and the promotion of Italian interests abroad. Italian business operators have become more and more interested in the markets of the Muslim world and have increasingly requested innovative instruments for internationalisation. The Ministries took note of the request submitted to the Italian Office for Patents and Trademarks by Co.Re.Is. to register a trademark 'halal', valid for the entire national territory, to certify the compliance of food, cosmetic and pharmaceutical products produced in Italy with Koranic rules (*sic*). Having in mind the positive results attained by the abovementioned pilot project on halal certification, they committed: 1) to promoting the trademark Halal Italia so that interested companies could be aware of the opportunities offered in terms of expansion into the markets of Muslim-majority countries; 2) to having this trademark accredited to the Islamic coun-

60 See http://www.halalitalia.org/b/index.php?p=promos (accessed 26 October 2020).

61 See https://www.exportiamo.it/aree-tematiche/12635/la-certificazione-halal-cose-e-come-si-ottiene (accessed 26 October 2020).

62 See, *inter alia*, Conte et al., 'Ritual Slaughter', 156.

tries' authorities as a certification of quality recognised by the Italian state for the export of shari'a-compliant products; 3) to organising training courses for the business operators interested in obtaining the halal certificate. As should be expected, the Convention specifies that the certified Italian companies continue to have an obligation to abide by all the rules stipulated by the Italian legal system concerning production, distribution, sale, hygiene, and safety, as well as the related rules and procedures envisaged by the European Union.

The link between the importance of the economic factor, the promotion of the 'made in Italy', and halal certification has been highlighted also by Elena Toselli, an official at the Ministry of the Economic Development. As she has written, the strong power of attraction exercised by 'made in Italy' resides in the attention to detail and the handcraft skills commonly associated with Italian products and, more generally, the Italian lifestyle. In common opinion, 'made in Italy' means beautiful and well produced, and it is related to a heritage of arts and crafts, mistrust of homogenisation, and the search for excellence. 'Made in Italy' has such an evocative power that it may be regarded as a trademark itself—the most copied and exploited in the world. The agri-food sector is historically one of the four pillars of Italian excellence (along with the automotive, clothing, and design sectors). However, the economic crisis of the last decade has badly affected the agri-food sector and has reduced Italian companies' competitiveness in the international market. In this context, halal certification can be an effective instrument to strengthen Italian companies and, more broadly, to promote 'made in Italy', by favouring the meeting between the offer of Italian excellence and the demands for halal-compliant products.[63] Scholars have further noted that 'Italian food products have 264 EU quality schemes of which 160 Protected Designation of Origin (PDO), 103 Protected Geographical Indication (PGI) and 2 Traditional Speciality Guaranteed (TSG). EU awarded them only to high quality products as a guarantee of the protected origin, the authentic taste, the typicality and the high physical-chemical characteristics (MIPAF 2014). If halal certification is added to EU quality ones the product could be a complete set of guarantees for Muslims and why not non-Muslims consumers.'[64]

As mentioned, the acceptability of the halal certificate obtained by an Italian company depends also on the credibility of the halal certifying body in import countries. 'More diffused is the acceptability of halal certificate larger will be

63 Toselli, *Le diversità convergenti*, 131 and 225–227. See also Rios et al., 'Do Halal Certification Country of Origin and Brand Name Familiarity Matter?', 665–686, one of the very few studies on the importance of the country of origin in halal certification.

64 Amicarelli et al., 'The Influence of Halal Certified Products', 15–16.

the possibility to export.'[65] The Inter-Ministerial Convention aims to provide Italian companies certified by Halal Italia with greater opportunities for market penetration. At the same time, it should be stressed that its purpose is not to endorse a specific interpretation of what halal is, as this matter ultimately belongs to the religious authorities concerned. The content of Halal Italia's technical guidelines has not been the result of negotiations with ministerial authorities. These rules must be consistent with the general provisions (stipulated by both Italy and the European Union) on health, safety, hygiene, and so on, but, within this legal framework, it belongs to religious authorities to define the standards for halal certification.

3.2 Spain and the Marca de Garantía Halal de Junta Islámica

The Islamic Commission of Spain (ICS) is the most important representative body of Islamic communities in Spain. It was originally founded in 1992 by the two major Muslim federations in Spain, the Union of Islamic Communities of Spain and the Spanish Federation of Islamic Religious Entities, both of which group together a number of Muslim entities. In particular, the latter includes the Junta Islámica, which founded the Halal Institute in 1998, a private body pioneer in the certification of halal products.[66] Its creation met a need that up to then had not been satisfied, and it has since provided Spanish food companies with the unparalleled opportunity to expand their business into international markets.[67]

According to Art. 1 of its Statute, the ICS was founded in order to negotiate, sign, and supervise the implementation of a bilateral agreement with the state, which was willing to cooperate with only one representative body.[68] Art. 14 of the Cooperation Agreement Between the Spanish state and the ICS, signed and entered into force in 1992, stipulates that

> 1. In accordance with the spiritual dimension and specific peculiarities of Islamic Law, the denomination HALAL serves to distinguish food products prepared in accordance therewith. 2. In order to protect the proper use of such denominations, the Islamic Commission of Spain must apply for and obtain registration of the corresponding trademarks from the Patent and Trade Mark Office, pursuant to the legal standards in force. Once the above requirements are met, products bearing the Islamic Commis-

---

65 Amicarelli et al., 'The Influence of Halal Certified Products', 12.
66 González Santamaria, 'La empresa española', 143.
67 Corpas Aguirre, *Las comunidades islámicas*, 114.
68 Mantecón, 'El status legal', 173.

> sion of Spain mark on the package shall be guaranteed, for the intents and purposes of marketing, import and export, to have been prepared in accordance with Islamic Law.[69]

This provision has recognised the right, but not the obligation, of the ICS to register a halal trademark bearing its own denomination, in order to enable Muslims to distinguish food products prepared consistently with Islamic rules.[70] However, the ICS has not made use of this opportunity, possibly because of its 'double-headed' situation.[71] The fact that the ICS was founded in a hurry in order to sign the cooperation agreement with the state and not to pursue a rooted, common vision, helps to explain why its activity has long been blocked by internal divisions. It was thus the Halal Institute that registered in 2003 the first halal trademark (Marca de Garantía Halal de Junta Islámica), and certified approximately 300 firms and 600 products.[72] It is especially interesting that the Halal Institute has presented its initiative as the implementation of Art. 14 of the cooperation agreement, despite the fact that this provision expressly mentions the ICS.[73] Scholars have debated whether the registration of halal trademarks by entities different from the ICS may be regarded as legitimate. On the one side, the cooperation agreement does not stipulate that the ICS should be the *only* authorised subject to register a halal denomination.[74] On the other side, the ICS has not taken any opposing actions in this regard.[75]

In the subsequent years, other halal certifying bodies were created. By 2008, as many as 17 trademarks including the denomination 'halal' had been registered; by 2015, they were about 50.[76] As in Italy, the economic crisis of the last decade has been a major factor explaining the interest of many Spanish—and especially Catalan—firms in being certified.[77] However, in Spain the state has cooperated with a Muslim federation for the primary purpose of guar-

---

69 English translation at https://original.religlaw.org/content/religlaw/documents/coagrspst islamiccom1992.htm (accessed 26 October 2020).

70 Coglievina, 'La tutela delle diversità alimentari', 409.

71 Corpas Aguirre, *Las comunidades islámicas*, 115.

72 González Santamaria, 'La empresa española', 143.

73 Jiménez-Aybar, 'La alimentación "halal"', 664.

74 Coglievina, 'La tutela delle diversità alimentari', 411; Rossell Granados, 'Prescripciones alimentarias', 215–216.

75 Mantecón, 'El status legal', 194.

76 Coglievina, 'La tutela delle diversità alimentari', 410.

77 Liñán García, 'Aspectos controvertidos', 348–349. See also Bolifa El Gharbi, 'Productos y servicios', 86–89; Calvar, 'Halal', 122–124; Guerrero Blanco, 'La certificación Halal', 821–827; Lora Álvarez and Amaya Gil, 'El mercado Halal', 62–83; Sánchez González, *Marketing Halal*; Santos Miranda and Rubio Canales, 'Las oportunidades', 34–41.

anteeing the right to religious freedom, by enabling Muslims to distinguish food products prepared consistently with Islamic rules. While recognising the ICS's authority to define what halal is, the state has retained its competence in the regulation of patents and trademarks: the ICS's authority to register a halal trademark has been recognised, but this is not a special mark. Any entity registering a halal trademark must respect the conditions prescribed by law and applying to any trademarks,[78] including those regulating invalidity and revocation.[79]

4 Conclusions: A Comparative View

The Italian and Spanish legal experiences with halal certifying bodies are characterised by two main differences. From a substantive point of view, the rationale for the endorsement of a specific Muslim organisation's halal certifying body has been the protection of religious freedom in the Spanish case and the promotion of economic interests in the Italian one. From a formal point view, the two countries have chosen different legal instruments with which to pursue their respective aim: a bilateral agreement between the government and the representative body of Muslim communities in Spain and an Inter-Ministerial Convention signed to support a specific initiative of halal certification in Italy. The Italian agreement was signed by four ministries (instead of the government), in order to endorse the certifying body created by a Muslim organisation, which the Italian authorities have recognised as a worthy spokesperson, but not necessarily as the representative body of all Muslim communities in Italy. This solution has allowed the problems that arose in Spain to be avoided, where the implementation of the agreement has been impaired by internal disagreements and rivalries within the Muslim federation. On the other hand, the Spanish arrangement was never an option for Italy, where the state has signed no bilateral agreement with a representative entity of the Italian Muslim communities. But even if such an agreement had been signed, it might still have lacked influence on the regulation of halal certification. None of the draft bilateral agreements prepared by Muslim organisations included a

78 Law no. 17 of 7 December 2001 on trademarks (especially Arts 68 and 69), published in the State Official Gazette no. 294 of 8 December 2001; and Royal Decree no. 687 of 12 July 2002 approving the regulation to implement Law 17/2001 published in the Official Gazette of the Italian Republic no. 167 of 13 July 2002.

79 Coglievina, 'La tutela delle diversità alimentari', 409–412; Lojacono, 'La rilevanza dei simboli religiosi', 160.

norm on halal certification. Further, as noted, unlike the bilateral agreements signed between the Spanish government and the Islamic Commission of Spain and Federation of Jewish Communities of Spain, the one signed between Italy and the Union of Italian Jewish Communities does not include any provision on the registration of religious trademarks. This omission has been regarded as a sign of insufficient sensitivity towards such an important religious need, if not as a lack of protection of the right to religious freedom.[80] Nevertheless, the bilateral nature of the agreement may also suggest that a similar provision has not been included because, at least at the time of negotiation, it was not crucial for the Union of Italian Jewish Communities.

There are also significant analogies between Italy and Spain. Neither legal system provides a definition of halal. Any active involvement by secular authorities to impose a standard would be liable to breach the principle of religious organisations' autonomy. In both countries, general rules on trademarks, which also apply to halal trademarks, seem to be—at the moment—the most effective legal instrument that, on the one hand, guarantees Muslim consumer protection and, on the other hand, prevents an ambiguous involvement on the part of the state in religious organisations' autonomy. Although halal trademarks appear to be the most appropriate legal instruments to achieve a fair balance between the principles at stake, this may be still difficult to reach, as proven by the Spanish case. Where there exists a plurality of Muslim communities certifying halal products, public authorities may feel it is convenient to encourage the profession of the same religious doctrine or the recognition of the same religious authorities. This attitude is a product of history; in the European context, where states have traditionally had relationships with hierarchical churches or with religious organisations having one, clearly identifiable representative, the Spanish experience highlights the problems of building an authentically representative Muslim body, able to speak with one voice and to act jointly. Although halal certification raises new issues and challenges, secular authorities may not impose in any way religious uniformity.

Consistently with the principle of selective cooperation, Spain has recognised the right of, but not the obligation for, a specific Muslim organisation to register a halal trademark. As a matter of fact, it has been a different Muslim body to first make use of this opportunity. In Italy, by virtue of a convention signed by four ministries, public authorities have promoted a specific halal trademark, Halal Italia. However, in both countries, the preference accorded to a Muslim organisation has not prevented other subjects (including those with

80 Lojacono, 'La rilevanza dei simboli religiosi', 153.

no clear link to a religious authority) to register their own halal trademark. In Italy as well as in Spain, all interested parties may register a halal trademark, provided that they comply with the requirements laid down by law. In this regard, it has been stressed that respect for religious organisations' autonomy in defining halal and registering halal trademarks does not imply the public authorities' abstention from any forms of control. The latter, in fact, retain their competence to regulate trademarks, and general rules applying to trademarks also apply to halal trademarks. Halal certifying bodies autonomously define their halal guidelines but are required to respect both national and European Union legal norms on health, food safety and hygiene, consumer protection, and so on.

In the case of fraud, Italy's and Spain's public authorities apply general rules concerning food mislabelling and, if this is the case, the Penal Code. Unlike the previously mentioned case of Singapore, which is concerned with providing the conditions for correct Islamic practice, Italy and Spain have left the task of guaranteeing and verifying compliance with Islamic norms to the competent religious authorities. The sanctions envisaged by the Italian and Spanish legal systems for the violation of the rules on trademarks, labelling, consumer protection, and so on are the same, and apply irrespectively of the 'orientation' of the actors or products concerned—be they halal, kosher, or organic.

Bibliography

Al-Teinaz, Yunes Ramadan, Stuart Spear and Ibrahim H.A. El-Rahim, eds. 2020. *The Halal Food Handbook*. Hoboken: Wiley-Blackwell.

Aluffi Beck-Peccoz, Roberta. 2004. 'Islam in the European Union: Italy'. In *Islam and the European Union*, edited by Richard Potz and Wolfgang Wieshaider, 181–198. Leuven: Peeters.

Amicarelli, Vera, Teodoro Gallucci and Giovanni Lagioia. 2014. 'The Influence of Halal Certified Products in Italian Food Market'. In *Towards Quality-Management Systems and Solutions*, edited by Tadeusz Sikora and Joanna Dziadkowiec, 7–17. Cracow: Polish Society of Commodity Science.

Baldassarre, Fabrizio and Raffaele Campo. 2015. 'Influences of Islamic Culture in Marketing and the Role of Halal Certification'. Conference Paper presented at the 10th International Forum on Knowledge Asset Dynamics, Bari, Italy 10–12 June.

Barreiro, David. 2019. 'Halal: un mercado en auge'. *Eurocarne: La revista internacional del sector cárnico* 278: 84–92.

Benali, Foaud. 2017. *El crecimiento de la banca y las finanzas islámicas en Europa y sus estrategias de expansión*. PhD Dissertation. Universidad Autónoma de Madrid.

Bergeaud-Blackler, Florence. 2016. 'The Halal Certification Market in Europe and the World: A First Panorama'. In *Halal Matters. Islam, Politics and Markets in Global Perspective*, edited by Florence Bergeaud-Blackler et al., 105–126. New York: Routledge.

Bergeaud-Blackler, Florence. 2016. 'Who Owns Halal? Five International Initiatives of Halal Food Regulations'. In *Halal Matters. Islam, Politics and Markets in Global Perspective*, edited by Florence Bergeaud-Blackler, Johan Fischer and John Lever, 192–197. New York: Routledge.

Biancone, Paolo Pietro, et al. 2019. 'Halal Tourism: An Opportunity for the Global Tourism Industry'. *Tourism Analysis* 24, no. 3: 395–404.

Bolifa El Gharbi, Fadoua. 2017. 'Productos y servicios Halal en España: ¿Un paso hacia una sociedad heterogénea?'. In *Jornadas Marruecos y España ante los retos migratorios de la Nueva Era*, edited by Hassan Arabi and Alfonso Vázquez Atochero, 85–98. Badajoz: Departamento de Estudios Hispánicos.

Bolifa El Gharbi, Fadoua and Pedro Cuesta-Valiño. 2017. 'Razones para apostar por el Turismo Halal'. *International Journal of Scientific Management and Tourism* 3, no. 4: 175–185.

Bonne, Karijn and Wim Verbeke. 2008. 'Religious Values Informing Halal Meat Production and the Control and Delivery of Halal Credence Quality'. *Agriculture and Human Values* 25: 35–47.

Bottoni, Rossella. 2017. 'I recenti decreti delle Regioni vallona e fiamminga sulla macellazione rituale nel contesto dei dibattiti belga ed europeo in materia'. *Quaderni di diritto e politica ecclesiastica* 2: 523–558.

Bottoni, Rossella. 2015. 'La disciplina giuridica della macellazione rituale nell'Unione europea e nei paesi membri'. In *Cibo, religione e diritto. Nutrimento per il corpo e per l'anima*, edited by Antonio G. Chizzoniti, 479–516. Tricase: Libellula Edizioni.

Calvar, César. 2017. 'Halal, un mercado regulado y en expansión'. *Eurocarne: La revista internacional del sector cárnico* 260: 122–124.

Carmona Barrero, Juan Diego, Juan Rebello Bote and Pilar Sánchez González. 2017. 'La virtualización del Legado Andalusí de Cáceres como oportunidad para el Turismo Halal'. *International Journal of Scientific Management and Tourism* 3, no. 4: 205–229.

Ceserani, Alessandro. 2016. 'Cibo "religioso" e diritto: a margine di quattro recenti pubblicazioni'. *Quaderni di diritto e politica ecclesiastica* 2: 369–384.

Chizzoniti, Antonio G. 2000. *Le certificazioni confessionali nell'ordinamento giuridico italiano*. Milano: Vita e Pensiero.

Coglievina, Stella. 2015. 'La tutela delle diversità alimentari religiose in Spagna'. In *Cibo, religione e diritto. Nutrimento per il corpo e per l'anima*, edited by Antonio G. Chizzoniti, 401–436. Tricase: Libellula Edizioni.

Conte, Francesca, Valeria Quartarone, Giovanni Maria Cubeddu and Annamaria Passantino. 2012. 'Ritual Slaughter: Regulatory Responses, Consumer Choice and

Labelling Strategies'. *Maso International Journal of Food Science and Technology* 2: 153–158.

Corpas Aguirre, María de los Ángeles. 2010. *Las comunidades islámicas en la España actual (1960–2008). Génesis e institucionalización de una minoría de referencia*. Madrid: UNED.

Cuesta-Valiño, Pedro, Fadoua Bolifa, Estela Nuñez Barriopedro. 2020. 'Sustainable, Smart and Muslim-Friendly Tourist Destinations'. *Sustainability* 12, no. 5: 1778.

Doe, Norman. 2011 *Law and Religion in Europe. A Comparative Introduction*. New York: Oxford University Press.

Ferrari, Silvio and Iván C. Ibán. 1997. *Diritto e religione in Europa*. Bologna: il Mulino.

Ferrari, Silvio and Rossella Bottoni. 2010. Legislation Regarding Religious Slaughter in the EU Member, Candidate and Associated Countries. https://issuu.com/florencebergeaud-blackler/docs/report-legislation (accessed 26 October 2020).

Ferrari, Silvio. 2010. 'Islam and the European System of State-Religions Relations Throughout Europe'. In *Cultural Diversity and the Law: State Responses from Around the World*, edited by Marie-Claire Foblets, Jean-François Gaudreault-DesBiens and Alison Dundes Renteln, 477–502. Brussels: Bruylant.

Fischer, Johan. 2012. 'Branding Halal. A Photographic Essay on Global Muslim Markets'. *Anthropology Today* 28, no. 4: 18–21.

Fischer, Johan. 2011. *The Halal Frontier. Muslim Consumers in a Globalized Market*. New York: Palgrave Macmillan.

Fuccillo, Antonio. 2015. *Il cibo degli dei. Diritto, religioni, mercati alimentari*. Torino: Giappichelli.

Fuccillo, Antonio, Francesco Sorvillo and Ludovico Decimo. 2016. 'Diritto e religioni nelle scelte alimentari'. *Stato, Chiese e pluralismo confessionale. Rivista telematica* 18: 1–34.

Fuseini, Awal, Steve B. Wotton, Toby G. Knowles and Phil J. Hadley. 2017. 'Halal Meat Fraud and Safety Issues in the UK: A Review in the Context of the European Union'. *Food Ethics* 1: 127–142.

Germanò, Alberto. 2010. 'Informazione alimentare halal: quale responsabilità per un'etichetta non veritiera?' *Rivista di diritto alimentare* 4, no. 3: 1–10.

Giuffrida, Armando. 2017. 'La certificazione di conformità del c.d. Halal Food'. *Il diritto dell'economia* 30, no. 1: 95–135.

González Santamaria, Ana Isabel. 2016. 'La empresa española frente al mercado halal'. In *Ética, marketing y finanzas islámicas. El consumidor musulmán*, edited by Pilar Sánchez González and María del Carmen de la Orden de la Cruz, 137–150. Madrid: ESIC Editorial.

Greenawalt, Kent. 1998. 'Religious Law and Civil Law: Using Secular Law to Assure Observance of Practices with Religious Significance'. *Southern California Law Review* 71: 781–843.

Guerrero Blanco, Tomás. 2018. 'La certificación Halal: impulsando la internacionalización del sector cárnico'. In *Alimentación y bebidas*, Vol. 1, edited by Enrique Ortega Burgos and Eduardo Muñoz del Caz, 821–827. Pamplona: Aranzadi.

Halkias, Daphne, Emmanuela Pizzurno, Alfredo de Massis and Mirka Fragoudakis. 2014. 'Halal Products and Services in the Italian Tourism and Hospitality Industry: Brief Case Studies of Entrepreneurship and Innovation'. *Journal of Developmental Entrepreneurship* 19, no. 2: 1450012-1-1450012-12.

Hall, C. Michael and Girish Prayag, eds. 2020. *The Routledge Handbook of Halal Hospitality and Islamic Tourism*. New York: Routldge.

Havinga, Tetty. 2010. 'Regulating Halal and Kosher Foods: Different Arrangements Between State, Industry and Religious Actors'. *Erasmus Law Review* 3, no. 4: 241–255.

Inter-Ministerial Convention for the Support of the Initiative 'Halal Italia'. 30 June 2010. http://www.halalitalia.org/documenti/Conv.%20Interm.firmata.pdf.

Italy's National Bioethics Committee. *Alimentazione differenziata e interculturalità. Orientamenti bioetici* [*Food differences and interculturality. Bioethical orientations*]. 17 March 2006. http://bioetica.governo.it (accessed 26 October 2020).

Jiménez-Aybar, Iván. 2005. 'La alimentación "halal" de los musulmanes en España: aspectos jurídicos, económicos y sociales'. *Ius canonicum* 15, no. 90: 631–666.

Kayadibi, Saim. 2014. 'A Way Forward to European Standard on Halal Food'. *Journal of Asian Development Studies* 3, no. 2: 105–116.

Khan, Mohd Imran and Abid Haleem. 2016. 'Understanding "Halal" and "Halal Certification & Accreditation System"—A Brief Review'. *Saudi Journal of Business and Management Studies* 1, no. 1: 32–42.

Laurence, Jonathan. 2015. 'Muslim Mobilization Between Self-Organization, State-Recognized Consultative Bodies and Political Participation'. In *After Integration. Islam, Conviviality and Contentious Politics in Europe*, edited by Marian Burchardt and Ines Michalowski, 59–78. Berlin: Springer.

Leonini, Fernando. 2018. 'La certificazione del rispetto delle regole alimentari confessionali: norme statuali e libertà religiosa'. In *Cibo e religione: diritto e diritti*, edited by Antonio G. Chizzoniti and Mariachiara Tallacchini, 143–154. Tricase: Libellula Edizioni. 2010.

Lever, John and Johan Fischer. *Religion, Regulation and Consumption. Globalising Kosher and Halal Markets*. Manchester: Manchester University Press.

Lever, John, Maria Puig de la Bellacasa, Marie Miele and Marc Higgin. 2010. 'From the Slaughterhouse to the Consumer. Transparency and Information in the Distribution of Halal and Kosher Meat'. http://orca.cf.ac.uk/20492 (accessed 26 October 2020).

Liñán García, Ángeles. 2017. 'Aspectos controvertidos de la libertad religiosa en España y Europa. Alimentación halal y casher'. *Estudios constitucionales* 15, no. 2: 331–364.

Lojacono, Pietro. 1999. 'I marchi "casher" e "halal" tra "ius singulare" e "diritto comune".

(Con riferimento alla situazione italiana e spagnola). *Anuario de derecho eclesiástico del Estado* 15: 15–38.

Lojacono, Pietro. 1997. 'La rilevanza dei simboli religiosi nel campo economico e commerciale: il marchio e la pubblicità (traendo spunto dagli Accordi spagnoli con ebrei e islamici)'. *Il diritto ecclesiastico* 108: 152–222.

Lora Álvarez, Beatriz and Maria del Carmen Amaya Gil. 2019. 'El mercado Halal como oportunidad de negocio y mejora de la internacionalización para la empresa española'. *Revista de Administración y Dirección de Empresas* 3: 62–83.

Malkawi, Bashar H. 2014. 'Food Labeling and Halal Mark'. *Intellectual Property Rights* 2, no. 1: 103.

Mangano, Stefania, Mauro Spotorno and Gian Marco Ugolini. 2016. 'Il turismo halal: una nicchia di mercato che può crescere anche in Italia'. *Annali del turismo* 5: no. 1: 57–76.

Mantecón, Joaquin. 2006. 'El status legal del Islam en España'. *Derecho y Religión* 1: 165–208.

Masoudi, Gerald F. 1993. 'Kosher Food Regulation and the Religion Clauses of the First Amendment'. *The University of Chicago Law Review* 60, no. 2: 667–696.

Milne, Elijah L. 2007. 'Protecting Islam's Garden from the Wilderness: Halal Fraud Statutes and the First Amendment'. *Journal of Food Law and Policy* 2, no. 1: 61–83.

Minns, Rain Levy. 2001. 'Food Fights: Redefining the Current Boundaries of the Government's Positive Obligation to Provide Halal'. *Journal of Law & Politics* 17: 781–843.

Morgan, Kristin. 1993. 'The Constitutionality of New Jersey Kosher Food Regulations under the Establishment Clause' *University of Cincinnati College of Law* 62, no. 1: 247–282.

Pointing, John. 2014. 'Strict Liability Food Law and Halal Slaughter'. *The Journal of Criminal Law* 78, no. 5: 387–391.

Pointing, John, Yunes Teinaz and Shufa Shafi. 2008. 'Illegal Labelling and Sales of Halal Meat and Food Products'. *The Journal of Criminal Law* 72, no. 3: 206–213.

Popovsky, Mark. 2010. 'The Constitutional Complexity of Kosher Food Laws'. *Columbia Journal of Law and Social Problems* 44: 75–107.

Rasul, Tareq. 2019. 'The Trends, Opportunities and Challenges of Halal Tourism: A Systematic Literature Review'. *Tourism Recreation Research* 44, no. 4: 434–450.

Riaz, Mian N. and Muhammad M. Chaudry, eds. 2019. *Handbook of Halal Food Production*. Boca Raton: CRC Press.

Rios, Rosa E., Hernan E. Riquelme, and Yasser Abdelaziz. 2014. 'Do Halal Certification Country of Origin and Brand Name Familiarity Matter?' *Asia Pacific Journal of Marketing and Logistics* 26, no. 5: 665–686.

Rosenthal, Stephen F. 1997. 'Food For Thought: Kosher Fraud Laws and the Religion Clauses of the First Amendment'. *George Washington* Law *Review* 65: 951–1013.

Rossell Granados, Jaime. 2004. 'Prescripciones alimentarias en el Islam. Sacrificio ritual y alimentación "halal"'. In *Los musulmanes en España. Libertad religiosa e identidad cultural*, edited by Agustín Motilla de la Calle, 205–227. Madrid: Trotta.

Saint-Blancat, Chantal. 'Italy'. 2015. In *The Oxford Handbook of European Islam*, edited by Jocelyne Cesari, 265–310. Oxford: Oxford University Press.

Sánchez González, Pilar. 2017. *Marketing Halal: un estudio empírico en España*. PhD Dissertation. Universidad Rey Juan Carlos, Madrid.

Sanchez, Pilar and Ruth Fernandez-Hernandez. 2019. 'Mayrit on: un nuevo turismo cultural-religioso'. *International Journal of Professional Business Review* 4, no. 1: 81–93.

Sandıkcı, Özlem and Gillian Rice, eds. 2011. *Handbook of Islamic Marketing*. Cheltenham: Edward Elgar.

Santos Miranda, Máximo and Helena Rubio Canales. 2007. 'Las oportunidades que la economía halal ofrece a la empresa española'. *Estrategia financiera* 351: 34–41.

Savorani, Giovanna. 2015. 'Il diritto all'informazione del consumatore di alimenti: un complesso sistema di regole con indice di protezione incerto'. *Politica del diritto* 4: 575–598.

Scopel, Laura. 2016. *Le prescrizioni alimentari di carattere religioso*. Trieste: Edizioni Università di Trieste.

Steiner, Kerstin. 2015. 'Governing Islam: The state, the Administration of Muslim Law Act (AMLA) and Islam in Singapore'. *Australian Journal of Asian Law* 16, no. 1: 1–16.

Sullivan, Catherine Beth. 1993. 'Are Kosher Food Laws Constitutionally Kosher?' *Boston College Environmental Affairs Law Review* 21, no. 1: 201–245.

Talib, Mohamed Syazwan Ab, Abu Bakar Abdul Hamad and Thoo Ai Chin. 2015. 'Motivations and Limitations in Implementing Halal Food Certification: A Pareto Analysis'. *British Food Journal* 117, no. 11: 2664–705.

Tirabassi, Mariagrazia. 2014. *Macellazione rituale e certificazione delle carni kasher e halal: i modelli francese e statunitense*. PhD Dissertation. Università Cattolica del Sacro Cuore, Piacenza.

Toselli, Elena. 2015. *Le diversità convergenti. Guida alle certificazioni kasher, halâl e di produzione biologica*. Milano: FrancoAngeli.

Van der Spiegel, Marjolein, H.J. van der Fels-Klerx, P. Sterrenburg, S.M. van Ruth, I.M.J. Scholtens-Toma and E.J. Kok. 2012. 'Halal Assurance in Food Supply Chains: Verification of Halal Certificates Using Audits and Laboratory Analysis'. *Trends in Food Science & Technology* 27: 109–119.

White, Gareth R.T. and Anthony Samuel. 2016. 'Fairtrade and Halal Food Certification and Labeling: Commercial Lessons and Religious Limitations'. *Journal of Macromarketing* 36, no. 4: 388–399.

Zergane, Slimane. 2017. 'The Retard of the Positioning of Spain on Developing Halal Tourist Products'. PhD Dissertation. Universidad Las Palmas de Gran Canaria.

CHAPTER 9

The Process of Eating Ethically: A Comparison of Religious and National Food Certifications in Italy

Lauren Crossland-Marr

1 Introduction

Production processes can be difficult to untangle for many consumers who wish to lessen environmental destruction, to live piously, or to ensure everyone in the commodity chain is treated fairly. Food activism movements have increasingly promoted a return to local food production.[1] Movements such as Slow Food resonate with a global audience because they actively promote transparency in the food system by emphasising local cultural heritage.[2] At the same time, production stages of a food's manufacture can take place across different locations. For example, *bresaola*, an Italian cured meat, can be made with beef sourced from Brazil, then manufactured in Italy, then sold in the United Arab Emirates.

Given the ambiguous origins of many foods, consumers across the globe who are concerned with eating ethically often consult third-party certifications when making buying decisions. For example, some Chinese consumers interpret the 'organic' label as shorthand for healthy.[3] Scholars have also show that consumer buying decisions can also be more complex. For example, anthropological studies have demonstrated that Italian consumers sometimes assume producers hold third-party certifications such as organic because they trust the producers at their local, open-air market.[4] Moreover, supermarkets are setting new ethical and sustainable guidelines that allow access to many different forms of ethical consumption.[5] However, sites of ethical meaning-making are

1 Grasseni, *Beyond Alternative Food Networks: Italy's Solidarity Purchase Groups*, 168–175.
2 Parasecoli, 'Postrevolutionary Chowhounds: Food, Globalisation, and the Italian Left', 37.
3 Jakob, 'Creating Ethical Food Consumers? Promoting Organic Foods in Urban Southwest China', 84.
4 Giovanni, 'Offsetting Risk: Organic Food, Pollution and the Transgression of Spatial Boundaries', 49.
5 Hatanaka, Carmen Bain and Lawrence Busch, 'Third-party certification in the global agrifood system', 365.

 | DOI:10.1163/9789004459236_010

not limited to physical commercial locations; they are also found in the institutions that build third-party certifications.

The development of religious certifications such as halal and kosher are part of the larger shift to the institutionalisation of morality in food consumption.[6] Many active in the halal industry see the parallels between it and other non-religious third-party certifications. Maryam Attar et al. write, 'halal food should be produced—much like organic food—in ways that are good for human, animal, and environmental health'.[7] Even though third-party certification processes are similar, social scientists rarely compare them across contexts, although social scientists have importantly compared kosher and halal markets across national contexts.[8] I extend this work to compare religious institutionalisation of ethical foodways[9] with secular forms in the same national context.

Findings for this article were collected during a 12-month research period, from September 2017 to September 2018. During this time, data was primarily collected through two 10-month internships at two certifications (a halal certification (Halal Italia) and a Made in Italy certification (Food Italy)). I supplemented the internships with interviews, trainings, focus groups, and attendance at public and religious events.

I centre on ethics as a commitment to consuming foods that align with ideas about 'good', 'healthy', and 'correct' production, processing, and distribution at many levels (local, regional, national, and global) and across religious and secular food certifications. Questions about consumable foods allow insight into concrete practices at the nexus of institutional and national food cultures. Put another way, by examining how actors understand what 'good' or 'consumable' foods are, this chapter will highlight that the process of deciding what warrants these categories shift depending on one's position and national context.

Italy is an important case study with which to investigate questions about ethical eating. Not only have many global food movements started in Italy, such as Slow Food, but also books, movies, and other forms of popular culture underscore Italy as *the* centre of farm-to-table foodways and traditional, regional cuisine. This status, however, is ironic, as the ability to meet basic food

6 Lever and Fischer, *Religion, Regulation, Consumption: Globalising Kosher and Halal Markets*, 8–9.
7 Attar, Lohi, and Lever, 'Remembering the Spirit of Halal: An Iranian Perspective', 55–71.
8 Lever and Fischer, *Religion, Regulation, Consumption*, 8–9.
9 Foodways refers to the study of the connections between social, cultural and economic practices in food, from production to consumption.

needs was long reserved for the Italian upper class.[10] Shortly after the country's unification in 1861, malnutritional diseases like pellagra were widespread.[11] At the turn of the nineteenth century, the lack of access to basic foodstuffs precipitated one of the largest migrations in modern history. More than 2 million Italians from rural northern and southern areas migrated to the United States between 1900 and 1910.[12] It was only after the Second World War, with heavy economic investment from the Marshall Plan, that Italians began to enjoy *la dolce vita*.[13] During this period, referred to as the 'economic miracle', the majority of the population gained access to regular meals that included previous rarities such as meats and fats (e.g. butter, olive oil).[14] Historically, anxieties about eating in Italy centred on meeting basic nutritional needs. The modern shift towards plenty emerges from a history plagued by anxieties surrounding scarcity.[15] Further, the association between good food and the Made in Italy brand is based on imaginings of the *bel paese* outside of Italy in places like the United States. Successful immigrant chefs, for example, Ettore Bioardi—the namesake of Chef Boyardee—found ways to adapt traditional, regional Italian dishes for the American palate. Bioradi and others modified traditional Italian recipes not only by using local spices and vegetables but also by incorporating meat, which was easier to come by in the United States. In summary, Italian food is not the result of endemic invention but, rather, a result of the circulation of Italian people and their foods.

While the origins of Italian food are complex, many businesses that deal in Italian-made worry about an increase in 'fake' Italian products. These businesses disparage 'Italian-sounding' products such as the green, grated parmesan cheese shakers; a popular fixture of American tables on spaghetti night. Producers argue that this is not just a matter of national heritage but also of cold, hard cash. The network of Italian Chambers of Commerce abroad, Assocamerestero, found in a survey that Italian-sounding products cost Italy €90 billion last year.[16] In June 2017, the Italian government attempted to create an overarching, governmental certification for Made in Italy foods. Represent-

10 Moyer-Nocchi, *Chewing the Fat: An Oral History of Italian Foodways from Fascism to Dolce Vita*, xxi–xxv.

11 Ginnaio and Jacobs, 'Pellagra in Late Nineteenth Century Italy: Effects of a Deficiency Disease', 583.

12 Wills and Grubin, 'PBS: Destination America', 2005.

13 Counihan, *Around the Tuscan Table: Food, Family, and Gender in Twentieth Century Florence*, 177–191.

14 Moyer-Nocchi, *Chewing the Fat*, 288–289.

15 Counihan, *Around the Tuscan Table*, 23 and 179.

16 'Italian Sounding: A €90 Billion Problem', ItalianFOOD.Net, 20 August 2018. https://ne

atives from the Italian food industry (*agroalimentare*) worried that the regulation might not be strict enough and halted legislation.[17] Despite the emphasis on heritage, standards are difficult to pin down, not least because what can be considered made in Italy is unclear. This parallels the halal sector in Italy because the sector also incorporates a plethora of international, national, and regional standards, a point I will develop further.

Both Made in Italy and halal realms are left relatively untouched by national legislation. In an interview with the Italian governmental accreditation agency, Accredia, I was told they have no direct control over the use of the Made in Italy and halal designations, though attempts to regulate both sectors are in process. Both sectors cater to an international audience and follow similar International Standards Organization (ISO) guidelines. Due to this reliance on broader international food safety guidelines, both entities structure the process for the release of certification similarly for most food products.

It is in this opaque food certification environment that this chapter attempts to intervene. Of particular interest is the ways in which the social life of institutions create ethical standards for many different audiences in Italy and beyond. I begin by comparing a Made in Italy certification with a halal certification in Italy not only to uncover the rich detail of each case but also to speak to larger questions critical to studying global foodways, specifically how standards work across differences in global markets, and the categories that emerge.[18] The small-scale critical comparison[19] presented here is meant to develop a fuller picture of the practices and processes embedded in building ethical foodways for markets outside of the place of manufacture. This chapter examines how food certifications set ethical standards and ask questions about the nature of institutional demands, which vary across religious, international, and national markets. Moving from the institutional realm, I look at how ethical standards are discussed by and between individual consumers, some of whom are also active in the certification industry.

---

ws.italianfood.net/2018/08/20/italian-sounding-90-billion-problem/ (accessed April 28, 2019).

17 Francesca Landini, 'What's truly Italian? Food fight foils 'Made in Italy' plan', Reuters, 2 June 2017, http://www.reuters.com/article/us-italy-food-idUSKBN18T1ER (accessed July 25, 2017).

18 Tsing, *The Mushroom at the End of the World: On the Possibility of Life in Capitalist Ruins*, 23.

19 Bowen and Petersen, 'Introduction: Critical Comparisons', 1–20.

2 Sites of Comparison

In 2015, I began working and conducting ethnographic field research on the two food certification sectors in Milan, Italy. In 2017, I returned for a full year of research, collecting the data that make up this chapter. I worked approximately 40 hours a week in Food Italy and Halal Italia, which translated to about two to three days a week at each site. My hours increased if there was a need, such as a deadline, an event, or an important meeting. In addition to ethnographic data collected, I also conducted a focus group with young Italian Muslim consumers at the University of Milan to understand further how they conceptualise halal and their access to halal foods. The first section of this chapter examines eating ethically as it becomes institutionalised in certifications through data collected through my daily work at the two institutions. The second part of the chapter follows how the process of eating ethically operates for individual consumers of halal foods. Through engagement with these two scales, I show that the turn to eating ethically is a contested process because it relies on local values, which is made semi-static for institutions, while it is left unfinished for consumers.

As Florence Bergeaud-Blackler et al.[20] show, from a technical point of view, the standardisation of halal is similar to that of organic foods. The two diverge, however, because organic foods are enforced by international agreements and governmental departments.[21] Unlike organic foods (known as *bio* in Italy), the Made in Italy sector is left fairly unregulated by government oversight, making it a good comparative site in the Italian case. Let us now turn to the history of each sector in Italy.

Made in Italy certifications have been in use since the 1980s: halal certifications developed later, primarily out of a need for an exportation mechanism for Italian businesses wishing to sell goods in Muslim-majority markets. In this chapter, halal refers to a dietary standard as prescribed by Islamic canons (Qur'an and hadith) and Islamic Law (*fiqh*). At a very general level, halal denotes the proscription of blood, pork, and carrion. The dietary laws also include the avoidance of copious amounts of alcohol.[22]

---

20 Bergeaud-Blackler, Fischer, and Lever, *Halal Matters: Islam, Politics and Markets in Global Perspective*, 14–15.

21 Bergeaud-Blackler, Fischer, and Lever, *Halal Matters*, 122.

22 A discussion of the harmful effects of wine (*khamr*) are in the Qur'an (surah 5:90). The surah was likely revealed only a few years before the Prophet's death. Previous discussions of wine were generally positive. Through the Islamic notion of abrogation (*naskh*) all previous interpretations of wine as consumable were nullified.

Halal certification in Italy developed within the last 15 years. In Italy, Muslims make up 2.6 per cent of the population and nearly 33 per cent of all foreigners.[23] The majority of Muslims live in the north of the country, making their home in the Lombardy region, the capital of which is the city of Milan.[24] While there is a growing second generation, the majority of Muslims are first-generation economic migrants from North Africa.[25] For the most part, halal certifications are used by companies for export and have only a small presence in the Italian market.[26] For example, a wholesaler in Saudi Arabia might decide to sell Italian-made mozzarella. The wholesaler suggests that the mozzarella maker seek a halal certification both as a value-add to consumers as well as a way to ease the product shipment through Saudi Arabian customs.

Co.Re.Is, the Islamic association that runs Halal Italia, is primarily made up of Italian-born converts from Catholicism to Islam. In 2009, the Ministry of the Interior sought out the community to begin a halal label to help ease the path for Italian products into markets abroad in Muslim-majority countries. Following the Halal Italia example, other communities established halal certifications. Another major contender in the Italian halal sector is the World Halal Authority (WHA). As of this writing, WHA is the only halal certification in Italy to hold the coveted accreditation from MUI (Majelis Ulama Indonesia), the Indonesian council of Muslim scholars responsible for accrediting halal certifiers. Halal International Authority (HIA), was a major player in the Italian halal realm until recently. In 2018, the president of HIA (2010–2017) and Imam of Bari, Sharif Lorenzini, was arrested on embezzlement charges.[27] The entity

23 Barbie Latza Nadeau, 'Milan's New 'Anti-Mosque' Law' *The Daily Beast*, 28 January 2015, http://www.thedailybeast.com/articles/2015/01/28/milan-s-new-anti-mosque-law.html (accessed January 28, 2015).

24 Barbie Latza Nadeau, 'Italy Drives Muslims Underground' *The Daily Beast*, 1 December 2015, http://www.thedailybeast.com/articles/2015/12/01/italy-drives-muslims-underground.html (accessed January 11, 2017).

25 Conrad Hackett, '5 Facts about the Muslim Population in Europe'. Pew Research Centre. Fact Tank: News in Numbers (blog), 29 November 2017, http://www.pewresearch.org/fact-tank/2017/11/29/5-facts-about-the-muslim-population-in-europe/ (accessed March 4, 2019).

26 This is not to say there have been no attempts to create access to halal-certified foods in Italy. In 2017, the Halal International Authority (HIA) certified the first halal retail store in Italy. The store, Ithaly, is based in Bari.

27 *Corriere del Mezzogiorno*, 'Appropriazione indebita e frode Agli arresti l'imam Sharif Lorenzini', 2 June 2018, http://httpf889269a-0b18-11e8-a159-261a041af718.shtml last retrieved 29 April 2019.

still exists though the scandal has greatly affected its standing.[28] The majority of halal certifications have either their primary offices or at least one office in the northern part of the country.

Beyond these larger players, a handful of smaller entities also administer halal certifications as part of their suite of certification services. The non-Muslim owner who runs a halal certification as one of the certification services his company offers explained that his halal certification is based primarily on the implementation of international standards. This business perspective of halal is fairly common, particularly as Muslims are not the only ones building these institutions nor are they the only ones operating production processes.

Certifiers in the halal and Made in Italy realms are creating new ways to eat ethically, while also helping others do the same. In the following sections, I begin with an overview of the varying regulations and standards. The first section ends with how certifications are influenced by local concerns when creating standards. Next, I turn to how young Italian Muslim consumers decide what to eat. Based on the ethnographic examples, I argue that eating ethically in Italy not only lessens anxieties about where food comes from but also has produced a new way certifiers and consumers understand the foods they eat.

Through small-scale interactions, both working in institutions and talking with consumers, I look at how certifiers and consumers grapple with what it means to deem a food consumable through modes of ethical reasoning. As a result, the research also grapples with the question: are both of these third-party certifications 'ethical'? Food Italy certifiers position themselves as authorities dedicated to transparency in the modern food system. Yet theirs is a national orientation, one that takes as its foundation the assumption that food produced within the nation is inherently ethical. Halal certifications have different orientations. A key takeaway from my research is that while the two certifications may differ in function, they begin from similar point of origin, namely how can we ensure consumers outside of the local context eat ethically?

3 Standardisation of Ethical Foodways

Halal certifications have struggled with the plethora of standards, which vary across Islamic juridical schools (sing. *maḏhab*) as well as across Muslim majority governmental accreditation bodies (e.g. MUI, JAKIM (Jabatan Kemajuan

28 Multiple requests for interviews were not answered.

Islam Malaysia), etc.). Legitimacy is further complicated because the halal economy, which includes Islamic banking and halal food certification, developed in Southeast Asian countries[29] while religious legitimacy remains in the Middle East. Diasporic Muslims are at the centre of the institutionalisation of halal food, because they are often the ones called on to start halal certifications in the West. These entities guarantee that foods made outside of Muslim-majority countries meet the standards of halal. Boğaç A. Ergene and Febe Armanios argue that 'diasporic Muslims … play an equal (and sometimes greater role) than their co-religionists in majority-Muslim countries with regard to how halal food is consumed and molded in today's world'.[30] Italian halal certifications draw on many criteria to write their own standards. They incorporate international halal accreditation standards and national and international food safety guidelines, international health and food safety standards, including Hazard Analysis and Critical Control Points (HAACP), ISO 9001, and regional EU benchmarks.

Standards for halal also vary between local certifications because every certification body interprets their own regulations. For example, there are varying standards between two local halal certifications in Italy: Halal Italia and the World Halal Authority. Halal Italia allows food products to contain trace amounts of alcohol. Acceptable traces of alcohol may come from cleaning the production line but cannot originate from additives or flavourings. A member of the Halal Italia audit team explained that the alcohol percentage is low enough that it is practically undetectable and cannot inebriate the consumer. The staff member believed that alcohol goes through a process of *istihlāk*, meaning forbidden substances become so diluted that they can be deemed halal. On the other hand, the World Halal Authority forbids any alcohol on the production line. The degree to which impure substances can be diluted is only one example of the many differences found across local standards.[31]

Made in Italy certifications also interpret global standards and are similarly diverse. The English phrase 'Made in Italy' similarly illustrates the major role played by Italian diasporic communities in developing a demand for these products abroad. Made in Italy certifications, such as Food Italy, guarantee products are fully produced in Italy. Food Italy creates standards based on international regulations (such as ISO 9001 and HAACP). Food Italy distinguished itself from other Made in Italy certifications by emphasising their stricter inter-

29 Bergeaud-Blackler, Fischer, and Lever, *Halal Matters*, 8–9.

30 Armanios and Ergene, *Halal Food: A History*, 6.

31 Husseini de Araújo, 'Assembling Halal Meat and Poultry Production in Brazil: Agents, Practices, Power and Sites', 220.

pretation of international guidelines, which to those working in Food Italy, imparted legitimacy. The owner of Food Italy complained that, without strict oversight, olives could be grown elsewhere, then shipped to Italy, and finally sold and marketed as 'Made in Italy'. Food Italy went a step further than current recommendations, ensuring that all steps of production are completed within Italy.[32] Olives must be grown in Italy in order for an olive oil to qualify for certification.

While halal certifications emphasise religious ethics, Food Italy recognises ethical foundations found in the national realm. Two of Food Italy's three main rules are that all raw materials must be Italian, and production must be fully carried out in Italy. When I asked the owner of Food Italy about these first two rules he replied:

> It is difficult to find social consciousness when food is grown/cultivated elsewhere … For example, [a large Italian pasta producer] is an important brand that is connected to Italian cultural heritage, but most of the production is done in Turkey. Without production in Italy, there is no responsibility. They can have awful working conditions, crowding workers and not allowing them to be content. The packaging in Italy allows for it to be 'Made in Italy'. We hope to go against this tendency.

Ethical food requirements include the humane treatment of not only animals but individuals involved in the process. The ethical treatment of people is front and centre and, to the owner, guaranteed within the boundaries of the Italian nation. However, recent scholarship on other Made in Italy sectors, namely fast fashion, shows that this is not the case. Many workers from China make clothing in Prato, Italy and are forced to work long hours in squalid conditions.[33] Immigrant labour is also used to produce olive oil or San Marzano tomatoes that boast a 'Made in Italy' labels. A *Guardian* article title from 2019 says it all: ''You're Lucky to Get Paid at All': How African Migrants are Exploited in Italy'.[34] According to a report by OXFAM, there are between 405,000 and

32 International guidelines also refer to the World Trade Organization's (WTO) agreement on Trade-Related Aspects of Intellectual Property Rights (TRIPS). The EU guidelines for a Protected Geographic Indication (PGI) allow foreign raw materials to be produced in Italy with this designation. For example, bresaola with PGI designation can be processed with meat from Brazil. The strictest designation is the Protected Designation of Origin (PDO) in which all raw materials must be from the designated area; for example, only grapes grown in the Champagne region of France may be used to make champagne.

33 Krause, *Tight Knit: Global Families and the Social Life of Fast Fashion*, 238.

34 Hsiao-Hung Pai, ''You're Lucky to Get Paid at All': How African Migrants Are Exploited

500,000 immigrant workers in Italian agriculture, which is just about half of the sector's total workforce. Additionally, around 80 per cent of these workers do not have legal contract arrangements.[35] This demonstrates that for most certifiers attempts to oversee all stages of production is difficult, if not impossible.

Despite the labour issues in Italy, the owner of Food Italy continued to express concerns about place of production. He explained that:

> [e]ven with DOP [labelling guaranteeing geographic origin] there isn't a production line. [There's] no traceability. For example, I visited a producer who made tomato sauce. I asked him where they get their tomatoes, and I was told 'from China'. If the last stage of production is done in Italy, then it is Italian.

To the owner, forms of ethical eating are found within Italy. Yet, much of the desire for Italian-made food products comes from outside national boundaries. This tension between local production and the global demand produces new meanings. This is not just a question of ethics though this is how it is often conveyed. It also helps the owner sell products and distinguish his certified products in a global marketplace. Ethical claims such as these, produce economic value by emphasising 'Italian' values surrounding food, which resonates with the world outside of Italy.

4 Ethics in Negotiating Standards

Those involved in the halal industry in Italy spoke at length about the ethics of eating to audiences they hoped to convert to implementing halal oversight practices. This technique was especially pronounced during a two-day training for businesses interested in seeking halal certification. Training for quality managers and employees before a company can be certified is typical for the food certification (halal and Made in Italy) model in Italy. Employees came from a variety of companies that produce cosmetics, parmesan, baby

---

in Italy'. *The Guardian*, sec. Opinions, 9 February 2019, https://www.theguardian.com/commentisfree/2019/feb/09/african-migrants-italy-hard-right-authorities (accessed August 6, 2019).

35 Giorgia Ceccarelli, 'Human Suffering in Italy's Agricultural Value Chain', Oxfam Case Study, Oxfam, 14 June 2018, https://oxfamilibrary.openrepository.com/bitstream/handle/10546/620479/cs-human-suffering-italy-agricultural-value-chain-210618-en.pdf?sequence=4. 2 (accessed August 6, 2019).

food, chocolate, tea, milk-derived substances, and ice cream (*gelato*). During the training, representatives covered the meaning of halal, the types of services they offered, and an overview of halal standards. In one of the sessions, a halal expert described the ritual slaughter process. He explained that the animal must be well taken care of prior to slaughter; for example, the animal cannot consume any animal by-products. After the halal expert finished, the milk-processing representative commented, '[I]f vegetarians and vegans knew about halal meat, they may become meat-eaters again'. The issue for the milk-processing representative is not the meat itself but the process of raising and slaughtering animals. The process of halal slaughter meat is understood as similar to other forms of ethical eating, specifically, the fair and ethical treatment of animals.

While this ethical orientation can be translated with relative ease, standards can be complex for food producers to understand. As a result, food producers looking to gain certification can navigate differing standards in practical ways. A quality manager for an ice cream company explained that her company maintains two halal certifications because the Indonesian Scholar Council, MUI,[36] recognises the WHA and Indonesia is a critical market for their ice cream products. Her company complied with the eased customs restrictions that came from this particular halal certificate. She said her firm needed two halal certifications because they use alcohol to clean one of their halal production lines. To the quality manager this was not an ethical or religious issue but a practical one. Her approach illustrates how, through the implementation of halal certification standards, producers strategise to achieve practical ends not necessarily ethical ones. Certifications, whether they be halal or Made in Italy, therefore, must find ways to resonate with diverse audiences.

Comparing halal and made in Italy sectors brings to light the commitments brought about by the Italian context. Workers in both sectors highlighted the value of Made in Italy artisanal products. In terms of marketing products, halal certifiers urged producers to highlight the 'made in Italy' aspects of products to avoid stereotypes. This was often discussed in the marketing phase, because the packaging of all certified halal products had to be evaluated and approved by the halal certification body. For example, a company used the name of an Ottoman dignitary for their Italian-made halal line and this was considered

36 MUI has recently undergone a major overhaul due to corruption charges. Other issues such as the discovery of trace amounts of pork in certified products led the Indonesian government to set up the Halal Product and Security Agency in 2014. However, the roles of MUI and The Halal Product and Security Agency remain unclear. For more information, see Armanios and Ergene, *Halal Food*.

an example of bad or irresponsible marketing. The halal certifiers believed the company should avoid stereotypes such as these when marketing a halal line of products to audiences in Muslim-majority countries. Rather, the halal certification body urged companies to promote the regional character of products and, therefore, the 'quality' of the product. This example shows that ethical orientations are standardised for diverse audiences and, for both sectors, Italian-made regional products are an important way to ease these diverging tensions. Eating ethically is articulated in this encounter between broader imaginaries and local institutional practices.

Ethical claims are not separate but are incorporated, challenged, and reinterpreted in the process of overseeing foodways. The lack of a global, unified standard in both Made in Italy and halal certifications means that standards vary and are influenced by the local cultural attitudes regarding the value of certain foods. The next section explores the ways consumers strategise to eat according to halal rules in Milan.

5 The Development of Ethics for Consumers

Similar to the interpretation of standards, consumers are incorporating knowledge about standards to navigate what is halal. While the institutionalisation of halal makes these debates about what can be considered halal semi-static, consumers expressed that foods were provisional in their categorisation of what can be considered a halal food.

Although many people work in certification sectors, in Italy, the majority of Muslims rarely use halal certification labels when making buying decisions because halal certifications are mostly found on products meant for export markets. To expand on this point, let's turn to an example of an Italian candy called Rossana. Rossana is widely available across Italy and carries a halal certification label on packaging, even in the domestic market. Yet, those working in the organisation that certified the candy as halal did not know that it held their halal certification. While the amount of labelled halal-certified food available to the average consumer is increasing, it remains only a small fraction of what can be purchased at grocery stores. This means Italian Muslim consumers do not typically look for halal certification when purchasing foods. In this section, I show that that what halal means is not only defined by institutions but also by the eating decisions and habits of consumers, who do not, and oftentimes cannot, rely on halal labels to navigate their foodscape.

The following relies on findings from a focus group held at the Università degli Studi di Milano. The focus group included three student participants, two men and one woman, ranging from 18 to 20 years old. Two of the participants were second-generation Muslims while the other had immigrated to Milan a few months earlier.

Findings from the focus group showed that many of the young Muslims relied heavily on internet research. While at first this may seem like an individual process, I found that they often speak to one another about current debates and issues. I also found that the second-generation Muslims in the group wanted to have more access to halal-certified products in grocery stores. The newly immigrated Muslim was less concerned about the availability of certified products.

The two second-generation Muslims spoke at length about the differences between their generation and their immigrating parents, to point out the need for access to in-country, certified foods. They also made it clear that eating halal is more important to them than it was for their parents. They believed that the rise of certifications like organic and vegan should also allow for halal to be present in the Italian context. As one participant explained:

> Something that comes to mind are vegan-made products, for example, an alternative for those who do not eat meat products and only eat it if they totally know that it is all vegetables … There are other examples, examples from other countries, so it's just a matter of taking that model there and making it … but I look around and say if there are vegans, organic, there are gluten-free products. There are many alternatives, certainly there should exist a [halal alternative].

For this participant, halal certification is another way to find food alternatives. The participants expressed that their parents did not worry about halal foods. Their parents' generation simply did their best to eat halal foods; similarly, the newly immigrated Muslim did not take as much interest in having certified products available in supermarkets. The second-generation participants viewed halal certification as a guarantee, a way to provide clarity on the hidden elements of processed foods. As one participant explained:

> They try much as they can to deceive you [through labelling]. You have to be really careful because then maybe you think there are chemical things, but in reality, it's just an acronym that hides another thing. There are so many things … for example, a snack. I never thought long ago that there could be something inside [that is non-halal], but … you should check after some time. Good or bad you buy the same things because you know you can recognise them. In this sense I'm telling you now in the first years

> [of immigrating] we did not know these things, but now with the internet everything is easier. It gives you a hand.

Indeed, for all Italian Muslim consumers the internet serves as an important tool in demystifying food labels. Notably, in this example the onus for information is on the individual consumer, but research is also a community endeavour. Research is disseminated to and from friends and family. When I asked where participants get their information, one explained 'from family and individually'. When I asked him to expand, he said:

> I'll research maybe [on the meaning of the labels]. You look for on the internet maybe on some things you have doubts and other things you don't doubt. You can manage. Then in general, for example, in my case I decide about halal based on the food. For example, returning to the meat discourse maybe there is also part of my family that pays attention to where you buy meat. I can't go to just any supermarket where one can buy meat. I go to the Islamic butcher who has it done in a halal way.

Research is a major component in understanding 'what's behind' the label at the supermarket. A consumer, in other words, depends on social relations: they trust their butcher and have discussions with their family about their buying decisions. Also striking is that knowledge about food is never fully complete. The participant says, 'You should check after some time', which suggests that halal is not static but can change and does change over time and through conversations with others. While it is better to know if something consumed is not technically permissible, participants repeated that one should do their best and continue to gain knowledge and awareness. To better understand how young Muslims do or do not come to consensus, I showed the focus group pictures of common Italian foods. I then asked if they would consume the food and why or why not. The first image of a cheese pizza was deemed halal by all participants. Below is their reasoning:

Moderator:	Why do you all say it is halal?
Participant #1:	Because there is no meat, it is vegetables and cheese, I don't see any meat that would make it not halal, I think.
Participant #2:	There might be lard used.
Participant #1:	I think lard does not come to mind because there is something … I want to expand on this point … for example, when someone maybe I do not know a Moroccan works with I

	don't know, an Egyptian who maybe works in a bakery when he works in a bakery he says 'look, I don't eat brioches that have lard', there is this tendency to warn others about certain things. In my opinion, for pizza there has never been a voice like that so ... pizza has nothing [non-halal] in its dough.
Participant #2:	I've never heard anything.
Participant #1:	Exactly.

While pizza is considered halal, one of the participants said that no one has *really* investigated what goes into pizza dough. Despite possible issues, there was a consensus that pizza may be consumed. Not all foods, however, were met with consensus. Interpretations varied regarding cannoli, a Sicilian pastry with a deep-fried shell filled with sweetened ricotta cheese. As it flashed on the screen, one youth said, 'Yes, it is halal', while another said, 'No'.

Participant #1:	I think it is halal because [the ingredients are] 100% ricotta and chocolate. There isn't a problem unless there is ... something that I don't know about.
Participant #2:	The dough has lard.
Participant #1:	What are you saying? Never ... I don't believe it.
Participant #2:	Your position doesn't work that way [just] because you would like that they are halal.
Participant #1:	But it's not true. There isn't alcohol. There isn't anything [non halal in it] ...
Participant #2:	In my opinion, alcohol maintains the sweetness longer, so ...
Participant #1:	No. I'm scared to do more research. I think it is halal because there isn't any alcohol. There isn't any meat. [Does some research on his phone] No there is lard!
Participant #2:	It's better to know.
Participant #1:	There is also 50 millilitres of marsala [a type of wine], whatever, this is not the original recipe. This is just a recipe therefore who knows? I will research it myself and make it at home.

The first participant is worried about what he might find with more research; the other participant responds, 'It's better to know'. The use of knowledge in navigating halal foods is complicated and can change perceptions of certain foods. For the first participant, the discovery that wine and lard are found in cannoli does not mean he will stop eating cannoli. Quite the contrary. He decides he will 'make it at home himself'. For the first participant, the issue of alcohol is reframed as an issue with the ingredients. This view contrasts with how alcohol is understood by certifiers. For consumers, the issue is not whether to allow trace amounts of alcohol because such amounts do not inebriate (*istihlāk*). In fact, the *amount* of alcohol is not debated. While certifiers incorporate scientific and Islamic debates to make their designations somewhat static, participants discuss the ingredient as something that can be substituted. For consumers, the skill of navigating what is halal or forbidden (ḥaram) is developed through internet research and discussions with family and friends. Knowledge about eating ethically is heavily influenced by what can be discovered online, but unlike in the process of institutionalisation, information does not always produce consensus.

6 Conclusion

My focus in this chapter is meant to help researchers think and theorise beyond consumption as subject-making or identity-affirming. Rather, as I have shown, the work of navigating food choices is complex and flexible. Local food culture also plays a major role in what both consumer and certifiers deem as halal. In terms of eating ethically, halal is closely related to the Quranic term, *ṭayyib*, which means good, wholesome, and clean. The term refers to a wide range of issues from how animals are raised to the healthfulness of the food in question.[37] While the consumption of food for many Muslims is a religious act, it is also an ethical expression. Many Muslims believe that *ṭayyib* encourages ethical food production,[38] an ideal that is also highlighted in other ethical eating certifications such as Made in Italy. Febe Armanios and Boğaç Ergene[39] call this turn to wholesome, local, widely accessible food a '*ṭayyib*-halal' ethos. Muslims advocating *ṭayyib*-halal find 'the mistreatment of farm animals and the manipulation of their food by chemicals or biological means as troublesome, abhorrent, and thus anything but *ṭayyib*'. This position has many parallels with other food movements that call for the humane treatment of animals, non-GMOs, or chemically engineered foods.

At the same time, technologies have propelled halal food bloggers—known as 'haloodies'—to the fore, writers like London-based Layla Hassanali, creator

37 Alzeer, Rieder, and Abou Hadeed. 'Rational and Practical Aspects of Halal and Tayyib in the Context of Food Safety', 265.

38 Adekunle and Filson, 'Understanding Halal Food Market: Resolving Asymmetric Information', 13.

39 Armanios and Ergene, *Halal Food*, 200–201.

of the 'Halal Girl About Town' blog. Haloodies not only guide consumers to halal food choices but they also expand notions of what is halal outside of Muslim-majority countries and beyond restaurants associated with diasporic populations. The tension between an expanding definition of halal along with the limitations of *ṭayyib*-halal fits well within the food culture of Italy because Italians take the ethical sourcing of their food seriously and rely heavily on networks to access it.[40] Trust networks support access to foods deemed consumable; at the same time, they help consumers understand and gain information about possible risks.

As discussions with halal consumers demonstrate, the limits of eating ethically are never fixed indefinitely across time and space. For halal consumers, pizza is halal today but may not be tomorrow. Shifting concerns are stabilised through trust in others, research, and discussion with peers, family, and religious leaders. During this process collective beliefs may be challenged; such challenges are central to eating ethically.

Tensions permeate the diverse interpretations of what is permissible and what defines halal even within the same certification environment. For example, Halal Italia allows trace amounts of alcohol whereas the World Halal Authority does not. The local context creates a degree of uncertainty; thus, certifications remain flexible in their interpretations of regional and global standards. But they must make a decision about what can and cannot be considered halal. This is not to say institutional categories do not change but to highlight that the processes take two different forms in the same context, though the function remains the same.

In the background of these debates is how the global food system has changed the ways consumers investigate what they consider permissible through their buying choices. The use of technology to uncover the doubtful aspects of a food along with discussion is key because, as one focus group participant said, producers are 'trying to deceive you'. The ethnographic examples expanded on in this chapter illustrate the cultural work of eating ethically, showing that the practice is truly a process. The possibility of getting it wrong now and again is an accepted and expected part of the process.

---

40 Grasseni, *Beyond Alternative Food Networks: Italy's Solidarity Purchase Groups*, 13–15; Counihan, *Italian Food Activism in Urban Sardinia: Place, Taste, and Community*, 23.

Acknowledgements

Thank you to John Bowen for his comments on my many drafts. Thank you to the organisers and participants for their invaluable insights on this chapter during the 'Rethinking Halal: Genealogy, Current Trends, and New Interpretations' conference held in Belgium from 18–19 June 2018. Many thanks to the editors of this volume, Ayang Utriza Yakin and Louis-Léon Christians, for their patience and support. Lastly, thank you to the anonymous reviewers in 2019 and 2020 for their careful reading and helpful comments.

Bibliography

Adekunle, Bamidele and Glen Filson. 2020. 'Understanding Halal Food Market: Resolving Asymmetric Information'. *Food Ethics* 5, nos 1–2: 13.

Alzeer, Jawad, Ulrike Rieder, and Khaled Abou Hadeed. 2018. 'Rational and Practical Aspects of Halal and Tayyib in the Context of Food Safety'. *Trends in Food Science & Technology* 71 (January): 264–267.

Armanios, Febe and Boğaç Ergene. 2018. *Halal Food: A History*. New York: Oxford University Press.

Attar, Maryam, Khalil Lohi, and John Lever. 2015. 'Remembering the Spirit of Halal: An Iranian Perspective', in *Halal Matters: Islam, Politics and Markets in Global Perspective*, edited by Florence Bergeaud-Blackler, Johan Fischer, and John Lever, 55–71. London; New York: Routledge.

Baume, Maia de la. 2010. 'France's Palate Acquires a Taste for Halal Food, to the Delight of Its Muslims'. *The New York Times*, September 8, 2010, sec. Europe.

Bergeaud-Blackler, Florence, Johan Fischer, and John Lever, eds. 2015. *Halal Matters: Islam, Politics and Markets in Global Perspective*. London, New York: Routledge.

Black, Rachel. 2012. *Porta Palazzo: The Anthropology of an Italian Market*. Philadelphia: University of Pennsylvania Press.

Bowen, John, Christophe Bertossi, and Jan Willem Duyvendak, eds. 2013. *European States and Their Muslim Citizens*. Cambridge: Cambridge University Press.

Bowen, John and Roger Petersen. 1999 'Introduction: Critical Comparisons'. In *Critical Comparisons in Politics and Culture*. Cambridge: Cambridge University Press: 1–20.

Ceccarelli, Giorgia 'Human Suffering in Italy's Agricultural Value Chain'. Oxfam Case Study, Oxfam, 14 June. https://oxfamilibrary.openrepository.com/bitstream/handle/10546/620479/cs-human-suffering-italy-agricultural-value-chain-210618-en.pdf?sequence=4 (accessed August 6, 2019).

Corriere del Mezzogiorno. 2018. 'Appropriazione indebita e frode Agli arresti l'imam Sharif Lorenzini', 2 June. http://corrierefiorentino.corriere.it/bari/cronaca/18_febbr

aio_06/arresti-domiciliari-ieri-l-imam-sharif-lorenzini-f889269a-0b18-11e8-a159-261a041af718.shtml last retrieved 29 April 2019.

Counihan, Carole. 2018. *Italian Food Activism in Urban Sardinia: Place, Taste, and Community*. London: Bloomsbury Academic.

Counihan, Carole. 2004. *Around the Tuscan Table: Food, Family, and Gender in Twentieth Century Florence*. London: Routledge.

Ginnaio, Monica and Amy Jacobs. 2011. 'Pellagra in Late Nineteenth Century Italy: Effects of a Deficiency Disease'. *Population* 66, no. 3: 583–609.

Grasseni, Cristina. 2013. *Beyond Alternative Food Networks: Italy's Solidarity Purchase Groups*. New York: Bloomsbury Academic.

Hackett, Conrad. 2017. '5 Facts about the Muslim Population in Europe'. *Pew Research Centre. Fact Tank: News in Numbers* (blog). 29 November. http://www.pewresearch.org/fact-tank/2017/11/29/5-facts-about-the-muslim-population-in-europe/ (accessed March 4, 2019).

Hatanaka, Maki, Carmen Bain, and Lawrence Busch. 2005. 'Third-party certification in the global agrifood system' *Food Policy* 30, no. 3 (June): 354–369.

Hatanaka, Maki. 2015. 'Organic Certification and the Rationalisation of Alternative Food and Agriculture: Sustainable Shrimp Farming in Indonesia', in *Re-Thinking Organic Food and Farming in a Changing World*, ed. Bernhard Freyer and Jim Bingen, 45–60. New York: Springer.

Husseini de Araújo, Shadia. 2019. 'Assembling Halal Meat and Poultry Production in Brazil: Agents, Practices, Power and Sites'. *Geoforum* 100 (March): 220–228.

'Italian Sounding: A € 90 Billion Problem'. 2018. ItalianFOOD.Net. 20 August. https://news.italianfood.net/2018/08/20/italian-sounding-90-billion-problem/ (accessed April 28, 2019).

Klein, Jakob. 2009. 'Creating Ethical Food Consumers? Promoting Organic Foods in Urban Southwest China'. *Social Anthropology* 17, no. 1: 74–89.

Krause, Elizabeth. 2018. *Tight Knit: Global Families and the Social Life of Fast Fashion*. Chicago: University of Chicago Press.

Landini, Francesca. 2017. 'What's truly Italian? Food fight foils 'Made in Italy' plan', *Reuters*, 2 June 2017. http://www.reuters.com/article/us-italy-food-idUSKBN18T1ER (accessed July 25, 2017).

Lever, John and Johan Fischer. 2015. *Religion, Regulation, Consumption: Globalising Kosher and Halal Markets*. Oxford: Manchester University Press.

Moyer-Nocchi, Karima. 2015. *Chewing the Fat: An Oral History of Italian Foodways from Fascism to Dolce Vita*. Ohio: Medea.

Nadeau, Barbie Latza. 2015. 'Milan's New 'Anti-Mosque' Law' *The Daily Beast*, 28 January. http://www.thedailybeast.com/articles/2015/01/28/milan-s-new-anti-mosque-law.html (accessed January 28, 2015).

Nadeau, Barbie Latza. 2015. 'Italy Drives Muslims Underground' *The Daily Beast*, 1 December. http://www.thedailybeast.com/articles/2015/12/01/italy-drives-muslims-underground.html (accessed January 11, 2017).

Orlando, Giovanni. 2018. 'Offsetting Risk: Organic Food, Pollution and the Transgression of Spatial Boundaries'. *Culture, Agriculture, Food and Environment* 40, no. 1: 45–54.

Pai, Hsiao-Hung. ''You're Lucky to Get Paid at All': How African Migrants Are Exploited in Italy'. *The Guardian* (London), 9 February. https://www.theguardian.com/commentisfree/2019/feb/09/african-migrants-italy-hard-right-authorities (accessed August 6, 2019).

Rudnyckyj, Daromir. 2012. *Spiritual Economies: Islam, Globalisation, and the Afterlife of Development*. Ithaca: Cornell University Press.

Tsing, Anna. 2015. *The Mushroom at the End of the World: On the Possibility of Life in Capitalist Ruins*. Princeton: Princeton University Press.

Wills, Chuck and David Grubin. 2005. *PBS: Destination America*. New York: DK.

CHAPTER 10

Halal Certification as a Source of Intra- and Inter-group Tensions among Muslims in Poland

Konrad Pędziwiatr

There has been unprecedented growth and development of halal (Islamically 'permissible' or 'lawful') goods and services markets across Europe[1] and beyond the continent.[2] This has been happening within a wider transformation of religions by contemporary consumer society forcing them to engage in marketing and branding.[3] These processes have emerged in Europe with diversified intensity not only in countries with significant Muslim populations (e.g. Germany, France, and the UK), but also in countries with smaller but historically more anchored Muslim communities such as Poland.

Although Muslims make up only around 0.1 per cent of the Polish population, that is c. 40,000 people and the majority of them arrived in Poland only in the last decades,[4] they play (if not directly then indirectly by legitimising it) a crucial role in the country's halal meat and other food production and certification businesses. Two major Polish Muslim organisations, the Muslim Religious Union (*Muzułmański Związek Religijny w Rzeczpospolitej Polskiej*, hereafter MZR) and the Muslim League (*Liga Muzułmańska w Rzeczpospolitej Polskiej*: hereafter LM) have developed their own halal certification strategies and smaller groups of Ahmadi and Shia Muslims, as well as Muslim organisations not affiliated with any legally recognised religious unions (e.g. Polish Halal

1 Fischer, *The Halal Frontier: Muslim Consumers in a Globalized Market*; Lever and Miele, 'The Growth of Halal Meat Markets in Europe: An Exploration of the Supply Side Theory of Religion', 528–537; Kurth and Glasbergen, 'Serving a Heterogenous Muslim Population? Private Governance Arrangements of Halal Food in the Netherlands', 103–118.

2 See, for example, Bergeaud-Blackler et al., *Halal Matters: Islam, Politics and Markets in Global Perspective*; Fischer, *Islam, Standards, and Technoscience: In Global Halal Zones*; Tayob, '"O You Who Believe, Eat of the Tayyibāt (Pure and Wholesome Food) That We Have Provided You"—Producing Risk, Expertise and Certified Halal Consumption in South Africa'; Voloder, 'The "Mainstreaming" of Halal: Muslim Consumer-Citizenship in Australia'.

3 Stolz and Usunier 2019, 'Religions as Brands? Religion and Spirituality in Consumer Society', 6–31.

4 Pędziwiatr, 'Muslims in Contemporary Poland', 10–11; Pędziwiatr, 'Imigranci Bliskowschodni i Północnoafrykańscy, a odrodzenie islamu we współczesnej Polsce', 241; Nalborczyk, 'Relations between Islam and the State in Poland: The Legal Position of Polish Muslims', 343–359.

 | DOI:10.1163/9789004459236_011

Institute (PIH)), have been trying to follow their tracks.[5] The fact that Poland is one of the biggest meat producers in Europe and exports 80 per cent of its beef abroad[6] is not without importance here. A significant part of this meat is halal-certified and is being sold not only to numerous European countries (e.g. Germany, France, and the Netherlands) but also to Africa and Asia (e.g. Algeria, UAE, and Saudi Arabia).[7] According to some experts, the value of halal and kosher meat exports has reached almost €0.5 billion.[8] Other agricultural products and cosmetics that receive halal certificates (or tend to be viewed as halal products[9]) are also being successfully exported. This lucrative business has been a source of numerous controversies and disputes in Polish society and within the wider Muslim community in Poland and some specific groups within it.

Many studies show how religiously inspired food standards assist in the creation of group boundaries[10] and help immigrants forming religious minorities in the new host countries to reconnect with their original culture and maintain distinctive religious and cultural identities.[11] At the same time, the aforementioned and other research also demonstrates that these practices might be a source of tensions between a minority group and the larger society as well as within a given minority. As John Lever rightly notices, the controversies over halal meat and Muslim (*dhabīḥa*) slaughter practice are complex and involve not only the elements of food production but also religion. In such a context the

---

5 Interviews with TM, YC, AM and AMM2.

6 Rzeczpospolita, 'Eksport służy wołowinie'.

7 How big proportion of the beef production is halal-certified is unknown but according to the employee of the General Veterinary Inspectorate this might be much more than 50 per cent of the total production (interview with AE).

8 Ferfecki, 'Zakaz uboju rytualnego do poprawki'.

9 I refer here for example to a breathable nail polish, a product that was designed by the Polish cosmetic company Inglot to be above all 'more healthy' but turned out to be very popular in Muslim countries. The cosmetic company promoted it later as world's first 'wudu-friendly' nail polish. While using the product, praying with nail polish (usually impermissible because of the waterproof barrier it creates on nails, which prevents the wudu ritual from being completed five times a day) becomes possible (Cieszak 'Inglota nie powstrzyma nawet bomba w salonie w Bengazi'; Kari, 'Inglot Releases Halal Nail Polish').

10 See, for example, Fischler, 'Food, Self and Identity'; Mintz and Du Bois, 'The Anthropology of Food and Eating', 99–119.

11 Jacobson, *Islam in Transition: Religion and Identity among British Pakistani Youth*; Weller and Turkom, 'Contextualizing the Immigrant Experience: The Role of Food and Foodways in Identity Maintenance and Formation for First- and Second-Generation Latinos', 57–73.

category of 'halal' is viewed frequently as an indicator of the growing power of Islam, linked with concerns about integration of some groups of immigrants and the presence of what are seen to be 'barbaric' Muslim practices.[12] Thus, public debates about it frequently do not concern halal goods or services as such, but other issues outside these categories (e.g. the wearing of the hijab or niqab in the public space).

The chapter sheds light on the key dimensions of the halal tensions in Poland that directly or indirectly involve the Polish Muslim community or various groups within it. Although it focuses on one Central European country, the processes it analyses are also to be found in other post-communist societies (e.g. Ukraine[13] or Russia[14]), as well as in other parts of the world where individuals (including religious leaders) and groups holding opposing views (for instance, on animal rights) compete for influence, power, and resources. It argues that halal food production and certification has been both a blessing and a curse for Muslims in Poland. It has provided additional source of funding for some Muslim organisations to run their activities (e.g. MZR and LM) and allowed several members of the community to achieve a higher standard of living and sometimes even generate significant profits, but it has also significantly reconfigured the larger Muslim community and various groups within it, in particular the oldest Muslim community in Poland—Tatars living within the Polish borders since the fourteenth century. The conflict within the last group, to a large degree linked with halal certification, is so severe that some members of it and experts see as the worst in the group's history and threatening its very existence.[15]

The chapter begins by drawing a larger picture of Muslims in Poland and context within which halal certification emerged. Then, it briefly analyses its economic and legal opportunity structures[16] and legal disputes over the legality of the ritual slaughter in which some leaders of the Muslim community have taken an active part, while the main lobbyists from the agricultural sector remained largely in the shadows. The main part of the text analyses the divisions within the Muslim community and its various groups emanating from halal certification or closely linked with it.

---

12 Lever, 'Halal Meat and Religious Slaughter: From Spatial Concealment to Social Controversy—Breaching the Boundaries of the Permissible', 1–2.

13 Brylov. 'Halal Industry of Ukraine in the Period of Independence', 238–241.

14 Silantev, *Sovet muftiev Rossii: istorija odnoj fitny*, 559–563.

15 *Inter alia*, interviews with KR, DB, DS, AFM, AMM1 and JA.

16 Hilson, 'New Social Movements: The Role of Legal Opportunity'; Sperling, *Organizing Women in Contemporary Russia*.

The article is based on the analysis of the existing sources, including halal certificates published on the websites of Polish companies, as well as extensive fieldwork in Poland, including participant observations of Muslim community life in various parts of the country. In the course of the research the author also conducted 25 in-depth interviews with representatives and members of the various groups within the Muslim population in Poland, as well as the anonymous employee of the General Veterinary Inspectorate (GVI). The fieldwork was carried out in those cities with the largest Muslim communities and where the most active Islamic centres supervised by the Arab-Muslim organisations in the country are to be found, that is in: Warsaw, Kraków, Gdańsk, Poznań, Wrocław, and Białystok.[17] The fieldwork data were mainly collected between June 2016 and June 2018. All interviews were carefully transcribed, and then coded and analysed with the help of the NVivo 11 software.[18]

1 Muslims in Poland and Halal Certification

For centuries, the Polish Muslim community was almost exclusively made up of the Tatars who had already settled within the Polish-Lithuanian borders in the Middle Ages. Before the Second World War the Muslim population in Poland was made up of around 6,000 people, among whom the Tatars constituted the vast majority. They lived in 19 communities with about 250 members each and prayed in 17 wooden mosques and two prayer halls.[19] Only around 10 per cent of the Tatar settlement territories remained in the post-war Poland.[20] In addition, post-war migrations led to the further fragmentation of the small Tatar community. Apart from their traditional settlements in Białystok, Białostocczyzna, and Warsaw, there were also new ones in Gdańsk, Gorzów Wielkopolski, Szczecin, and Oleśnica. This dispersion made it difficult not only to build even the basic structures of religious validation (so-called plausibility structures) but also maintain religious practice.

As a result of the immigration processes already starting to emerge in the late 1950s (mostly in the form of student migrations) and conversions to Islam, the Muslim community revived and started to become increasingly diversified.[21] At the beginning of the twenty-first century, the largest group within the Muslim

17 Except one interview that was carried out in Birmingham, UK.

18 The full list of the project interviews is to be fund at the end of the text.

19 Chazbijewicz, 'Islam i Środowiska Muzułmańskie We Współczesnej Polsce', 337.

20 Nalborczyk and Gródź, 'Poland'. 401–411.

21 Pędziwiatr, 'Muslims in Contemporary Poland'. 10–13.

population in Poland are no longer Tatars, but immigrants and their children and grandchildren as well as Polish citizens who have embraced Islam. It is estimated that the very diverse Muslim community of around 40,000 people is made up of immigrants from around the world and their offspring, Tatars, and Polish converts. They are students, entrepreneurs, manual and intellectual workers, refugees,[22] and diplomats. Thus, the character of Islam in Poland is mediated not only through influences of many ethnic groups but also wide range of religious currents from Sufism, through Gulenism and Ikhwanism, to Salafism, to name only a few. It is also important to remember about the remote influences from outside of Poland *inter alia*, from the Polish diaspora. For many of about 2,500 Polish Muslims living in Great Britain, the separation from their country of origin was also associated with the adoption of a new faith in the form of Islam.[23]

At the time of writing, the largest Muslim group in Poland is made up of more than 10,000 Arabs or people of Arab origin.[24] In this group the most important role is played by former students from Syria, Lebanon, Yemen, Iraq, Jordan, Occupied Palestinian Territories, Algeria, Egypt, and Tunisia, who have settled in Poland over the past 30–40 years. To date, most of them have already acquired Polish citizenship and substantial cultural capital. They identify strongly with their new nation/country, while maintaining contact with families and friends in their countries of origin.[25] These people played a key role in the creation of numerous Muslim organisations (e.g. the first immigrant Arab-Muslim organisation in Poland, the Association of Muslim Students (SSM), in 1991[26] and the Muslim Association of Education and Culture (MSKK) in 1996)[27] and management of the most dynamic Muslim Centres in the major Polish

---

22 Among the refugees the Chechens were the most numerous group in the last decades. Only some of them remained in Poland, and most left for Western European countries, including France, Austria, Belgium, and Germany Górny et al., 'Uchodźcy w Polsce: Sytuacja prawna, skala napływu i integracja w społeczeństwie polskim oraz rekomendacje'.

23 Pędziwiatr, 'Islamophobia in Poland: National Report 2016'.

24 According to Office for Foreigners (UDSC), there are currently slightly over 8000 citizens of the countries of the Arab League residing in Poland. These statistics though do not take into account many citizens of Arab countries who were naturalized and their children who are Poles. Own elaboration of the data available on the UDSC-maintained site www.migracje.gov.pl. Available also in Pędziwiatr, 'Transformacje postaw wobec Arabów w społeczeństwie polskim'.

25 Interview with YC, IK, NZ.

26 Information about the association is available on http://dziedzictwo.ekai.pl/text.show?id=25 (accessed 20 May 2018) and from interviews with SI, IK, YC, AWW.

27 The organisation was founded in 1996 by the SSM circle to carry out various projects for the Arab community and to manage Muslim centres in various parts of the country (interviews with SI, IK).

cities. In 2001 they also set up the Muslim League in the Republic of Poland. As one may read in its brochures, they aspire to 'promote awareness about Islam' and 'to exercise Muslim religious rights', among other things. The organisation was recognised as a 'religious community' in 2004 by the Department of Denominations and National Minorities at the Ministry of Internal Affairs and Administration. Since then the LM has been competing with the Tatars for influence in the Polish Muslim community and representation of it in contacts with the state administration and vis-a-vis other Muslim and non-Muslim countries of the world, *umma* and the international community.[28]

Like the Tatars, the Muslim League has also created the position of mufti (with the title Mufti of the Muslim League),[29] whose responsibilities are similar to those of the Polish Mufti (an institution reactivated by the Polish authorities in agreement with the Tatars in 2004). By creating this position, the league wanted to at least partially challenge the authority of the Tartar Mufti of Poland, Tomasz Miśkiewicz, in matters concerning the Muslim community in Poland. At the same time, my research shows that, in the era of relatively easy access to religious knowledge from outside of the country, Mufti Tomasz Miśkiewicz and Mufti Nidal Abu Tabaq are not necessarily perceived as the most important instances of religious authority.[30] Importantly, from the moment of its creation the LM began to develop its own halal certification strategy and compete with other Muslim organisations on the certification market, which will be elaborated in more detail below.[31]

Although Tatars, who trace their roots to fourteenth-century Poland, are one of the smaller groups (between 3,000 and 5,000 people) within the broader Polish Muslim community, their position in it is strongly secured not only as a legally recognised historical ethnic minority but also as the only Muslim group in the country whose relations with the state are regulated by the special bill passed by the Polish Parliament before the Second World War (in 1936). This bill continues to be legally binding in spite of the completely changed polit-

---

28 For more information about the context of creation of LM in 2001 and its recognition by the state as religious association in 2004, see Pędziwiatr, 'The Established and Newcomers in Islam in Poland or the Inter-Group Relations within the Polish Muslim Community', 169–182.

29 From the moment of its creation this position was held by medical doctor by profession Nidal Abu Tabaq who passed away on 30th November 2020. As of January 2021 the new Mufti of the Muslim League was not selected.

30 Pędziwiatr, 'Imigranci Bliskowschodni i Północnoafrykańscy, a odrodzenie islamu we współczesnej Polsce', 261–263.

31 The basic information about the halal certification process within the LM can be found at http://islam.info.pl/?page_id=928 (accessed 1 October 2018).

ical, social, and even geographical realities.[32] The oldest Muslim organisation in the country, the Muslim Religious Union in the Republic of Poland (MZR), was established in 1925 and since then it has been always led by a Tatar. It plays the role of organisational *primus inter pares* within the Muslim population in Poland and has been acting as the representative of the Polish Muslims. Provisions from the 1936 law stipulate that the Mufti of Poland, as well as imams and muezzins, are chosen from the ranks of the MZR and that their salaries are paid by the Polish state.[33] After 1989, when new legislation allowing the establishment of new Muslim organisations was introduced, MZR lost its monopoly as the sole representative body of Muslims in Poland, though it maintained privileged relations with the state. The first Mufti of Poland after the Second World War was elected in 2004. Since then this position has been held by Tomasz Miśkiewicz—a Tatar imam from Białystok (born in 1977), who completed a degree in Shari'a law in Saudi Arabia. Until the end of 1990s, membership of the MZR was open only to Muslims with Polish citizenship, a fact that has partially contributed to the creation of a much more inclusive organisation, the Muslim League.[34] The MZR has been looking after two historic mosques from the sixteenth and seventeenth centuries in Kruszyniany and Bohoniki and a small but modern purpose-built mosque in Gdańsk. It maintains a vibrant publishing activity[35] that, as well as providing religious education, plays an important role in Islam in Poland.[36]

Although some imams of the MZR issued halal certificates during the Communist period, this was mostly on the incidental basis.[37] This situation changed after the re-establishment of the institution of the Mufti of Poland in 2004. Since then, the new Mufti, Tomasz Miśkiewicz, has been very actively building structures for halal certification in close cooperation with state authorities (e.g. General Veterinary Inspectorate, Ministry of Agriculture, Ministry of Foreign Affairs, and Polish Embassies). Before setting up a private company (Halal

32 For example, it talks about Vilnius, now the capital of Lithuania but in Polish hands before the Second World War, as the seat of the Tatar organisation.

33 This was at least the case before the Second World War. The Communist regime ceased to support any religious group after the end of the war.

34 Pędziwiatr, 'Imigranci Bliskowschodni i Północnoafrykańscy'.

35 Two of the journals published by the MZR, *Przegląd Tatarski* and *Muzułmanie Rzeczpospolitej* can be downloaded from its well-maintained website. More information about the organisation can be found at http://www.mzr.pl (accessed 1 June 2019).

36 For more information about Islamic religious education in Poland, see Nalborczyk and Pędziwiatr, 'Between Old Traditions and New Diversities—Islamic Religious Education in Poland'.

37 Interview with TŻ and TM.

System), owned by his wife to manage business contacts and the certification process 'more professionally' in 2011, he had been doing it as part of MZR's activities.[38] This move was one of the reasons for internal tensions within the Tatar community, which are elaborated at more length below.

Other smaller Muslim groups within the Polish Muslim community have also developed their own halal certification policies. In fact, one of the leaders of the small Shia Muslim community, Imam Mahmoud Taha Żuk (born in 1939), who embraced Islam in the mid-1960s, was one of the pioneers of halal certification in Poland. Some of the first halal certificates issued for Polish companies exporting their products abroad were prepared by him initially, even without stamps. He recalled that one of the firms for which he was issuing certificates in the mid-1970s was Animex, a company created in 1951 and now the biggest employer in the meat industry in Poland.[39] Imam Żuk had led the Association of Muslim Unity (Stowarzyszenie Jedności Muzułmańskiej[40])—one of the Shia organisations[41] in the country recognised in 1989 by the state authorities as a 'religious community'[42]—until 2010, when he was replaced in the leadership position by imam Rafał Berger.[43] However, he continued issuing halal certificates until 2016 and played a key role in an internal halal dispute within the Muslim League between 2010 and 2014, which will be analysed in the last section of this chapter.

Another Muslim group that has been developing a halal certification strategy is the Ahmadiyyas.[44] They have been trying to tap into the halal certification market through their organisation, Muslim Association Ahmadiyya (Muzułmańskie Stowarzyszenie Ahmadiyya), recognised by the state as a 'religious community' in 1990. The group, however, is very small in Poland (officially it has only 45 members) and its influence on halal certification is rather lim-

38 Interview with TM.

39 More information about the company Animex is available on its website at http://www.animex.pl/ (accessed 1 October 2018) and interview with TŻ.

40 More information about the association and its publishing activity can be found on its website at http://www.shiapoland.com/ (accessed 1 October 2018).

41 More information about the second Shia Muslim organisation in Poland, Ahl-ul-Bayt Islamic Assembly of Poland (Islamskie Zgromadzenie Ahlul-Bayt) can be found on its website at http://www.abia.pl/ (accessed 1 October 2018).

42 GUS, *Wyznania Religijne: Stowarzyszenia Narodowościowe i Etniczne w Polsce 2007–2011*, 122.

43 Interview with RB.

44 More information about its certification process can be found at https://www.alislam.pl/certyfikacja_halal/zasady_systemu_halal (accessed 1 October 2018).

ited.[45] Other Muslim organisations in the country are either not interested in dealing with halal certification or do not have clear policies in this domain.

2 Changing Legal and Economic Opportunities for Ritual Slaughter

The emergence of the halal certification in Poland has been linked not only to the significant changes within the Polish Muslim community (in particular with revival of Islam in Poland, its diversification, democratisation and globalisation explored in more depth elsewhere (Pędziwiatr 2011b)) but also to the wider systemic transformations taking place in Poland after the collapse of the communism. The changes linked to this transition led to a general improvement of economic indicators, significant growth of number of people entering institutions of tertiary education (Polish Gross Enrolment Index was below 10 per cent in 1990 and increased to above 40 per cent in 2016 (MNiSW 2016)), rising living standards and life expectancy (from 70 years in 1990 to almost 78 in 2016 (GUS 2016)). Some of the key changes that enabled the emergence of the halal certification market had to do with the sphere of economy and law. One may consider them as specific legal and economic opportunity structures which inhibit or support the development of the social phenomenon in question—halal certification—similarly to the way these forces act with regards to a given social movement (Hilson 2002; Sperling 1999). In the case of the halal certification the first one—that is economic context within which it operates—is greatly influenced by the later one, i.e. the legal context.

Because the majority of the halal market in Poland has been linked with ritual slaughter its legal frame is of paramount importance to its existence. Up until the end of 1936 there were no specific practice barriers for the religious communities in highly multiethnic and multi-religious pre-war Poland.[46] This situation changed from the beginning of 1937 when a 1936 law came into force that requested that the ritually slaughtered animals needed to be unconscious so as not to feel pain and suggested quotas of the animals that Jews and Muslims could slaughter for their own use. Just before the war this law was made even more restrictive by banning ritual slaughter all together. Although the arguments used against the ritual slaughter at that time referred to the

45 GUS, *Wyznania Religijne*, 124.

46 Less than 70 per cent of the citizens of the country were ethnic Poles and over 10 per cent were followers of Judaism.

rights of animals and economic reasons (the supposed rising price of meat as a result of it), the anti-Semitic sentiments played the major role in it.[47]

After the Second World War the 1936 bill significantly restricting the ritual slaughter became part of the legal framework throughout the Communist period. This situation was not conducive to the development of the halal market. It changed only in 1997, when several bills passed through Parliament made ritual slaughter possible again. One of the most important developments was a new Polish Constitution with special provisions regarding not only the protection of the rights of national and ethnic minorities but also the protection of religious freedom. Article 35 of the Constitution of the Republic of Poland guarantees Polish citizens belonging to national and ethnic minorities, among others, freedom to maintain their customs, language, and traditions. Article 53 of the Constitution stipulates that the state must ensure that believers are free from obstacles to express and practise their religion (Constitution of Poland 1997). Ritual slaughter has been interpreted here as part of this guaranteed practice. Apart from these very important constitutional provisions the Animal Protection Act of 21 August 1997 enabled the religious communities recognised by the state to practice ritual slaughter without the necessity of pre-stunning the animals.[48] They all served as important stimuli for the groups that were not yet registered as religious communities (e.g. LM) to organise themselves and apply for such a status. They also constituted an important incentive for the dynamically growing agricultural sector searching for new export possibilities.

---

47 Similarly today, some aspects of the opposition to Muslim ritual slaughter have clear Islamophobic connotations (see, for example, Mann, 'Campaign to Boycott Halal Food Gains Momentum in Australia,' or Lever, 'Halal Meat and Religious Slaughter'). Although Muslims make up only around 0.1 per cent of the Polish population, a recent study showed that Poles believed that Muslims made up 7 per cent of total population of the country in 2016 and that the size of the community would grow up to 13 per cent by 2020 (Narkowicz and Pędziwiatr, 'Between Old Traditions and New Diversities'). This discrepancy can be explained by the high level of fear of Muslims and Islam in a society that is one of the most ethnically and religiously homogenous in Europe and with high levels of religious services participation. The anti-Muslim fears were particularly strongly politicised and instrumentalised by right-wing and far-right parties before and after the parliamentary elections in 2015. More information about various dimensions of Polish Islamophobia can be found in Pędziwiatr, 'Islamophobia in Poland: National Report 2015' and 'Islamophobia in Poland: National Report 2016'. Szostkiewicz, 'Ubój rytualny: prawa ludzi czy zwierząt?' *Gra w klasy*,' Nalborczyk 'Ubój Rytualny w Polsce—Zagadnienia Religijne, Obecny Stan Prawny i Jego Historia', 366–367; Szumigalska and Bazan 'Ritual Slaughter Issue in Poland: Between Religious Freedom, Legal Order and Economic-Political Interests', 55–56.

48 Drath, 'Ubój Rytualny w Polskim Systemie Prawnym'; Nalborczyk, 'Ubój Rytualny w Polsce—Zagadnienia Religijne, Obecny Stan Prawny i Jego Historia'.

In the 1990s and at the beginning of 2000s one may observe also the dynamic growth and institutionalisation of animal rights and animal welfare activism. A large number of organisations and initiatives were either set up or undergoing the process of professionalisation or 'ngo-isation'.[49] They form the basis of the larger animal rights movement united in their aversion to all forms of animal abuse.[50] Some of the organisations that make up part of this movement are the Animal Liberation Front, Klub Gaja, Empathy Association, Foundation Viva!, The All Polish Association for Animal Protection (OTOZ), and Animal Guard, to name only a few. They have all exercised increasing pressure on the political and legal system to limit the practice of ritual slaughter, viewed by them as cruel and harming the rights of animals.

The result of this pressure was the amendment of the Animal Protection Act of 1997, which came into force in 2002 and made ritual slaughter illegal again. As Agata Nalborczyk rightly notes, at that time this radical legal change passed almost without protest as it was legitimised by the assumed necessity of the legal adjustments linked with Polish accession to the European Union in 2004. Yet another major reason why these 'legal adjustments' have not resulted in Muslim protests was that hitherto there were only a few businesses linked with halal food production and the formalisation and professionalisation of halal certification had not yet started.[51]

The ban on ritual slaughter was short-lived. In September 2004 the Minister of Agriculture and Rural Development issued a regulation according to which the obligation to pre-stun the animals before the slaughter did not apply to the killing of animals slaughtered in accordance with religious practices of registered religious associations. This decision de facto restored the legal status from before the 2002 amendment.[52] From that moment, meat from ritual slaughter gradually became an increasingly important export product. This regulation is closely linked in time with the re-emergence of the position of the Mufti of Poland and significant diplomatic activism of the new young Mufti, strengthening economic cooperation with numerous Muslim countries that begun to import Polish halal certified products.[53] Meat from ritual slaughter started to make up an increasingly important part of the Polish beef export.

---

49 Jacobsson and Saxonberg, *Beyond NGO-Ization. The Development of Social Movements in Central and Eastern Europe*.

50 Jacobsson, 'Fragmentation of the Collective Action Space: The Animal Rights Movement in Poland'.

51 Nalborczyk, 'Ubój Rytualny w Polsce', 268.

52 Drath, 'Ubój Rytualny w Polskim Systemie Prawnym', 74.

53 Interviews with TM, MSM, JA.

The animal rights groups, however, did not surrender but only prepared for the next legal battle that emerged eight years later when the Prosecutor General (on behalf of, among others, Foundation Viva!) asked the Constitutional Tribunal to investigate if the adoption of the minister's regulation from 2004 regarding ritual slaughter violated a higher-ranking document; that is, the amendment to the Animal Protection Act of 1997 from 2002. The Tribunal ruled on 27 November 2012 that such a violation indeed did have a place and set the date of expiry of the contested paragraph of the regulation for 31 December 2012. At the same time the Tribunal did not consider the relation between ritual slaughter and the constitutionally guaranteed freedom of religious practices but only called upon the legislator to make decisions regarding the manner of shaping animal protection regulations, including regulating the issue of ritual slaughter. The result of this Tribunal decision was legal chaos regarding ritual slaughter. Muslim and Jewish organisations claimed that there is no ban on it since the Constitution guarantees freedom of worship, while the animal rights groups claimed the opposite.

An important clash between the Mufti of Poland, by then very deeply involved in the halal certification business, and the animal rights activists took place in September 2013 during the Eid al-Adha celebrations. When the Mufti and his Tatar congregations in a village of Bohoniki decided to publicly slaughter an animal, activists from the All Polish Association for Animal Protection (OTOZ) tried to prevent them from doing so. Through this highly mediatised event, Mufti Miśkiewicz has become the face of the struggle for ritual slaughter in Poland, although the main group that lobbied for the maintenance of this practice were farmers and the agricultural sector, who remained largely invisible in it.[54]

The final episode of this legal battle of the Muslim-Jewish forces aligned with agricultural lobby against the Animal Rights Movement came with the 10 December 2014 decision of the Constitutional Tribunal on the case brought by the Union of Jewish Religious Communities in Poland. The court found that the amended Animal Protection Act banning ritual slaughter was inconsistent with the constitutional provisions of freedom of conscience and religion, including freedom to exercise religious rites even if these rites are unpopular within the wider society. It also reaffirmed that the freedom to manifest religion may be limited only by law and only when it is necessary to protect the security of the state, public order, health, morals, or the freedoms and rights of

54 TVN, 'Obrońcy Praw Zwierząt Kontra Polscy Muzułmanie. Awantura Podczas Kurban Bajram'.

others.[55] What is very important with this decision is that the tribunal not only re-established the legal and economic opportunities for Muslims to perform ritual slaughter but also cancelled earlier regulations stating that only recognised religious communities were eligible for issuing halal certifications.[56] This has been particularly important information for one of the actors in the halal market (Polish Halal Institute) who had only loose relationship with one of the recognised religious unions (SJM).[57] Since this verdict the Institute has not needed to align itself with the Shia Organisation to be able to issue halal certificates that are valid under Polish law.

3 Impact of Halal Certification on Muslims in Poland

As mentioned earlier, although some halal certificates were issued by the members of the Muslim community in Poland under Communist rule, this was mostly incidental. The growth of the Polish economy after 1989, its opening up the global markets, the new legal framework, and the aforementioned changes within the Muslim community (in particular its diversification and growth) created a new and conducive environment for the development of the halal certification strategies by various Muslim groups within the Muslim community in Poland.[58] Very early in this process, however, conflicts begin to emerge, at first mostly inter-group and then also intra-group.

The first type of dispute, apart from the Muslims versus animal rights groups dimension analysed above, has Muslim inter-group character. It emerged after 2004, when the newly elected Mufti of Poland, Tomasz Miśkiewicz, who, before becoming a Mufti, had already designed a clear plan for the development of halal certification in Poland,[59] tried to have the market monopolised by the MZR and, within the MZR, link it to the position of Mufti and the Chairman of the Highest Collegium.[60] He did it in 2006 by signing an agreement between the MZR and the Chief Veterinarian giving the right to issue halal certificates only to the MZR. This agreement was legally challenged by the LM, who

55 Drath, 'Ubój Rytualny w Polskim Systemie Prawnym', 79.

56 Interview with EA.

57 Interview with TŻ and MSM.

58 Here it is worth pointing out that some Polish companies in recent years have also managed to obtain halal certificates from foreign certification institutions. (e.g. from Germany and Austria) where most probably they export their products.

59 Interview with TM.

60 Two positions of the highest authority within the MZR are held by one person—Tomasz Miśkiewicz.

argued that it violated the constitutional provisions about religious freedom and the equality among the religious unions. This action was successful and the LM also received the right to issue halal certificates in 2007. In the following years, other recognised Muslim organisations in the country followed suit.[61]

In October 2010, representatives of the all Muslim organisations registered by the state as religious associations (MZR, LM, SJM, Ahmadiya, and Ahl ul-Bayt) were invited to the headquarters of the General Veterinary Inspectorate in Warsaw to sign two documents. The first document outlined the procedures for issuing a 'certificate of a company's readiness for slaughter and production in the halal system'. It stipulated *inter alia* that: 'The certificate is issued for one year by an authorised Muslim Religious Association acting on Polish territory and may be cancelled if in the protocol after unannounced inspection, shortcomings will be noted in adapting of the company to production in accordance with the rules and requirements of Halal.' The second document described in detail 'the rules and conditions for slaughtering of animals in accordance with the requirements of Islam (Halal System)'. Thus, the agreement between the GVI—a state agency—and the Muslim organisations has reconfirmed the existing practice of issuing by them two types of certificates, a) for companies and b) for part of their production. More importantly, it has standardised and regulated the market, also indicating the actors eligible to issue halal certificates.[62]

Although Muslim religious associations in the country managed to reach agreement among themselves in 2010, in cooperation with the GVI, and established uniform procedures for the certification purposes, the detailed mechanisms of the certification and, in particular, the income generated from it, remained unclear. They eventually became a very important source of inter- and intra-group disputes. From the perspective of Mufti Miśkiewicz, who introduced the certification to MZR:

> Halal system was stabilised in 2011, including by appointing a company to service it (Halal System—KP). Earlier in the Muslim Religious Union there was neither a paid position nor a secretariat, and by 2012 at the headquarters of the Supreme College there was one person who was involved in everything: the secretariat, the mufti's writings and the preparation of certificates on behalf of the mufti. It was quite a nuisance, because not everything could be done on time. From that perspective I

61 Nalborczyk, 'Ubój Rytualny w Polsce', 369.

62 The documents from this meeting can be found on http://blog.boz.org.pl/uboj/101027_umowa_halal.pdf (accessed 30 May 2018).

> knew that the Muslim Religious Association could not cope with all the tasks involved with certification (preparing the legal part of it, supervising the persons who carry out slaughter, supervising food production, contacts with companies etc.), and if MZR could cope it would do so only in a very small perspective. Clients or companies that are looking for a given system, would go to other organisations, such as the Muslim League, because at the same time, in 2004, they started issuing certifications.[63]

However, taking over a significant part of this lucrative market from the LM was not without cost for the MZR and Miśkiewicz himself. Importantly, after outsourcing halal certification to a separate company outside of the supervision of the leadership of the MZR, the Tatar leaders lost control over money transfers for the certificates. The internal conflict within the Tatar dominated organisation seemed inevitable.

The rivalry between the MZR and LM and the disputes between the leaders of Tatar and Arab communities from 2001–2012 weakened after this period due to the internal problems in both organisations. Regarding the MZR and the Tatar community, the internal dispute became particularly visible during the Congress of the Supreme Muslim College that took place in November 2012. Delegates then decided to separate the function of the Chairman of the Supreme College (Przewodniczący Najwyższego Kolegium) from the function of mufti, thus removing Mufti Tomasz Miśkiewicz from the role of Chairman. The main reason for this change was dissatisfaction with the Miśkiewicz's rule and allegations of a lack of transparency regarding the revenues from halal certification conducted by the external company—Halal Poland System (HP), belonging to the Miśkiewicz's family—on behalf of the MZR.[64] These actions started a legal battle in which one party decided (in favour of Mufti Miśkiewicz) that in the light of the current regulations, Congress could not deprive him of the function of Chairman, and the other party which claimed that Congress had the right to do so. Subsequently, the entire community was divided into two camps: one in favour of Miśkiewicz and the other that did not support him. This has led to the emergence of two separate MZR boards, two Białystok religious communities, and even two Tatar folklore dance groups—both called 'Buńczuk'.[65] The latest episode of this dispute took place in 2017, when the second mufti—Janusz Aleksandrowicz, imam of Kruszyniany—was

63 Interview with TM.
64 See the company's website at http://www.halalpoland.pl/ (accessed 30 May 2018).
65 Radłowska, *Tatarzy Polscy: Ciągłość i Zmiana*, 141.

appointed. This triggered yet another unresolved legal battle in which Mufti Aleksandrowicz sued the Polish state for interference in the internal affairs of the religious community.[66]

The ongoing dispute is so deep that it even threatens the possibilities of the future survival of the Tatar community. As one of my interlocutors sympathetic to Mufti Miśkiewicz observed:

> Through this conflict, the youth also broke up. Let's face it—they do not meet now as they used to. After all, in our time ... we were meeting all the time. And that's how we knew each other. Later, marriages from these groups were also created. And now I'm scared that it will all blur. That young people see it all. They will go away from it. And here I regret. I'm afraid to think about it.[67]

Endogamy, thanks to which the Tatar community was able to survive for several centuries, is obviously undermined not only by the intra-group conflict but also by other social processes, including globalisation and democratisation. However, the seriousness of the dispute has also been noticed by members of the group opposing the leadership of Mufti Miśkiewicz. One of them said: 'Even in families people argue. He divided them ... Parents are arguing with children about Miśkiewicz'.[68] As Karolina Radłowska aptly notes, the conflict in the Tatar community cannot be reduced to only a financial dispute, it is also an effect of conflicting interests of individual Muslim communities, polarisation of the Tatar community, weakening of the importance of the religious factor, and the growth of democratisation processes in the group; however, halal certification is of key importance to that.[69]

Although the issue of halal certification has not been so divisive within the Arab Muslim community linked with the LM as it has been inside the MZR, the LM has not been fully spared. One of the pioneers of the certification system within the community, Mohammad Saleh Messikh, who in the eyes of the leadership of the organisation wanted to connect too closely the religious and business activities (*inter alia*, 'by registering the private company under the address of the Muslim Centre') was removed from the organisation and banned from issuing the certificates in 2010[70]. This has not prevented him, however,

66 Interview with JA.

67 Interview with AFM and AMM1.

68 Radłowska, *Tatarzy Polscy: Ciągłość i Zmiana*, 141.

69 Radłowska, *Tatarzy Polscy: Ciągłość i Zmiana*, 141.

70 Interview with SI and TŻ.

from continuing his business and certification activities. He has actually extended them even further by setting up in the same year the Polish Halal Institute (PIH) with, among other things, such ambitious objectives as:

> monitoring halal products and the market; supporting development of Polish halal business; creating opportunities and developing domestic and international halal trade; coordinating activities for the development of halal trade; extending access to financing sources of the Polish halal economy; participating in the creation of a unified—internationalized global halal system; providing help and support to institutions and establishments that run the halal program, and Polish companies to reach new customers and outlets; promotion of halal products in Poland and abroad; scientific research in the field of halal, healthy, ecological products.[71]

Dr. Messikh could launch this ambitious project thanks to unexpected help from the leader of the Shia Muslim community, imam Taha Żuk (Chairman of SJM), who agreed to certify the products and companies passing through the PIH.[72] According to the existing legal basis, between 2010 and 2014 the PIH could not issue legally-binding halal certificates since this privilege belonged at that time only to the religious unions.[73] As shown above, with the ruling of the Constitutional Tribunal in 2014 the legal basis changed and also opened up opportunities for organisations such as the PIH.

The creation of the Polish Halal Institute has taken part of the market traditionally serviced by the LM[74] to the organisation of the former member of the LM. The organisation has developed dynamically since 2010. In 2017, it organised the World Halal Convention East Europe, which brought companies, institutions, and organisations involved in the halal certification and production to Poznań not only from the Central and Eastern Europe region but also from other parts of Europe (e.g. Italy or Bosnia and Herzegovina) and the Muslim world (e.g. Jordan, UAE, and Turkey). Among the speakers of the conference were the Mufti of Bosnia and Herzegovina Mustafa Ceric, Director of the Halal Science Centre at the Chulalongkorn University in Thailand Winai Dahlan, and President of Polish Union Meat Witold Choiński. The convention sessions dealt with not only halal food and beverages but also halal ingredients,

71 NGO.pl, 'Polski Instytut Halal, Poznań'.
72 Interview with TŻ.
73 Interview with AE.
74 Interview with AE.

cosmetics, and pharmaceuticals as well as Islamic finance.[75] The PIH managed to carry out this ambitious project in spite of an unfavourable social climate and a high level of Islamophobic sentiments in the country.[76]

At the time of writing, the PIH claims to be 'number one in the region', 'the leader in halal field in Poland', and an organisation 'recognized by several accreditation bodies from around the world'. In contrast to the company Halal System, certifying products on behalf of the MZR, the PIH does not share the profits with any Muslim organisation. It presents itself as the institution that has 'provided more than 150 halal certification in Poland' and that 'offers the best qualified and confirmed halal auditors in Poland'.[77] According to the founder of the PIH, the majority of the products it currently certifies are exported to Western European countries (e.g. Denmark, Sweden, UK, France, and The Netherlands), but it also has the right to certify halal products for numerous Muslim countries and, as the only Polish organisation, to the United Arab Emirates. Apart from meat it also certifies milk products and sweets.[78]

Neither the HP nor the PIH disclose financial information about the revenues from halal certification, claiming that it would expose them to their competitors and breach confidential contracts with the business partners.[79] Historic material concerning revenues from certification of the MZR mention around €50,000 annual revenue in 2011.[80] According to Miśkiewicz, the profits that his company (the HP) generates from halal certification are shared (supposedly on a 50/50 basis[81]) with the MZR. They are said to constitute around 20 per cent of the budget of the MZR in the last few years.[82]

4 Conclusion

As shown above, the development of the halal market in Poland, mainly oriented towards export, has not progressed without problems and controversies. The legal opportunity structure has played a key role in its expansion and brief

75 More information about the Convention is available at https://www.polandhalalconvention.com last retrieved 30 May 2018.

76 Pędziwiatr, 'Islamophobia in Poland: National Report 2015' and 'Islamophobia in Poland: National Report 2016'.

77 Information from http://www.institutehalal.com/#about (accessed 30 May 2018).

78 Interview with MSM.

79 Interview with TM and MSM.

80 Krasnowska, 'Mufti Niezgody'.

81 With no budgetary transparency for either the MZR or the HP, this information cannot be verified.

82 Interview with TM.

moments of decline. The state, and in particular various lobbyists from the agricultural sector, have enabled its establishment and do not hide their strong interest in its maintenance. The growth of the market has also caused significant tensions between Muslim groups and members of the broader society involved directly or indirectly in the animal rights movement. Thus, it has acted as one of the major factors reconfiguring some groups within a diverse Muslim community in Poland, the community as a whole, and its relations with broader society.

On the one hand, the development of halal certification opened new markets for Polish products. In this process various Muslim groups in the country have also gained additional political importance in the eyes of political and economic elites. The certification procedures have empowered them and injected novel agency into the groups aware of their economic value. Thanks to the revenues from halal certification, some of the Muslim groups in the larger Polish Muslim community have become stronger economically and have been able to expand their cultural and religious activities.

On the other hand, very early in the process of development and professionalisation of halal certification, inter- and intra-group rivalry started to play an important role. The individuals directly linked to the halal market, mainly as certifiers (or in rare cases also as producers of halal products or, as in the case of the founder of the Polish Halal Institute, in both roles), have been particularly closely scrutinised. Partly as a result of the limited transparency of their actions and other factors explored above, halal certification has also weakened the Muslim community internally, especially affecting the Tatar community.

At present the legal and economic opportunity structures are conducive to further development of the halal market in Poland. However, animal rights groups continue to lobby for a change of the law that would at least partially limit the rights to ritual slaughter for Jewish and Muslim communities. The planned amendments to the Animal Protection Act may become another turning point in the (de)regulation of the halal market in the country.[83] Some of the actors involved in halal certification have expressed fears about the prospective changes, which may hinder their chances for further business expansion.[84] At the same time they may be beneficial from the point of the Muslim community and various groups within it, reducing the space for internal competition and at least partially weakening the intra- and inter-group tensions.

---

83 Spożywczy 'Zakaz uboju rytualnego—Cios w interesy branży czy nieunikniona zmiana? —Mięso/wędliny'.

84 Interviews with TM and MSM.

Bibliography

Bergeaud-Blackler, Florence, Johan Fischer, and John Lever, eds. 2015. *Halal Matters: Islam, Politics and Markets in Global Perspective*. London: Routledge.

Brylov, Denys. 2018. 'Halal Industry of Ukraine in the Period of Independence'. *Philosophical Sciences* 132: 238–241.

Chazbijewicz, Selim. 2016. 'Islam i Środowiska Muzułmańskie We Współczesnej Polsce'. In *Badania Nad Światem Islamu: Dzieje, Dzień Dzisiejszy i Perspektywy*, edited by M. Woźniak and D. Ściślewska, 335–348. Łódź: Katedra Bliskiego Wschodu i Północnej Afryki UŁ.

Ciszak, Przemysław 2015. 'Inglota nie powstrzyma nawet bomba w salonie w Bengazi. Chce być najbardziej widoczną polską marką na świecie'. *WP money*. 13 December. http://www.money.pl/gospodarka/wiadomosci/artykul/inglota-nie-powstrzyma-nawet-bomba-w-salonie,242,0,1971442.html (accessed 1 October 2020).

Constitution of Poland. 1997. http://www.sejm.gov.pl/prawo/konst/angielski/kon1.htm (accessed 1 July 2020).

Drath, Jakub. 2015. 'Ubój Rytualny w Polskim Systemie Prawnym'. *Colloquium Wydziału Nauk Humanistycznych i Społecznych* 19 (3): 71–86.

Ferfecki, Wiktor 2018. 'Zakaz uboju rytualnego do poprawki'. *Rzeczpospolita*, 25 February. http://www.rp.pl/Spoleczenstwo/302259963-Zakaz-uboju-rytualnego-do-poprawki.html (accessed 1 October 2020).

Fischer, Johan. 2011. *The Halal Frontier: Muslim Consumers in a Globalized Market*. New York: Palgrave Macmillan.

Fischer, Johan. 2016. *Islam, Standards, and Technoscience: In Global Halal Zones*. London: Routledge.

Fischler, Claude. 1988. Food, self and identity. *Social Science Information/sur les sciences sociales* 27: 275–292.

Górny, Agata, Halina Grzymała-Moszczyńska, Witold Klaus, and Sławomir Łodziński. 2017. 'Uchodźcy w Polsce: Sytuacja prawna, skala napływu i integracja w społeczeństwie polskim oraz rekomendacje'. Ekspertyza Komitetu Badań nad Migracjami PAN. Warszawa.

GUS. 2013. *Wyznania Religijne: Stowarzyszenia Narodowościowe i Etniczne w Polsce 2007–2011*. Warszawa: GUS.

GUS. 2016. 'Rocznik Demograficzny 2016'. Warszawa: Główny Urząd Statystyczny. http://stat.gov.pl/obszary-tematyczne/roczniki-statystyczne/roczniki-statystyczne/rocznik-demograficzny-2016,3,10.html.

Hilson, Chris. 2002. 'New Social Movements: The Role of Legal Opportunity'. *Journal of European Public Policy* 9 (2): 238.

Jacobson, Jessica 1998. *Islam in Transition: Religion and Identity among British Pakistani Youth* (1 edition). London; New York: Routledge.

Jacobsson, Kerstin. 2012. 'Fragmentation of the Collective Action Space: The Animal Rights Movement in Poland'. *East European Politics* 28 (4): 353–370.

Jacobsson, Kerstin and Steven Saxonberg. 2013. *Beyond NGO-Ization. The Development of Social Movements in Central and Eastern Europe*. Farnham: Ashgate.

Kari, Maria. 2013. 'Inglot Releases Halal Nail Polish'. *The Express Tribune Blogs*. https://blogs.tribune.com.pk/story/15815/halal-nail-polish-say-what/ (accessed 1 July 2020).

Krasnowska, Violetta. 2017. 'Mufti Niezgody'. *Polityka*, August.

Kurth, Laura and Pieter Glasbergen. 2017. 'Serving a Heterogenous Muslim Population? Private Governance Arrangements of Halal Food in the Netherlands'. *Agriculture and Human Values* 34, no. 1: 103–118.

Lever, John. 2018. 'Halal Meat and Religious Slaughter: From Spatial Concealment to Social Controversy—Breaching the Boundaries of the Permissible'. *Environment and Planning C: Politics and Space* 37, no. 5: 1–19.

Lever, John and Mara Miele. 2012. 'The Growth of Halal Meat Markets in Europe: An Exploration of the Supply Side Theory of Religion'. *Growing Old in Rural Places* 28 (4): 528–537.

Mann, Alex. 2014. "Campaign to Boycott Halal Food Gains Momentum in Australia." Text. ABC News. November 20, 2014. https://www.abc.net.au/news/2014-11-20/campaign-to-boycott-halal-food-gains-momentum-in-australia/5907844. (accessed 1 October 2020)

Mintz, Sidney W. and Christine M. Du Bois. 2002 'The Anthropology of Food and Eating'. *Annual Review of Anthropology* 31: 99–119.

MNiSW. 2016. 'Szkolnictwo Wyższe w Polsce'. Warszawa: Ministry of Science and Higher Education.

Nalborczyk, Agata. 2011. 'Relations between Islam and the State in Poland: The Legal Position of Polish Muslims'. *Islam and Christian–Muslim Relations* 22 (3): 343–359.

Nalborczyk, Agata. 2015. 'Ubój Rytualny w Polsce—Zagadnienia Religijne, Obecny Stan Prawny i Jego Historia'. In *Badania Nad Światem Islamu: Dzieje, Dzień Dzisiejszy, Perspektywy*, edited by M. Woźniak and D. Ściślewska, 358–375. Łódź: Katedra Bliskiego Wschodu i Północnej Afryki UŁ.

Nalborczyk, Agata and Stanisław Gródź. 2010. 'Poland'. In *Yearbook of Muslims in Europe*, edited by Jorgen S. Nielsen, Samim Akgönül, Ahmet Alibašić, Brigitte Maréchal, and Christinne Moe, 401–411. Leiden: Brill.

Nalborczyk, Agata and Konrad Pędziwiatr. 2018 'Between Old Traditions and New Diversities—Islamic Religious Education in Poland'. In: Jenny Berglund ed. *European Perspectives on Islamic Education and Public Schooling*, 136–156. London: Equinox.

Narkowicz, Kasia and Konrad Pędziwiatr. 2017. 'Why Are Polish People so Wrong about Muslims in Their Country?' *Open Democracy*. 13 January. https://www.opendemocracy.net/can-europe-make-it/kasia-narkowicz-konrad-pedziwiatr/why-are-polish-people-so-wrong-about-muslims-in (accessed 1 August 2020).

NGO.pl. 2010. 'Polski Instytut Halal, Poznań'. http://bazy.ngo.pl/profil/206906/Polski-Instytut-Halal (accessed 1 August 2020).

Pędziwiatr, Konrad. 2011a. 'Muslims in Contemporary Poland'. In *Muslims in Visegrad Countries*, edited by J. Bureš, 10–24. Prague: Anna Lindh Foundation and Visegrad Fund.

Pędziwiatr, Konrad. 2011b. 'The Established and Newcomers in Islam in Poland or the Inter-Group Relations within the Polish Muslim Community'. In *Muslims in Poland and Eastern Europe. Widening the European Discourse on Islam*, edited by K. Górak-Sosnowska, 169–182. Warszawa: Impuls.

Pędziwiatr, Konrad. 2012. 'Imigranci Bliskowschodni i Północnoafrykańscy, a odrodzenie islamu we współczesnej Polsce'. In *Czy Polska Leży Nad Morzem Śródziemnym?*, edited by R. Kusek, 240–265. Kraków: Wydawnictwo Międzynarodowe Centrum Kultury.

Pędziwiatr, Konrad. 2016. 'Islamophobia in Poland: National Report 2015'. In *European Islamophobia Report 2015*, edited by F. Hafez and E. Bayrakli, 423–441. Istanbul: SETA.

Pędziwiatr, Konrad. 2017a. 'Conversions to Islam and Identity Reconfigurations among Poles in Great Britain'. *Studia Religiologica* 50, no. 3 (December): 221–239.

Pędziwiatr, Konrad. 2017b. 'Islamophobia in Poland: National Report 2016'. In *European Islamophobia Report 2016*, edited by F. Hafez and E. Bayrakli, 411–443. Istanbul: SETA.

Pędziwiatr, Konrad. 2020. 'Transformacje postaw wobec Arabów w społeczeństwie polskim z perspektywy członków społeczności arabskiej i muzułmańskiej'. Studia Humanistyczne AGH 2020;19(2): 89–106.

Radłowska, Karolina 2017. *Tatarzy Polscy: Ciągłość i Zmiana*. Białystok: Fundacja Sąsiedzi.

Rzeczpospolita. 2017. 'Eksport służy wołowinie'. http://www.rp.pl/Przemysl-spozywczy/307309962-Eksport-sluzy-wolowinie.html (accessed 01.08.2020).

Silantev. R.A. 2015. *Sovet muftiev Rossii: istorija odnoj fitny*. Moskva: RISI.

Sperling, Valerie. 1999. *Organizing Women in Contemporary Russia*. Cambridge: Cambridge University Press.

Spożywczy Portal. 2018. 'Zakaz uboju rytualnego—Cios w interesy branży czy nieunikniona zmiana?—Mięso/wędliny', www.portalspozywczy.pl. http://www.portalspozywczy.pl/mieso/wiadomosci/zakaz-uboju-rytualnego-cios-w-interesy-branzy-czy-nieunikniona-zmiana,152925.html (accessed 01.08.2020).

Stolz, Joerg and Jean-Claude Usunier. 2019. 'Religions as Brands? Religion and Spirituality in Consumer Society'. *Journal of Management, Spirituality & Religion*. vol. 16, issue 1, 6–31 doi.

Szostkiewicz, Adam 2013. 'Ubój rytualny: prawa ludzi czy zwierząt?' *Gra w klasy*. https://szostkiewicz.blog.polityka.pl/2013/03/24/uboj-rytualny-prawa-ludzi-czy-zwierzat/ (accessed 01.08.2020).

Szumigalska, Agnieska and Monika Bazan. 2014. 'Ritual Slaughter Issue in Poland: Between Religious Freedom, Legal Order and Economic-Political Interests'. *Religion and Society in Central and Eastern Europe* 7, no. 1: 53–69.

Tayob, Shaheed. 2016. '"O You Who Believe, Eat of the Tayyibāt (Pure and Wholesome Food) That We Have Provided You"—Producing Risk, Expertise and Certified Halal Consumption in South Africa'. *Journal of Religion in Africa* 46, no. 1: 67–91.

TVN. 2013. 'Obrońcy Praw Zwierząt Kontra Polscy Muzułmanie. Awantura Podczas Kurban Bajram'. *TVN24.Pl.* 15 September. https://www.tvn24.pl/r/363050 last retrieved 1 August 2020.

Voloder, Lejla. 2015. 'The "Mainstreaming" of Halal: Muslim Consumer-Citizenship in Australia'. *Journal of Muslim Minority Affairs* 35 (2): 230–244.

Weller, Danieal L. and David Turkon. 2015. 'Contextualizing the Immigrant Experience: The Role of Food and Foodways in Identity Maintenance and Formation for First- and Second-Generation Latinos in Ithaca, New York'. *Ecology of Food and Nutrition* 54: 57–73.

Interview

1. Arkadiusz Miernik—AM—Birmingham (UK), 8 June 2016
2. Samir Ismail—SI—Warszawa, 20 September 2016
3. Ahmed Abdal—AA—Warszawa, 20 September 2016
4. Dżafar Alizade—DA—Gdańsk, 14 October 2016
5. Olgierd Chazbijewicz—OC—Gdańsk, 15 October 2016
6. Abdelwahab Bouali—AWB—Katowice, 9 March 2017
7. Agata Bouali—AB—Katowice, 9 March 2017
8. Adham Abd El Aal—AEA—Warszawa, 20 March 2017
9. Tomasz Miśkiewicz—TM—Białystok, 12 January 2018
10. Artur Konopacki—AK—Białystok, 12 January 2018
11. Karolina Radłowska—KR—Białystok, 12 January 208
12. Ibrahim Khartouma—IK—Białystok, 12 January 2018
13. Dagmara Sulkiewicz—DS—Białystok, 13 January 2018
14. Halina Szahidewicz—HS—Białystok, 13 January 2018
15. Anonymous female member of the Muslim community—AFM—Białystok, 13 January 2018
16. Anonymous male member of the Muslim community—AMM1—Białystok, 13 January 2018
17. Dżenneta Bogdanowicz—DB—Kruszyniany, 15 January 2018
18. Janusz Aleksandrowicz—JA—Białystok, 17 January 2018
19. Rafał Berger—RB—Poznań, 30 January 2018
20. Youssef Chadid—YC—Poznań, 30 January 2018
21. Mohammad Saleh Messikh—MSM—Poznań, 2 February 2018

22. Nezar Cherif—NC—Warszawa, 17 February 2018
23. Anonymous member of the Muslim community—AMM2—Warsaw, 12 May 2018
24. Anonymous employee of the General Veterinary Inspectorate—AE—Warsaw, 22 May 2018
25. Mahmoud Taha Żuk—MTŻ—Krakow, 12 June 2018

CHAPTER 11

Living Halal in the Volga Region: Lifestyle and Civil Society Opportunities

Matteo Benussi

1 Introduction

Soon after arriving in Kazan in September 2014, I became aware of the strikingly pervasive presence of the Islamic concepts of 'halal' (permissible) and 'haram' (forbidden) across many of the city's social spaces. Kazan, despite its Tatar heritage, looks less stereotypically 'Islamic' than quaintly Russian, grandiosely Soviet, and ambitiously modern. Yet, over the past few years, an Islamic subtext has been woven directly into the city's fabric—an urban network of people, places and events, continuously bustling with activity.[1]

After the dissolution of the Soviet order in central Russia's multi-ethnic and multi-religious Povolzhye region, a galaxy of interrelated scripturalist Sunni piety trends coalesced amongst the area's Muslim, predominantly (though not exclusively) Tatars and Bashkirs. I collectively refer to these ethical trends as Povolzhye's 'halal movement' or 'halal milieu'. The halal milieu is a loose, theologically diverse network of faith communities defined by self-chosen adherence to strict Islamic precepts of virtue as well as by heightened mindfulness of Islamic purity. Commitment to a halal lifestyle implies being constantly alert to spiritual purity and potential sources of pollution or sin (from pop music, to gossip, to indecent sights), pursuing exactness in ritual conduct, and accumulating Islamic theological knowledge to use as guidance in one's choices.

The term 'halal movement' (Rus. *khalyalnoe dvizhenie*, Tat. *xäläl xäräkäte*) was used by one of my key respondents—a Tatar *abıy* (uncle, 'veteran') with two decades of experience in Muslim civic activism—and some of his closest associates. While not all interlocutors would necessarily use it, I find it captures the essence of this phenomenon: a dynamic, grassroots network of communities, unified, in spite of many internal differences, by the common goal of

1 Benussi, 'Public Spaces and Inner Worlds: Emplaced Askesis and Architecture of the Soul among Tatarstani Muslims', 685–707 and 'Pietaskscapes of Halal Living: Subjectivity, Striving and Space-Making in Muslim Russia'.

 | DOI:10.1163/9789004459236_012

following the Qur'an and the Sunna in pursuit of purity and avoidance of anything sinful. It is not, however, an organised front campaigning over explicitly political issues.[2]

The halal milieu thrives amongst youthful, aspirational, and upwardly mobile urbanites. It operates in (partial) opposition to the popular devotion practices tolerated during the late Soviet times and currently promoted by the authorities as 'traditional', i.e. discursively constitutive of ethnic 'identities' positioned within a secular order.[3] This perceived opposition has earned the halal movement a dubious reputation with the state's security organs. As a result, this community is faced with considerable political opposition from Russian state authorities. On the other hand, vast sectors of the halal milieu are at the forefront of a remarkable economic boom, as their economic philosophy urges Muslims to pursue achievement 'in both this world and the other' (*uspekh v oboikh mirakh*). Thus, this newly born community oscillates between subalternity and success, political marginalisation and economic flourishing.

In this chapter, I will offer an ethnographic account of the 'halal boom' in Povolzhye, a phenomenon that, while connected to the region's long Islamic history, take this history in a new direction, defined by novel circumstances. The spread of halal will be considered in the light of the emergence of an energetic Muslim middle class, the success of ethical-cultivationist approaches to religion, the new opportunities (and risks) afforded by capitalism, and the scope for timid civil-society experimentation opened by the socio-political restructuring of Russia.

I conducted 16 months of ethnographic fieldwork in Povolzhye between 2014–2015. This long-term stay was followed by shorter research visits in 2018 and 2019. During fieldwork, I recorded over fifty semi-structured interviews, observed social life in a variety of settings (from halal cafes to large Muslim gatherings), diarised countless informal conversations and spontaneous discussions, attended public seminars, conferences, and religious lectures organised by various religious bodies (from the state-backed Muftiate, to *de facto*

2 In light of its quietism and emphasis on individual religiosity (rather than on state religion), religious rights (rather than duties), and cultural action under a secular/pluralist framework (rather than political militancy), the halal milieu could perhaps be described as a post-Islamist phenomenon, see Bayat, 'The Coming of a Post-Islamist Society', 43–52 and *Post-Islamism: The Changing Faces of Political Islam*, 2013. My terminology should therefore not be mistaken, as some Tatarstan-based academics appear to do in their reading of my work, as indicating a political or social organisation that uses this expression as a collective self-designation or to define an 'ideology'. See Almazova and Akhunov, 'In Search of "Traditional Islam" in Tatarstan: Between National Project and Universalist Theories', 11–46.

3 Benussi, 'Public Spaces', 685–707.

autonomous mosque communities and preachers, to informal faith-based groups), and collected written materials ranging from Salafi pamphlets to best-selling Islamic self-help volumes. While this contribution takes a diachronic dimension into consideration by considering the 'halal boom' in the historical context of post-socialist social change and contemplating its implication for the prospects of the region, an anthropological approach means that what follows is primarily a snapshot of religious dynamics among Volga region Muslims at a specific moment in time, the mid-to-late 2010s.

This is a period marked by economic dynamism and excitement about social mobility opportunities (including Islamic business), illiberalism and political centralisation, and, concomitantly, an increasing visibility of Islam in Russian public sphere.[4] Given the complexities of the period and the fast pace of social, political, and cultural change, no individual account can aspire to exhaust the 'big picture'—and what follows makes no exception. Rather, this chapter aspires to add further elements of conversation to a young, but growing, scholarly trend focusing on Muslim's moral economies and civic participation in Russia and the former Soviet space,[5] as well as contributing to our understanding of halal-related dynamics in a neoliberal global ecumene.[6]

2 The Setting

The Volga region, also known by its official Russian equivalent 'Povolzhye' and the Turkic toponym 'Idel-Ural' (Idel being the Volga river's Turkic name), has a complex history.[7] Sunni Islam reached the shores of the Volga in the early Middle Ages, becoming the official religion of Volga Bulgaria, a multi-ethnic yet predominantly Turkic polity, in the tenth century. Despite the devasta-

4 Laruelle, 'How Islam Will Change Russia'.

5 Rabinovich, 'Living the Good Life: Muslim Women's Magazines in Contemporary Russia', 199–214; Biard, '"Bourgeois" Islam, Prosperity Theology and Ethics in Muslim Eurasia'; Botoeva, 'Islam and the Spirits of Capitalism: Competing Articulations of the Islamic Economy', 235–264; Turaeva, 'Informal Economies in the Post-Soviet Space: Post-Soviet Islam and Its Role in Ordering Entrepreneurship in Central Asia', 208–230; Kaliszewska, 'Halal Landscapes of Dagestani Entrepreneurs in Makhachkala', 708–730.

6 See this volume's Introduction and other essays; Brose, 'China and Transregional Halal Circuits', 208–227; Tayob, 'Molecular Halal: Producing, Debating and Evading Halal Certification in South Africa', 108–118.

7 Rorlich, *The Volga Tatars: A Profile in National Resilience*; Shnirelman, *Who Gets the Past? Competition for Ancestors among Non-Russian Intellectuals in Russia*; Faller, *Nation, Language, Islam: Tatarstan's Sovereignty Movement.*; Bukharaev, *Islam in Russia: The Four Seasons.*

tions caused by the Mongol conquest (thirteenth century), Islam was subsequently adopted by the Golden Horde's Turkicised Mongol rulers, which brought Povolzhye into the orbit of the Central Asian Turko-Persianate world. Islam remained a hegemonic civilisational force until the Russian conquest of Idel-Ural in the sixteenth century. Russian rule was characterised by an alternation of anti-Islamic (and subsequently anti-religious) campaigns and more accommodating policies.[8] While Russian, and later Soviet, domination partly diluted the region's Islamicate character, religion remains a bastion of Tatar self-identification.

With their long tradition of statehood and regional hegemony, the Volga Tatars constitute the most numerous, historically most powerful, and best-organised ethnic community in Povolzhye after the Russians. Over five million Tatars live in the Russian Federation, of which two million live in Tatarstan (amounting to 53 per cent of the republic's population against 39 per cent of Russians) and one million in Bashkortostan. A sizable Tatar diaspora extends from Central Asia to Russia proper, into Finland and beyond. The composite religious and ethnic makeup of Povolzhye is reflected in the current administrative structure, set up by the Soviet government. It features six national republics at the region's core: Tatarstan, Bashkortostan, and Chuvashia, named after their Turkic titular nationalities; and Udmurtia, Mordovia, and Mari El, administrative embodiments of the region's Uralic ethnic components. Unsurprisingly, Soviet-era borders do not mirror the territory's ethnic complexity. Chuvash villages exist in Tatarstan, Tatar villages in Mordovia, and so on—while Kazakh settlements add to the ethnic variety of the lower Volga region, which is also an intermediate stop on the new migration routes from the Caucasus to Moscow. Today, the Russians are Povolzhye's largest ethnic group, though they remain a minority in ethnic republics, notably Tatarstan.[9]

---

8 Rorlich, *The Volga Tatars: A Profile in National Resilience*; Kappeler, *The Russian Empire: A Multiethnic History*; Kefeli, *Becoming Muslim in Imperial Russia: Conversion, Apostasy, and Literacy*.

9 The Russians migrated into the region over the course of the last four centuries, radically changing its demographic balance. Today, they demographically dominate all Povolzhye's administrative regions with the exception of Chuvashia, Bashkiria, and Tatarstan. A short-lived political experiment of an independent Turkic Idel-Ural state was attempted during the 1917–1922 Civil War and disestablished by the Bolsheviks immediately after their victory. After Soviet-led modernisation, the Russian element definitively overtook the Tatars as the region's hegemonic element. The subdivision of Idel-Ural into several oblasts and ethnic republics further weakened its regional identity. Today, the name 'Povolzhye' evokes more of an administrative entity than a culturally bounded space endowed with a distinct history. The Idel-Ural idea remains alive amongst a minority of Tatar national activists.

Tatarstan—strategically located between Russia proper, Siberia, and Central Asia, and endowed with rich supplies of natural resources—is the Volga region's most economically and infrastructurally advanced subdivision, as well as the main geographic focus of my research. My base and one of my main research sites were in Kazan: Tatarstan's capital, Povolzhye's major urban centre, and Russia's official 'third capital'. Today's Tatar public culture comes across as characteristically secular (*svetskaya*), unsurprisingly in light of four centuries of Russian domination, which systematically undermined Povolzhye's Islamic juridical and political institutions, and the thorough anti-religious campaigns carried out by the Soviets. During my fieldwork, numerous participants expressed the view that the Tatars are the most 'Europeanised' (*evropeizirovannaya*) amongst the world's Muslim nations.[10] The emergence of the halal milieu at the turn of the century is thus all the more intriguing if considered against the backdrop of Povolzhye's secularised and Russianised social setting.

3 The Spread of Halal

Adopting rigorous Islamic conduct entails not overstepping the boundaries of what is permissible (halal) and avoiding exposure to all things defiling (haram), which is not always simple in the un-Islamic environment of post-Soviet Povolzhye. Notions of halal and haram began gaining currency in the 1990s, at first amongst segments of the uprooted urban youth and ethnic intelligentsia, and gradually amongst the Tatar population at large—until halal awareness became something of a mass phenomenon.[11] As mentioned earlier, it was the sheer striking pervasiveness of halal talk that directed my attention to this topic. Halal-related neologisms pepper the language of young, citified Muslims, more at ease using Russian than their grandparents' Turkic tongue: thus, an appealing Muslim-friendly restaurant can be defined as *khalyalnenko*, 'cosily Muslim-y', and a clip of a cute kid reading the Qur'an can be commented on in social media by saying 'Aw, that's so halal!' Importantly, the concept of halal has come to indicate a veritable 'art of living', encompassing spiritual and material, ethical and aesthetic dimensions. This art of living animates bearded

10 Humphrey, Marsden, and Skvirskaya, 'Cosmopolitanism and the City: Interaction and Coexistence in Bukhara', 208.

11 Maevsky, 'Letter From: Halal Haircuts in the Capital of Tatarstan', *The Calvert Journal*, 23 September 2014, https://www.calvertjournal.com/articles/show/3117/letter-from-kazan-Tatarstan-halal (accessed 26/10/2020).

young men in smart suits who can be spotted as they gather in cafes to talk business after evening prayer, and elegantly dressed hijabis walking in and out the glass entrances of business centres.

Two related consequences emerged from this scenario: first, halal was adopted by the market. As a result of the halal milieu's dynamism, concerns about halal and haram spread spectacularly amongst Povolzhye Muslims, while halal business increased dramatically in importance and size. The success of Islamic piety movements engendered a boom in Russia's halal industry. By the mid-2010s, Povolzhye had consolidated its position as a hub for 'halal' capitalism in Russia. A spate of halal services and establishments catering to demanding Muslim customers had sprung up altering the landscape of Tatarstani cities.[12] This enabled mass production/import/distribution of halal goods and services catering to local Muslims—food, cosmetics, and clothes to leisure activities, and even financial consulting. (Meanwhile, in a largish town in the vicinity of Kazan, the community's only liquor shop was renamed 'Haram'.)

Second, as halal became a fashionable buzzword, a large number of forgery scandals occurred. In the most outrageous cases, unscrupulous producers and retailers introduced non-halal products (mainly processed food containing pork meat) into the market under 'halal' labels. Other more ambiguous cases feature products such as bottled water or eggs being pitched in the marketplace as 'halal' so as to attract concerned Muslim buyers—at least those willing to accept inflated prices in order not to jeopardise their spiritual efforts towards salvation—while leaving other shariʿa-conscious consumers puzzled or annoyed at what some perceive as a scam. Water or eggs are unmarked, permissible items under normal conditions, e.g. unless they are spoilt or contaminated. Tatarstan's supporters of 'total halalification' emphasise that resorting to the halal brand is legitimate: halalness encompasses ideas of wholesomeness, salubriousness, and proper quality (polluted water or poor-quality eggs, the theological reasoning goes, cannot be halal), as well as taking into account shariʿa compliance at the supply chain level (e.g. no Islamically forbidden financial practices, like *ribā*, being involved in the handling of these products). Sceptical Muslim consumers, however, stress the opaqueness of tracking mechanisms, (what is perceived as) excessive, even fanatical casuistry, and the high prices of halal-logoed products.

12 Benussi, 'Public Spaces and Inner Worlds', 685–707.

4 Halal as Historical Novelty

The halal movement is, in many respects, a novelty. Even though categories of pure/impure and lawful/unlawful were known by pre-revolutionary and Soviet-era Muslim literati, it is dubious that they enjoyed wide currency amongst the Muslim populace.

Historical accounts of pre-revolutionary everyday life amongst urban Tatars suggest that Povolzhye Muslims assessed the acceptability of certain products, foods, and behaviours on the grounds of custom, national culture, and ethnic origin, in ways that were not necessarily always congruent with theological/juridical categories. For instance, foods consumed by Russians such as potatoes, mushrooms, and other vegetables, or certain kinds of fish, were groundlessly (from a *fiqh* viewpoint) considered unlawful by some Muslims. On the other hand, some booze-loving Tatars might claim that certain types of alcoholic drinks were not forbidden to Muslims as long as they were not explicitly mentioned in Qur'anic sources.[13] As far as the socialist era is concerned, my participants confirmed that the words 'halal' and 'haram' had little currency in Soviet Idel-Ural, at least at the level of everyday religiosity.[14] During the Soviet times, consuming 'Tatar' food (technically halal, but not typically understood in those terms) was an (occasional) practice carried out privately, within the framework of vernacular devotion. While dietary differences between Tatars and Russians existed, it seems that they were conceptualised and negotiated in terms of custom and ethnic belonging rather than as part of an all-encompassing ethical (and legal) paradigm.

---

13 Gabdrafikova, *Povsednevnaya zhizn' gorodskikh tatar v usloviyakh burzhuaznykh preobrazovanii vtoroy poloviny XIX—nachala XX veka*, 97 and 'P'yanstvo tatar 100 let nazad: Kurban-bayram s ryumkoy vodka, netrezvye shakirdy i tletvordnoe vliyanie Zapada. Problema alkogolizma v tatarskom musul'manskom obshchestve vo vtoroy polovine XIX—nachale XX veka'. *Real'noe Vremya*, 7 November 2016, https://realnoevremya.ru/articles/47290 (accessed 26/10/2020).

14 For one exception, see Bustanov 'Against Leviathan: On the Ethics of Islamic Poetry in Soviet Russia', 210. In Bosnia-Herzegovina, by contrast, the word 'halal' has long become part of an emic vernacular language of morality and mutuality. David Henig has described how the word, having become partly detached from its theological meaning, is used by Bosniaks to describe gratuitous deeds and acts of forgiveness that may or may not have an explicitly religious inflection. Both the Tatar and the Bosniak case, albeit different, reveal that an identification of the word halal with its *exact theological meaning* and with *precise ethical procedures* is not a stable construct across the Muslim world, having in fact gained traction in both the Volga region and Bosnia only recently. Henig, 'A Good Deed is not a Crime: Moral Cosmologies of Favours in Bosnia-Herzegovina', and personal communication.

Halal [as an idea] appeared in the 1990s. It appeared when people began to go to Turkey or Arab countries. Before that, nobody used the word 'halal'. If someone says otherwise, they are not telling you the truth. In the Soviet times, back in the old days, most village elders would not even think of eating pork. The Soviets deliberately opened pork meat factories in Tatarstan, but most elders would not have any of that. [Elders] would say that eating pork is a sin (*gönah*), but they wouldn't say it's haram or halal.

Jamila-*apa*,[15] aged 70, retired music teacher, Kazan

[In the 1970s and 1980s,] *babays* (elders) were already telling their fellow Tatars not to eat pork. For average Soviet citizens, drinking vodka and eating pork sausages were completely common habits. But *babays* organised funeral banquets and demanded that only special meat, from the countryside, should be served on these occasions. These elders were the first to remind their fellow Tatars [of dietary norms]. Back then, there wasn't any understanding of halal, but *babays* knew that only village meat could be considered permissible. This is just because the immemorial Tatar [slaughtering] traditions had survived only in villages, although villagers themselves followed [*dhabiḥa* rules] just because this was the only way they knew. Fathers taught sons how to slaughter animals—[saying,] 'Bismillāhi Allāhu akbar', [facing the] *qibla*, and draining all the blood—generation after generation. That was it, without special knowledge or religious explanations. They didn't know why, they only knew that these words *must* be said.

Since life [under Soviet rule] was frugal, a lot of people got their meat mostly this way, from villages. And when elders came visiting, or to attend a *mäclis* (commemorative meal), people knew that he'd want special food. It was *ğadät* (customary). People would even cook a separate meal, using separate pots and separate tableware, for visiting *babays*. They knew that there was a different way to eat—even if they didn't pray or anything. As regards the word halal, people didn't use it. They said *kurban ite* (festive meat), or *bismilla äytep suılğan it* (meat slaughtered uttering *bismillah*), or *bismilla äytep çalğan it* (meat cut uttering *bismillah*). This is the way Soviet people talked about this.

Salih-*hazrat*, imam, Yar Çallı

15 Ethnographic interlocutors are anonymised or pseudonymised throughout the text.

Halal-milieu Muslims reject understandings of halal in mere terms of Tatar food, rather than an ethical-juridical framework based on Scripture (see below), as misinformed and parochial. Ethnography thus suggests that the halal boom, with its scriptural, cultivational bent, is better framed as a novel development rather than the mere re-appearance of pre-existing religious identities/sensitivities. The halal milieu ought to be understood as a specifically late-modern phenomenon that can be more fully accounted for through an 'anthropology of discontinuity' rather than continuity.[16] This view is consistent with Mathijs Pelkmans' observation that 'the forms in which religion re-entered the public sphere [after socialism] are not (or are only indirectly) related to the pre-Soviet past'.[17] This approach challenges the assumption that the post-Soviet boom of religious movements can be explained as merely a consequence of the disappearance of anti-religious governmental control—a simplistic approach aptly dubbed 'cold storage hypothesis' by Pelkmans.[18] A more nuanced view needs to take into account the existential and ethical needs of the new social groups that emerged from transition-era societal restructuration.

Of course, continuity cannot be completely discounted in a discussion on Sunni Islam. Sunnism has long been concerned with the preservation of the original spirit of its founders. It is not a coincidence the most influential paradigm for the anthropological study of Islam, Talal Asad's notion of discursive tradition,[19] brings to the fore the Islamic body of texts as a relatively stable matrix for diverse and dynamic social formations throughout history and across geography. I am ready to agree that continuity plays a role in my field site too—something made manifest by the fact that Russia's halal movement made its most spectacular inroads in a region with a long Islamic history.

Yet, in this chapter, I wish to emphasise the innovative, unprecedented aspects of the halal milieu as a social phenomenon—aspects that a 'continuity' paradigm would struggle to account for. Collectively taken, the halal milieu

---

16 Robbins, 'Continuity Thinking and the Problem of Christian Culture: Belief, Time, and the Anthropology of Christianity'.

17 Pelkmans, *Defending the Border: Identity, Religion, and Modernity in the Republic of Georgia*, 163. After 1991, the multi-confessional region Adjara (Georgia), witnessed a surge in Orthodox Christianity and a near-definitive discursive erasure of Islam from its collective memory. While the case of Muslim Povolzhye presents profoundly different dynamics and a radically divergent treatment of the Muslim past (ideologically recuperated and idealised, rather than erased), Adjara's experience of discontinuity exposes the deep transformative potential of Soviet socialism and the difficulties of drawing any direct line between pre-revolutionary religious landscapes and those of today.

18 Pelkmans, 'Defending the Border', 10 and 218.

19 Asad, 'The Idea of an Anthropology of Islam', 1–30.

is a cosmopolitan, individual-centred, puritanical-conservative yet glamorous ethical self-cultivation trend, attracting persons of diverse ethnic background, including Russians and members of Povolzhye's smaller nationalities. Its participants, despite the region's Muslim heritage, often come from irreligious, agnostic, or spiritually turbulent pasts, and frame their relationship with Islam in terms of conversion: as several respondents pointed out, '[I]n Russia, all true Muslims are converts (*neofity*)'. Adherence to faith rests on personal, free, self-reflexive choice, rather than enculturation or essentialist logics according to which Muslimness 'runs in blood'.[20] More often than not, in fact, choosing a life of piety runs counter to the expectations of a predominantly secular society. However, this piety movement thrives on a series of virtuous engagements with the market, and is characterised by a powerful drive to enrichment describable in Weberian terms as a 'capitalist' bourgeois spirit.

It is important to stress that the halal milieu appears to be doing quite well without the civilisational institutes and apparatuses that characterised Povolzhye's pre-revolutionary Islamicate[21] society—Sufi brotherhoods, elder councils, shariʿa councils, Qur'anic schools, and religious foundations—and in fact does not seem to need them at all.[22] In fact, the halal milieu appears to acquire part of its appeal precisely from its exceptionality vis-à-vis a mainstream perceived and described as 'spiritually numb'. It is therefore the *absence* of an Islamicate culture based on historical continuity that fuels the success of Povolzhye's virtue movement.

5 Halal and *Ḥarām* as Tools for Ethical Self-Cultivation

The recent success of a halal discourse can be interpreted as a sign of transformation in Volga Muslims' religious experience. As I have begun to illustrate, the

20 Benussi, "Ethnic Muslims and the "Halal Movement" 88–93.

21 The adjective 'Islamicate' refers to social, political, and cultural phenomena associated with contexts where Muslims are dominant. Such phenomena are indirectly inspired by Islam, but not specifically religious ('Islamic') in nature. They include poetry, architecture, customs and social institutions, etc., see Ahmed, *What Is Islam? The Importance of Being Islamic*, 158–160. For the first use of the term: Hodgson, *The Venture of Islam, Volume 1: The Classical Age of Islam*. In the case at hand, the term 'Islamicate' refers to political-civilisational historical formations that include both religious and non-religious dimension (the Golden Horde, the Kazan Khanate, pre-Soviet Central Asia, etc.).

22 Some of these institutions have reappeared in some form or another in the post-atheist phase, but their role is ancillary, rather than key to the existence of a community of believers.

halal milieu's ethos entails a purposefully-chosen path of self-transformation, the autonomous pursuit of spiritual stimuli beyond local traditions, and reform in all spheres of human activity, in disregard of the secular/religious divide. In the context of post-Soviet Idel-Ural, the categories of 'halal' and 'haram' equip cultivationists with a guide for Islamically permissible conduct in a predominantly non-Muslim social landscape. Halal and haram are tools for *askesis*, guidelines for the construction of the self through the development of Islamic virtues, such as God-awareness, charity, and modesty[23]—as well as 'Islamised' middle-class virtues such as enterprise, respectability, sobriety, and healthiness.[24] My participants' pursuit of a saintly this-worldly life, oriented towards the goal of salvation in the afterlife, unfolds through a 'Weberian' rational ethic of everyday life based on what Marsden and Retsikas have called 'systematicity':[25] as one of my respondents put it, borrowing an expression from Russian political jargon, 'believers must live according to a plan' (*veruyushchie dolzhny zhit' po planu*)—or at least try their best in this endeavour.

> This material world (*dunya*) is like a computer programme. We are like pixels living in a computer programme. Quantum physics says that matter is in fact made of energy—this is how Allah created us, from his breath into matter. Everything is already prearranged (*predupreleno*), like in a programme. Through prayer and sincerity (*iskrennost'*) we can interact with the programmer. But He has set clear rules that we are to follow if we want to succeed.
>
> Arslan-*hajji*, aged 45, businessman, Saratov

Halal movement participants emphasise halal as a tool for self-legislation,[26] at once global and intimately personal, and encompassing a wide range of areas of existence. The conceptual framework Povolzhye Muslims most often utilise to describe their relationship with halal builds on notions such as 'form of life' (Rus. *khalyalnyi obraz zhizni*, Tat. *xäläl tormış räveşe*), 'halal living' (*zhit' po*

23 Mahmood, *Politics of Piety: The Islamic Revival and the Feminist Subject*. Also see Foucault, *The Courage of the Truth: The Government of Self and Others II: Lectures at the Collège de France 1983–1984* and, *The Government of Self and Others: Lectures at the Collège De France 1982–1983*, 343–354.

24 Compare with Biard, 'Bourgeois Islam'; Botoeva, 'Islam and the Spirits'; Kaliszewska, 'Halal Landscapes'.

25 Marsden and Retsikas, 'Introduction', 10–11. Cf. Osella and Osella 'Muslim Entrepreneurs in Public Life between India and the Gulf: Making Good and Doing Good', 202–221.

26 Mahmood, *Politics of Piety*.

khalyal'nomu), and 'halal as a code for living' (*khalyal'nye pravila zhizni*). These concepts convey the sense of embracing halal a deep, totalising, and substantive life choice.

> Halal is a complex of rules for life (*zhiznennye pravila*). It encompasses all aspects of the life of a Muslim. For this reason, I call [halal] the Constitution of the believer.
>
> Foat-*äfände*, religious activist, aged 52, Yar Çallı

> If Islam is a form of life (*obraz zhizni*), then halal refers to food, employment, relationships … it's everything permitted by Allah. Halal is a global thing, it has to do with [a Muslim's] mental activity, nutrition, professional sphere, and way of living in general.
>
> Alina, designer, aged 25, Kazan

> Halal is a form of life (*obraz zhizni*). Year after year, I delve deeper into it (*vnikayu v eto*). Year after year, I pay more and more attention to prohibitions. To what is forbidden and what is not (*na zapretno I ne zapretno*). To haram and halal. I am more aware of the minute actions that expose me to sinfulness, I am more watchful. I endeavour to really pay attention to how to live a halal life (*zhit' po halyal'nomu*). I try to stay farther away from haram (*ot kharama derzhat'sya po dal'she*).
>
> Ismail, food retailer, aged 34, Kazan

Theological notions of halal and haram are relevant to multiple spheres of life. Besides food, halal *obraz zhizni* include: money and finance; intimate relations (spousal, parental, and filial); language (control over one's speech, avoidance of voluntary or involuntary falsehood); fitness (care of one's own health/body); free time and leisure (pursuing spiritually sound entertainment); space, place, and time management; decorum and beauty; and names/naming.[27] Especially amongst the younger generations, this kind of spirituality has an edge over 'traditional' forms of religiosity predominant amongst those who are not involved in the halal milieu, and especially Soviet-educated older Tatars. The latter is

27 I.e., choosing Muslim first names for one's children and/or adopting Muslim nicknames (Muhammad, Fatima, or Abdurrashid) in addition to/instead of Turkic (Aygul, Edigey, Candemir) or European (Marsel, Rafaelya, Rinat) traditional Tatar names. Muslim names bear direct connection to Islam's discursive tradition: they may be the names of prophetic figures or signify commitment to Islam (e.g. *'abd* (slave) + one the names/attributes of God).

a religiosity largely based on essentialist understandings of Muslimness, fragments of received custom (now perceived by some pious-oriented urbanites as old-fashioned and parochial), life-cycle ceremonies, and vernacular rituality.[28] By contrast, for halal-minded religionists, Islamic piety is 'good to act by'—a practice-oriented and holistic toolkit that, having an immediate operative aspect and virtually limitless scope, offers concrete answers to the existential needs of Tatarstan's Muslims who yearn for a 'good life' infused with spiritual fulfilment.[29] Like analogous Islamic virtue movements across the world, thus, Povolzhye's halal milieu furnishes Russia's Muslims with concrete instruments that help deal with the ethical and existential quandaries of late modernity.

Additionally, halal's focus on personal choice, conduct, and rectitude in a less-than-perfect world (implied in its conceptual twin-cum-reverse, haram) helps understand the success of this specific Islamic idiom over, say, shariʿa-centred discourses. Granted, shariatic awareness is capillarily widespread within text-oriented halal milieus.[30] In terms of public discourse, however, halal has all the limelight. 'Shariʿa talk' has a distinctly civilisational-juridical bent, prone to evoke grand scenarios of societal reformation and Islamic utopias. While such visions are not absent amongst my interlocutors, the halal milieu's post-Islamist emphasis on *the reform of one's self* (and immediate community) by striving towards 'halal lives', rather than 'establishing shariʿa', enables adherents to pursue goals that are both achievable and politically sustainable in the fraught scenario of Russia's illiberal public sphere. As we shall see in the final section of this chapter, halal makes for a suitable framework for fostering civic society initiatives shared by both state-controlled Islamic organisation and grassroots piety communities—unlike shariʿa which, being discursively bound up with state anxieties over Muslim disloyalty, extremism, and separatism, would come across as a thornier item in the context of an already fraught public conversations.

6 The Halal Milieu and the Emergent Muslim Middle Class

It is worth noting that the halal framework's emphasis on individual self-cultivation and alternative forms of subjectivity is bound up with the emer-

---

28 Benussi, 'Ethnic Muslims and the "Halal Movement" in Tatarstan', 88–93; Di Puppo, 'The Paradoxes of a Localised Islamic Orthodoxy: Rethinking Tatar Traditional Islam in Russia', 311–334.

29 Cf. Rabinovich, 'Living the Good Life', 199–214.

30 Bekkin, *Shariat dlya tebya. Dialogi o musul'manskom prave.*

gence of new, Muslim middle classes in post-Soviet Russia.[31] As a socio-ethical phenomenon, the halal movement has gained special traction, over the past two decades, amongst businesspeople, students, professionals, and young, mobile strata. Significantly, it appears particularly strong in Idel-Ural's urban areas. Young Povolzhye Muslims represent a particularly entrepreneurial and economically successful slice of the Volga region's population, akin to the global 'Muslim yuppies' roaming other corners of the Muslim world—idealist yet pragmatic 'saints/merchants' whose natural environment is Islamised neoliberal modernity.[32] Respondents in this group explicitly associate Islam with notions of progress, innovation, and development.

The Bourdieusian notion of distinction is useful in framing two conjoined dimensions of virtuous life: the moral/ethical ability of *discernment*, on the one hand, and the social ability of *distinguishing oneself*, on the other:[33] the existential enterprise of becoming good Muslims appears to coincide with a form of bourgeois self-edification. The ethos of this emerging middle class, focused on ethics as reflexive self-perfecting, stand in contrast with both the pre-existing paternalist Soviet ideology of mass mobilisation, collective obligations, horizontality, and conformism, as well as the organicist moralism of traditional Tatar custom. A streak of spiritual and moral snobbishness might be detected among some sectors of Povolzhye's Muslim middle class vis-à-vis the religiously 'ignorant' and socially inert Soviet-bred generations, as well as the hedonistic and vulgar *nouveaux riches* who emerged from the ruins of the old order.[34] Many of my interlocutors entertain the conviction that in Islam they may find instruments for moral perfecting that they could not find in Russia's mainstream society, plagued by evils such as disorderly gender and family dynamics, fatalism/lack of initiative, ethnic and national parochialism, and excessive tolerance for corruption.

Samuli Schielke has argued that 'revivalist Islam is not an alternative to nor a corrective for capitalism. Rather, [*revivalist Islam*] *is an especially compelling way to live capitalism*, and vice versa'.[35] Schielke identifies capitalist modernity as a specific 'sensibility of being in the world' that conditions the existences

31 Benussi, 'Public Spaces', 685–707.

32 Rajaee, 'A Thermidor of "Islamic Yuppies"? Conflict and Compromise in Iran's Politics', 222; Rouhani, '"Islamic Yuppies"? State Rescaling, Citizenship, and Public Opinion Formation in Tehran, Iran', 169–182.

33 Carrier, 'Introduction', 24.

34 Barker, *Consuming Russia: Popular Culture, Sex, and Society Since Gorbachev*; Patico, *Consumption and Social Change in a Post-Soviet Middle Class.*

35 Schielke, *Egypt in the Future Tense. Hope, Frustration and Ambivalence before and after 2011*, 119 (emphasis added).

of his virtuous and less virtuous Egyptian interlocutors. These considerations apply easily to Povolzhye's halal milieu: in fact, the connection between halal and capitalist/neoliberal modernity is particularly visible in a post-socialist context like Russia. In the same decade that ushered in the halal milieu, pious believers were, for the first time in the country's history and despite an economic crisis, faced with the joys and pains of mass consumption. Not only did categories of halal and haram gain mass currency on the 'immaterial' impulse of religious fervour: they also became attached to the new wealth of consumables on display in shops, supermarket, and internet catalogues.

My ethnographic material shows that halal consumption is an important area in which Idel-Ural Muslims express their religious discernment. Scrutiny does not stop at subtleties, from companies' sourcing of supplies and capital, to manufacturing methods, to packaging styles. Is a halal café really halal if the shop owner has taken on a loan from a conventional bank? Is it permissible for believers to buy halal foodstuffs from a company that also processes conventional meat? Are Muslims allowed to purchase biscuits sold in packages carrying human representations or, even worse, depictions of characters from Russian folklore? Should not the latter be interpreted as 'elements of polytheism' and avoided as such? Questions like these are routinely discussed within the halal milieu.

That practices of consumption (of food and nonfood goods) have a central role in ethical self-making has been recognised well beyond this case-study.[36] While ethical consumption projects often possess an explicitly *religious* connotation, and not just in Muslim settings,[37] this religious dimension might coexist with other, 'secular' moral discourses about desirable/distinguished personhood: cosmopolitan, sophisticated, and affluent. Like other sectors of the emergent global middle class, Tatarstan's halal milieus appear inclined to operate under such a 'morality of quality'—a endeavour to achieve higher standards of living than previous generations on the grounds that affluent consumption is both a 'right' and necessary to materialise 'middle-class romantic ideas of "the good life"'.[38] Ammara Maqsood's work on the new

36 For 'serious consumption' practices in the global West, see De Solier, *Food and the Self: Consumption, Production and Material Culture*; for the morality of food in post-Soviet Russia, see Caldwell, 'Gardening for the State: Cultivating Bionational Citizens in Postsocialist Russia'.

37 For an account of upmarket Buddhism-inspired Taiwanese restaurants in mainland China that combine vegetarian/organic menus with cultural activities informed by Buddhist and Confucian ideals, see Klein, 'Creating ethical Food Consumers? Promoting Organic Foods in Urban Southwest China', 74–89.

38 De Solier, 'Food and the Self', 99.

Pakistani middle class shows how, through consumption, Muslims forge 'modern' subjectivities in keeping with a global dreamworld of prosperity, glamour, and respectability.[39] Similar dynamics are at play in Povolzhye. As one of my respondents told me:

> Allah (subḥānahu wa taʿālā) is beautiful—this is one of His names [attributes]—and He loves beauty. Therefore, it is permissible for Muslims to love and respect themselves, and desire beautiful things, be it with regards to apparel, accommodation, cars ... Prophet Muhammad (*ṣallaLLāhu alayhi wa sallam*) said that a Muslim should look tidy and neat. I do not say you should be a poser (*shikovat'*), no, but you definitely ought to look respectable (*solidno*), neat (*chetko*). Because people will judge you as a Muslim, and other Muslims thereby, accordingly.

7 Working Halal in Post-socialist Russia

The previous section showed that partaking in consumption is seen as acceptable and indeed Islamically commendable—provided that one's spiritual obligation in the pursuit of the good life are not forgotten. Let us now observe how halal money is made amongst Povolzhye Muslims.

Making (a lot of) money is not considered a religious obligation, strictly speaking, by halal milieu Muslims, yet in light of the 'morality of quality' discussed above, it won't come as a surprise that many respondents see becoming rich as an ethical duty towards themselves as well as a moral incumbency vis-à-vis their community. A much-quoted maxim goes, '[T]here can be poor Muslims and rich Muslims, but a rich Muslim is better than a poor one'. Material aspirations are more than welcome, they are actively incentivised across different sectors of the halal milieu. Theological justifications for the pursuit of riches are drawn from the rich discursive tradition of Sunnism, for instance by referring to the lives of the Prophet and his wealthy first wife, Khadijah, who were partners in business. When it comes to moneymaking, though, not everything goes:

> Muslims must remain within the framework (*ramki*) of Islam, and not trespass the boundaries of what is permissible. Then business will be

---

39 Maqsood, ''Buying Modern': Muslim Subjectivity, the West and Patterns of Islamic Consumption in Lahore, Pakistan', 84–107.

> halal, whatever it is—restoration, education, trade, anything. As an example, halal business implies the absence of interest loans. If I lend you money and ask exactly the same amount of money back, and we seal the deal preferably in front of witnesses, then we are doing halal business. If I buy a car for you and tell you exactly how much you are going to pay in advance, that is halal business, too.
>
> Sultan, aged 29, halal food entrepreneur, Kazan

Wealth accumulated in Islamically illicit ways—for instance by stealing or gambling, but also by trading non-halal goods such as alcohol, immodest clothes, or conventional financial products (interest-based loans, insurances)—lacks *barakat*, i.e., in this context, God's blessings or grace. This is a very common risk. The halal market is rife with uncertainties and deceptions, while practical theological information to help orient one's choices is sometimes scarce or contradictory. As a result, in spite of their genuine zeal, large numbers of Muslim entrepreneurs struggle to keep up with halal norms while moving across the rugged terrain of Russia's economic landscape. As the imam of a Salafi-oriented community in eastern Tatarstan explained to me:

> It isn't easy, we all know that—young brothers want a lot of things, they want to make money (*okhota zarabotat'*), for instance to go on hajj. They want to set up their own businesses. And we understand perfectly well that doing business in Russia without trespassing somewhere haram is almost impossible. Haram is connected to business in many ways—banking, insurance, secular laws. There is almost always some illicit profit (*likhva*) somewhere, some subterfuge (*ulovka*). For this reason, for the time being, doing 100 per cent halal business is enormously complicated. But at least people are learning how not to fool themselves or get fooled if they come across anything illicit. [Our mosque] organises Islamic business classes, where what we try to get across is that, however bad the outside world might be, *we have to be different*. We need to strive towards halal income. But as I said, that isn't easy. Taxes to pay, salaries to fork out, if you want to get big you need to take this into account.

In Russia's Muslim-unfriendly business environment, being exposed to blatant or hidden (*skrity*) haram is very easy—especially in cases of lack of knowledge or lack of viable choices. However, as one interlocutor put it, 'it is key that one does not take into account exclusively what one is going to earn. Muslims must sincerely (*iskrenno*) desire that everything be halal. Intention, *niyat*, is what we shall be judged on in the afterlife'. Moreover, money earned by non-fully-halal means can be partly purged of its impurity (if not fully halalified) by good deeds, such as charity, patronage, and support of local Muslim communities.

A very specific obstacle to halalness in business is corruption, a widespread practice in free-market Russia as well as an illicit one under shariʿa. As one of the imams I interviewed commented: 'We all know that in Russia there is corruption. Now, there exists a counter-corruption programme, but it is nobody's secret that there is a lot of corruption in this country. This, too, makes it almost impossible to carry out halal business in Russia.' By and large, fully halal entrepreneurship is vastly perceived as unrealistic,[40] and much less attainable than halal consumption. This perception, however, does not discourage business-like Povolzhye Muslims from engaging with the market in order to make money—in ways that should be ethically as consistent as *possible* but also, and primarily, economically sensible. As a result, in business, the imperative of material success and the push to possessive individualism appear to override the principles of avoidance and precaution that condition halal consumption so heavily. In the sphere of moneymaking, halalness seems to configure itself as a distant ideal, a polar star that may orient—at least as much as is financially reasonable—one's steps across the rugged terrain of Russia's economy, yet that remains as of now unattainable.

8 Questions of Trust

> I know people who avoid buying anything, even bread, from supermarkets, including halal supermarkets. That's because these businesses made their initial money by selling alcohol and cigarettes, prior to opening their halal branches. In fact, I too get myself bread from the city industrial bakery (*khlebzavod*) whenever possible. But then again, the *khlebzavod* might be involved in *ribā* [interest-based loan]. To be 100 per cent safe, one should get flour from farmers and bake at home. Indeed, there are brothers here who never ever eat out. I've heard of people [travelling to Russian regions] who bring food with them and drink only bottled water for days because they don't dare buying anything local. Anyway, excessiveness (*cherezmernost'*) is discouraged in Islam, too. This is why I personally get my groceries in halal supermarkets most of the times.
>
> Amir, aged 31, programmer, Kazan

40 On the difficulties of ethical life in and beyond Islam, see Osella and Osella, 'Muslim Entrepreneurs'; Schielke, 'Egypt in the Future Tense'.

The excerpt above shows how difficult it can be for Muslim consumers to navigate a post-socialist market rife with sin, corruption, and unethicality. Trust plays a great role in orienting Muslim consumers' choice, particularly in a still-evolving sector like that of Povolzhye's halal goods. Personal connections, word-of-mouth, and specific individuals and communities' reputation—which were key assets in the Soviet-era informal economy—are still immensely important.[41] This, however, might be about to change, at least to a degree. In 2008, a Halal Standard Committee was established under the aegis of Tatarstan's Muslim Spiritual Directorate or Muftiate (see below) as an organ entitled to issue certifications and carry out audits to protect Muslim buyers. The advent of an 'audit culture'[42] of certification in the halal sector is perceived as a necessity by growing numbers of religionists.

> On the one hand, one cannot just trust anybody when it comes to halal. Unless you personally know the butchers, you'll never be 100 per cent sure. On the other hand, not trusting a fellow Muslim is *makrūh* (disapproved)—even more so if he takes offence at your scepticism. So Muslim consumers are between a rock and a hard place. Some prefer to rely on reputation. Yet it is increasingly hard to know each other personally in urban areas. More and more people now want to see the 'halal' mark printed on food packaging.
>
> Malik, aged 34, halal retail sector worker, Kazan

Halal consumers bear no spiritual responsibility for being deceived, particularly in an infamously fraught environment like the post-Soviet halal market; according to Islamic theology, one's soul will be judged in accordance to the goodness of one's intention (*niyya*). Yet there remains a great deal of anxiety about involuntary consumption of haram goods. Some of my respondents voiced the idea that 'if you consume non-halal food by mistake, you still risk losing your [spiritual] strength. The haram will get into your veins'. I also came across the notion that involuntary haram consumption renders one more vulnerable to possession by spirits. Although these views of the perils of haram are not universally held, it is still assumed that watchfulness is an ethical duty incumbent on all sincere Muslim consumers, as the following interview excerpt shows:

---

41 On 'wealth in people' among another Russian religious minority, see Rogers, *The Old Faith and the Russian Land: A Historical Ethnography of Ethics in the Urals.*

42 Strathern, *Audit Cultures: Anthropological Studies in Accountability, Ethics and the Academy.*

> If one trusts the halal stamp on packaged food and is mistaken, technically they're not committing sin. But then again, there is this story about Abu Hanifa ... he caught wind of a sheep in town that ate carcass [polluting and forbidden under shariʿa]. To avoid the risk of eating meat from that [impure] sheep, he abstained from sheep meat for five or six years, the average life span of sheep. This story is to inspire us to steer clear of anything dubious.
>
> Rifat, aged 28, translator and activist, Kazan

Particular suppliers or even entire villages—especially Mishar (Western) Tatar communities—are renowned for their 'strong faith' and 'sincerity', so that the quality of processed food hailing from there is hardly ever questioned. *Sarafannoe radio* (word of mouth) works only in the case of small-scale businesses, though. Things are more complicated when it comes to large food factories without religious or ethnic connotations that cater to a broad range of buyers. State-backed halal certification agencies play a huge role in these scenarios, although their effectiveness and good faith are routinely debated.[43] In 2013, a major scandal befell both food company Tsaritsyno, whose halal sausages were exposed on TV as containing pork DNA, and the state-run Council of Russian Muftis that had cleared those sausages as halal.

The Council was not necessarily in bad faith: as a halal certification specialist explained to me, manufacturers can change production methods without advising them, and constant auditing is complicated and costly. Dishonest manufacturers oftentimes try to deceive Islamic control boards:

> Sometimes we call over to some, say, Saint Petersburg company before striking a deal: 'Hi. Could you send us a scanned copy of your certificate?' And they are all like, 'Assalaaaamu aleykuuum. We are all Muslim here, we pray five times a day'. And we are like, 'Er, wa aleykum as-salaam. That's wonderful, but wouldn't you mind sending us some piece of evidence [issued by a local auditing body]?' And they go, 'Assalaaaaaaamuuu aleykuuuuum. Our cows are fit and fat, and everything is homemade up here'.
>
> Marat-*äfände*, head of Tatarstan's Halal Certification Committee, Kazan

43 See Fischer, *The Halal Frontier. Muslim Consumers in a Globalized Market*, on halal certification; also cf. Jung, 'Re-Creating Economic and Cultural Values in Bulgaria's Wine Industry: From an Economy of Quantity to an Economy of Quality?', 298–299, on the role of the state in post-socialist consumption scenarios.

Halal-related anxieties are the main source of inspiration for of the ambitious *Halal Guide* project—a website and smartphone app allowing Muslim users to locate a range of places of interest ('halal places') on a map. These include mosques and madrasahs as well as cafes, grocery shops, restaurants, hotels, healthcare facilities, clothes retailers, bookshops, and all manners of commercial activities specifically catering to Muslim consumers. HalalGuide, born in 2010, is the main search engine for Muslims in Eastern Europe and Central Asia, and is now expanding in Western Europe and North America. Amir explained that HalalGuide addresses the issue of trust in halal consumption by establishing different 'levels of trustworthiness' (*kategorii doveriya*).[44]

Let us consider food-related businesses: low trustworthiness implies storing and selling certified halal products alongside hon-halal products (e.g. bottled alcoholic drinks, common meat). A business' halalness can be contested in such cases, especially by buyers of Salafi persuasion. However, as long as halal and haram products are separated, there are theological grounds for considering establishments of this kind (that include most Povolzhye supermarkets and grocery shops, as well as most restaurants and trattorias) viable for Muslims customers. Intermediate trustworthiness is attributed to establishments that explicitly cater to a Muslim clientele (e.g. do not sell alcohol) but cannot offer proof of halalness (e.g. a Muftiate-issued certificate). In Tatarstan/Povolzhye, this tends to apply to small family businesses run by Central Asian immigrants or rural Tatars who rely on reputation rather than certification. The most trustworthy businesses combine self-proclaimed Muslimness and possession of certificates issued by state-approved Islamic boards. The latter formula is gaining prominence in Povolzhye's cities, with growing numbers of cafes and restaurants that are both explicitly and officially Muslim-friendly, and supermarket chains opening completely haram-free retail points under the aegis of Tatarstan's Muftiate.

9 Halal and Civil Society

In the previous sections, I have described the halal milieu (or 'movement') as a post-Islamist phenomenon equipping an emerging urban middle class with tools for ethical self-cultivation. Even its most conservative segments tend

44 Initially, these categories were referred to as 'levels of faith', but this problematically judgemental faith-based terminology was later ditched in favour of more neutral phrasing.

towards political quietism. Nonetheless, many of my respondents have experienced, with varying degrees of intensity, an uneasy relationship with the Russian state—in particular, the risk of being branded 'non-traditional' (*netraditsionnie*) Muslims, a label that in the political parlance of post-Soviet Russia typically implies fanaticism, foreignness, and potential dangerousness. As piety trends made their appearance, scripturalist Sunnism—especially, though not exclusively, its Salafi/Athari theological declination—came to become identified as 'non-traditional for Russia' (*netraditsionny dlya Rossii*), an obscurantist ideology prompting unruly youths to absorb the poisonous influence of foreign countries and cultural worlds.[45] While this narrative is evolving rapidly, it remains contentious amongst the many Muslims who follow autonomous paths to Islamic virtue.

This diatribe is a recent development in a long history of state intervention in the affairs of Russia's Muslims. Since the late eighteenth century, the Russian state's governmental intervention in the sphere of Islam has been primarily carried out though ideological apparatuses called Muslim Spiritual Directorates (*dukhovnie upravleniya musul'man*) or Muftiates. These institutions, established in the Tsarist era, remained active even during the Soviet period.[46] After the breakdown of the Soviet order, over 50 local Muftiates—with varying degrees of autonomy—emerged in the Russian Federation, along with two competing all-Russian Spiritual Directorates. Muftiates constitute a possibly unique example of a Christian-majority, secular state endowed with official apparatuses active in the sphere of Muslim affairs, including theology.

Being a cosmopolitan grassroots phenomenon, the halal milieu has developed in large part independently from state-backed Spiritual Directorates, which amplifies the risk of being branded 'non-traditional' and thus undesirable. In spite of this fraught situation, the halal issue has become the

---

45 Benussi, '"Sovereign" Islam and Tatar "Aqīdah": Normative Religious Narratives and Grassroots Criticism amongst Tatarstan's Muslims', 111–134. Bustanov and Kemper, 'Valiulla Iakupov's Tatar Islamic Traditionalism', 818. For a reflection covering Central Asia, see Montgomery and Heathershaw, 'Islam, Secularism and Danger: A Reconsideration of the Link between Religiosity, Radicalism and Rebellion in Central Asia', 192–218. For an analysis of state-led 'domestication' attempts toward Western Europe's Muslim communities, look comparatively at Sunier, 'Domesticating Islam: Exploring Academic Knowledge Production on Islam and Muslims in European Societies', 1138–1155 and 'Beyond the Domestication of Islam in Europe: A Reflection on Past and Future Research on Islam in European Societies', 189–208.

46 Benningsen and Lemercier-Quelquejay, *Les musulmans oubliés. L'Islam en Union Soviétique*, 194–195; Ro'I, *Islam in the Soviet Union: From the Second World War to Gorbachev*.

setting for a series of encounters between official Islamic institutions and fledgling Muslim civil society as new state-supported initiatives that address the needs of halal milieu religionists are taking shape.

In 2008, for example, control boards like the Halal Standard Committee were established in Kazan under the aegis of Tatarstan's Muslim Spiritual Directorate. The Halal Standard Committee is entitled to issue certifications and carry out audits to protect Muslim buyers. In 2011, the republic's Islamic Directorate authorised the creation of Tatarstan's Muslim Youth Union, promoting 'halal' forms of sociality and fun made Islamically acceptable by upholding Islamic dress codes and controlled gender relations. Similarly, over the past few years, Tatarstan's Spiritual Directorate and Halal Standard Committee have been increasingly promoting halal business by organising numerous initiatives targeting pious-minded entrepreneurs and by fostering Muslim businesspeople networks at a trans-regional level.[47] Grassroots initiatives were inaugurated as well. In the mid-2000s, Muslims in an Eastern Tatarstani town agreed with the local municipality not to serve halal food in kindergartens and schools.

Although such encounters take place in a scenario still rife with tension and mutual scepticism, they are nonetheless significant developments. By addressing the needs of halal-conscious middle-class Muslims, segments of the official Islamic bureaucracy hope to meet the halal milieu outside the straightjacket of the traditional/non-traditional opposition, which many feel is increasingly inadequate, especially as Russia's diverse Muslim component grows in size, visibility, and protagonism.[48] Such a move appears conducive to the emergence of an idiosyncratic form of Muslim civil society based on state-engineered—through the mediation of Russia's Spiritual Directorates—civic activism combined with a boost in economic liberties. This development would be consistent with a broader, nation-wide project of 'managed', state-driven civil society in contemporary Russia. Without fully corresponding to Western liberal mod-

47 Russia's Association of Muslim Entrepreneurs (APM) is a particularly interesting case. The APM became operative in 2015, its focus the promotion of halal business both domestically and overseas. Its goal is connecting and coordinating Russian-speaking Muslim businesspeople, furnishing them with support and advice, and modernising the economy of Russia's Muslim-majority regions through an emphasis on halal business. Founded in Kazan, the APM has quickly established itself nationwide and its new headquarters are located in a prestigious historical building in Moscow. APM's representatives are operative in Northern Caucasus, Central Asia, the Arabian Peninsula, and Western Europe. Many pious entrepreneurs are interested in this organisation, which places a great deal of emphasis on sincerity and virtuous conduct, and possesses selective acceptance standards.

48 Laruelle, 'How Islam Will Change Russia'.

els of civil society,[49] this project appears nonetheless capable of intercepting authentic grassroots enthusiasm. By engaging religiously-minded middle-class Muslims as economic actors, concerned consumers, active citizens, and good-willed youths—rather than mere subjects to keep under control—and by taking their ethical positioning seriously, 'halal' initiatives for Muslims may offer a platform for Russia's Islamic officialdom to assert itself as a credible catalyst of civil energy in the eyes of the country's devout religionists.

10 Conclusion

In this chapter, I have offered an ethnographic analysis of the halal milieu in Central Russia's Idel-Ural region. I have adopted a 'discontinuity' approach, in order to illustrate that Povolzhye's 'halal boom', despite being steeped in the region's long Islamic history, represents a new chapter of that history. The success of halal discourses indicates a rise in ethicised religion at the expense of the vernacular devotionalism and localism which characterised Soviet-era approaches to Islam. The idiom of halal, with its universal categories, and its emphasis on conduct, personal choice, and individual rectitude, resonates deeply with the existential needs and aspirations of a bourgeoning, cosmopolitan Muslim middle class. At the same time, this success indicates Povolzhye Muslims' sincere commitment to ways of living Islam that, though scripturally informed, do not require organised political militancy or grand civilisational goals.

I have illustrated how Muslim consumers use halal as a guiding principle in a post-Soviet landscape of newly formed, still unruly markets, as well as a fertile ground for experiments in Islamic capitalism—another radically new development in the history of this Islamicate province. The contradictions and aporias faced by halal consumers and entrepreneurs have been highlighted alongside the opportunities that the spread of halal offers in terms of civil-society strengthening in Central Russia.

Most of these developments would have likely befuddled the great-grandparents of today's halal milieu religionists. This indicates that Islam is plastic, it changes across history, and is capable of changing configuration

49 Brunarska, 'Understanding Sociopolitical Engagement of Society in Russia: A View from Yaroslavl Oblast and Tatarstan', 315–326. On non-Western civil societies, see Comaroff and Comaroff, 'Millennial Capitalism: First Thoughts on a Second Coming', 40–44; Hann and Dunn, *Civil Society: Challenging Western Models*; Mandel, 'Introduction: Transition to Where? Developing Post-Soviet Space', 223–233.

according to the dynamics of the time. The halal milieu in Tatarstan is, thus, as much a product of social change in post-Soviet, neo-capitalist Russia as it is an heir to the many centuries of Muslim history unfolding on the shores of the Volga River.

Acknowledgements

I thank my internal and external reviewers in 2019 and 2020 for their excellent advice on earlier drafts of this chapter, the editors of this volume for their hard work, and above all my friends, acquaintances, and interlocutors in Povolzhye for their help and support during my fieldwork.

Bibliography

Ahmed, Shahab. 2016. *What Is Islam? The Importance of Being Islamic*. Princeton: Princeton University Press.

Almazova, Leyla and Almaz Akhunov. 2019. 'In Search of "Traditional Islam" in Tatarstan: Between National Project and Universalist Theories'. *Časopis za interdisciplinarne studije* 6, no. 1: 11–46.

Asad, Talal. 2009. 'The Idea of an Anthropology of Islam'. *Qui Parle* 17, no. 2: 1–30.

Barker, Adele Marie, ed. 1999. *Consuming Russia: Popular Culture, Sex, and Society Since Gorbachev*. Durham: Duke University Press.

Bayat, Asef, ed. 2013. *Post-Islamism: The Changing Faces of Political Islam*. Oxford: Oxford University Press.

Bayat, Asef. 1996. 'The Coming of a Post-Islamist Society'. *Critique: Critical Middle East Studies* 9: 43–52.

Bekkin, Rinat. 2015. *Shariat dlya tebya. Dialogi o musul'manskom prave*. Kazan: Smena.

Benningsen, Alexandre and Chantal Lemercier-Quelquejay. 1981. *Les musulmans oubliés. L'Islam en Union soviétique*. Paris: Maspero.

Benussi, Matteo. 2018. 'Ethnic Muslims and the "Halal Movement" in Tatarstan'. *Anthropological Journal of European Cultures* 27, no. 1 (2018): 88–93.

Benussi, Matteo. 2020. 'Public Spaces and Inner Worlds: Emplaced Askesis and Architecture of the Soul among Tatarstani Muslims'. *Ethnicities* 20, no. 4: 685–707.

Benussi, Matteo. 2020. '"Sovereign" Islam and Tatar "Aqīdah": Normative Religious Narratives and Grassroots Criticism amongst Tatarstan's Muslims'. *Contemporary Islam* 14: 111–134.

Benussi, Matteo. 'Pietaskscapes of Halal Living: Subjectivity, Striving, and Space-Making in Muslim Russia'. *Ethnic and Racial Studies*. Forthcoming.

Biard, Aurelie. 2018. '"Bourgeois" Islam, Prosperity Theology and Ethics in Muslim Eurasia'. Central Asia Program Paper 198.

Botoeva, Aisalkyn. 2018. 'Islam and the Spirits of Capitalism: Competing Articulations of the Islamic Economy'. *Politics & Society* 46, no. 2: 235–264.

Brose, Michael. 2018. 'China and Transregional Halal Circuits'. *Review of Religion and Chinese Society* 5, no. 2: 208–227.

Brunarska, Zuzanna. 2017. 'Understanding Sociopolitical Engagement of Society in Russia: A View from Yaroslavl Oblast and Tatarstan'. *Problems of Post-Communism* 65: 315–326.

Bukharaev, Ravil. 2013. *Islam in Russia: The Four Seasons*. London/New York: Routledge.

Bustanov, Alfrid. 2017. 'Against Leviathan: On the Ethics of Islamic Poetry in Soviet Russia'. In *The Piety of Learning: Islamic Studies in Honor of Stefan Reichmuth*, edited by Michael Kemper and Rolf Elger, 199–225. Leiden/Boston: Brill.

Bustanov, Alfrid and Michael Kemper. 2013. 'Valiulla Iakupov's Tatar Islamic Traditionalism'. *Asiatische Studien* 67, no. 3: 809–835.

Caldwell, Melissa. 2014. 'Gardening for the State: Cultivating Bionational Citizens in Postsocialist Russia'. In *Ethical Eating in the Postsocialist and Socialist World*, edited by Yuson Jung, Jakob A. Klein and Melissa Caldwell, 188–210. Berkeley: University of California Press.

Carrier, James. 2012. 'Introduction'. In *Ethical Consumption. Social Value and Economic Practice*, edited by James Carrier and Peter G. Luetchford, 1–36. Oxford/New York: Berghanh.

Comaroff, John and Jean Comaroff. 2001. 'Millennial Capitalism: First Thoughts on a Second Coming'. In *Millennial Capitalism and the Culture of Neoliberalism*, edited by John Comaroff and Jean Comaroff, 1–56. Durham: Duke University Press.

De Solier, Isabelle, ed. 2013. *Food and the Self: Consumption, Production and Material Culture*. London: Bloomsbury.

Di Puppo, Lili. 2019. 'The Paradoxes of a Localised Islamic Orthodoxy: Rethinking Tatar Traditional Islam in Russia'. *Ethnicities* 19, no. 2: 311–334.

Faller, Helena. 2011. *Nation, Language, Islam: Tatarstan's Sovereignty Movement*. Budapest: Central European University Press.

Fischer, Johan. 2011. *The Halal Frontier. Muslim Consumers in a Globalized Market*. London: Palgrave Macmillan.

Foucault, Michel. 2010. *The Government of Self and Others: Lectures at the Collège De France 1982–1983*. New York: Palgrave Macmillan.

Foucault Michel. 2011. *The Courage of the Truth: The Government of Self and Others II: Lectures at the Collège de France 1983–1984*. New York: Palgrave Macmillan.

Gabdrafikova, Liliya. 2013. *Povsednevnaya zhizn' gorodskikh tatar v usloviyakh burzhuaznykh preobrazovanii vtoroy poloviny XIX—nachala XX veka*. Kazan: Akademia Nauk.

Gabdrafikova, Liliya. 2016. 'P'yanstvo tatar 100 let nazad: Kurban-bayram s ryumkoy vodka, netrezvye shakirdy i tletvordnoe vliyanie Zapada. Problema alkogolizma v tatarskom musul'manskom obshchestve vo vtoroy polovine XIX—nachale XX veka'. *Real'noe Vremya*, 7 November. https://realnoevremya.ru/articles/47290 (accessed 26/10/2020).

Hann, Chris and Elizabeth Dunn, eds. 1996. *Civil Society: Challenging Western Models*. London/New York: Routledge.

Henig, David. 2017. 'A Good Deed is not a Crime: Moral Cosmologies of Favours in Bosnia-Herzegovina'. In *Economies of Favour After Socialism*, edited by David Henig and Nicolette Makovicky, 181–202. Oxford: Oxford University Press.

Hodgson, Marshall. 1974. *The Venture of Islam, Volume 1: The Classical Age of Islam*. Chicago/London: University of Chicago Press.

Hoesterey, James K. 2016. *Rebranding Islam: Piety, Prosperity, and a Self-Help Guru*. Stanford: Stanford University Press.

Humphrey, Caroline, Magnus Marsden, and Vera Skvirskaya. 2009. 'Cosmopolitanism and the City: Interaction and Coexistence in Bukhara'. In *The Other Global City*, edited by Shail Mayaram, 202–231. London/New York: Routledge.

Jung, Yuson. 2016. 'Re-creating Economic and Cultural Values in Bulgaria's Wine Industry: From an Economy of Quantity to an Economy of Quality?' *Economic Anthropology* 3, no. 2: 180–292.

Kaliszewska, Iwona. 2020. 'Halal Landscapes of Dagestani Entrepreneurs in Makhachkala'. *Ethnicities* 20, no. 4: 708–730.

Kappeler, Andreas. 2001. *The Russian Empire: A Multiethnic History*. London/New York: Routledge.

Kefeli, Agnes. 2014. *Becoming Muslim in Imperial Russia: Conversion, Apostasy, and Literacy*. Ithaca: Cornell University Press.

Klein Jakob. 2009. 'Creating Ethical Food Consumers? Promoting Organic Foods in Urban Southwest China'. *Social Anthropology* 17, no. 1: 74–89.

Laruelle, Marlene. 2014. 'How Islam Will Change Russia', *The Jamestown Foundation—Global Research and Analysis*, 13 September. https://jamestown.org/program/marlene-laruelle-how-islam-will-change-russia/ (accessed 26/10/2020).

Maevsky, Kirill. 2014. 'Letter from: halal haircuts in the capital of Tatarstan'. The Calvert Journal, 23 September. https://www.calvertjournal.com/articles/show/3117/letter-from-kazan-Tatarstan-halal (accessed 26/10/2020).

Mahmood, Saba. 2005. *Politics of Piety: The Islamic Revival and the Feminist Subject*. Princeton: Princeton University Press.

Mandel, Ruth. 2012. 'Introduction: Transition to Where? Developing Post-Soviet Space'. *Slavic Review* 71, no. 2: 223–233.

Marsden, Marsden, and Konstantinos Retsikas, eds. 2013. *Articulating Islam: Anthropological Approaches to Muslim Worlds*. Amsterdam: Springer Press.

Maqsood, Ammara. 2014. '"Buying Modern": Muslim Subjectivity, the West and Patterns of Islamic Consumption in Lahore, Pakistan'. *Cultural Studies* 28, no. 1: 84–107.

Montgomery, David, and John Heathershaw. 2016. 'Islam, Secularism and Danger: A Reconsideration of the Link between Religiosity, Radicalism and Rebellion in Central Asia'. *Religion, State and Society* 44, no. 3: 192–218.

Osella, Filippo, and Caroline Osella. 2009. 'Muslim Entrepreneurs in Public Life between India and the Gulf: Making Good and Doing Good'. *Journal of the Royal Anthropological Institute* 15, no. 1: 202–221.

Patico, Jennifer. 2008. *Consumption and Social Change in a Post-Soviet Middle Class*. Palo Alto: Stanford University Press.

Pelkmans, Mathijs. 2006. *Defending the Border: Identity, Religion, and Modernity in the Republic of Georgia*. Ithaca: Cornell University Press.

Rabinovich, Tatiana. 2017. 'Living the Good Life: Muslim Women's Magazines in Contemporary Russia', *European Journal of Cultural Studies* 20, no. 2: 199–214.

Rajaee, Farhang. 1999. 'A Thermidor of "Islamic Yuppies"? Conflict and Compromise in Iran's Politics', *Middle East Journal* 53, no. 2: 217–231.

Robbins, Joel. 2007. 'Continuity Thinking and the Problem of Christian Culture: Belief, Time, and the Anthropology of Christianity', *Current Anthropology* 48, no. 1, February: 5–38.

Ro'i, Yaacov. 2000. *Islam in the Soviet Union: From the Second World War to Gorbachev*. New York: Columbia University Press.

Rogers, Douglas. 2009. *The Old Faith and the Russian Land: A Historical Ethnography of Ethics in the Urals*. Ithaca: Cornell University Press.

Rorlich, Azade-Ayşe. 1986. *The Volga Tatars: A Profile in National Resilience*. Stanford: Hoover Institution Press.

Rouhani, Farhang. 2003. '"Islamic Yuppies"? State Rescaling, Citizenship, and Public Opinion Formation in Tehran, Iran'. *Urban Geography* 24, no. 2: 169–182.

Rudnyckyj, Daromir. 2010. *Spiritual Economies. Islam, Globalization, and the Afterlife of Development*. Ithaca: Cornell University Press.

Schielke, Samuli. 2015. *Egypt in the Future Tense. Hope, Frustration and Ambivalence Before and After 2011*. Bloomington: Indiana University Press.

Shnirelman, Victor. 1996. *Who Gets the Past? Competition for Ancestors among Non-Russian Intellectuals in Russia*. Baltimore/London: The Johns Hopkins University Press.

Strathern, Marilyn, ed. 2000. *Audit Cultures: Anthropological Studies in Accountability, Ethics and the Academy*. London/New York: Routledge.

Stratton, Allegra. 2006. *Muhajababes: Meet the Middle East's Next Generation*. London: Constable and Robinson.

Sunier, Thijl. 2012. 'Domesticating Islam: Exploring Academic Knowledge Production on Islam and Muslims in European Societies'. *Ethnic and Racial Studies* 37, no. 6: 1138–1155.

Sunier, Thijl. 2012. 'Beyond the Domestication of Islam in Europe: A Reflection on Past and Future Research on Islam in European Societies'. *Journal of Muslims in Europe* 1, no. 2: 189–208.

Tayob, Shaheed. 2019. 'Molecular Halal: Producing, Debating and Evading Halal Certification in South Africa'. In *Insatiable Appetite: Food as Cultural Signifier in the Middle East and Beyond*, edited by Kirill Dmitriev, Julia Hauser, and Bilal Orfali, 100–118. Leiden/Boston: Brill.

Tobin, Sarah. 2016. *Everyday Piety. Islam and Economy in Jordan*. Ithaca: Cornell University Press.

Turaeva, Rano. 2018. 'Informal Economies in the Post-Soviet space: Post-Soviet Islam and Its Role in Ordering Entrepreneurship in Central Asia'. In *Being Muslim in Central Asia: Practices, Politics, and Identities*, edited by Marlene Laruelle, 208–230. Leiden/Boston: Brill.

Index

9/11 113–116, 162

accreditation 8, 17, 198, 224, 226, 227–228, 258
ʿadl 117, 124
ʿAbdillāh, Jābir bin 97
ʿAbduh, Muḥammad 63, 64
ʿīna 40
Abdel-Meguid, Ahmed Asmat 113
Abū Bakr 32
Afghanistan 115
Africa 118, 139
  Africa, North 158, 174, 226, 242
Agamben, Giorgio 29, 30
agency 25–55, 259
ahilik 49
aḥkām al-shārʿīa 85
Ahl ul-Bayt 54
Ahmad, Abdullah 66, 71–72, 73–74
Ahmad, Ilyas 29, 41
Ahmadi 241
Ahmadiya 254
aḥyaṭ 101
Ajinomoto case 140–145, 146
al-Mālibārī, Zayn al-Dīn 69
al-Suyūṭī, Jalāl al-Dīn 69
Albania 159
alcohol 67–68, 70, 99, 100, 138, 173, 175–176, 225, 228, 231, 235–236, 237, 281, 282, 285
Aleksandrowicz, Janusz 255–256
Algeria 159, 242, 245
ʿālim see ʿulamaʾ/ulama
American Animatograph 71
American Biograph 71
Amidhan 97
Amin, Ma'ruf 97
Amsterdam 197, 204
animal rights 166, 243, 251–252, 253, 259
animal rights movements (Poland) 251, 252, 259
  All Polish Association for Animal Protection (OTOZ) 251, 252
  Animal Guard 251
  Animal Liberation Front 251
  Empathy Association 251
  Foundation Viva! 251, 252
  Klub Gaja 251
animal welfare 16, 18, 128, 161, 198, 203, 251
ʿaql 33, 36
Arab League 113, 114, 245n24
Arab Spring 116
Arab-Israeli peace process 120
Argentina 128
ari-ari 59
Armanios, Febe 228, 236
Arslān, Amīr Shakib 65
Asad, Talal 273
Asia 139
  Central 268–269, 274n21, 285, 287n47
  East 108, 141, 242
  Southeast 12, 56–79, 80, 85, 129, 131n7, 141, 156, 163, 166, 167, 168, 174, 228
al-Aṣl fī al-Ashyāʾ al-Ibāḥa 103
Association of Muslim Students (SSM) 245
Association of Muslim Unity (Stowarzyszenie Jedności Muzułmańskiej: SJM) 248, 253, 254, 257
Asutay, Mehmet 45
Attar, Maryam 222
Austin, John 29
Australia 128, 139
autonomy 16, 109, 113, 200, 201–204, 214, 215, 286
al-Azhar 60, 62, 63, 72

Badan Penyelenggara Jaminan Produk Halal *see* National Agency of Halal Product Assurance (BPJPH)
Bahsul Masa'il 86, 87
baḥth al-ʿilm 84
Bashkortostan 268
al-Baṣrī, Abū'l-Ḥusayn 33, 84
Batavia 66 71
Bāṭinīs group 36
Beijing 108, 113, 114n15, 118, 119, 120, 122, 123
Beijing Consensus 112
Belgian Muslims (l'Exécutif des musulmans de Belgique: EMB) 162, 164, 179
Belgium 16–17, 153–195, 245n22
Belt Road Initiative (BRI) 108, 116, 119, 122, 123

Bentham, Jeremy 174
Bergeaud-Blackler, Florence 130, 131, 173, 225
Berger, Rafał 248
Bertrand, Jacques 145
Białostocczyzna 244
Białystok 244, 247, 255
bioethics 2, 18, 201
biotechnology 14, 98, 104
Bodin, Jean 28–29
Bogor Institute of Agriculture (IPB) 137
Borneo 64
Bosnia and Herzegovina 257, 271n14
Bourdieu, Pierre 278
Bowen, John 171, 238
Brazil 221, 229n32
Brunei 156, 163, 168
Bush, GeorgeW. 115
al-Būṭī, Ramaḍān 25

Cairo 12, 57–58, 60, 62–67, 70–74, 76
Cambodia 60, 61
capitalism 3, 4, 5, 8, 10, 11, 21, 25, 26, 27, 31–32, 38, 41, 42, 43, 45–46, 47, 50, 51, 52, 112, 113, 155, 266, 270, 274, 278–279, 288
Centre for Islam and Culture of Belgium (Centre Islamique et culturel de belgique: CCIB) 159–162, 164
Centro Islamico Crema 208
Centro Islamico Culturale d'Italia (Islamic Cultural Centre of Italy) 205
Ceric, Mustafa 257
China 14–15, 108–127, 130, 131n7, 229, 230, 279n37
Chinese Communist Party 112, 123
Choiński, Witold 257
Chuvashia 268
civil society 11, 21, 26, 46, 47–51, 88, 90, 265–292
Codex Alimentarius 165, 167–168
Codex Alimentarius Commission 165n83, 199
Comitato per l'Islam italiano (Committee for Italian Islam) 206
Community-Supportive Agriculture (CSA) 117
Comunità Religiosa Islamica (Co.Re.Is.) 18, 205, 208, 209, 226
Consulta Islamica (Islamic Council) 206
consumer ethics *see* eating ethically
consumer protection 6, 18, 203, 214, 215
corruption 145, 231n36, 278, 282, 283
Council of Indonesian Ulama (MUI) 13–14, 15, 80n2, 81–82, 84, 87, 89, 90–92, 94–102, 103–104, 132, 134–135, 136, 137, 139, 140, 142–145, 146–147, 154n8, 166, 167, 175, 198, 226, 227, 231
  Fatwa Commission 82, 89, 94, 95, 98
Council of Russian Muftis 284
COVID-19 108, 111, 123

Daḥlān, Aḥmad ibn Zainī 58
Dahlan, Winai 257
dalils 95
Dār al-Iftā' (House of Fatwa, Egypt) 89
ḍarūra 8, 13, 98, 100–101, 124
ḍarūriyyāt 33
Dassetto, Felice 153n4, 160
Dawud, Abū 97
Deng Xiaoping 112
Denmark 258
Department of Islamic Development (JAKIM) 13, 81, 82, 84, 89, 90, 93–103, 104, 153n1, 166, 167, 168, 175, 198, 227
dhabīḥa 242, 272
dīn 33, 36
Djalaluddin, Thaher 62–63
Dubai 208

East Indies 59, 61, 64, 68, 90
eating ethically 221–240
Egypt 1, 57, 65, 73, 74, 89, 92, 114, 245
Eid 117, 252
Embassy Islam 205
England 30
Epstein, Steven 155, 157
Ergene, Boğaç A. 228, 236
essentialism 5–22, 38, 41, 43, 47, 49, 274, 277
ethics 6, 7, 10, 19, 93, 174, 221–240, 265, 269, 271, 273, 274–277, 278, 279, 280, 282, 283, 285, 288
EuroHalal 164, 166–167, 169, 172, 176n142, 182
Europe 3, 113, 139, 156, 165, 166, 167, 168, 172, 241, 242, 250n47, 257
  Central 257
  Eastern 257

European Certification and Control of Halal (EICH) 170, 172n121, 176n142, 180
European Committee for Standardization 166
European Convention on Human Rights 200
European Court of Human Rights (ECtHR) 1, 199, 200
European Islamic Halal Certification (EIHC) 164, 167, 169, 175n132, 182
European Parliament 203
European Single Market 5
European Union (EU) 6, 122, 161, 162n57, 196, 199, 201–202, 203, 210, 211, 215, 228, 229n32, 251
Court of Justice 6, 162n57, 196
exception 11, 26–32, 37, 38–43, 51

fair trade 27, 46, 50
falāḥ 50
farā'id 61
farm-to-table 222
see also farm-to-fork
al-Fāsī, Allāl 37
al-Fatani, Ahmad ibn Muhammad Zain 58–61
al-Fatani, Shaykh Da'ud 59–60
al-Fatāwā al-Faṭāniyah 58, 59, 61–62
fatwa (pl. fatāwā) 2, 3, 9, 11, 12, 13–14, 15, 25, 26, 32, 33, 43, 51, 52, 56–79, 80–107, 132, 135, 137, 142–145, 146, 175, 176
Fawzi, Ahmad 64
Federation of Jewish Communities of Spain 206, 214
Ferrari, Silvio 200, 204
Fiji 128
fiqh 1, 3, 9, 25, 46, 50, 60, 61, 85, 96, 99, 100, 175, 176, 225, 271
see also Islamic law
Fischer, Johan 83, 132, 156
Food Italy 19, 222, 225, 227, 228–230
Foucault, Michel 158, 174
Foundation of Consumers' Institution (Yayasan Lembaga Konsumen) 137
France 30, 119n32, 158, 175n138, 184, 229n32, 241, 242, 245n22, 258
fraud 6, 18, 144, 202, 204, 207, 215
from-farm-to-fork 16, 198
see also farm-to-table

*furū*ʿ 86, 102
fuzzy logic 11, 27, 45, 46–50, 51, 53

Gajah Mada University (UGM) 132, 144
Gdańsk 244, 247
Gembloux 158, 160
General Veterinary Inspectorate (GVI) 242n7, 244, 247, 254
Germany 30, 155n8, 241, 242, 245n22, 253n58
gharār 124
al-Ghazālī 30, 31, 33, 34, 35–36, 84, 102
Girindra, Aisjah 140, 144
Global Action in the Interest of Animals (GAIA) 166
globalisation 9, 45, 121, 249, 256
glocalisation 3–5, 9, 17, 163
Gorzów Wielkopolski 244
Gratian (Flavius Gratianus Augustus) 30
Gulf Cooperation Council (GCC) 166
Gulf Cooperation Council Standardization Organization (GSO) 166, 167
Gulf countries 108, 117, 118, 120, 123, 160, 164, 167, 208

ḥadīth/hadith 2, 34, 35, 71, 97–98, 142, 143, 156, 176, 225
ḥājiyyāt 33
ḥajj 58, 59, 74, 281
hakim kafir 59
halal
halal authentication 15–16, 128–150
halal awareness 129, 130–132, 135, 269
halal certification 1–22, 80n2, 81, 82, 87, 94, 103, 104, 117, 120, 124, 129–134, 136, 137, 138–140, 141, 144, 146–147, 153–195, 196–240, 241–264, 264–293
halal market 1–22, 25–150, 153, 154, 156, 163, 165, 196, 197, 208, 222, 249, 250, 253, 258, 259, 281, 283
halal norms 10, 154, 155, 157, 168, 173, 281
pluriversality 17, 153, 156, 173–177
Halal Act 2011, Indonesia 146–147
Halal Advocates of America 117
Halal Certification Bodies (HCBs) 3, 8–9, 15, 16, 17, 19, 124, 153, 155, 156–158, 163–165, 166–168, 170–173, 174–176, 178–187
Halal Expertise 164, 166, 167, 169–170, 172n121, 175, 176n142, 184

Halal Federation of Belgium (HFB) 167, 168, 180
Halal Food Council of Europe (HFCE) 164, 166–170, 172n121, 176n142, 182
Halal Guide 285
Halal Institute (Italy) 211, 212
Halal Institute (Poland) (PIH) 20, 241–242, 253, 257–258, 259
Halal International Authority (HIA) 208, 226
Halal Italia 18, 19, 206–211, 214, 222, 225, 226, 228, 237
Halal Italia 2010 Inter-ministerial Convention 206–211, 213
Halal Poland System (HP) 255, 258
Halal Research Group (HRG) 132
Halal Standard Committee (Tatarstan) 283, 287
Halal Stock 166
Halal System 247, 254, 258
halalness 9, 47, 129, 134, 136, 146, 154n8, 198, 270, 282, 285
Halim, Sheikh Abdul 92
Hallaq, Wael 29, 84
Han Chinese 114
Ḥanīfa, Abū 32, 284
ḥarām/haram 8, 10, 12, 15, 27, 46, 47, 51, 56, 93, 95, 97, 98, 99, 102, 103, 133–134, 135, 138, 139, 143, 147, 173, 198, 209, 236, 265, 269, 270, 271, 272, 274–277, 279, 281, 283, 285
Hasanuddin, Maulana 98
Hassan, Ahmad Fahmi 42
Hassanali, Layla 236
hegemony 11, 25–55, 268
ḥisba 49, 94
Hobbes, Thomas 28
Hong Kong 15, 108, 116, 123
Hosen, Nadirsyah 83, 142
Hui 14, 108–127
  Hui Autonomous Region 118
ḥujjiyya 33, 35
Hurayrah, Abū 97
Hurgronje, Snouck 59
Hussein, Y.A.B. Tun Abdul Razak bin Dato' 93

Ibn Qayyim 102
Ibn Taymiyyah 99
Ibrahim Husen, H. 135, 136
Idel-Ural 21, 267, 271, 275, 279, 288
  see also Povolzhye
identity 1, 6, 7, 18, 20, 21, 26, 37, 52, 83, 108, 114, 201
Idris, Mahmud bin Shaikh Muhammad 74
iḥsān 50
iḥtiyāṭ 8, 13–14, 101–102
iḥtiyāṭ wājiba 101–102
ijmāʿ 29, 34, 95, 143
ijtihad 12–14, 29, 30, 80–107, 124
ʿilla 34
impurity (of materials) 98, 99, 100, 102, 282
  see also najs
Imran, Basyuni 63–65, 70, 72
Imran, Muhammad 64
Indonesia 13–16, 57, 58, 59, 64, 65, 66, 69, 75, 80–107, 109, 123, 128–150, 153n1, 154n8, 156, 163, 166, 167, 168, 175, 176n142, 198, 226, 231
Indonesian Council of Religious Scholars, Food, Drug, and Cosmetics Section (Lembaga Pengkajian-Pangan, Obat-Obatan, dan Kosmetika, Majelis Ulama Indonesia: LPPOM-MUI) 92, 94, 95, 132, 137, 143, 144, 146, 147, 148, 153n1
Indonesian Halal Standard (HAS-MUI 2008) 167
Industrial Property Code 206, 207
instrumentalization 5–22, 250n47
International Criminal Court 1
International Standards Organization (ISO) 224, 228
intifāʿ 97
Iqbal, Muhammad 89
Iran 119n32, 128, 155n10
Iranian Revolution (1979) 128
Iraq 245
Islamic Association for the Student and Youth of BENELUX 160
Islamic banks 38, 39–42, 51
Islamic Commission of Spain (ICS) 19, 211–214
Islamic Financial Institutions (IFIS) 2, 11–12, 25, 26–27, 37, 40, 43, 44, 45, 46–51
Islamic Food and Nutrition Council of America (IFANCA) 167, 182
Islamic legal theory *see uṣūl al-fiqh*

Islamic Moral Economy (IME) 8, 12, 41, 47, 48–50
Islamic reformism 62–66, 72, 76
Islamophobia 162, 250n47
Ismail, Nik Mahmud bin Nik 60
Israel 114, 119, 145
istiftā' 63, 65, 94
istiḥāla 13, 83, 96–100, 101, 102, 142
istihlāk 13, 96–100, 102, 228, 236
istiḥsān 32, 95
istinbāṭ 13, 86, 88
Italy 16, 18, 19, 30, 196–220, 221–240, 257

Jaafar, Syed Mohd Jeffri Bin Syed 83
Jabar, Khatib 60
Jabatan Agama Islam Negeri (State Department of Islamic Affairs, JAIN) 93, 95
Jakarta 82, 132, 134, 144
Jam'iyya al-Khayriyya al-Talaba al-Azhariyya al-Jawiyya 67
Jamiah Setia Pelajar 67
Jamiyat Khayr 65
Java 61, 68, 70, 89, 133, 140, 141, 142, 144
Jawa 58, 59, 62, 63, 65–66, 67
Jawatan Kemajuan Islam Malaysia *see* Department of Islamic Development (JAKIM)
Jawatankuasa Fatwa Majlis Kebangsaan Bagi Hal Ehwal Ugama Islam Malaysia 93
Jaw 60, 62, 64, 65, 67
al-Jawi, Abd al-Hafiz 5
Jiang Zemi 114
Jordan 245, 257
al-Juwaynī, Abu Muḥammad 84
Juwaynī (Dhia' ul-Dīn 'Abd al-Malik ibn Yūsuf al-Juwaynī al-Shafi'ī) 32–33
al-Juwaynī, Imam Ḥaramyn 84
juz'iyyāt 35

al-Kabūlī, Shaykh 'Abdu al-Rahīm 60
Kamali, Mohammad Hashim 84
Kāmil, Muṣṭafā 73
Kaptein, Nico 59, 90
Kasali, Rhenald 138
kaum kafir Olanda 59
Kazan 265, 269, 270, 287
Kelantan 60, 61, 92
Kementerian Wilayah Persekutuan 93
Kenali, Tok 60
  see also Yusuf, Muhammad
Kes, M. 141
khalīfa 50
Khallāf, 'Abd al-Wahhāb 37
Khatib, Ahmad 62, 64
khilāfa 124
Khnifer, Mohammed 40
King Mohamed VI (Morocco) 119
kitab 59, 60, 69, 75
Kraków 244
kulliyyāt 35
Kupang 67, 68, 69
Kuwait 97, 142, 160

labelling 6, 14, 16, 18, 20, 27, 46, 123, 136, 140, 147, 209, 215, 230, 233
  'fake' 14, 109, 123
Lard Scandal (1988) 132, 135, 137, 138–139
law
  consumer 5
  European Union 7, 201
  international 1
  Islamic 1, 11, 13–14, 25, 26, 27, 30, 31, 37, 41, 43, 73, 82, 83–88, 90, 92, 95, 96, 98, 99, 100, 102–104, 129, 131, 211–212, 225
    see also law, shari'a/sharia; *fiqh*
  positive 1, 5, 29, 94
  Shari'a/sharia
    see also law, Islamic; *fiqh* 88, 96, 247
  trademark 5, 19
Lebanon 245
Lembaga Bahsul Masa'il (LBM) 91
Lembaga Tarjih Muhammadiyah (LTM) 91
Lever, John 242
Locke, John 28
London 83, 236
Lorenzini, Sharif 226
Luxembourg 160

Made in Italy 19, 209–210, 222, 223, 224, 225, 227, 228–229, 230, 231–232, 236
maḏhab 85, 96, 101, 227
madhāhib 13, 83, 95, 96–97, 101–102
mafsada 36
Majelis Hisbah 91
Majelis Ulama Indonesia *see* Council of Indonesian Ulama (MUI)
Majlis Agama Islam 93, 95

Majlis Agama Islam Neger (State Council of Islamic Affairs, MAIN) 95
Majlis Kebangsaan bagi Hal Ehwal Ugama Islam Malaysia (National Council for Islamic Affairs (MKI)) 93
Majlis Ugama dan Adat Istiadat Melayu 61
Majlis Ugama Islam Singapura (MUIS) 153n1, 166n89, 167, 168, 198
Majmaʿ al-Buhūth al-Islāmiyyah (Islamic Research Academy, Azhar University) 89
Majmaʿ al-Fiqh al-Islāmiyy (Fiqh Research Academy) 89
Malay 56, 59, 60, 61, 64, 73, 75, 83, 92, 132
Malaysia 13–14, 15, 40, 42, 60, 61, 80–107, 109, 120, 123, 129, 131n7, 153n1, 156, 163, 165, 166, 167–168, 175, 176n142, 198, 228
Malaysian Halal Standard (MAS 1500–2009) 167
Malik, Imam (Malik ibn Anas) 32, 95
Man, Saadan 83
maqāṣid 36, 49–50
  see also shariʿa, objectives of
Maqsood, Ammara 279
Marca de Garantía Halal de Junta Islámica 18–19, 211–213
Mari El 268
Marmosoedjono, Soekarton (Attorney General) 136–137
maṣāliḥ mursala 95
maṣlaḥa 11, 13, 27, 30–37, 40, 41–43, 50, 88
  delusional 8, 11, 25–26, 38, 41, 42, 43, 45, 50–51
Mecca 39, 58–61, 62–66, 97, 112, 116
media 144, 147, 162
  journals and magazines
    Canopy Bulletin 133, 138
    al-Imam 63, 73, 75
    al-Manār 12, 31, 56–79
    al-Munir 66, 73, 74, 75
    Pengasoh 61
    Tempo 132, 144
  newspapers
    Guardian, The 229
    Islam Bergerak 75
    Kompas 132, 135, 136
    Republika 147
  printed and electronic 73, 74, 75
  social 52, 53, 269
Megawati 145
Messikh, Saleh 256–257
Middle East 13, 65, 71, 92, 98, 100, 108–127, 128, 131n7, 139, 208, 228
Middle East and North Africa (MENA) 14, 108–127
Mignolo, Walter D. 157
Milan 208, 225, 226, 232, 233
Misbach, Hadji 75
Miśkiewicz, Tomasz 246, 247, 252–256, 258
mīzān 117, 124
Mochammad, Agus Krisno Budiyanto 141
modernity 12, 25, 43, 56–79, 155, 171, 277–279
Mordovia 268
Morocco 119, 159
muʿāmala 61
mufti 58, 61, 74, 84, 88, 89, 90, 92, 94, 246, 254, 255
  see also shariʿa experts/scholars
Muftiate 266, 285
  see also Spiritual Directorate
Muhammadiyah 86–87, 90, 91
Muhimmat al-Nafāʾis 58, 59, 61–62
mulkiyya 33, 36
Munji, Salim 68–69
mushtabihāt 15, 135
Muslim Association Ahmadiyya (Muslim Association Ahmadiyya) 248
Muslim Association of Education and Culture (MSKK) 245
Muslim League (Liga Muzułmańska w Rzeczpospolitej Polskiej: LM) 20–21, 241, 243, 246, 247, 248, 250, 253–255, 256, 257
Muslim Religious Union (Muzułmański Związek Religijny w Rzeczpospolitej Polskiej: MZR) 241, 243, 247, 253, 254–255, 256, 258
Muslim Youth Union 287
mustaftī 59, 63, 64, 65, 66, 69, 94
mustawriq 39, 40
mutawarriq 38

nafs 33, 36
Nahdlatul Ulama (NU) 86–87, 90, 91, 146
najs/najis 98, 99, 102
  see also impurity
Nalborczyk, Agata 251
Nana, Shaykh Abdulla 117

nasl 33, 36
Nasser, Gamal Abdel 112
National Agency of Halal Product Assurance (BPJPH) 14, 81, 92, 94
National Bioethics Committee (Italy) 18, 201
National Fatwa Council of Malaysia (NFC) 89, 93, 98, 100
Nederlandsche Bioscoop Maatschaapij 71
neoliberalism 112, 113, 267, 278, 279
Netherlands, The 160, 242, 258
New Order regime 134, 136, 137, 145
New Zealand 128, 155n10
nikāḥ 61
Ningxia 108, 118
Non-Aligned Movement (NAM) 110, 112

Occupied Palestinian Territories 245
Office for Patents and Trademarks (Italy) 207, 209
Oleśnica 244
Oman 40
One Belt, One Road (OBOR) *see* Belt Road Initiative (BRI)
Opwis, Felicitas 35, 36
Organization of Islamic Cooperation (OIC) 39, 165–167
  International Council of Fiqh Academy (ICFA) 39–40, 51
  Standards and Meteorology Institute for Islamic Countries (SMIIC) 165, 166, 167
Ottoman 49, 231
OXFAM 229

Pancasila state 90
Paris Court of Appeal 7
Patani 59, 60, 61
Pauzi, Norhidayah 83
Pejabat Mufti Wilayah Persekutuan (Department of Mufti of Federation) 87
Pelkmans, Mathijs 273
Pengesahan Halal Malaysia (Malaysia Halal Legalisation Panel) 95
Perintah Perihal Dagangan 93, 101
Persatuan Islam (Persis) 91
Philippines, The 156, 163, 166
pluralism 104, 196–200, 266n2
Poland 16, 20–21, 241–264
politics 15, 27, 45, 128–150
  ethno-religious 15, 16, 128–150
  national 145–148
positivisation 1–2, 11
Povolzhye 265–271, 273n17, 275, 278, 280, 282, 285, 288, 289
  see also Idel-Ural
Poznań 244, 257
public interest/utility *see maṣlaḥa*
purity (of materials) 70, 89, 99, 265

al-Qaraḍāwī, Yūsuf 84, 99, 100
al-Qarāfī 31, 34
al-Qāsimī, Jamāladdīn 31, 50
qaṭʿiyya 85
qawāʿid 34
qawāʿid fiqhiyya 96
qawl muʿtamad 88
qiyās muʿtabar 95
Qur'an 2, 11, 25, 26, 29, 30, 31, 32, 34, 35, 37, 41, 50, 51, 56, 64, 70, 76, 85, 86–87, 94, 95, 96, 142, 225–226, 269, 271, 274

Radłowska, Karolina 256
al-Rāzī 30, 31, 33, 34, 35
regulatory mechanisms 11–12, 26–27, 46, 47, 50
ribā 68, 69, 270, 282
Rida, Rashid 12, 31, 37, 50, 57, 58, 63, 64, 65, 71, 72, 73–74, 76, 89
ritual slaughter 6, 16, 17, 20, 93, 117, 129, 154, 160–162, 166, 196, 199, 201n22, 204, 223, 231, 242, 243, 249–253, 254, 255, 259, 272
Riyadh 119
Rousseau, Jean-Jacques 28
Russia 16, 21, 243, 265–293
Russia Volga region 21, 265–291
  see also Povolzhye

Saʿid, Shaykh Mahmud 60
al-Sarawaki, Umar al-Sumbawi, Uthman 64
Saʿud, Ahmad 64
sadd al-dharīʿah 95, 100–101
ṣahāba 156
Salafi 4, 267, 281, 285, 286
salam 41
Salih, Haji Muhammad 60
Sarekat Islam 75

Saudi Arabia 112, 119, 226, 242, 247
Schielke, Samuli 278
Schmitt, Carl 26, 29, 30, 37, 41, 51
schools of law
  Ḥanafī 13, 32, 83, 88, 95, 96, 99, 102
  Ḥanbali 32, 88, 95, 96, 102
  Mālikī 13, 32, 83, 88, 95, 96, 102
  Shafiʿi 13, 32, 58, 82, 85, 86, 87–88, 95, 96, 98, 99, 101, 102, 104, 142
science 3, 15, 16, 17, 22, 89, 104, 128–150, 170, 171, 174
Science and Technology Studies (STS) 133
Shabbar, Said 85
shak 124
Shariʿa Advisory Board of Bank Negara Malaysia 42
shariʿa/sharia/Shariah 1, 2, 11, 29, 30, 33, 35, 37, 40, 42, 44–46, 48, 49, 51, 81, 82, 84, 89, 92, 93, 95, 104, 142, 153, 277, 282, 284
  boards (SBS)/committees 2, 3, 9, 10, 11, 26, 41, 46
  compliance 11, 25, 26, 27, 38, 40, 41, 44, 46, 47, 48, 51–53, 113, 117, 118, 120, 124, 202, 207, 210, 270
  experts/scholars 11, 13, 25, 26, 27, 30, 37–38, 40, 41, 42–43, 43–45, 47–48, 51, 52, 94
    see also *muftī*
  morality of 12, 27, 29, 37, 46–47, 48, 50, 51
  objectives of 30, 33, 36, 41, 45–46, 48, 49, 50, 51, 52
    see also *maqāṣid*
  principles of 25
al-Shāṭibī 30, 31, 35–36, 37, 85
al-Shawkānī 102
Shia 241, 248, 257
Shihab, Hasan bin Alwi bin 70
shubha 102, 143n32
Siberia 269
Silk Road 110, 116, 124
Singapore 15, 61, 63, 70, 73, 109, 121, 123, 124, 138, 153n1, 156, 163, 166n89, 167–168, 176n142, 198, 202, 215
Single European Act 5
Sino-Arab Cooperation Forum (SACF) 122
Sino-Muslim relation 109, 112
al-Sisi, Abdel Fattah 119
sovereignty 11, 22, 26–32, 37, 38, 41, 45, 51, 110, 114
Spain 16, 18–19, 196–220
Spanish Federation of Islamic Religious Entities 211
Special Economic Zones (SEZS) 112
Spiritual Directorate 283, 287
  see also Mufitate
Sri Lanka 120, 124
standardisation 2, 9, 10, 19, 21, 134, 140, 155–156, 157, 164, 165, 167–168, 173, 196–200, 225, 227–232
standards 1, 2, 3, 4–5, 8–9, 16–17, 19, 113, 117, 120, 129, 153–195, 197, 198–199, 202, 204, 211, 224, 227–228, 230–232, 237, 242, 249, 279, 287n47
Stowarzyszenie Jedności Muzułmańskiej (SJM) 257
stunning 16, 17, 20, 128, 129, 161–162, 196, 197, 199, 201n22, 203, 204, 250, 251
Sudomo 139
Sufi 73, 102, 274
Suharto 16, 89, 91, 134, 136, 137, 145
Sulayman, Abdul Hamid Abu 85
Sultan Muhammad I of Kelantan 92
al-Sumbawi, Umar 64
sunat 59
sunna 2, 25, 26, 29, 30, 31, 32, 34, 35, 37, 41, 51, 64, 85, 86, 87, 94–96, 98, 156, 266
Sunnism 17, 95, 119, 157, 158, 175, 176, 205, 265, 267, 273, 280, 286
Surabaya 66, 68, 69, 134
Soesanto, Tri 89, 132, 133–134, 136–138, 140, 147
Sweden 258
Switzerland 30
Syria 245
Szczecin 244

Tabaq, Nidal Abu 136
tābi' al-tābi'īn 156
tābi'īn 156
taḥqīq 13, 86
taḥsīniyyāt/taḥsīniyya 8, 12, 33, 47
ṭalāq 61
taqnīn 84
taqrīr 13, 86
tarjīḥ 13, 86
Tatar 20–21, 243, 244–245, 246–248, 255–256, 259, 265, 268, 269, 271–273, 276, 278, 284, 285

Tatarstan 21, 266n2, 268–270, 272, 277, 279, 281, 283, 285, 287, 289
taṭhīr 98
tawarruq 11, 25, 38–43, 51
ṭayyib 8, 10, 15, 117, 236, 237
technology 14, 17, 68, 70, 71, 104, 118, 119, 128, 131, 138, 148, 170, 171, 237
technoscience 16, 132, 148
Teheran 119
Thahir, Muhammad bin Hashim bin 66, 70, 71
Thailand 60, 156, 163, 257
Tiananmen 114
Timmermans, Stefan 155, 157
Toselli, Elen 210
trademarks 19, 202, 206–211, 212, 213, 214, 215
Trump, Donald 119
trust 15, 20, 57, 109, 111, 121, 123, 124, 128, 207, 221, 234, 237, 282–285
al-Ṭūfī 31, 34–35, 36, 37, 41–42, 50
Tunisia 159, 245
al-Turābī, Ḥasan 37
Turkey 159, 167, 229, 257, 272

Udmurtia 268
Uighur 14, 108–127
Ukraine 243
ʿulamaʾ/*ulama* (sing. *alim*) 3, 9, 12, 13, 17, 56–62, 63, 64, 71–76, 84, 85, 87, 91, 95, 97, 98, 128, 143, 145, 147, 156, 157, 158, 173–174, 176
umma 40, 85, 91, 124, 174, 246
Union of Islamic Communities of Spain 211
Union of Italian Jewish Communities 206, 214
Unione delle Comunità Islamiche d'Italia (Union of Islamic Communities of Italy) 205
United Arab Emirates (UAE) 160, 167, 208, 221, 242, 257, 258
United Kingdom (UK) 241, 258
United Nations 199
  Educational, Scientific and Cultural Organization (UNESCO) 116
United States of America (USA) 18, 30, 108, 112, 113, 115, 117, 119, 122, 124, 128, 129, 163, 167, 169n99, 202, 223, 285
uṣūl 86
uṣūl al-dīn 60, 61
uṣūl al-fiqh 11, 69, 96

Van Klinken, Gerry 145

Wahid, Abdurrahman 144, 145–146
War on Terror 115–122, 163
Warsaw 244, 254
Washington Consensus 112
West Sumatra 62, 66, 71, 72, 73, 74
West Timor 67, 68
World Halal Authority (WHA) 226, 228, 231, 237
World Halal Conference 97
World Halal Convention East Europe 257
World Halal Council 129
World Halal Food Council 129
World Health Organization (WHO) 142, 165n83, 199
Wrocław 244

Xi Jinping 108, 118, 119, 124
Xinjiang 109, 114, 118, 122

Yahya, Sayyid Aqil bin Uthman bin 67–68, 69
Yaquby, Nizam 40
Yemen 245
Yogyakarta 132
Yusuf, Muhammad 60
  see also Kenali, Tok

Ẓāhirī group 36
Zain, Muhammad 60
zakat 61
Zaman, Muhammad Qasim 88
Zhou Enlai 112
al-Zuḥaylī, Wahbah 98
Żuk, Mahmoud Taha 248, 257

Printed in the United States
by Baker & Taylor Publisher Services